*To Don, Stella,*
*Anne Carol, Joe and Bobbie*

Other books by Lydia Dotto

*Canada in Space*
*The Ozone War*
*Planet Earth in Jeopardy*
*Thinking the Unthinkable: The Social Impact of Rapid Climate Change*

# CONTENTS

PREFACE *vii*

ACKNOWLEDGMENTS *ix*

## INTRODUCTION

1: Fifty Hours without Sleep  *3*
2: Cheating on Sleep  *15*

## SECTION 1: THE PROBLEM OF SLEEP

3: Still a Mystery After All These Years  *25*
4: The Time of Your Life  *41*
5: Out of Time  *65*
6: Trouble at Night, Trouble during the Day  *83*
    I. Can't Fall Asleep  *89*
    II. Can't Stay Awake  *104*
    III. Adventures in the Night  *116*

## SECTION 2: SLEEP AND WORK

7: An Epidemic of Sleepiness  *123*
8: Sleepiness and Performance  *147*
9: A Little Bit of Sleep  *168*
10: Caught Napping?  *199*
11: Toughing It Out  *213*
    I. Shift Work: Circadian Chaos  *222*
    II. Jet Lag: Shift Work with Wings  *249*
12: Asleep in the Fast Lane  *259*
    I. Medicine  *279*
    II. Transportation  *285*
    III. Sports  *310*
    IV. The Space Program  *316*

CONCLUSION  *327*

REFERENCES AND BIBLIOGRAPHY  *329*

INDEX  *333*

# PREFACE

Sleep loss is one of the more predictable side effects of writing a book. Usually, this is something you just accept, something that goes with the territory. But writing a book about sleep is different, I discovered. It's disconcerting, for example, to be sitting in front of your word processor at three o'clock in the morning, trying to make sense of scientific studies demonstrating the negative effects that sleep loss can have on intellectual performance.

Fortunately, there are also studies demonstrating that even short naps can restore and sustain performance. During the most intense period of writing, I was able to practice what I was preaching, with great success: for several months, I followed a sleep schedule that involved taking two or three 2-hour naps each day, and after a period of adjustment, I found that this routine sustained me while working long hours every day. It was also gratifying to learn that the type of work schedule I prefer — working late into the night and sleeping during the afternoon — is neither as bizarre nor as harmful as "normal" people usually consider it to be.

From the outset, I decided to limit the scope of this book to dealing with urban lifestyles characteristic of advanced industrialized societies. In part, this was dictated by necessity; it would be impossible to examine the entire range of socioeconomic circumstances in which human beings find themselves. But this decision was prompted by more than mere practicality: there's also the fact that industrialized societies are the ones most divorced from the natural, primitive cycle of day and night and they are also the most dependent on — and vulnerable to — complex technologies whose failure (often brought about by human error) can exact a huge social and economic toll. Moreover, the urban industrial lifestyle is (for better or worse) being spread rapidly throughout the world by social, economic and, particularly, technological forces such as sophisticated new computer, communications and transportation systems.

The major focus of this book is on the impact of sleep deprivation, sleep disturbances and sleep disorders on alertness and performance on the job. In order to examine this question, however, it is necessary first to provide the reader with some basic background on theories about why we sleep, and what is known of the nature of sleep and its stages, and to examine the current understanding of the role of biological clocks and circadian rhythms. Doing this presents certain difficulties because sleep research, like any complex field of science, is fraught with unknowns, uncertainties and controversies, and it is beyond the scope or intention of this book to examine these complexities in exhaustive detail. This is a book for nonspecialists, and my objective is to provide lay readers with enough of the basic scientific groundwork needed to gain a better understanding of the impact of sleep problems on their daily lives. Accordingly, it has been necessary to generalize a good deal — but I have tried nevertheless to reflect the range of current scientific thinking on these complex issues as accurately as possible. I should mention also that it was impossible to deal adequately with two related subjects — dream research and the effects of drugs on sleep — and still keep the length of this book within reasonable limits. I leave these important subjects to other writers.

We have learned a great deal about sleep, especially in the past few decades, but perhaps the most amazing thing about it is that so ancient and basic a function — one that consumes a third of our lives — remains so much a mystery.

# ACKNOWLEDGMENTS

A science writer is always dependent on the cooperation and good will of the scientists who do the studies on which a book like this so critically depends. I owe a great debt to all the researchers who shared their knowledge with me, many in personal interviews, others through the provision of research papers and other documentation.

I'm grateful to all of them, but I must mention several whose assistance and encouragement were especially helpful: Bob Angus, Harvey Moldofsky, Roger Broughton, David Dinges and Claudio Stampi. In particular, I would like to thank Bob Angus and his colleagues at the Defence and Civil Institute of Environmental Medicine in Toronto for going to the trouble of having me participate in one of their sleep-deprivation experiments so that I could provide readers with a first-person account of this experience in Chapter 1.

I must also express my appreciation to him and to Harvey Moldofsky for reading the manuscript and offering many good suggestions; however, the responsibility for accuracy and completeness is, of course, ultimately mine.

I would also like to acknowledge financial support from the Ontario Arts Council, which helped with research expenses. And, finally, I'd like to thank my editors, Donald G. Bastian, Greg Ioannou and Alison Reid; this was a difficult book to write and their encouragement and support were greatly appreciated.

# INTRODUCTION

# CHAPTER 1

# 50 HOURS WITHOUT SLEEP

I BLINK TWICE, SUPPRESS A YAWN and try desperately to concentrate on the words written on the computer screen in front of me. They say:

*B is not preceded by A (T/F?)*

Beneath this cryptic statement are two letters:

*A B*

I blink again. Succumb to the yawn. Mumble "B is not preceded by A" to myself, enunciating each word carefully, as though saying them aloud will somehow untangle my befuddled thoughts. True or false? It's a simple choice, or so I tell myself, but by now I am too far gone for these little pep talks to have much effect. The meaning of the words, and especially their truth or falsity, completely eludes my comprehension.

I think longingly of the war. I know it would perk me up — it always does. But, alas, the war is on hold while I grapple with these exasperating A's and B's. Doggedly, I say again, "B is not preceded by A," this time more loudly and emphatically, hoping that repetition and assertiveness will force some sense into the words. My finger hovers over the keyboard as my mind drifts off into a white fog. I'm not asleep exactly — at least, I don't think so, though it occurs to me I may be dreaming that I'm awake. It hardly matters — I am, at the very least, in a not-all-there kind of daze. With an effort, I force myself to snap to attention, thinking that this experience is beginning to resemble a routine by comedian Dave Broadfoot, in which he starts every few sentences with "When I regained consciousness . . . "

I don't know how long I was "out" this time, but it can't have been very long or one of those who are monitoring me on the closed-circuit TV would have appeared to rouse me. Did my eyes actually close? I don't think so, but I can't be sure. The white mist in front of my eyes is dissipating, coalescing into solidity again — walls and a desk and, of course, the computer terminal, the inescapable terminal that has been my constant companion and implacable taskmaster for the past 37 hours. I find my finger still poised over the keyboard and the screen still issuing the inscrutable demand: *B is not preceded by A (T/F?)*. I still can't figure out what the hell it means — and, more to the point, I don't really care anymore. I can't imagine why I ever did. I hit F just to make it go away.

Not that this does much good. The screen clears for only a moment, then presents another set of letters and demands another decision: *A does not follow B (T/F?)*. I groan to myself. This one makes no more sense to me than the last. Nor does *A is followed by B* or *B follows A* or any of the rest of the statements the computer throws at me in rapid succession. In this task, there are, unbelievably, 32 distinct ways to describe the combination of the two letters. As I struggle on through the A's and B's that march relentlessly across the screen, some still-functioning part of my brain recalls bemusedly that there was a time — now seemingly aeons ago — when I could do this test with an almost instinctive assurance.

It is — though I don't know it — about nine o'clock in the morning and I have been awake for nearly 50 hours, except for a 2-hour nap some 22 hours ago. Not counting the nap and the approximately 20-minute breaks I'm allowed every 90 minutes or so, I've been sitting at this computer keyboard for about 37 hours, responding to its aggravatingly peremptory demands with deteriorating patience and skill. The 19 electrodes glued to my scalp, feeding readings of my brain-wave activity into three tape recorders slung around my waist, aren't helping matters any: at times, I feel as though someone has clamped two large hands around my head.

My feelings of sleepiness and fatigue are fluctuating dramatically, depending on which tasks I'm doing and how long it's been since my last brief respite from the computer. There are times when I feel surprisingly alert, cheerful and competent, and other times when I think I would readily sell my soul for a chance to lay my head down on the desk and go to sleep. "My eyes keep wanting to shut all the time . . . . It's just a relentless need for sleep," I mutter into the small tape recorder I'm using to record my impressions. My voice is low-pitched and sluggish, my sentences fragmentary and punctuated by long pauses as I grope for the words my brain refuses to supply. "I can barely function . . . can barely . . . can't remember numbers, uh . . . it takes me a long, long time to look things up on the screen . . . Just generally nonfunctional . . . . Unable to concentrate . . . I'm blanking out." I conclude by stating the obvious: "I am just about reaching the end of my rope."

I'm trying not to think about how much longer this is going to go on, but I can't help it — I just want it to be finished. The tests I'm doing are many things — repetitive, boring, exasperating — but, unfortunately, finished is the one thing they are not. As soon as the A/B test, known as the "logical reasoning" test, is done, another appears on the screen. This one is called the "serial reaction time" test. The computer randomly spits out four numbers — 11, 12, 13 or 14 — and I respond by hitting appropriate keys on the keyboard as fast as I can. The computer is measuring both reaction time and accuracy and will score me on the number of correct responses per minute. This test is, in my expert opinion, the hands-down winner in the tedium category, yet it still requires a high level of vigilance, sharp reactions and excellent motor control. I barely survived one long session — 10 unbelievable minutes — by adopting a combative it's-you-against-me attitude toward the computer, but even with my competitive nature, I'm finding it increasingly difficult to care any longer how well I'm performing this test.

The computer moves on to tests that involve fairly complex adding and subtracting problems. These cause me no great emotional distress because I have long since given up on them. My native ability to do such math problems in my head is iffy at the best of times — and the best of times vanished many hours ago.

"I am falling asleep in the middle of doing all my tasks," I report wearily in the early morning after the second night of lost sleep. "Almost none of the tasks are possible. The logical reasoning problem is almost incomprehensible . . . . I can still do the serial task very slowly. The addition and subtraction tasks are becoming almost impossibly hard . . . . Lack of motivation . . . . I just don't care. Reaction time very slow . . . motor skills very poor . . . extremely poor memory for numbers. It just reaches the point where you don't really care anymore and you're always, always fighting off that heavy-lidded . . . It feels as though someone's snatching at your head."

A few more tests — a time-estimation task and another involving word associations — and finally, it's time to get back to the war. My interest picks up instantly and the fatigue, though it cannot be entirely banished at this stage, retreats to the background of my mind. For the purpose of this test, I am assuming the role of an operations duty officer whose function is to monitor communications relating to a battle in progress. The computer has been programmed with the battle scenario, and as it feeds messages to me, I write down the relevant information on slips of paper, file them in a box with little pigeonholes and then use the information to update the tactical map on the wall beside me, moving colored pins around to mark the movement of troops and equipment. A related test involves pinpointing coordinates supplied by the computer on a grid map, using a special electronic pen that enables the computer to score my accuracy.

Even in my sleep-deprived state, I find this exercise interesting enough to keep me reasonably alert most of the time. "The interest level really has a major impact on my ability to stave off the sleepiness and to function," I report into the tape recorder after one session near the end of the experiment. "I wasn't working on the grid maps as fast as I had been before. I was making mistakes, having to think twice, go back and do things again, but I didn't have sleep grabbing at me the way it does when I'm doing some of the other tasks. I felt fairly alert and able to cope. So I think interest level and diversity of tasks and having something challenging to do is very important to keep up the alertness."

Nevertheless, there are times when even having an interesting and challenging task to do isn't enough to keep my reactions from slowing to the pace of molasses or to maintain my motivation to perform. It is this last sensation that I find most disconcerting. I've worked through fatigue before — as a university student, I did my share of all-night cramming, and as a journalist, I often worked long hours with little sleep — but still, I'm disturbed by the loss of the will to persevere that accompanies my extreme sleep-deprived state.

I can't help wondering what would happen if I were called upon now to perform tasks or make decisions with life-or-death consequences.

. . . . . . .

It has taken just two days and two nights to reduce me to this sorry state — a fact that annoys me no end, because I'd started the experiment determined not to let it get the better of me. How difficult can it be to last two days without sleep, I'd asked myself as I checked in at the Defence and Civil Institute of Environmental Medicine (DCIEM) in Toronto shortly before noon on a Tuesday in early April. At that point, it was not hard to feel self-confident. I'd been awake only four hours, having awakened at 8:00 a.m. after sleeping a full eight hours the night before. I felt alert and mentally geared up for the challenge ahead.

The researchers are rather bemused by my enthusiasm for this project. Most of their subjects are paid volunteers recruited from the ranks of the Canadian Forces. "We don't usually get subjects who are looking forward to the experience," Bob Angus, Head of Applied Psychology at DCIEM, comments wryly.

He takes me down to the sleep lab, located in the basement off a drab, narrow hallway barricaded at both ends with Do Not Disturb signs. The lab consists of a suite of four small rooms in which the subjects work and a control room filled with computer equipment as well as a bank of small closed-circuit TV monitors lining one wall. Here the researchers, working in shifts, maintain an around-the-clock watch on the subjects. Drooping eyelids and nodding heads are picked up by wall-mounted TV cameras in each room, and within moments, one of the researchers is headed down the hall to nudge the subject awake. As the hours wear on, these trips become more frequent. "I just kind of scratch on the door before I go in, to give them a chance to fool me," says Bob.

He introduces me to his colleagues, Ross Pigeau, Ron Heslegrave and Bob Stretch, a U.S. Army scientist who is working in Canada on an exchange program. Along with the support staff, they take turns monitoring subjects during the experiment.

Out in the hallway, against one wall, is a table cluttered with the paraphernalia needed for attaching electrodes (used to record brain-wave and heart activity) to the subjects' heads and chests. A television set and VCR sit on a small stand off to one side; they'll be used during the breaks, when subjects can watch movies in 20-minute doses. Across the hall there's a lunchroom equipped with a microwave oven and a well-stocked refrigerator. Subjects are allowed to eat whatever they want during the breaks, so that meals won't give them clues as to the time of day or night.

I'm introduced to Julia Rylands, a physiologist from a British Army research laboratory who is working in Canada on a scientific exchange program. She'll also be a subject, and we spend most of the afternoon learning the tasks we'll be required to perform. Before rehearsals begin, we're asked to fill out a questionnaire about our normal sleep habits, but in my case, the word *normal* isn't quite apropos. As a freelance writer, I don't lead a 9-to-5 existence; I follow an irregular sleep/wake cycle, involving frequent overnight work sessions and daytime napping. Such a pattern is not unheard of, particularly among self-employed writers, artists and entertainers, but it's not common in the general population.

Finally, we're asked to hand over our watches; for the next two days, we'll have to rely on our internal sense of time to mark the passage of the hours.

About 6:00 p.m., after I've eaten a light supper, the task of attaching the electrodes begins. Normally, only three or four electrodes are used, but in a rash moment I'd agreed to have a "full-head" complement of 19 electrodes, which will allow the researchers to follow waves of drowsiness across different parts of my brain. Attaching the electrodes involves a tedious and mildly painful process that takes about two hours. I watch the science fiction movie *Tron* on the VCR while Ross meticulously plots points on my head with a tape measure and scrubs little patches of my scalp with alcohol before attaching the electrode contacts, tiny metal cups, with a special glue that he assures me will wash out — eventually. I am momentarily disconcerted to see him brandishing a huge hypodermic syringe with what appears to be a long, wicked-looking needle; but the needle is blunt tipped and used merely to insert a dollop of sticky material into tiny holes in the metal cups, which will enable the electrodes to pick up the brain-wave readings that will provide a record of my state of alertness throughout the experiment.

The electrode wires are strung through tiny loops in a collar around my neck and then attached to the three tape recorders slung around my waist. (I will soon discover that going to the washroom tangled up in wires and carrying a weight belt of bulky tape recorders is not the simplest task in the world.) As a fashion statement, this get-up leaves everything to be desired; trussed up like this, I feel like some weird electronic Medusa. I climb out of the chair and Julia climbs in. Everyone cheerfully waves me off to my rendezvous with the computer.

It's about 8:00 p.m. on Tuesday night, and I have now been awake for 12 hours.

During the first 90-minute session, I feel very alert — quite hyped up, in fact, and ready to face whatever challenges the computer throws my way. At the first break, between 9:30 and 10:00 p.m., I'm still feeling pretty good, and I note into the tape recorder that my motivation remains strong: "I really want to keep things under control and to keep myself awake and alert." But by the time the second break rolls around, just before midnight, I'm beginning to feel fatigued and my concentration is slipping. I become annoyed and frustrated if I can't understand something right away. The repetitive tasks are becoming both boring and irritating, eliciting a reaction of "Oh, Lord, not this one again." Being confronted with a test that I don't like to do provokes a few episodes of fist-waving at the terminal. Ross later observes that the frequency of these displays of temper, which have been duly witnessed on the closed-circuit TV, seem to be increasing.

Periodically during sessions, the computer instructs me to sit with my eyes closed for 4 minutes. Now, as I enter the wee hours of the first night of sleep loss, I find myself drifting toward sleep during these closed-eyes sessions and I comment that although "I still feel I'm on top of the tasks, I'm glad when the breaks come." The computer also inquires solicitously from time to time about my mood and the degree of sleepiness and fatigue I feel. The sleepiness scale contains seven statements, starting with *alert, wide awake* through *foggy, slowed down, beginning to lose interest in remaining awake* to *fighting sleep, losing the struggle to remain awake*. The fatigue checklist asks me to record whether I am *better than, the same as* or *worse than* a series of statements ranging from *very lively* and *extremely peppy* to *slightly pooped* and *ready to drop*. And the mood scale asks me to describe my feelings in terms such as *carefree, cheerful* and *full of pep* or *dull, drowsy* and *defiant*.

By 7:00 a.m. on Wednesday, *dull, drowsy* and *defiant* don't even come close to describing how I feel. Now approaching 24 hours without sleep, I am not in a happy frame of mind. My subjective feelings of sleepiness and fatigue have increased sharply, and my mood, along with my performance, has begun to deteriorate badly. The words *cheerful* and *peppy* are no longer in my vocabulary. Although I can still remain reasonably alert during the war game exercises, I'm beginning to struggle against falling asleep during the more boring tasks. "Sleep is starting to ambush me," I report into the tape recorder. "I find myself staring into space. I just kind of blank out; it's like I vanish, disappear."

I know that sometime during this experiment, I'll be allowed to have a nap. Periodically, the computer taunts me with questions like "If you could sleep now, would you do so?" For the first time, I start hinting that I wouldn't turn down a nap if it were to be offered. It isn't. The computer, it seems, is only interested in knowing if I'd *like* a nap, not in actually satisfying my wish.

During the next break, which I have calculated occurs during early morning, Ross appears looking suspiciously well scrubbed and wearing a cheerful grin. He does not look like a sleep-deprived person and this makes me feel distinctly grumpy. I find that I'm also depressed. I "hit the wall" during the last work session, and as a result, I've broken my rule not to think too far ahead. The certain knowledge that there's at least another full day and night of this to get through induces a state of mild despair, and for the first time I wonder if I'm going to make it. Julia is also beginning to despair about her ability to carry on, reflecting, "It's this rough now and I have to make it through another night." Ours is a typical response to "the first-night effect." Subjects hit a low point between about 4:00 and 6:00 a.m. after the first night of lost sleep, says Ross. "They feel very depressed because they think, 'If I'm feeling this tired and it's only the first night, I'll never make it. I'm going to die.'"

Certainly, I'm beginning to wonder how I'm going to marshal the resources needed to go back into that room. As it happens, however, I don't have to. At the end of the break period, about 10:00 a.m. on Wednesday, Ross announces that it's nap time. When I was six years old, these were dreaded words; now they couldn't have been more welcome.

Julia and I bed down on cots in two of the unused rooms. We're allowed to remove the belts of tape recorders, which are laid beside the beds trailing their wires. The electrodes have to stay on, of course, but it hardly matters; I've reached the stage where nothing's going to keep me awake, not even the sensation of having my head in a vise.

The nap occurs between 10:00 a.m. and noon on Wednesday. For me, it comes at just the right time, rescuing me as I'm about to hit rock bottom. As I settle gratefully into the bed and close my eyes, I experience a momentary anxiety that I won't be able to sleep on demand, even though — or perhaps because — I desperately want to. But, given my advanced state of exhaustion, and perhaps the fact that I am used to napping in my "regular" life, I manage to fall asleep very quickly, even under these unusual circumstances.

Julia, though also highly fatigued, is less happy than I about the timing of the nap. She's a morning person and by midmorning is usually at the height of alertness. Even though she's in a sleep-deprived state, her biological rhythms had begun to climb by 10:00 a.m. and she had trouble falling asleep. "I'd have preferred the nap earlier on, say at 4:00 a.m., because that was my really low point," she commented later. But she began to pick up after the early-morning break during which we had breakfast: "I was awake by the time the nap came along because that's my high point of the day. It wasn't when I craved sleep. I hadn't geared up to having a nap; I was not thinking, 'I've just got to last till the nap.' I think that's why I had such difficulty getting to sleep." She too put psychological pressure on herself, knowing the nap would be her only opportunity to sleep until the end of the experiment. "I knew the nap was two hours long and I was saying, 'C'mon, got to get to sleep, got to make the most of this two hours of sleep.' " In the end, she managed about 1½ hours of sleep.

The nap helped both of us tremendously. I woke up feeling completely refreshed and in a greatly improved frame of mind — feeling, in fact, pretty much as I had when the experiment began. Even though she did not sleep for the full 2 hours, Julia felt the nap helped her too. "If I hadn't had it, I'd be dead by now," she said during the last break before the end of the experiment. Ross asked her if she felt the nap had allowed her to do better on the computer tasks. "I felt better, yes, but whether I did better or not, I don't know."

In fact, the nap had a significant impact on our performance of the tasks. Our scores on the logical reasoning and serial reaction time tasks improved by more than 40 percent after the nap, and in one case, Julia's score almost doubled. Equally important, for a period of more than 12 hours after the nap, our performance was maintained well above the levels to which they'd dropped before the nap. At times, our performance after the nap was nearly equal to — and occasionally even better than — our performance when we first started the experiment. In some cases, our scores did not fall below their prenap lows until about 5:30 a.m. on the second night of lost sleep, some 17½ hours after the nap.

Studying the effect of napping on performance was the whole point of this experiment, one of a series of such studies conducted by Angus and his group in recent years. They're focusing on factors that affect the performance of military personnel under battle conditions (referred to as "sustained operations"), when they might have to function for days on end with only brief snatches of sleep. However, these studies on napping — currently one of the hottest new fields of sleep research — have much wider implications. The knowledge gained about human sleep/wake patterns may someday help others — doctors, pilots, athletes, air traffic controllers, firefighters, nuclear plant operators and astronauts, to name just a few — whose jobs demand high levels of alertness over long periods of time and/or sustained high-quality performance under extremely demanding conditions. These studies may also help people with more normal but still stressful jobs, such as executives who work long hours or travel a lot, and millions of people trying to cope, often unsuccessfully, with shift work.

Reviewing the data from my experiment, Angus noted with satisfaction that "the nap seemed to give you almost a whole day. It really helped." But it couldn't sustain me indefinitely. Both Julia and I began to disintegrate during the early-morning hours after the second night of sleep loss, and toward the end, we both exhibited a sharp roller-coaster pattern on the tests, performing moderately well — though with ever-diminishing accuracy — immediately after a break but falling apart rapidly in the middle of the 90-minute work sessions. These extreme swings are a striking feature of work sessions during the second day or so without sleep. Ross commented that when subjects are well rested, breaks don't make much difference in their performance because they're already very alert. But as time wears on and fatigue starts to build, the breaks do have a brief noticeable effect, causing the roller-coaster performance pattern. Ultimately, however, they lose their effectiveness and "after you've been awake two or three days, they don't make much difference."

There were many similarities in the way Julia and I reacted to extreme sleep deprivation, but there were also some intriguing differences. While I experienced sensations of blanking out and "disappearing," Julia felt that her thoughts were wandering aimlessly. "My mind would shoot off and I had no control over it," she said. "My thought patterns were going off in different directions." Often, she could not comprehend words printed on the screen because they seemed to be spelled wrong. "They looked totally weird and I thought, 'What is this word?' When you look at a word for a long time, it just appears to be odd. That kept capturing my attention, rather than what I was supposed to be doing." She also had some mild hallucinatory experiences; sometimes she was uncertain whether she was actually doing a task or merely dreaming that she was doing it, and at times she felt as though there was someone in the room. "I got quite worried about the shadows around me. I kept on thinking that somebody's in the room with me because I see shadows on the walls. My vision's a bit iffy."

Like me, she was easily annoyed by the computer's "damn fool questions," but, she added, "I was less grouchy than I thought I was going to be."

We were sprung from the sleep lab around noon on Thursday. I didn't feel drop-dead tired — in fact, I felt surprisingly alert — but I was grateful that arrangements had been made for a friend to drive me home. Still feeling strangely energized, I puttered around for a while, catching up on chores that had accumulated during my two-day absence, but I finally conked out around 2:00 p.m. I slept until about 7:00 p.m., woke up to have some supper, listened to a baseball game on the radio and went back to bed at 11:00 p.m. The next morning I got up at 7:00 a.m. and attended meetings from 9:00 that morning till 7:00 at night. I had not been looking forward to this unavoidably busy day, coming hard on the heels of two days of sleep deprivation, but my night of recovery sleep seemed to have restored me to normal and the experience did not appear to have left me too much the worse for wear.

I admit to feeling just a little smug about my resiliency, but it didn't take Bob very long to deflate me. In an overly innocent tone of voice, he asked whether I'd be willing to do the experiment again, and grinned knowingly when I hesitated.

I suspect he doesn't get very many repeat customers.

# CHAPTER 2

# CHEATING ON SLEEP

IT IS SURELY NOT COINCIDENTAL that Thomas Edison, the inventor of the electric light bulb, had a thing about sleep — or, more specifically, excessive sleep, by which he meant 8 to 10 hours a night. He regarded oversleeping as a waste of time and a sign of weakness and stupidity — an indulgence that could be overcome by willpower and discipline. He would have been right at home in today's modern industrial society, where the prevailing work ethic is "anywhere, anytime" and sleep is perceived by a generation of fast-trackers as unproductive down time.

"Sleep's the thing we cheat on," says David Dinges, a researcher at the Institute of Pennsylvania Hospital and the University of Pennsylvania. "It's what we cut out to get the car to the repair shop, to do our taxes, to have a party. We have more and more segments of our society under some sort of chronic sleep deprivation."

Edison believed that his light bulb would liberate us from the night and in the process transform our lives. It certainly did that — but what it did *not* do was transform human physiology. The fact that the light bulb served as a reliable, inexpensive and easily controlled way to, in effect, banish the night did not, as Edison perhaps hoped it would, banish our need for sleep.

In fact — although the suggestion would no doubt outrage Edison — the light bulb can be considered one of three major technological "curses" of the modern age, says sleep researcher Harvey Moldofsky, chief psychiatrist at Toronto Western Hospital. The other two are the jet engine, which gave us jet lag, and the continuous conveyor belt, which gave us rotating shift schedules. In the past two decades, the trend toward the 24-hour lifestyle has been greatly accelerated by the advent of sophisticated computer-communications devices such as cellular phones and portable computers and fax machines. Together, these technologies have permitted — indeed, forced — dramatic changes in our work patterns and lifestyles. They have made possible our attempt to override what Moldofsky calls "biologic time." Western civilization, he says, has "done everything possible to eliminate sleep."

But the attempt seems doomed to failure. Technology evolves much faster than biology and our hunter-gatherer physiology is increasingly hard pressed to keep up. For the overwhelming part of the millions of years the human body has been evolving, it was not required to cope with working the graveyard shift, cramming all night for exams, preventing a nuclear meltdown, launching a space shuttle or zapping halfway around the world faster than the speed of sound. We were, for most of our history, a primitive species living lives far more tied to the natural cycle of day and night than we are today. We hunted and gathered mostly by day, and since we simply did not function very well at night (certainly not nearly as well as some of our predators), we slept — with luck, tucked somewhere out of harm's way. Indeed, it has been suggested that early in our history sleep served as a survival mechanism, preventing us from blundering off cliffs or bumping into saber-tooth tigers in the dark, forcing us to be inactive when our ability to find food and defend ourselves against predators is at its daily nadir.

"Our sleep system obviously evolved to meet the demands of man the hunter and man the gatherer in his original natural state. That's the first million or million and a half years of human evolution," says Roger Broughton, a sleep researcher at Ottawa General Hospital. "The evolutionary pressure was for very different work and lighting circumstances than exist today." The light bulb, he says, is "very much a Johnny-come-lately."

Dinges comments that humans, like all other creatures, are adapted to their ecological niche and "that doesn't easily change — yet we're living in a world that no longer acknowledges that." These days, people work (and play) every day of the week and at all hours of the day and night. Mortimer Mamelak, director of the Sleep Disorders Centre of Sunnybrook Medical Centre in Toronto observes that our lives have become increasingly separated from the natural rest/activity cycle dictated by the sun, and this has strained the ability of our sleep/wake system to adapt.

Consider the following examples:

• In 1978, a commercial airliner scheduled to land at Los Angeles International Airport passed over the airport at 32,000 feet and unaccountably headed out over the Pacific. Flying on automatic pilot, the plane was about 165 kilometers (100 miles) out to sea before air traffic controllers found a way to sound an alarm in the cockpit. The entire crew had fallen asleep on the flight deck. In another incident, a pilot flying a Honolulu-bound jet with 150 people on board fell asleep at the stick when the aircraft was just 200 feet off the ground. The co-pilot realized what was happening in time to make a safe landing.

• On the night of January 27, 1986, a dozen key managers involved in the U.S. space shuttle program held a three-hour teleconference during which the ill-fated decision was made to launch the shuttle Challenger the next day. That day had been a long and difficult one, involving the latest in a long series of launch delays, and the managers had been on duty for periods ranging from 12 to 19 hours. The two managers who had been on duty the longest time had slept only about two hours each the night before.

• In New York City, a grand jury found that fatigue among doctors was a major contributing factor in the death of a young woman admitted to a New York hospital with a high fever. In many North American hospitals, interns and residents are on call for up to 36 hours at a time. New York state subsequently passed a law limiting interns and residents to an 80-hour work week and to no more than 12 consecutive hours of duty in the emergency department and no more than 24 consecutive hours in other departments.

• In December 1987, the U.S. Congress, pressing to end a session for the Christmas break, worked feverishly around the clock for a week to pass a $604-billion omnibus appropriations bill, representing two-thirds of the fiscal 1988 budget. One senator commented that his days became 17- to 18-hour marathons, during which he was making decisions on projects worth hundreds of millions of dollars.

• Regulations governing the duty hours of North American truck drivers force them to follow a schedule that produces disruption of their sleep/wake cycles equivalent to that caused by flying across the continent or across the Atlantic every day.

• The Three Mile Island nuclear accident occurred at 4:00 a.m., in the middle of the "trough" in the human sleep/wake cycle that typically occurs in the early morning hours. The crew on duty had been on the night shift only a few days and had been on a rapidly rotating shift schedule for six weeks, a situation that is known to contribute to high levels of fatigue and lack of alertness. Two other serious incidents at U.S. nuclear plants — and the Chernobyl nuclear accident in the Soviet Union — occurred between 1:30 and 4:30 a.m. A Pennsylvania reactor was shut down and its owners fined $1.25 million after operators were found sleeping on the job.

• In the United States, an estimated 6,500 automobile-related deaths each year — 13 percent of the annual toll — may be caused by people falling asleep at the wheel.

Incidents and statistics like these raise serious questions as to whether the human sleep/wake cycle is really up to life in the fast lane. Can our physiology cope with the mixture of endurance and high performance needed to achieve what we deem to be success in our society? Should it be required to? Is it equal to the challenge of monitoring, managing and controlling the vast array of often dangerous technologies that are supposed to make life better and more productive, but are just as likely to make it more hazardous — as often as not because of human error?

Despite the mounting evidence that sleep problems can cause serious social and economic disruption, we still tend to dismiss them as small potatoes. With the likes of cancer, heart disease and AIDS lurking about, this indifferent attitude toward sleep is perhaps not surprising. But, even though sleep problems may not terrify us the way cancer and AIDS do, they can nevertheless destroy lives and careers and cost billions of dollars in lost property and reduced productivity of the work force. An article in *The Wall Street Journal* estimated the cost to U.S. industry from reduced alertness in the workplace at about $70 billion a year. And though sleep is rarely thought of as a life-threatening activity, sleep problems directly or indirectly cause thousands of deaths each year. As our lives become ever more dependent on sophisticated and potentially dangerous technologies, the threat posed by the lack of restful sleep increases apace.

Certainly, there's far more to the problem than the occasional bout of insomnia or jet lag; nor are those afflicted confined to the ranks of factory workers. We've all received admonishments to get a good night's sleep — the magic panacea offered by doctors, mothers and well-meaning friends to revive sagging spirits and restore a sense of perspective — but for millions of people, maintaining a regular routine of 6 to 8 hours of sleep a night is a next-to-impossible task. According to various estimates, perhaps as many as 20 to 25 percent of the working population in industrialized countries now works shifts. Millions more are awake in the hours after midnight — not only working, but spending money in restaurants, stores or while traveling. Boston University sociologist Murray Melbin, who describes the night as a new frontier, has called this the age of incessance.

We appear to be evolving toward a 24-hour economy and with it a 24-hour lifestyle. Many industries and essential services already operate around the clock and the trend is increasing: these days, everything from brokerage firms to grocery stores and hairdressing salons is open 24 hours a day. Many people have jobs that involve not only working shifts but also working for long hours for days or weeks at a time, or jobs that dish up a steady diet of demanding but unpredictable crises, often in situations with many lives or millions of dollars in property at stake. Technological advances in communications and transportation are changing the time/space coordinates of our lives, spawning a work ethic that demands that people be able to function at any hour of the day or night in any circumstances virtually anyplace on earth. Articles in newspapers and magazines tout the advent of "the mobile executive" who, armed with cellular phones and portable computers and fax machines, can do business from a car, a hotel room, a ski resort — even from an aircraft 30,000 feet over the ocean. There is no refuge; some executives have even installed these technologies in their vacation "retreats."

But, unlike tireless technologies, the human body is not made of wires, plastic and computer chips, so it comes as no surprise that sleep problems are widespread. A 1987 survey conducted by several groups of U.S. sleep researchers revealed that fully two-thirds of the American population reported having problems with sleep on a regular basis. About half of those surveyed said that they are less than "very satisfied" with the quality of their sleep and that their daily activities are affected at least once a week as a result of a poor night's sleep. There's evidence to suggest that by the mid-1970s, Americans were sleeping about an hour less a night on average than they did in the early part of the century.

In industrialized societies, we live in a workaholic, achievement-oriented, time-obsessed culture. According to a Harris poll, the leisure time of the average American shrank about 37 percent — from about 26½ hours a week to about 16½ hours a week — between the mid-1970s and the late 1980s, and the work week increased from an average of less than 41 hours to more than 47 hours. In a cover story on "how America is running itself ragged," *Time* magazine (appropriately) suggests this is the era of "time famine" and says that time will be in the 1990s what money was in the 1980s — what Harris calls the "most precious commodity." Chronic fatigue and daytime sleepiness are now so common that they are, for the most part, simply accepted as the unavoidable price of demanding modern lifestyles — as the unsurprising consequence of working too hard at all hours of the day or night, chasing too many deadlines, coping with too many crises with too little opportunity to "get away from it all."

It is a society in which the ability to forgo sleep and soldier on in the face of pressing deadlines is taken as a measure of dedication and determination — as a sign of having the "Right Stuff" work ethic that results in corporate, professional or political success. But does it have to be this way? Sleep scientists say no. Decades of research into biological rhythms and the human sleep/wake cycle have enabled them to devise therapies and practical techniques for helping people cope with sleep problems and maintain alertness on the job. Recent research into the complex relationship between work and sleep suggests that even more radical changes in sleep/wake/work cycles may be possible and desirable.

Many industries and businesses — particularly those involving shift work — have started to seek the advice of sleep researchers to stem the losses in productivity and cut the accident rates that result from disruptions of the sleep/wake cycles of their workers. In recent years, dozens of companies have hired sleep consultants to analyze and rearrange shift-work schedules, most of which were established long before much was known about human circadian rhythms and their limitations. Certainly, circadian principles were not used in devising these schedules, and in most cases the schedules could not have had a worse effect on workers' alertness and productivity if they'd been deliberately designed that way.

Sleep doctors have also been able to help many people whose ability to work — or to do much of anything else — has been seriously compromised by a variety of sleep disorders. Although some of these maladies are rare and rather bizarre, others are far more common in the general population than previously suspected. These disorders often cause sufferers to experience devastating problems at work and in their personal lives. In the past, these people were often regarded as malingerers, hypochondriacs or neurotics and their sleep problems went unacknowledged and untreated; now, many disorders can be diagnosed in the sleep lab and often treated well enough to give those who suffer from them some semblance of a normal life.

More recent research has raised intriguing new questions about our ability to cope with the demands of modern lifestyles by adopting a strategy of multiple naps rather than sleeping for a single long period every 24 hours. These studies suggest that human physiology, like that of other animals, may be naturally suited to napping — that our sleep/wake cycle may not be quite so bound to the 8-hours-at-night regimen that has long been regarded as the norm for humans. Several research projects now under way are investigating the nature of naps, their effect on mood and performance and whether they can be used to reduce the total amount of time we sleep and still maintain a high level of alertness and performance on the job, particularly while doing demanding work.

Fatigue on the job — and the human error that results from it — exacts a high price, one that is measured not only in dollars and cents but also in human dimensions: job burnout, family disintegration and even the loss of life. It is inevitable that our growing knowledge of the human sleep/wake cycle will be put to practical use in the workplace, not only to increase productivity but to reduce these human costs.

But like most other applications of scientific and technological knowledge to our daily lives, this trend will probably create a host of new and thorny social, economic and labor/management issues. For example, it may one day be possible to have machines monitor workers' levels of sleepiness or fatigue and measure the impact on job performance — perhaps far better than workers themselves can do using only the subjective measure of how they feel. But how will workers react to the idea of a machine telling them they're too tired to do their job? Or worse, telling their *boss* that they're too tired to work? Will such technological intervention affect job security or promotions? Will workers accept such monitoring more readily if lives are at stake than if they perceive that the system is intended primarily to benefit the company financially? Will management be prepared to adopt innovative shift-work schedules or incorporate scheduled napping into the workday? Are such measures even practical? What will they cost — and will the costs be offset by gains in productivity and safety? Are we headed into a 24-hour economy when most businesses and services will be expected to operate around the clock seven days a week? Would such a system allow many more people to work — and sleep — at any time of the day or night that best suits their individual physiology? Would this result in greater safety, productivity and worker satisfaction or less? What will be the net effect of new technologies that give people greater flexibility and freedom in planning their work schedules to suit their biological rhythms, but at the same time make it nearly impossible for them to truly escape from work?

These are some of the questions sleep researchers are just beginning to ask. But perhaps there are some even more fundamental questions: Should we even be attempting to tinker with our sleep/wake patterns in this way? Are we already "cheating on sleep" far too much? Should we be directing our efforts instead to finding ways to slow down the pace of modern life, to allow ourselves the amount of sleep that our rather primitive physiology demands? Is this even possible?

Will the findings of sleep researchers and their application to the workplace help us to live better, more productive and more rested lives, or will we simply use this knowledge to push our sleep/wake system harder than ever — and continue rushing along in the fast lane, fast asleep?

# SECTION 1:
# THE PROBLEM OF SLEEP

# CHAPTER 3

# STILL A MYSTERY AFTER ALL THESE YEARS

*If sleep does not serve an absolutely vital function, then it is the biggest mistake the evolutionary process ever made.*
UNIVERSITY OF CHICAGO SLEEP RESEARCHER ALLAN RECHTSCHAFFEN

I<small>T'S NO WONDER THAT SLEEP</small> fascinates us. It is something we all do virtually every day of our lives and yet it's still such a mystery. In fact, for most of human history the only thing we've really known for certain about sleep is that we need it — that trying to do without it will drop us in our tracks in very short order.

In recent decades, with the advent of new technologies that allow researchers to monitor electrical activity in the brain, scientists have discovered a great deal about sleep. But for all these advances, the answer to one central question has proved frustratingly elusive: the precise function of sleep — what it actually does to or for our brain and our body — remains a puzzle. We spend a third of our lives in a mysterious, dangerous and seemingly unproductive state of unconsciousness — and no one knows exactly why.

"It's a huge biological mystery, a staggering mystery of monumental proportions," says David Dinges. "That's why there are so many scientists studying it now. It's a great big Nobel Prize sitting out there."

Could sleep be only a "vestigial remnant" that has outlived its usefulness? asks Allan Rechtschaffen. For scientists, this idea goes very much against the grain; instinctively, they reject the suggestion that sleep might be nothing more than what many workaholic over-achievers believe it to be: a waste of valuable time. If that were the case, evolution would surely have stamped it out by now — for sleep definitely has its down side. Besides the fact that it consumes a large portion of every creature's life, sleep is a state of extreme vulnerability, one that greatly increases susceptibility to attack from enemies. In fact, says Rechtschaffen, sleep is "so apparently maladaptive" that we must ask why some other behavior did not evolve to do whatever it is that sleep does.

Consider the giraffe, for example. So ungainly that it takes a life-threatening risk practically every time it lies down (it needs about 15 seconds just to stand up again), the giraffe can't afford to sleep very much. Giraffes have been observed to lie down three to eight times a night for periods ranging from 3 to 75 minutes, but most of that time is spent awake; on average, they sleep for only about 2 hours out of every 24. Sleep researcher James Horne of Loughborough University in England notes that giraffes spend most of the night relaxed but awake and that if sleep were not an essential function it would have been a rather trifling evolutionary matter for this resting phase to have been extended by a few hours and sleep eliminated altogether.

It's also remarkable that aquatic mammals such as dolphins, porpoises and seals engage in the risky behavior of sleep, says Dinges. "Aside from the fact that they can be eaten, they can drown. They've got to breathe air." These species have developed remarkable ways of coping. For example, the blind Indus dolphin, which lives in danger-ous, muddy waters, sleeps frequently but for only about 90 seconds at a time — a pattern that appears to provide a total of about 7 hours of sleep in every 24. Studies of other dolphins and porpoises have revealed the existence of an unusual 3-hour sleep/wake cycle, re-peated several times a night, during which one hemisphere of the brain sleeps for an hour, then the other sleeps for an hour and during the third hour, both hemispheres are awake.

Humans too have found ways to reduce the vulnerability caused by sleep; it's even been suggested that social institutions like the home and family may have evolved in part from the need for protection during sleep. Today, modern technology has removed most of the environmental barriers to being awake 24 hours a day for hundreds of millions of people. Yet still we sleep and still we falter if we don't.

The simple, inexplicable fact is that the one sure-fire way of eliminating the risks inherent in sleep and the "waste" of time it involves — the simple expedient of eliminating sleep altogether — has never materialized. "For [sleep] not to have evolved away means that it is doing something very major, but we can't find what it is," says Dinges. "We can't figure out why organisms would do it. Why would nature permit that?"

There are many different theories about the purpose and function of sleep but most fall into one of two broad general categories. The first, says Dinges, is that sleep is a "forced time out" that makes up part of the daily rhythms that govern many biological processes and behaviors. Most creatures experience daily peaks and troughs in performance and alertness; some are better at night, others during the day. Sleep may have evolved as a way of precluding activity at the wrong time, which would be inefficient and increase the likelihood of being eaten or killed.

One variant of this theory is that the function of sleep is to conserve the energy needed for physical exertion and thereby reduce our need for food. Biologist Ralph Berger of the University of California at Santa Cruz suggested that sleep and hibernation may have a common evolution. However, Horne argues that energy conservation may now be only a minor function of human sleep. While small-brained mammals appear to need sleep in order to relax — when they're awake, they're always active — humans can and do rest physically while awake, so they may no longer need to sleep for this purpose, he suggests.

Dinges questions the "time-out" theories another way: if sleep does nothing more than force us to rest and conserve energy, why is it that when we rest but don't sleep, we're still not alert the next day? "If it's just a matter of not being active at that phase, why aren't you up and at 'em?" Laboratory studies have shown that resting while awake simply does not do whatever sleep does to restore mood and performance; when subjects lie in bed all night without sleeping, they still feel sleepy and tired the next day and their ability to do various tasks is impaired.

There is a second major group of theories about the function of sleep based on the concept that sleep performs a major biological restorative function. To most of us, the idea that sleep restores the body and mind makes intuitive sense; we've all experienced its effects in banishing fatigue, restoring alertness and improving mood. We also know that if something is wrong with our sleep, or if we don't get enough of it, we become seriously grumpy individuals who are inefficient, hard to live with and often downright dangerous to be around. And, in recent years, laboratory experiments have shown that even comparatively small amounts of sleep can make a big difference in maintaining or restoring performance in sleep-deprived subjects.

It seems clear, then, that sleep does *something* restorative. But what, exactly? We simply don't know yet, says Moldofsky, who is doing research on the problems of people who suffer from unrefreshing sleep, who seem to get enough sleep, but wake up tired and complaining of chronic, diffuse aches and pains, and who literally drag themselves through their lives. Unrefreshing sleep is a major problem, he says. "The importance of the quality of sleep is vastly underestimated. You can sleep for 8 hours, but how do you feel when you get up? What is it that makes sleep refreshing?"

In their search for answers, scientists are turning to the biochemistry of the brain. Many have speculated about the possible existence of a "hypnotoxin" or chemical "sleep factor" — or perhaps several such chemicals working together. The idea is that these sleep factors build up in the body during wakefulness, causing sleepiness and finally inducing sleep, and then diminish during sleep. Or the process might work the other way around: perhaps the depletion of certain chemicals during wakefulness forces sleep, which then restores the levels of these chemicals needed for alertness.

Do sleep factors really exist? If so, what is their chemical nature and how do they act on the brain? These are questions that have tantalized scientists for a long time; in fact, attempts at an explanation date back to Aristotle, who suggested that sleep was induced by gases that "evaporated" from digested food. But so far there are no conclusive answers, and the scientific evidence is somewhat contradictory. However, several studies have shown that certain biological chemicals isolated from sleeping animals and injected into ones that are awake can cause the latter to fall asleep.

Peter Hauri, director of the Dartmouth-Hitchcock Sleep Disorders Center in New Hampshire, says in a booklet called *The Sleep Disorders* that a combination of various chemicals in the brain, known as neurotransmitters, is believed to be responsible for modulating the balance between sleep and wakefulness. We appear to have two systems within our brains, one that promotes sleep and the other wakefulness. In order for us to fall asleep, the wakefulness system must diminish in strength because "only then can the weaker sleep system actively start to dominate." He suggests that insomnia may result either from too much strength in the wakefulness system (excessive arousal) or too little strength in the sleep system.

Researchers have found that the patterns of secretion of a number of important biological chemicals change radically during sleep and some of these substances have been shown to be sleep promoting; but scientists are still a long way from fully understanding the biochemical mechanisms involved in the control of sleep and wakefulness. "We know something about it, but we don't know everything we need to know," says Moldofsky. "It's unlikely there is a single sleep factor, but there might very well be a cascade phenomenon of various factors that come together at a particular time that might be related to the induction and preservation of sleep." And what starts the cascade? "That's what we have to find out."

And what is it that sleep restores? Our body? Our brain? Both? And how? Again, there are more theories than there are conclusive answers. Some scientists speculate that sleep plays a role in metabolic buildup and the regeneration of cells and tissues, that it helps to consolidate memories, or to develop and "repattern" neurological pathways in the brain or to update the "data banks" in our brains. Allan Rechtschaffen and his colleagues have done sleep-deprivation studies with rats suggesting that regulation of body temperature and energy expenditure is a major function of sleep — although they say that it remains unclear why a condition as complicated and time-consuming as sleep is needed to do this.

James Horne has proposed a provocative theory that sleep in humans and other advanced mammals primarily restores not the body but the brain — in particular, the cerebral cortex, which controls complex mental processes. Horne says that muscles can relax and recover as much when we simply rest as when we sleep, but the cerebral cortex cannot; even in waking restfulness, it is active with thoughts and awareness of the outside world. In mammals, he suggests, only sleep provides a significant amount of cerebral "shutdown" and, thus, "some form of essential restitution for the brain." There may be some support for this idea in the fact that people who stay in bed 24 hours a day, and therefore indulge in very little tiring physical activity, do not sleep much less than active people. This suggests that the brain needs a kind of restoration provided uniquely by sleep, even when the body is physically at rest.

Horne concludes that for humans and other advanced mammals the benefits of sleep for restoring the body are doubtful. Noting that an inherent circadian (approximately 24-hour) sleep/wake cycle clearly exists, he suggests that *both* this innate cycle and the requirement for cerebral restoration are responsible for our need to sleep. (The circadian sleep/wake cycle and the effect of sleep loss on mood and performance will be discussed in later chapters.)

Other researchers challenge Horne's theory, however. For example, Roger Broughton points out that there's strong evidence that sleep loss affects other portions of the brain, e.g., subcortical areas known to be involved in the regulation of sleepiness and alertness. "These are all brain functions, so why say [sleep] only has to do with cortical function?"

Moldofsky adds that his research suggests strongly that sleep does have a biological/physiological restorative function. Nonrestorative sleep is one of the major symptoms in people who suffer from chronic widespread pain and chronic fatigue that cannot be attributed to disease or to structural damage of the body. Patients are often diagnosed as having rheumatic pain (known as fibromyalgia) or chronic fatigue syndrome ("yuppie flu"). But Moldofsky and his colleagues have found that regardless of how they're labeled, these people have one thing in common: there's something abnormal about their sleep. "What we've discovered is that altered sleep physiology is related to this sense of unrefreshing sleep and daytime fatigue and it's ubiquitous throughout these disorders, which are characterized by chronic fatigue, diffuse aches and pains and unrefreshing sleep." The brain-wave patterns observed in these people while they're asleep suggest that they are practically on the threshold of being awake. They typically report that their sleep is light and restless; they refer to "skimming across the surface" of sleep, Moldofsky says. And they wake up feeling tired and complaining of aching and stiffness all over, localized tender spots and persistent fatigue — a feeling of being "run over by a truck."

On rare occasions when they do sleep deeply, they report little pain and fatigue on awakening. These findings suggest an association between nonrestorative sleep and the symptoms of chronic diffuse pain and fatigue. Recent studies indicate there is an intimate connection between the immune system and the sleep/wake system in the brain, but how disturbances in these two systems contribute to chronic fatigue and pain "remains to be unraveled," Moldofsky said.

Even more tantalizing are indications from his studies and others that during sleep major changes occur in the levels of many biochemicals known to play an important role in the body's physical well-being — hormones and chemicals associated with the endocrine and immune systems, for example. "Certain immune functions dramatically change when you're asleep," said Moldofsky. For example, the activity of natural killer cells, which fight off infection, increases before sleep and drops off precipitously immediately after a person falls asleep. But these patterns of activity are altered when subjects are deprived of sleep (even a single night of sleep loss causes marked changes) and "when you return to sleep, there's a prolonged decline in natural killer cell activity," Moldofsky said.

What this means isn't clear; it's impossible to tell, for example, whether sleep loss causes a weakening of the immune system. "After all, all of us have stayed up all night and we don't get sick," Moldofsky comments. Nevertheless, people often complain of catching a cold or the flu when they're tired and run-down. "We hear over and over again, 'I've been working so hard and then when I want to relax, I get sick.'" But he has no answer as to why people should be more prone to succumbing to a flu virus when they're sleep deprived than when they're rested. "Relating the changes that we see [in the immune system] to causing disease is a big jump."

· · · · · · ·

These issues are by no means the end of the mystery surrounding sleep. One major problem with all current theories about the purpose of sleep, according to Dinges, is that neither the "forced time-out" variants nor the "restoration" theories can explain "what the hell we're doing with two kinds of sleep, REM and non-REM — why they're so incredibly different and why they vary throughout the night. So we're a long way from understanding this mystery yet."

## TWO KINDS OF SLEEP

Sleep research took a major step forward in the 1930s when noninvasive techniques were developed for measuring electrical activity in the brain. Before this, researchers had to resort to ineffective observational techniques that usually woke subjects up — for example, prying open eyelids to observe whether the pupils were dilated. Today, subjects in sleep labs are monitored remotely. Electrodes placed on the scalp and face feed information into a polygraph machine that records electrical activity going on not only in the brain but in the eyes and muscles as well. The record of brain-wave activity is called an electroencephalogram (EEG), that of eye movements an electrooculogram (EOG) and that of muscle activity an electromyogram (EMG). Electrodes are usually placed on the chest so that a record of heart activity — an electrocardiogram (EKG) — can also be made. In many cases, particularly in diagnosing sleep disorders, measurements are also made of snoring and breathing patterns, limb movements and changes in oxygen and carbon dioxide levels in the blood.

The output of the polygraph is a series of jagged lines trailing across long continuous sheets of graph paper that show wavelike patterns of peaks and troughs indicating the state of alertness or sleepiness of the subject. The amount of data gathered is huge; a single night's output from one subject can consume 300 meters (1,000 feet) of paper. These tracings show marked differences not only between the waking and sleeping states, but at various times during sleep as well. As a result, polygraph records have become the basic tool researchers use to plumb the depths of the sleep state.

One of the most significant things found in humans and other mammals is that there are two distinct types of sleep — REM and non-REM (NREM).* REM stands for rapid eye movement, a designation that stems from a discovery made by researchers at the University of Chicago in 1952. Nathaniel Kleitman, a sleep research pioneer, was curious about the slow, rolling eye movements that usually accompany falling asleep. He assigned a graduate student, Eugene Aserinsky, to watch for the occurrence of these movements in subjects throughout the night. Much to everyone's surprise, As-

---

* Studies indicate that REM sleep seems to be largely confined to mammals. Reptiles clearly experience NREM sleep and so do birds, which also occasionally experience very brief episodes of a state that might be a precursor to REM sleep. Only mammals show a distinct pattern of REM/NREM sleep. Research projects involving everything from elephants to mice indicate that all mammals spend a substantial amount of their sleep time in REM.

erinsky found evidence in the polygraph records that at various times during sleep the subject's eyes would dart around rapidly rather than rolling slowly. The scientists were skeptical about this finding until they directly observed the rapid eye movements in sleeping subjects, according to William Dement, then a medical student studying under Kleitman and now director of the Stanford University Sleep Disorders Clinic and Research Center. In his book *Some Must Watch While Some Must Sleep,* he comments that these movements, which had "no business" showing up during sleep, were not only highly coordinated, but were often faster and sharper than subjects could accomplish while awake. He adds that this discovery, which belied the conventional wisdom that sleep was a state of total quiescence, changed the entire course of sleep research.

Dement subsequently found that the eye movements were accompanied by distinctive brain-wave patterns and other physiological changes that indicated a departure from quiet sleep. The polygraph data also revealed the presence of a regular cycle of REM/NREM sleep that recurs four to six times a night — a finding that demonstrated conclusively that sleep is not a quiet, uniform state of rest. In fact, it turns out that REM sleep is as different from non-REM sleep as sleeping is from waking, and its presence and purpose are as much a mystery as sleep itself. The discovery of REM periods had a major impact on sleep research because it made the sleep state much more intriguing to scientists than it had been before. The realization that sleep was not just a boring, unchanging state of inactivity prompted the establishment of a wide range of research programs that have resulted in an ability to diagnose and treat many sleep disorders and other sleep-related problems of modern life.

## THE STAGES OF SLEEP

When you fall asleep, you lose awareness of the world around you. And, despite the fact that we commonly talk about "falling" asleep, the onset of sleep is not a gradual process; it happens very abruptly. This has been observed in the laboratory when subjects lying in bed with their eyes taped open are subjected to bright light flashes every second or so. Instructed to press a switch every time they see the flash, they will do so for a time and then suddenly they'll just stop. Awareness of the outside world has vanished literally from one second to the next.

As you fall asleep, you enter the first non-REM phase of the sleep period. In humans, non-REM sleep is divided into stages, each one deeper than the one before and distinguished by brain waves of progressively slower frequency. Non-REM is known as "quiet sleep" because breathing is slow and even, the heartbeat is regular, blood pressure is at its daily minimum, brain temperature decreases and blood flow to the brain is reduced. There is also little body movement and EEG patterns are slow and regular.

Stage 1 is light sleep — a transitional stage that most people call drowsiness. Awakened at this point, you might say that you weren't sleeping, just "drifting off." In adults, it typically lasts up to about 10 minutes and is characterized by changes in the EEG readings, by slow, rolling eye movements and by relaxed muscle tension in most of the body. Fragmentary thoughts often swirl around in your head, progressing from realistic to fantastic; sensations of floating or falling or feelings of anxiety or peacefulness are common. Some people who suffer from depression, schizophrenia or a sleep disorder called narcolepsy may experience frightening hallucinations during this twilight zone between waking and sleeping.

From Stage 1, you descend through ever-deeper stages of sleep, during which you become progressively more detached from the outside world and more difficult to wake. Stage 2, intermediate sleep, lasts about 20 minutes and is followed by the deep-sleep phase (once divided into Stages 3 and 4), beginning 30 to 45 minutes after falling asleep. Deep sleep is characterized by large, slow brain waves and thus is often called slow wave sleep (SWS). This final stage of the non-REM period may last only a few minutes or up to about an hour, depending on the age of the sleeper. (Children spend more time in slow wave sleep than adults.)

During slow wave sleep, the sleeper is virtually "shut down" — largely cut off from sensory contact with the outside world. It's the kind of sleep that elicits the description "dead to the world." Arousing a sleeper from slow wave sleep is very difficult, and those who do awake often feel groggy, confused and disoriented — a state sometimes called "sleep inertia" or "sleep drunkenness." It's worst when someone is awakened from deep sleep in the first third of the night. Children in particular may be nearly unwakable, and if they are roused they may be so dazed that they won't even remember having been wakened. Some childhood sleep disorders such as bed-wetting, sleepwalking and night terrors are believed to occur during incomplete arousal from slow wave sleep. (It has been suggested that this period of low arousability may be a way of ensuring the continuity of sleep, which some scientists argue is necessary for sleep to be restorative.)

At the end of the first period of slow wave sleep, you ascend back to Stage 2 and then enter the first REM period of the night, which is brief. The two types of sleep alternate four to six times a night, with each cycle lasting from 70 to 110 minutes, averaging about 90 minutes in adults. Slow wave sleep dominates the first two sleep cycles in adults, but as the night wears on, it decreases markedly and the time spent in REM sleep increases. Toward morning, slow wave sleep virtually disappears and REM sleep dominates, lasting up to 45 to 60 minutes a cycle and becoming more intense.

## REM SLEEP: A THIRD STATE OF CONSCIOUSNESS

REM is a curious state: it is different from both slow wave sleep and from wakefulness, but in some respects resembles both. In fact, EEG patterns during REM are quite similar to those that occur when you're awake; it's been suggested that one purpose of REM may be to counterbalance the vulnerability caused by deep sleep by permitting periodic vigilance of the outside environment. Some researchers suggest that, in fact, there are three separate states of consciousness: waking, sleeping and REM.

REM is sometimes referred to as "active sleep" because it is characterized not only by rapid eye movements but also by irregular breathing and heart rate and by increases in oxygen consumption, brain temperature and blood flow to the brain. Blood pressure becomes variable, sometimes increasing significantly, and there is speculation that this can trigger heart attacks. Regulation of body temperature is impaired; both shivering and sweating stop and internal temperature moves in the direction of ambient temperature. Penile erection in males and clitoral engorgement in females often occurs.*

Convulsive twitching of the face and fingers also occurs, but the torso, arms and legs literally *cannot* move because the large muscles

---

* This fact can be used to test whether male impotence is physiological or psychological in nature. If erection does not occur during REM sleep, the cause of the impotence is likely organic. If it does, psychological factors are more likely to be causing the problem.

of the body are paralyzed. This paralysis is different from the type of immobility that occurs during non-REM sleep; in that case, the relative lack of movement occurs because the brain does not command it, not because the body is actually incapable of moving, as is the case during REM sleep.

The purpose of this sleep paralysis may be to preclude a dangerous acting-out of dreams* — for it is during REM sleep that most dreaming occurs. This was first documented in Nathaniel Kleitman's lab in the late 1950s, when the researchers wakened subjects during both REM and non-REM sleep and asked them what they recalled. About 80 percent of those awakened from REM sleep recalled vivid dreams, compared with only about seven percent of those awakened from non-REM sleep.

It's now known that dreams recalled after awakening from REM sleep have a markedly different character than those recalled after awakening from non-REM sleep. They tend to be more vivid and visual, more emotional and sometimes frightening, and they usually have a continuous, detailed and often bizarre story content. Dreams reported after non-REM sleep are usually disjointed and fragmentary, more like a vague, drifting kind of thinking than what most people would call dreaming. Nevertheless, it cannot be said that dreaming occurs *only* during REM sleep.

Many people, especially those with little interest in dreams, claim they "never" dream, but this is not true — it's just that they forget most of them. Dreams are elusive, usually dissipating within seconds of awakening unless a special effort is made to remember them; thus, although we spend about 10 percent of our lives dreaming, most of this experience is lost to us. However, researchers have found they can increase dream recall significantly by using polygraph information to wake subjects in the middle of REM periods in order to elicit dream reports from them.

It's beyond the scope of this book to discuss the nature, content and meaning of dreams. However, it is important to focus briefly on REM sleep, which is as much a puzzle as sleep itself. Although scientists don't know why it exists or exactly what purpose it serves, it too seems

---

* Scientists recently discovered a rare new sleep disorder, called REM behavior disorder, in which patients are able to act out their dreams because of a malfunction in the system that normally maintains paralysis during REM sleep. This is discussed further in Chapter 6.

to be necessary. Sleepers deliberately deprived of REM sleep will try to make up for it (a phenomenon known as REM rebound). If sleepers are prevented from obtaining REM sleep by being awakened as soon as it begins, they will enter REM sleep more rapidly the next time they're allowed to sleep and these REM periods will be more intense than normal. If deprivation continues, subjects soon start going into REM virtually immediately on falling asleep; ultimately it becomes impossible to further deprive them without keeping them awake all the time. When subjects take naps shorter than the 90 minutes it usually takes for the first REM period to occur, REM sleep shows up sooner in the sleep period.

These studies show clearly that we cannot go long without REM sleep; selective deprivation invariably increases the pressure for this type of sleep. But why? Contrary to theories that such deprivation might precipitate psychotic behavior, there's no evidence that it causes serious or long-lasting psychological problems in otherwise normal, healthy people. And in some depressed patients, REM deprivation actually *improves* mood and performance.

There are numerous theories about the possible physiological function of REM sleep (quite aside from theories about the purely psychological dimensions of dreams). It has been speculated, for example, that REM sleep may play a role in brain development and maintenance — for example, in restoring or "repatterning" nerve connections in the brain and nervous system. Sleep researcher Richard Coleman, president of a California consulting firm, Coleman & Associates, suggests that the computer provides a useful analogy here: just as reorganizing, updating and erasing of files must be done periodically in a computer system, so REM sleep and dreams may be a manifestation of the brain's effort to perform a similar kind of housekeeping. He proposes that dreams might be "remembered fragments" from a nocturnal data-processing effort, in which the "off-line brain assimilates the day's experiences and updates old 'programs.'" He says this theory is interesting because it provides a possible explanation for sleeping and dreaming: they put the brain into "off-line mode" and protect it from outside distractions while it engages in information-processing and retraining. "It would be difficult to update our memory bank while we are awake and functioning."

A controversial theory along these lines has been put forward by British molecular biologists Francis Crick (co-winner of the Nobel

Prize for the discovery of the structure of the DNA molecule) and Graeme Mitchison. They've suggested that the purpose of REM sleep is a kind of "reverse learning" — that it allows us to "unlearn" or discard useless or disturbing thought patterns and thereby prevent the brain's storage capacity from being overloaded. They argue that the failure of this process could lead to waking disturbances including obsessions, delusions and hallucinations. They even suggest that it's *not* a good idea to try remembering dreams because this could result in retaining the very thought patterns that the brain is working so hard to throw out — an idea that, not surprisingly, finds little support among scientists who believe in the psychological benefits of dream recall. One of the difficulties with this theory is that there's no evidence of psychological ill effects in long-term users of antidepressant drugs, which are known to have a powerful effect in inhibiting REM sleep.

## SLEEP PATTERNS CHANGE WITH AGE

Sleep patterns change significantly as we age. Both total sleep time and the continuity of sleep decrease steadily with increasing age and significant changes occur in the relative amounts of different sleep stages obtained, particularly slow wave sleep.

Newborn infants sleep about 17 to 18 hours a day, but total sleep time drops to about 10 to 12 hours by age four and to about 9 to 10 hours at age 10. At the onset of adolescence, there's another major drop to an average of about 7½ hours and, after that, a gradual decline during young adulthood and middle age to an average of about 7 hours. By the seventh decade, the average drops to about 6 to 6½ hours.

Preadolescents sleep more efficiently than any other age group. In general, they experience little disruption, sleeping soundly and continuously during the night and remaining alert and active all day. They maintain a regular sleep/wake pattern with little effort. By adolescence, however, sleep begins to lose its continuity, nighttime awakenings become more frequent and a tendency toward daytime sleepiness develops.

The incidence of insomnia increases with age. Sleep efficiency — the percentage of time in bed spent asleep — decreases after about age 30 in men and after age 50 in women and the number of nighttime awakenings increases in men after age 40 and in women after age 70.

These problems are even more pronounced among the elderly. The nature of insomnia also changes with age; young adults typically have trouble falling asleep, while the elderly experience more nighttime awakenings and tend to wake up earlier in the morning. "The deterioration of nighttime sleep is mirrored in increased pressure for sleep during the day," notes Mortimer Mamelak in a paper on insomnia. "The degenerative brain diseases of old age only exaggerate these physiological changes."

The incidence of sleep disorders also varies with age. Sleepwalking, bed-wetting and night terrors occur more frequently in children. Adolescents and young adults often have problems with daytime sleepiness, and the onset of several major sleep disorders often occurs during this period. The incidence of sleep disorders increases with age and is most pronounced in the elderly.

Finally, there are marked changes in the structure of sleep as we get older. Newborn infants have shorter sleep cycles of about 50 to 60 minutes (instead of the 90 to 100 minutes typical in adults), and they spend nearly half of their total sleep time in REM.* In fact, in premature babies, REM sleep can take up as much three-quarters of total sleep time, and it has been suggested that in the womb it may dominate completely. The percentage of REM sleep drops to about 25 to 30 percent by the first year and to about 20 percent after puberty. In view of the dominance of REM sleep in early life, scientists have speculated that it may play a role in maturation of the brain.

Aging brings an even more dramatic decline in slow wave sleep — from about 20 to 25 percent in childhood to about 10 to 15 percent in adulthood and five percent or less in old age. In the elderly, slow wave sleep may be completely absent — probably the result of aging of the brain cells. This decrease in the amount of deep sleep may account for the fact that as people grow older they have increasing problems with insomnia and nighttime awakenings.

These normal changes in sleep patterns result in increasing complaints of insomnia among older people, but most healthy elderly people "sleep well and do not complain about their sleep," notes Mamelak.

. . . . . . .

---

* In some species — cats, dogs and hamsters, for example — REM sleep is the only kind of sleep in newborns.

So far, scientists have failed to come up with a simple, unifying theory to explain the function of sleep. A number of single-purpose theories have been advanced, but many researchers now question whether the answer can be that simple. Perhaps, they suggest, sleep serves more than one purpose — or perhaps its purpose or purposes have changed over the course of hundreds of millions of years of evolution. "If you asked me what is *the* purpose of sleep, I would have to say I don't know," says Mary Carskadon of the Bradley Hospital, Brown University, in Providence, Rhode Island. "The bottom line is that no one would tell you *the* function of sleep because I think there are many functions."

Broughton adds that although scientists may have a "tremendous need" to find a neat, simple answer, "that's not the way biology works." He recounts the story of a graduate student who, in the midst of a debate over competing theories about the function of REM sleep, asked, "What is the function of wakefulness?" And, indeed, since wakefulness serves many purposes, "why would any biological state be any different?" Broughton says. "A state can be used for multiple functions."

While researchers continue to struggle with some of these fundamental questions, their efforts have nevertheless revealed a great deal about the essential nature of sleep and its effect on mood, behavior and performance in humans. Among the most significant of their findings is that sleep and sleepiness are inherently cyclical phenomena; they are among the many natural rhythms controlled by an internal timing mechanism known as a biological clock. This important discovery, which will be discussed in the next chapter, has opened the door to a greater understanding of the physiological effects of jet lag, shift work and certain sleep disorders and their debilitating impact on work and performance. And it has inspired research on innovative new sleep/wake strategies that may one day help many people cope with extraordinary demands on the job.

# CHAPTER 4

# THE TIME OF YOUR LIFE

IN 1729, A FRENCH SCIENTIST, JEAN Jacques d'Ortous de Mairan, performed a simple but intriguing experiment: he put a plant into a room where no light penetrated and then observed its behavior. Although he was an astronomer, not a biologist, his curiosity had been piqued by the fact that certain plants open their leaves during the day and close them at night. The existence of this phenomenon had been known for a long time, but it had always been assumed that this behavior was simply a reaction to the presence or absence of sunlight. (These plants are, in fact, called "heliotropes," meaning to turn toward the sun. Helios was the Greek sun god.)

De Mairan decided to test this assumption. He put his plant in a dark closet, reasoning that the opening and closing of its leaves would cease to occur if this behavior were indeed triggered by light. To his surprise, he found that the leaves continued to open during the day and close at night, even though the plant remained in darkness all the time.

This was the first scientific demonstration of the operation of an internal biological clock. The fact that the leaves continued to open and close in the absence of external cues showed that some internal mechanism — and *not* merely a passive response to the outside world — was controlling its behavior. It has since been demonstrated that virtually all living things, from single-celled algae to human beings, have internal clocks that drive the patterns of rhythmic peaks and troughs that occur in a wide range of biological/physiological behaviors and processes.

There is a distinction between a biological *clock* and a biological *rhythm*. The clock, as its name implies, is an actual time-keeping mechanism inside the brain. Scientists believe that in mammals these clocks are located within a small cluster of cells in a part of the brain known as the hypothalamus. Although a great deal remains to be learned about the exact way biological clocks work at the biochemical level, their action can be compared to that of a pacemaker controlling the timing of biological behaviors and processes, including the sleep/wake cycle. These behaviors and processes are called biological rhythms; they can be compared to the hands of a clock because they are the observable results of the action of the biological pacemaker.

Rhythms that fluctuate on a roughly 24-hour frequency are known as *circadian* rhythms (from the Latin *circa*, meaning "about," and *dies*, meaning "day"). Typically included in this category are sleep/wake cycles, metabolism, fluctuations in body temperature and the secretion of hormones and several other important biochemicals. Other biological rhythms occur over much shorter periods; for example, heartbeat, respiration and electrical activity in the brain have frequencies on the order of seconds or less. These are called *ultradian* rhythms. The 90-minute NREM/REM cycle is also an ultradian rhythm. Still other rhythms, called *infradian* rhythms, have longer periods — for example, the monthly menstrual cycle of women and the seasonal hibernation cycle of some animals. The study of biological clocks and biological rhythms is known as *chronobiology.**

Scientists did not accept the concept of biological clocks easily or quickly. Although observations of rhythmic biological processes date back to Aristotle and Hippocrates, the existence of internal biological timekeepers was not fully embraced by the scientific community until some 250 years after de Mairan did his experiment. Indeed, his discovery was all but ignored at the time. A brief description of the experiment was published in the proceedings of the Royal Academy of Sciences of Paris, and de Mairan suggested further tests, but, pressed by other duties — he was, after all, an astronomer — he did not pursue this research. His suggestions were not followed up for about 30 years, when another scientist, Henri-Louis Duhamel, demonstrated that external temperature variations were not driving the plant's behavior. (It is crucial for the day-to-day reliability of biological clocks that their time-keeping abilities not be affected by such temperature changes. If your alarm clock ran faster or slower depending on the temperature, you'd have a hard time following a sched-

---

* Biological rhythms should not be confused with *biorhythms*, which are purported physical, intellectual and emotional cycles said to be determined by the date and time of a person's birth. Most scientists regard the study of biorhythms as a pseudoscience.

ule — although this would certainly provide a handy excuse for sleeping in on cold winter mornings.)

In 1832, botanist Augustin de Candolle discovered another curious fact: the plants not only followed a regular pattern of opening and closing their leaves in the dark, but the pattern repeated itself, not every 24 hours as might be expected, but approximately every 22 hours. This was a most significant finding: the first demonstration that biological clocks can "free-run" — that is, in the absence of external time cues, organisms will follow an internal or biological "day length," which is usually close to, but rarely exactly, 24 hours long. Internal day lengths vary from species to species and among individuals within species; typically they range from about 20 to 28 hours. Nocturnal animals generally have biological day lengths shorter than 24 hours and diurnal animals, including humans, usually have ones that are longer.

Subsequent experiments further validated the existence of truly internal time-keeping mechanisms in virtually all living things. In 1929, German scientists did a series of experiments with bees. They left out food at specific times of the day and soon the bees were arriving to feed at the designated times each day. Then the researchers stopped leaving food, but the bees arrived right on time anyway; they did this even when the experiment was conducted in an underground mine, away from all external cues. However, the bees would only perform in this way when the food was first offered at approximately 24-hour intervals; if the intervals were much longer or shorter, the bees never caught on to the schedule.

In 1955, a French scientist, M. Renner, carried this research one step further. First, he got the bees to feed between about 8:00 and 10:00 p.m. in France and then moved them overnight across the Atlantic to New York City. The next day the bees started feeding right on schedule — between 8:00 and 10:00 p.m., *French* time. The bees' internal clocks were working like . . . well . . . like clockwork. (In the bee, this internal timing system has an important practical benefit because it permits efficient nectar-gathering by allowing the bee to exploit the biological timing system in flowers.* Flowers are rather

---

\*   In the mid-1700s, C. Linnaeus, a Swedish scientist who documented the precise daily opening and closing times of the petals of many flower species, created a "flower clock" in his garden. He could tell the time of day merely by observing which flower species had their petals open and which had theirs closed.

like cafeterias that are open to bees only at certain times of the day; once the bee determines a flower's "open" hours, its internal timing system allows it to schedule nectar-gathering expeditions accordingly, regardless of external environmental conditions.)

Studies have shown that the circadian timing system in animals can be remarkably precise — within minutes a day. This reliability provides an important predictive capability that helps to liberate organisms from being held hostage by the whims of nature. Harvard University sleep researcher Martin Moore-Ede gives the example of an animal whose feeding area is some two hours distant from its nighttime shelter. This animal must be able to "predict" nightfall two hours in advance so it can get home without being caught out in the dark by predators. Using external environmental cues to make this prediction — e.g., temperature or the position of the sun — could be dangerous because other variables, such as cloud cover, make them unreliable. Instead, the animal uses an internal time-keeping mechanism that is precise enough to get home safely each day, yet still capable of adjusting to seasonal changes in day length. As we shall see later, the circadian timing system is flexible enough to be "reset" by changing environmental circumstances. This flexibility plays an important survival role by enabling organisms to respond and adapt to new conditions.

Throughout this century, scientists gradually uncovered more details about the workings of biological clocks. They demonstrated that learned behavior was not responsible for observed biological rhythms. They discovered that the natural day length of biological clocks is genetically inherited and unique from species to species. It has even been demonstrated that the earth's rotation does not affect circadian rhythms; when researchers took hamsters, fruit flies and a fungus to the South Pole and spun them around on a table rotating counter to the earth's rotation, no significant changes were found in the functioning of the creatures' biological clocks.

In the 1960s scientists performed experiments that confirmed that human beings also have internal biological clocks. This was done using a method not dissimilar to de Mairan's — isolating human subjects from the external world and observing changes in their biological rhythms. Though these experiments now take place mostly in modern, comfortable sleep labs, early tests were run in underground caves and bunkers. As early as 1938, two U.S. sleep researchers, Nathaniel Kleitman and B. H. Richardson, isolated themselves from the outside world for a month in a damp, chilly cave in Kentucky as they tried to adjust to a 28-hour sleep/wake schedule. In 1962, a French scientist, M. Siffre, spent two months in a cavern, and in the same year, two German researchers, Jurgen Aschoff and Rutger Wever at the Max-Planck-Institut, reported the results of experiments with subjects who had been isolated in a cellar and allowed to free-run for eight to 19 days.

This experiment and Siffre's were the first to demonstrate that the human biological clock has a natural period averaging about 25 hours. (It varies from individual to individual, but only rarely is it very much longer or shorter.) This finding has since been confirmed by numerous other studies in which subjects have lived in special isolation laboratories for periods of up to six months. Typically during this time they have no watches, no newspapers, magazines, radios or TV sets. They have little or no social contact with people outside, although they are continuously monitored remotely.* They eat and sleep when they want to and control light levels themselves. They also undergo repeated physiological measurements (e.g., blood and urine sampling, core body temperature and so on), brain-wave monitoring of their sleep periods and frequent evaluations of their moods and ability to perform various tests.

After a certain point during these tests, many subjects develop very long biologic "days" with sleep/wake cycles ranging from 35 to 50 hours, often interspersed with short "days" of about 25 hours. They also usually increase their total sleep time so that it maintains the usual ratio to waking time of approximately one-third to two-thirds of the "day." Long sleep periods of 12 hours or more are common in free-running situations, usually alternating with shorter sleep periods lasting less than 10 hours. Body temperature at the time of going to sleep appears to play a significant role in determining whether a sleep period will be long or short.

The major consequence of free-running on a 25-hour clock is that

---

\* It is critical that researchers conducting these tests avoid inadvertently giving the subjects time cues. As a result, support staff are usually put on a completely random work schedule and are not allowed to wear wristwatches. They are also instructed not to use phrases like "good morning" or "good night." These measures extend even to having male staff shave before entering the lab to eliminate the possibility that morning beards or five o'clock shadow could give the subjects time cues.

the circadian rhythms of time-isolated subjects rapidly start to drift out of phase with the external 24-hour day. Each day, they go to bed an hour or so later and also wake up later, until their sleep/wake cycle is completely turned around with respect to day and night in the outside world. Eventually, they drift back into phase, but in short order, the process of desynchronizing begins again. Since they lack external time cues, they are unaware of being out of phase; subjectively, their sleep/wake schedule seems quite normal, even when it stretches to 50 hours. In fact, subjects often report feeling generally more alert than they do in the outside world.

The fact that rhythmic behaviors persist in free-running conditions proves that they are driven by internal clocks, but it does *not* mean that biological clocks are utterly impervious to external influences. Quite the contrary; if they *were,* we'd be in serious trouble. What happens to people isolated in caves or sleep labs would happen to us in the real world: our 25-hour clocks would be constantly shifting out of phase with the external world and it would be virtually impossible to maintain an orderly day-to-day schedule. To prevent this from happening, our clocks must be "reset" (synchronized) to a 24-hour cycle every day by *zeitgebers* ("time givers"), such as light and dark, meals, work schedules, alarm clocks and so on. This process is known as *entrainment.* Its role in permitting us to adapt to modern lifestyles and work schedules — and the problems that can occur when entrainment breaks down — will be examined later.

## CIRCADIAN RHYTHMS IN HUMANS

We start and end life with our circadian rhythms in disarray. Biological clocks do not operate well in newborns until three or four months after birth; this is what produces the random sleeping and eating patterns that cause so much chaos in the lives of new parents.* In the elderly, the circadian sleep/wake system is often not strong enough to maintain a regular 24-hour rhythm. In between, our circadian system works hard to provide us with stability and routine, even though life in the fast lane seems particularly well designed to confound it.

In humans, biological clocks control literally hundreds of behaviors and processes that fluctuate between minimum and maximum values

---

* Stanford University psychologist Amy Wolfson has done a study in which 60 first-time parents were taught sleep-inducing techniques that helped babies between six and nine weeks old to sleep longer at night, wake less frequently and require fewer feedings.

on a daily basis. Each rhythm follows a distinctive pattern of daily peaks and troughs, which may or may not coincide with the peaks and troughs of other rhythms; some rhythms are strongly synchronized, while others follow independent patterns. The interplay of these rhythms with one another and with external factors weaves a complex tapestry that researchers have only begun to unravel.

The activities of all our most vital physiological systems are subject to circadian influences — the activity of the immune, reproductive and gastrointestinal systems, endocrine secretions, kidney and liver function, metabolism, digestion, body temperature and, of course, the sleep/wake cycle. Many hormones are secreted into the bloodstream intermittently, peaking at characteristic times of the day or night; their intricate choreography provides a method of synchronizing the functions of many body tissues. Circadian rhythmicity has been found in a wide range of hormones, such as insulin, growth hormone, sex and reproductive hormones and many others.

There are also daily rhythms in the way our body processes food and water. Eating a rich meal late at night often causes indigestion because production of digestive fluids and activity in the gut decreases at night. Kidneys produce less urine at night than during the day and, in fact, production of urine varies throughout the day as well; subjects given water to drink at different times will produce urine at 10:00 a.m. at twice the rate they do at 3:00 p.m. The concentrations of various constituents in the urine (e.g., potassium, calcium and sodium) also fluctuate over a 24-hour period.

Some rhythms are closely tied to the sleep/wake cycle. For example, the secretion of growth hormone increases substantially within the first hour or two after sleep onset. The secretion patterns of certain biochemicals associated with the immune system are dramatically different when we're asleep from when we're awake and they can also be altered by sleep deprivation. The implications of this are not fully understood, but it may have some bearing on the fact that deaths from illness and disease occur more often during the early-morning circadian trough than at any other time.

The finding that the sleep/wake cycle can affect the immune system prompts intriguing speculation about the extent to which biological clocks may be more widely implicated in human health. "Why do things happen occur at particular times in our life cycle?" asks Harvey Moldofsky. "Why do we grow at a particular rate and then stop? Why does menopause occur at a particular time? Why are we aging? These are all clocks. We see that throughout life, there are these clocks that affect us during sleep and during wakefulness." He speculated that clocks might also be implicated in the occurrence of diseases like cancer and AIDS. "When does AIDS begin? Here's this virus that's hanging around, and all of a sudden a person becomes sick. Why at that particular point?"

Life and death, it would appear, are very much a matter of timing. Moldofsky says the study of biological clocks gets to the "very root of our existence," but there are still few answers to some of the most fundamental questions: Why do they exist? Where do they exist? And what are the genetic mechanisms that cause them to evolve?

## A ROLLER-COASTER RIDE ON THE SLEEP/WAKE CYCLE

Circadian rhythms related to sleep include not only sleep itself but also the propensity or urge for sleep (i.e., the relative strength of sleepiness and alertness). Moreover, both slow wave sleep and REM sleep exhibit a daily cycle, in addition to their 90-minute ultradian cycle during the sleep period — that is, you're more likely to have slow wave sleep at certain times of the day or night and REM sleep at other times.

It is important to understand that these daily patterns of ups and downs in alertness and sleepiness occur in both well-rested and sleep-deprived people. In other words, this happens *regardless of the amount of sleep a person has had or not had*, although sleep loss can exacerbate the negative effects on mood and performance that typically occur during the circadian low points. (Scientists are still trying to sort out the relative contributions of circadian influences and prior sleep loss in determining when we fall asleep, how long we sleep and how sleepy we feel while awake — a subject that will be explored further in later chapters.)

When the sleep/wake cycle is entrained to the 24-hour day, the periods of greatest daytime alertness and the least urge to sleep usually occur in midmorning and early evening. Wakefulness is generally so strong during the evening circadian peak that most normal sleepers (i.e., those without sleep disorders) find it very difficult to fall asleep between about 7:00 and 9:00 or 10:00 p.m., even in a sleep-deprived condition. Even when subjects deliberately try to fall asleep during this period, it takes them longer than at any other time of the day — if they can fall asleep at all.

Israeli researcher Peretz Lavie describes the 2 to 4 hours before the normal overnight sleep period as a "forbidden zone" for sleep. He and his colleagues at Technion-Israel Institute of Technology conducted a study in which they asked subjects to try to sleep for 7 out of every 20 minutes over a 24-hour period. Despite the sleep loss caused by the fragmentation of their sleep, very few fell asleep in the evening forbidden zone.

Morning is also a time of peak alertness in most people; this too is a circadian effect that occurs regardless of sleep loss. Most people who have worked through the night with little or no sleep experience this "second wind" effect. Typically, they hit bottom in the wee hours of the morning but when dawn rolls around, their level of alertness picks up, despite the fact that they're even more sleep deprived than they were in the middle of the night. Sleep researcher Charles Czeisler of Brigham and Women's Hospital in Boston describes this as the "internal alarm clock going off."

This revival effect also occurs after the midafternoon dip in alertness; even without an afternoon nap, most people will start to pick up again by about 5:00 or 6:00 p.m.

In the entrained state, the strongest circadian pressure for sleep typically occurs between about 3:00 a.m. and 6:00 a.m. Under normal conditions, awakening at this time occurs so infrequently that it has been labeled a second "forbidden zone" — this time, a forbidden *wake-up* zone. Recently, scientists have also shown that another peak in the pressure for sleep occurs in midafternoon. The urge to have an afternoon nap is quite common in adults and it becomes stronger with age.* However, despite the fact that this phenomenon is sometimes called the "postlunch dip," it is not, as most people assume, primarily a postprandial effect — the price one pays for eating too heavily or having a few beers at lunch.

In 1975, Broughton proposed that the midafternoon increase in sleep tendency reflects a strong twice-daily biological rhythm involving a major sleep period at night and a minor sleep period in the middle of the afternoon. He argues that the existence of this midafternoon

---

* Children of about 10 to 12 years old, who are the most alert people of all, do not show an increased midafternoon propensity for sleep. In fact, given the opportunity to nap, they rarely fall asleep at any time of the day.

dip in alertness suggests that humans have a powerful natural propensity for sleeping twice every 24 hours (*biphasic* sleep) rather than once every 24 hours (*monophasic* sleep). Monophasic sleep is considered the norm in industrialized societies, but far from being physiologically driven, it appears to be purely social, Broughton argues. In short, humans may be natural nappers. The implications of this in the workplace will be examined more fully in later chapters.

Broughton says several lines of evidence support the idea of a midafternoon circadian dip: the afternoon nap is the last to be given up in childhood; adult napping, which is far more common than generally believed, is usually done in the afternoon; and napping in countries where the siesta is common also virtually always occurs in the midafternoon. "All the siesta cultures reduce their nighttime sleep. They eat very late in the evening, they often don't go to bed until well after midnight, they get up at the usual hours. So they've got to make up sleep at some other time of the day and they always choose to do it in the midafternoon." (Coleman suggests that in industrialized countries, coffee breaks have replaced the siesta by providing strategic jolts of caffeine to overcome drowsiness.)

More important, however, free-running laboratory studies have confirmed the existence of a twice-daily rhythm of increased sleep tendency.

One of these studies, done at Stanford University by sleep researchers Mary Carskadon and William Dement, demonstrated that the afternoon sleep tendency is not caused by food intake. Subjects were asked to try falling asleep at 2-hour intervals six times during the day following a full night's sleep; how fast they fell asleep was a measure of how sleepy they were at various times during the day. This is known as the Multiple Sleep Latency Test (MSLT), which has become a commonly used test of daytime sleepiness.

In one experiment, the subjects were fed three meals a day, at 8:00 a.m., noon and 6:00 p.m.; in another, they ate a small meal every hour during the day. In both cases, the subjects fell asleep much faster during the middle of the afternoon than they did during the morning or evening. (In fact, another study showed that subjects fall asleep in midafternoon almost as fast as they do in the middle of the night.) On days when the subjects received three meals a day, there was no sign of an increased sleep tendency after either breakfast or supper; in fact, those were the times when the subjects took the longest to fall asleep.

These results indicate that an internal rhythm, and not the midday meal, is the primary cause of the increased pressure for sleep in midafternoon. In other studies, a "postlunch" drop in performance has been shown to occur even if no lunch is eaten, and increased sleepiness has consistently failed to turn up in the postbreakfast or postdinner periods.

However, it does appear that the strength of the tendency to fall asleep in the afternoon can be affected by food. Carskadon says that carbohydrates and alcohol do seem to make the midafternoon trough deeper. However, there do not appear to be any foods that make the trough shallower, with the possible exception of those containing caffeine.

The effect of heavy food at lunch appears to be even more pronounced when combined with sleep loss, according to a study by James Horne. He asked student volunteers to perform a vigilance task between 2:30 and 3:15 p.m. in four different conditions: after a full night's sleep with a heavy lunch, and with a light lunch, and after a night of reduced sleep with a heavy lunch, and with a light lunch. Their overall performance was worst when reduced sleep was combined with a heavy lunch and best when normal sleep was combined with a light lunch. What was more surprising was that the students' fastest reaction time occurred in the "reduced sleep/heavy lunch" test; however, this was also when they recorded the highest number of false responses, which accounted for its being ranked the worst state for overall performance. Horne concluded that a heavy lunch improved response time after reduced sleep, but increased "carelessness."

Further support for the midafternoon dip in alertness comes from the analysis of sleep-related traffic accidents by Lavie and his colleagues, who found that these types of accidents peaked at 4:00 a.m., with a secondary peak occurring exactly 12 hours later at 4:00 p.m. (The total number of accidents from all causes did not show this 12-hour pattern; instead, the peaks occurred during the morning and evening rush hours and over the lunch period, presumably reflecting the fact that the greatest number of cars are on the road at these times.) The double peak in sleep-related accidents provides strong evidence for a 12-hour sleepiness cycle, Lavie says.

David Dinges observes that since daytime napping is not nearly as prevalent as nighttime sleeping this might suggest the afternoon sleep tendency is the weaker of the two. However, another possible explanation is that the stimulation provided by day-to-day activities helps us stay awake during the period of increased afternoon sleep tendency, reducing the desire (and often the opportunity) to nap.

In addition to 24-hour variations in sleepiness and alertness, there are ultradian ups and downs that occur, on average, about every 90 minutes throughout the day, according to a number of studies. Broughton says that the intensity of these fluctuations appears to depend a great deal on a person's relative level of arousal. They are more pronounced when a subject is bored or suffering from sleep loss or excessive daytime sleepiness caused by certain sleep disorders; on the other hand, if the subject is highly stressed or extremely motivated to perform, these 90-minute cycles of alertness may virtually disappear for long periods of time. Personality traits, such as emotional stability, may also play a role in preventing large swings in daytime alertness.

## CIRCADIAN VARIATION IN PERFORMANCE

Our ability to perform a wide range of physical and mental tasks also varies on a daily basis. The familiar roller-coaster effect is observed in the performance of many mental and psychomotor tasks, such as "flying" an aircraft simulator and tests of vigilance and reaction time. In studies of activities like answering phone calls, reading gas meters, falling asleep while driving, responding to warning signals and single-vehicle truck accidents, the pattern is consistent: performance is poorest in the middle of the night, mostly between 3:00 and 7:00 a.m., and best in the late afternoon/early evening. (Some studies indicate, however, that memory-related performance is more likely to peak in the morning.)

The poor showing in the middle of the night cannot be attributed solely to sleep loss because performance, like alertness, usually improves the next morning despite continued sleep deprivation. The same thing occurs after the midafternoon trough; performance typically improves during the early-evening circadian peak even without an afternoon nap. If sleep deprivation continues, the overall level of performance will deteriorate rapidly, but it will continue to show this persistent pattern of circadian-driven ups and downs over each 24-hour period.

In humans, psychological factors such as personality traits and motivation (e.g., the desire to pass an exam or to get into the *Guinness*

*Book of Records*) can override the circadian pressure to sleep and maintain performance, at least for a short time. The nature of the task (i.e., whether it is mentally challenging or tedious) can also affect performance and endurance. Nevertheless, alertness and performance appear to be inherently more impaired in the middle of the night and the middle of the afternoon, quite apart from the effects of sleep loss itself; however, this impairment can be greatly aggravated by sleep deprivation, sleep disorders, shift work and continuous work over long hours.

## CIRCADIAN TROUGHS: A MATTER OF LIFE AND DEATH

The circadian low points in the middle of the night and the middle of the afternoon have been called "zones of vulnerability" for good reason: these are the times when we're most likely to cause accidents or succumb to illness. Data from 50 studies of 437,000 deaths indicate that the chances of dying are greater between 4:00 and 6:00 a.m. and, to a lesser extent, between 2:00 and 4:00 p.m. than at any other time of the day or night.

Dozens of studies from all over the world have shown that transportation and industrial accidents resulting from human error are far more likely to occur during the two circadian troughs. For example, one study showed that more than half of 6,000 single-vehicle traffic accidents occurred between midnight and 7:00 a.m., with the peak occurring between 1:00 and 4:00 a.m. A second peak occurred between 1:00 and 4:00 p.m.

Death from illness and disease is also more likely to occur in the morning,* although peaks tend to occur somewhat later than for accidents. For example, the likelihood of both suffering a heart attack and dying from it is greatest between about 6:00 and 10:00 a.m. One survey of nearly 5,000 disease-related deaths in New York City showed that the incidence of these deaths (about half due to heart disease) starts to climb sharply between 3:00 and 6:00 a.m. and that most of them occurred between 6:00 and 9:00 a.m. The reasons why most of these deaths appear to occur a couple of hours after the lowest point in the circadian trough are not entirely understood, but it has been speculated that these patients may be sleeping later than other

---

* Ironically, births also occur most frequently in the early-morning hours, which, Moore-Ede notes, has prompted the observation that "we tend to live an exact number of days."

people, or that the data may reflect a "discovery artefact" — i.e., the deaths are more likely to be discovered by others in the morning than in the middle of the night. (It should be noted, also, that time-of-death patterns may be influenced by social factors, such as the relative availability of emergency medical care at different times of the day.)

Biological organisms are more susceptible to trauma, allergies and toxic substances at some stages of the circadian cycle than at others. Studies with mice have shown that 85 percent survived a dose of bacterial toxin injected at 4:00 p.m. while fewer than 20 percent survived the same dose injected between midnight and 4:00 a.m. Humans have shown acute susceptibility to illness and disease at certain times of the day; one study showed that people suffering from respiratory failure caused by bronchial asthma experienced abnormal bronchial constriction about 6:00 a.m. Respiratory arrests and deaths tended to occur mostly about this time of day.

Other studies indicate that there are time-of-day differences in human susceptibility to acceleration, decompression sickness (excess nitrogen bubbling out of joints and tissues as a result of reduced atmospheric pressure) and altitude tolerance (tolerance to decreased oxygen pressure, which can lead to oxygen starvation and a loss of consciousness).

In humans, circadian factors should be taken into account when doing tests to diagnose illnesses and disease and in the therapeutic administration of drugs and X-rays. Moldofsky notes that because the activity of the immune system is affected by sleep and by sleep deprivation, care must be used in interpreting test results. "If you take a blood sample at a particular time in the 24-hour cycle, and you study the immune characteristics, they'll be very different than at another time."

In the book *The Clocks That Time Us*, Moore-Ede and colleagues Frank Sulzman and Charles Fuller note that there are circadian variations both in toxic and therapeutic effects of many drugs, so care should be taken to administer them at times when they will do the most good while causing the fewest negative side effects. In one study, researchers injected mice with leukemia cells and then gave them drugs used in chemotherapy. One group of mice was given the drugs in a way that varied rhythmically, while a second group was given the drugs at a continuous level. Both groups of mice received the same total amount of the drugs. About 95 percent of the mice in the first group survived, compared with only 70 percent in the second group. In another test, mice exposed to X-rays while asleep died while those exposed while awake lived. Animal studies have also shown a marked rhythmicity in both the effectiveness and the lethality of chemicals used as anesthetics.

While this does not apply to all drugs, there may be situations in which there's only a narrow range between a drug's therapeutic and toxic doses and, in such cases, the timing of its administration may be extremely important, the researchers note. When the chances of recovery are marginal, circadian factors might "tip the balance."

Citing recent studies indicating that circadian variations in the effects of heart drugs may cause apparent abnormalities to appear in EKG readings, Moldofsky notes that "this kind of information is just coming out and I don't know how much doctors are paying attention."

## THE SLEEP/WAKE CYCLE AND BODY TEMPERATURE: AN INTIMATE RELATIONSHIP

Core body temperature was one of the first circadian rhythms to be observed and studied in humans (as early as 1778), and it is routinely monitored in sleep lab experiments. It typically peaks in late afternoon/early evening, usually sometime between 7:00 and 9:00 p.m. Then it starts to drop a couple of hours before sleep onset, and even more rapidly immediately afterward, reaching its lowest point in the middle of the night, usually sometime between 3:00 and 6:00 a.m. It starts to rise again prior to morning awakening and may reach a secondary peak in midmorning almost as high as the evening peak. It remains high throughout the day, although it may level off or even drop slightly in the afternoon before climbing again to the evening peak. (Noncircadian influences, such as heavy exercise or taking a bath, may cause temperature changes that would be superimposed on this circadian pattern.)

Sleep researchers have been investigating the relationship between core body temperature and sleep — in particular, the role that temperature plays in determining when we fall asleep, how long we stay asleep, how much REM versus NREM sleep we get and when we wake up. These studies form part of a larger effort to understand the extent to which circadian rhythms influence our sleep/wake patterns, compared with the effects of sleep loss and the length of prior wakefulness. An understanding of the relative contributions of these various factors is needed in order to find ways to help people with clinical sleep disorders and those who are suffering from work-related sleep problems. Sleep researcher Deborah Sewitch, at Yale University and the Griffin Hospital in Connecticut, says that there has been a steady accumulation of evidence for an inextricable link between the human body's temperature-regulation system and its sleep/wake system, so that studying one almost requires studying the other.

There are several lines of evidence for this link. For example, under normal entrained conditions, there is a strong parallel between highs and lows in the sleep/wake cycle and core body temperature. Researchers have also found that "night owls" have different temperature rhythms than "morning larks." And it's known that the elderly, who typically awake earlier than younger people, experience their temperature trough about 4:00 a.m., compared with 6:30 a.m. for young adults, and their temperature starts rising earlier as well.

Falling core body temperature is strongly associated with falling asleep, and it drops even more sharply after sleep onset. Sewitch has suggested that the failure of this rapid temperature drop to occur within the first hour or two after sleep may be implicated in causing insomnia in some people. One study found that people who reported sleeping poorly had significantly higher body temperatures during a period lasting from about 2 hours before falling asleep to about 4 hours afterward, compared with subjects who reported sleeping well. In his paper on insomnia, Mortimer Mamelak notes that in poor sleepers temperature remains significantly higher throughout the night than in good sleepers, and this causes an increased energy expenditure that may be manifested in daytime fatigue. He suggests that energy conservation, as much as the duration of sleep, may determine how rested you feel during the day.

There's little doubt that the relationship between body temperature and sleep is an intimate one, but it's not a simple one. For example, the correlation between sleep (or sleepiness) and low body temperature and that between wakefulness and high body temperature is not invariable: the midafternoon increase in sleepiness (and napping, if permitted by circumstances) occurs at a time when body temperature is high and approaching its daily peak. And then there's the fact that the two rhythms can decouple from each other altogether under free-running conditions — a process known as *internal desynchronization*.

In subjects isolated from external time cues, the internal relationship between various circadian rhythms (including body temperature and the sleep/wake cycle) persists for a month or more, but it usually breaks down after that. Groups of rhythms part company and start lapping each other, running on very different biological day lengths. In most cases, the sleep/wake cycle becomes longer — periods of up to 50 hours have been observed — and the temperature cycle settles between about 24 and 25 hours.

The fact that the temperature cycle and the sleep/wake cycle desynchronize during free-running indicates that humans must have at least two biological clocks, says Moore-Ede, because a single clock could not drive two independent rhythms. According to one model of the circadian system, an X-pacemaker drives the core body temperature cycle (and the timing of REM sleep), and a Y-pacemaker drives the circadian sleep/wake rhythm (and the timing of slow wave sleep). The brain centers responsible for controlling sleep and arousal receive input from both pacemakers. Under entrained conditions, the two are coupled, with the X (temperature) pacemaker exerting more control on the Y (sleep/wake) pacemaker than vice versa.

However, even in free-running conditions, there's still a strong relationship between sleep and temperature, according to a study done by a group of researchers including Charles Czeisler, Elliot Weitzman and Martin Moore-Ede. They found that that free-running subjects were far more likely to choose to go to sleep just after the low point in their circadian temperature cycle than when their temperature was high. When subjects chose to go to sleep during their temperature trough, they slept for under 10 hours and awoke as their temperature started rising again. Conversely, when they chose to go to sleep during their temperature peak, they slept for 12 hours or more; these sleep periods extended right through the subsequent temperature trough and the subjects did not wake up until the next temperature upswing.

Previously, the variations in sleep length that occur in free-running conditions were thought to be random and irregular, but this study showed that they reflected a consistent, predictable relationship to the temperature cycle. The researchers concluded that how long we sleep is determined primarily by the internal circadian system and not by how long we've been awake before the sleep period begins. (This conclusion is supported by the fact that when people resume sleeping after having been awake for a long time, they rarely extend even the first sleep period much beyond normal and go back to their usual sleep period quickly.) They argued that in humans the timing of sleep is never completely free from circadian influences related to the temperature cycle. These findings, as we shall see in later chapters, may have an important bearing on the ability of people to adapt to shift work and other unusual work schedules.

Subjective sleepiness — the sensation of *feeling* sleepy — is also under complex control by the circadian system, according to a study by University of Pittsburgh sleep researcher Timothy Monk. It is curious and seemingly paradoxical that many people, if asked how sleepy they feel, report low subjective sleepiness around midday or shortly thereafter. Yet, shortly after this, during the midafternoon trough, they exhibit a sleepiness peak when administered the Multiple Sleep Latency Test. Monk notes that it seems peculiar that people rate themselves as feeling least sleepy shortly before a peak in their *objective* sleepiness occurs. He suggests that objective sleepiness (how fast you fall asleep) is not related to the absolute level of subjective sleepiness (how sleepy you feel), but rather to its rate of change. "The rate of rise in subjective sleepiness may be the prime determinant of an individual's ability to fall asleep."

The sensation of feeling sleepy does not simply parallel the body temperature cycle; instead, Monk suggests, subjective sleepiness is controlled by a complex mixture of the temperature cycle and the sleep/wake cycle and this gives us much-needed flexibility in coping with our daily sleep needs. His reasoning goes this way: it has been shown that the length of time one will sleep is related to body temperature at the time of going to sleep; therefore, since feeling sleepy would tend to precipitate a decision to go to sleep, it's advantageous to have the variations in this feeling of sleepiness tied to the temperature cycle. However, free-running tests have shown that the temperature cycle does not vary as much as the sleep/wake cycle. Therefore, if the daily variation in feeling sleepy were completely controlled by the temperature cycle, it would not cope very well with changed circumstances, such as a night of missed sleep or shifting of the sleep period to earlier or later times than normal (as in jet lag or shift work). The mixture of control from both the temperature and the sleep/wake circadian systems "ensures that the subjective sleepiness rhythm can guide the individual toward the bedtime choices that are more suitable for a given routine, even when that routine is a changing one."

# Riding the Circadian Waves

When marathon swimmer Vicki Keith mounted an unprecedented assault on the five Great Lakes during the summer of 1988, she was fighting not only the currents, the distance, the heat and the cold, but her own sleep/wake system as well.

Sleep deprivation, hallucinations and a daily ride on the circadian roller coaster were among the challenges she faced during the record-setting swims, which were completed over a grueling two-month period and covered some 275 kilometers (171 miles). The tally: Lake Erie, 20 hours; Lake Huron, 47 hours; Lake Michigan, 53 hours; Lake Superior, 17 hours; Lake Ontario, 24 hours. Lake Michigan was particularly difficult because it was the longest of the five crossings and Keith was fighting a current the whole way. "I worked that entire 53 hours." Keith was the first person to swim Lake Huron and Lake Superior (which she dubbed "Lake Inferior" after her conquest).

Keith says she has more difficulty staying awake during lake swims than during pool marathons because she has to contend with the natural light/dark cycle outdoors. "As soon as it gets dark, that cues you to be tired. The first night I have some problem staying awake but usually I'm able to enter a trancelike state where I'm not really aware of the passage of time and therefore I don't have a lot of problems. Once I've entered that trancelike state, it's almost like sleeping. I sort of wake up every two hours to be fed. That makes the first night relatively easy."

As the swim progresses, Keith follows a classical circadian pattern of ups and downs in sleepiness and alertness. She slides into the circadian trough about 3:00 a.m. on the first night, and it usually lasts until about dawn. "I usually have a little bit of an up because the sun's coming up and I'm warming. I'm often very cold at night and it doesn't help that I sunburn all day. The second day, I find myself really tired for a while after the sun's come up and then I'm usually wide awake for a while. About eight or nine in the morning, I'll really start climbing and I can swim till about four o'clock in the afternoon really efficiently."

At that point, she has to contend with a midafternoon circadian dip, followed by an evening peak in alertness and performance. "About four o'clock in the afternoon, I start getting tired again to the point that I feel like falling asleep. I'm totally exhausted and that's when the battle starts. That lasts for maybe 2 or 3 hours and if I allow myself the freedom to talk to people and not swim quite as hard, then I usually hit a really strong period after that. Usually I swim strongly until 10 or 11 o'clock, sometimes as late as midnight, but once midnight passes, I start to feel tired again. The second night, it's a battle all night long trying to stay awake. A lot of the time it's confused with hallucinations due to sleep deprivation."

The hallucinations, which usually start at about four to six o'clock on the afternoon of the second day, are mild at first: "Patio stones, Aztec paintings. In Lake Huron, I started off with Aztec paintings in bright blues and greens and then, as it got dark, there was a forest. About midnight, one o'clock, is when I notice the full-blown hallucinations. They're very real. I'm in Lake Huron totally surrounded by trees at this point. I could see the boats, I could see the trees. I knew which was reality, which was fantasy and I had a lot of fun with it. I was joking around to my crew members, telling them to watch out for the trees.

"At one point, I noticed about 12 people underwater telling me that that I could go to sleep if I wanted to — which, of course, I decided not to do. Throughout that whole time, I had a terrible time trying to stay awake. I'll yell underwater sometimes, just out of frustration, sometimes just to keep myself awake. I'll allow myself to drift off, as long as my arms are still moving, hoping that I will become more alert after that.

"Sometimes I'd just stop moving. People have experienced the same sort of thing when they're driving — they doze off for a second and then they wake up. I'd still be swimming a bit, but I'd have one stroke being a really strong pull and then I'd fall asleep at that point, so I'd make a right-hand turn. I'd just start floating off in the wrong direction. Those were cues that I was having problems staying awake. [The crew] would yell my name and that usually worked. I'd wake up and I'd swear at myself and keep on going.

"The more tired I get, the more likely I am to say funny things between breaths. I'll say things to the people in the boat; I keep myself awake by talking back and forth with them. And of course the people on the boat help me to stay awake also. In Lake Ontario, when I swam overnight, they climbed out on one of the Zodiacs in a penguin costume. But once I start hallucinating, they don't have to entertain me anymore. I never try to fight off the hallucinations because I find them exceedingly amusing."

Keith did some research on the effects of sleep deprivation before her swims, so she knew she might start hallucinating and she warned her crew. "We have a lot of fun with it. People have noticed that if they say something, that's usually where I get my hallucinations from. We had a dog paddle race in the pool and all of a sudden, I saw dogs everywhere swimming with me. Anytime I see people or animals underwater they always have really large eyes. One of the hallucinations was little white fluffy animals with huge eyes and another was people playing golf underwater. All the players had large eyes."

Keith has found that contrary to the advice of other marathon swimmers, it's best for her to start her swims early in the morning. "It was recommended to me by many swimmers that I start about 11 o'clock at night. I disagreed with that. I've tested this out on a couple of swims. If I change the sleep pattern that day — say, go to sleep at two o'clock in the afternoon, sleep through to till nine o'clock at night or something like that — it doesn't do me any good. I will still enter the sleep-deprivation time 36 hours from the time that I would have regularly woken up. It's similar to jet lag. It would take two weeks or so to get used to it; I would have to sleep during the day for two weeks, so starting the swim at night isn't any good for me. I won't change my sleep pattern and swim at 11 o'clock. I try and start as soon as I wake up. The best situation for me is having a hotel on the beach. I like to be in the water within half an hour, 45 minutes of being awake, so that I have a full sleep period before I hit the water — so that I'm totally rested when I get into the water."

In order to cope with the fatigue and loss of drive that can accompany sleep deprivation, Keith mentally prepares herself ahead of time: "I set my goals before. I embed in my mind the necessity to stay moving, so when I get to the point that I'm falling asleep the only thing that's left in my mind is that I have to keep on going, I can't stop. It's all a matter of motivation. If the motivation means a lot to you, then staying awake is easier. My motivation was very strong in my mind."

Only after the last lake swim was completed could Keith loosen her grip: "I could let go and acknowledge that I was tired. All I wanted to do was lie down and sleep." Normally an 8-hour-a-night sleeper, she found herself sleeping "well over 12 hours a day. It was like that for the next two weeks. I was totally physically and mentally exhausted. Other than the appearances I had to make, I spent the whole time sleeping. I'd get up in the morning, I'd do the appearances, I'd take a nap, do some more appearances, go back to sleep that night."

The hardships obviously did not put a dent in Keith's determination: during the summer of 1989, she swam Australia's Sydney Harbour, the English Channel, the Strait of Juan de Fuca between Vancouver Island and Washington State, Lake Winnipeg, Lake Ontario and the Catalina Strait.

. . . . . . . . . . . . . . . . . . . . . . . . . . . . . .

# CHAPTER 5

# OUT OF TIME

TWO FRIENDS, SARA AND Angela, decide to take a ski holiday together. They arrive at the ski lodge in the late afternoon, and after unpacking and eating supper, they wander into the lounge to have a drink and listen to the band. Sara wearies quickly and heads off to bed before 11:00 p.m., but Angela is feeling too alert to sleep and lingers until nearly 2:00 a.m. Anxious to hit the slopes early, Sara sets the alarm for 6:30 a.m. When it goes off the next morning, she leaps out of bed full of anticipation, turns on the light, switches on the TV to a morning news show and is into the shower, humming, in 3 minutes flat. Angela cowers under the covers, groggy and disoriented, wondering what's hit her. Usually she's not even alive before 10:00 a.m.

Sara is out on the slopes by 8:00 a.m., aggressively tackling the expert runs. By 9:30, Angela, fortified by half a dozen cups of strong coffee, has managed to shake off her sluggishness enough to risk some of the easier runs. But by midday, the situation is reversing: Sara is flagging and decides to call it quits by midafternoon. Angela, only now hitting her stride, tears down the expert slopes until dusk.

## LARKS AND OWLS: AS DIFFERENT AS DAY AND NIGHT

Sara is a "lark" and Angela an "owl" — and they probably shouldn't be vacationing together if they want their friendship to survive. Their circadian rhythms dictate that their peaks of alertness and performance occur at very different times of the day, and they both have such a hard time functioning during their off-peak times that it's virtually impossible for either to adjust to the other's schedule. Extreme owls have great difficulty living or working with persons of the lark persuasion and vice versa — and, to make matters worse, they're often judgmental about each other's sleep/wake habits. "Larks see owls as lazy; owls see larks as party poopers," notes Richard Coleman.

Fortunately, only about 20 percent of people fall into either "extreme" category. Most are either moderate larks or owls or neutral types. These categories are determined by administering a "morningness/eveningness" questionnaire developed by James Horne of Loughborough University and O. Östberg of the Swedish National Board of Occupational Safety and Health. The form includes a series of questions asking subjects about their preferred times of waking, sleeping and working, their times of peak and low mental and physical performance, their feelings on awakening, the times when they feel fatigued or full of energy, and whether they consider themselves to be "morning" or "evening" people. The answers are scored on a morningness/eveningness scale, with the highest numbers indicating "definite" morning types (M-types) and the lowest "definite" evening types (E-types). Scores in between indicate moderate morning or evening types or neutral types.

Horne and Östberg found a number of distinct differences in sleep habits and daily body temperature rhythms among morning and evening types (including both the extreme and moderate types). Morning types tended to have a higher body temperature than evening types throughout the day and their temperature peak occurred much earlier — about 7:30 p.m., compared with about 10:40 p.m. for E-types. After the peak, the temperature of M-types fell below that of the E-types. The body temperature of intermediate types was generally between that of the two other groups, except that this group showed a substantial midafternoon temperature trough between about 3:00 and 6:00 p.m., which was not paralleled in either the M-types or the E-types (although M-types did show evidence of a very slight dip about 2:00 to 3:00 p.m.)

Intermediates reached their evening temperature peak at about 10:30, nearly the same time as evening types — but they went to bed at about the same time as M-types, about 11:30 p.m. E-types favored a bedtime about 1:00 a.m. All three groups slept nearly the same length of time — between 8 and 8½ hours. Evening types woke up later — after about 9:15, compared with about 8:00 a.m. for intermediates and about 7:30 a.m. for morning types. (These subjects were students, who are more likely to have the freedom to wake up later than people who have to be up in time for work.) Several other studies done in the United States, France, Italy, the Netherlands and Japan have confirmed these findings regarding the differences between morning types and evening types with respect to total sleep time and the times of going to bed and waking up.

Sleep researcher Kaneyoshi Ishihara and a group of his colleagues from four Japanese universities found other significant differences in the sleep/wake patterns of larks and owls. They surveyed nearly 1,500 university students and found that larks reported going to bed earlier, falling asleep more easily and getting up earlier than owls. They also reported being in a better mood on waking up; nearly all of them reported feeling "very good" or "fairly good." In contrast, about three-quarters of the owls reported feeling "fairly bad" or "very bad" on waking up. Larks were also more likely than owls to report getting adequate amounts of sleep. Owls reported taking longer and more frequent naps at a later time of day than larks, and nearly half said they stayed awake all night at least once a month, something that very few larks reported doing.

Similar results were obtained by American researchers Wilse Webb of the University of Florida and Michael Bonnet, now at Loma Linda VA Hospital in San Diego, who characterized owls as poor sleepers and larks as good sleepers. However, the Japanese researchers said it might be more appropriate to characterize owls as having more irregular or more flexible sleep habits than larks. They found that most of the owls in their study reported that during the week their bedtime and arising time could vary by an hour or more, whereas most larks varied these times by half an hour or less. On weekends and holidays, owls were far more inclined than larks to delay both bedtime and arising time, and the amount of delay was usually larger — about 2 to 3 hours, compared with less than 2 hours for those larks who delayed their sleep time.

When the Japanese researchers took EEG and body temperature readings of 10 larks and 11 owls, one significant difference they found was that the larks' middle-of-the-night temperature trough occurred earlier — at 4:17 a.m., compared with 6:10 a.m. for owls. Although larks reported subjectively feeling less sleepy and more mentally efficient after arising than owls did, the EEG measurements did not show any significant objective differences in sleep quality between the two groups. There were also no significant differences on personality tests, but the owls did show a somewhat greater tendency to be extraverted, neurotic and anxious.

Some researchers have suggested that owls might be more tolerant than larks of night work or shift work. Others have argued that flexibility of sleeping habits might be more important for predicting who can better tolerate this kind of work than whether a person is an owl or a lark. The Japanese study suggests that both groups could be right because "the people who have flexible sleeping habits are most probably owls . . . . Thus, the tolerance of owls to night and shift work may be greater than that of the larks."

Not surprisingly, however, owls have a hard time adjusting to a 9-to-5 existence. Many of those who can't — or choose not to — adjust to society's timetable select loosely structured or freelance occupations that permit them to follow their own circadian rhythms; writers, artists, musicians, actors and computer programmers, for example, are often owls. The emergence of 24-hour industrial, commercial and professional operations and the advent of new computer-communications technologies have enabled increasing numbers of people to follow a lifestyle that suits their particular circadian rhythm, but for most people, reality still consists of getting up early in the morning, working all day and going to bed (or trying to) by late evening. In short, the lark lifestyle still predominates — and, in industrialized societies, it's still looked on as more normal than the owl lifestyle. In fact, owls are often considered by larks to be quite eccentric and they often feel misunderstood and victimized by others who try to enforce conformity to the lark lifestyle. In particular, owls often suffer the disapprobation of employers and co-workers who consider sleeping in to be a sure sign of laziness.

"Other people do tend to look at you strangely and say, 'You slept all day?' " comments Mark Moraes, a graduate student in electronics at the University of Toronto who often works at night and sleeps during the day. He says there's a curious kind of double standard in operation here. People who get up and go in to work extremely early in the morning and leave about 4:00 in the afternoon are generally admired. But those who do the reverse, coming in at noon and working until after midnight, are often told their hours are "weird."

"They almost sound accusing, as if there's something wrong with you," Moraes said. "I always feel a bit defensive about that because I keep explaining that I'm in control of it. I have switched to ordinary daytime schedules for long periods. It's just that the sort of work I do I don't think is conducive to 9 to 5."

"I don't associate first thing in the morning with waking up," says Eric Geringas, another university student. "That doesn't happen until a couple of hours later." Geoff Collyer, a young computer programmer who also prefers to work at night and has difficulty getting into the office in the morning, agrees that "there's an assumption that getting up early is *a good thing* — that it's virtuous. I find if I do work 9 to 5, I can't get any serious work done. If I'm up at 9:00, I'm physically awake but I'm not good for much. I put in an 8-hour day, but I don't actually produce anything." He admits to feeling "a bit of culture conflict" with people who live a 9-to-5 life. "At my most cynical times, I tend to feel that they're just sort of robots." Nevertheless, he has sought help at a sleep clinic in the hope of finding some way to cope with getting in to work earlier in the morning.

## WHEN CIRCADIAN CYCLES GO AWRY

When there's a chronic mismatch between a person's circadian rhythms and society's timetables, that person may be suffering from a disorder of the sleep/wake schedule. Unlike people who have pathological problems falling asleep at night or staying awake during the day, people with disorders of the sleep/wake schedule *can* sleep normally and function efficiently while awake — as long as they sleep at times dictated by their own internal clocks and not those of society. "They are not bad sleepers," says Mortimer Mamelak, director of the Sleep Disorders Centre at Sunnybrook Hospital in Toronto. "Once asleep, they're very good sleepers — they'll get their seven or eight hours, but not at the time when conventional society demands it." Unfortunately, work schedules and family life often do not allow these people the luxury of following their internal clocks, and they run into serious trouble when they try to shoehorn themselves into a "normal" 9-to-5 existence. "Usually when they come here, they're desperate to hang on to their jobs," Mamelak says.

The treatment of these types of sleep disorders is relatively new, notes Peter Hauri, director of the Dartmouth-Hitchcock Sleep Disorders Center in New Hampshire, in his book *The Sleep Disorders*. While doctors have been treating insomnia and excessive daytime sleepiness for centuries, "physicians only recently became aware that the sleep/wake rhythm can also be disrupted." Circadian sleep/wake rhythms can be confounded by irregular sleep/wake habits, rotating work schedules and traveling across time zones — all of which cause a realignment of the rhythms relative to each other and to external time. In fact, wholesale scrambling of the circadian system can occur rather easily, often with dire consequences for alertness and performance. The two most common modern causes of this problem are jet lag and shift work. Czeisler has suggested that the electric light has contributed to the development of these disorders because it allows humans to self-select their light/dark cycle instead of being forced to follow the natural one resulting from the earth's rotation.

Problems with sleep/wake schedules can happen to just about anyone because most people have a biological day that is longer than 24 hours. Entrainment — the process of resetting our biological clocks to a 24-hour schedule — must occur every day if we want to avoid slipping out of synch with the external world, which is exactly what happens in free-running experiments in the sleep lab. Since most people have an internal biological day of about 25 hours, entrainment is usually a straightforward matter of establishing a fairly regular routine and using external time cues to set their biological clocks back by about an hour or so every day. Many of these time cues are social and behavioral — work, meals, TV, bedtime and wake-up time, and so on — but the light/dark cycle is a powerful environmental cue that is now being exploited therapeutically to help people who have trouble entraining their sleep/wake cycle.

If time cues are disrupted or irregular — as is the case with jet lag or shift work — the results are similar to what happens when subjects free-run in the sleep lab: they drift more and more out of synch with the external world. A variant of this problem occurs on weekends, when many people start to free-run by delaying bedtime on Friday and Saturday night and sleeping in the following mornings.* Come Sunday night, they have trouble getting to sleep because their clocks have drifted by 2 or 3 hours. They wake up on Monday feeling groggy

---

* Juan-Carlos Lerman of the University of Arizona has suggested that the seven-day week, which was probably adopted in prebiblical times and has been remarkably resistant to change, might have arisen as a way of coping with a sleep deficit caused by several days of entraining biological clocks to the demands of the 24-hour day. The Sabbath provides a "day off" from entrainment, an opportunity to catch up on lost sleep and perhaps our first attempt to periodically resynchronize the human internal pacemaker to the requirements of organized society. Seven days is an adequate week length to perform this function, says Lerman, who also suggests this may provide the rationale behind the biblical statement that "sleep is a delight on the Sabbath."

and sluggish, and no wonder — their bodies think it's 4:30 a.m. instead of 7:30 a.m.

"People are incredibly naive," says Charles Czeisler. "They'll say, 'I can't understand why I have so much trouble getting to work in the morning.' Sometimes they'll even have been to psychiatrists who will be trying to understand what aversion they have to working. But if you take a history of when they're sleeping and waking on Friday and Saturday — they're at Studio 54 in New York until six o'clock in the morning. And then they can't understand why on Sunday night they can't go to bed at 10 o'clock in the evening, which may be by that point the equivalent of 6:00 p.m., biological time. There's very little appreciation of the importance of regularity in sleep and waking."

(Mamelak notes, however, that Sunday-night insomnia can also be experienced by people who sleep poorly during the week because of job anxieties and who try to catch up with their sleep on weekends. In these cases, therapy is indicated.)

The weekend syndrome may also account for many of the sleep problems reported by adolescents, according to a study by Arne Henschel and Leon Lack of Flinders University of South Australia. In a survey of 387 adolescents 13 to 17 years old, they found that 57 percent reported at least one type of sleeping difficulty (the most common problem was falling asleep, followed by difficulty staying asleep). The researchers found that on weekends many of these adolescents went to bed and woke up about two hours later than they did on weekdays. These subjects reported experiencing not only daytime sleepiness during the week, but also feelings of depression, inferiority and loss of concentration. The researchers concluded that it was likely that bad sleep habits and resulting daytime sleepiness were detrimental to the productivity and sense of well-being of these students in school. They suggested that delayed-phase chronotherapy (described below) might help, but would be impractical to use on such a wide scale; counseling on better sleep hygiene "would be a more economic solution."

In most cases, when people revert to their normal weekday sleep/wake schedule, their clocks once again become entrained and their mood and performance pick up during the week. Many people, however, do not have work or school schedules or other social time cues to synchronize their clocks; for example, the elderly, the jobless or self-employed people who live alone can all too readily slip into a permanent free-running schedule that can completely disrupt their sleep/wake cycles. In addition, there are people who have circadian sleep/wake cycles that stubbornly resist being entrained to a 24-hour day — their cycle of sleepiness and alertness occurs at a later time than most people or their biological day is much longer than the normal 25 hours. In recent years, innovative new therapies have been developed to help these people, but many still have great difficulty adjusting to a regular schedule.

## DELAYED SLEEP PHASE SYNDROME

People who reach their peak of alertness and efficiency very late in the day (extreme owls) often have delayed sleep phase syndrome. They usually can't get to sleep until sometime between 2:00 and 6:00 a.m. and will sleep until late morning or early afternoon unless forced to get up earlier. The timing is the only thing that's abnormal about their sleep; unless they try to change this timing, they easily sleep for a normal amount of time and awake refreshed. Attempts to shift to an earlier sleep/wake schedule are usually futile; it's like a person with a regular 11:00 p.m. bedtime trying to get to sleep at 7:00 or 8:00 p.m. They end up lying awake for hours at night and fighting sleepiness for much of the day.

These people cannot simply switch voluntarily to an earlier bedtime, so sleep researchers tried a different tack: they got these patients to *delay* their sleep time even more — so much, in fact, that they eventually worked their bedtime right around the clock to a normal evening hour. This works because the human sleep/wake rhythm is usually longer than 24 hours, which makes delaying the sleep period easier than trying to move it earlier. This procedure, called chronotherapy, was first developed in the mid-1970s by sleep researcher Elliot Weitzman and his colleagues at Montefiore Hospital in New York City. Patients stayed for a week in an isolation lab without external time cues. Each day, they were instructed to go to sleep about 3 hours later than the day before. Seven days of this treatment moved a 3:00 a.m. bedtime around to a midnight bedtime — and made it possible for the patient to get up about 7:00 or 8:00 in the morning. (This disorder can also be treated by timed exposure to bright lights, which will be discussed in more detail below.)

Exactly the opposite situation occurs with advanced sleep phase syndrome — the patient habitually goes to sleep and wakes up very much earlier than normal. The condition is rare, and there is only one reported case of its being treated by *advancing* the sleep period around the clock — that is, progressively putting the patient to bed earlier until he has achieved a normal late-evening to early-morning sleep schedule. This therapy was carried out in 1985 by Harvey Moldofsky and his colleagues at Toronto Western Hospital on a 62-year-old man who complained of intractable, irresistible afternoon and early-evening sleepiness. This man would fall asleep while watching TV, eating meals or in the middle of conversations. Once he fell asleep while riding a bicycle and another time while driving his car, which resulted in an accident. He would usually go to bed about 6:30 p.m. and sleep until about 3:00 a.m. He would awake feeling refreshed and would be alert until early afternoon when he would again be overtaken by extreme sleepiness and would often nap for an hour or two.

An attempt to treat this patient by delaying his sleep period around the clock failed; if he went to sleep at 11:30 p.m., he woke up between 3:00 and 4:00 a.m. and continued to be uncontrollably sleepy in the afternoon and early evening. So his sleep period was moved forward by 3 hours every two days until, after two weeks, he was going to bed at 11:00 p.m. and waking at 7:00 a.m. A follow-up five months later showed that he maintained an 11:00 p.m. to 6:00 a.m. sleep schedule at home and had no daytime sleepiness. This demonstrated that phase-advance treatment is possible and can work. Unfortunately, after about a year, other medical problems caused this patient to again experience difficulties with his sleep/wake pattern, although Moldofsky said they were not as bad as they'd been before.

. . . . . . .

For patients suffering from delayed sleep phase syndrome, one week of treatment in the lab will provide the initial shift in their sleep/wake schedule but it will not in itself provide a long-term solution to their sleep problems. The key to success is faithful adherence to the new schedule at home; they cannot slide back into late-night living and "they can't fall off the wagon on weekends," says Mamelak, who puts patients on a strict seven-days-a-week, late-evening-to-early-morning sleep schedule at home. Motivation is the major problem with these techniques, he says. "A great deal depends on the patient. A lot of people don't cooperate. These are people who like to be up at night; they do all the important things in their lives at night."

Hauri notes that people who suffer from delayed sleep phase syndrome differ from people who have a habit of going to bed late and arising early on weekdays, then making up for lost sleep by sleeping longer on weekends. These people can generally be shifted to an earlier bedtime by consistent enforcement of an early wake-up time seven days a week. In people with delayed sleep phase syndrome, "consistent wake-up times seem inadequate to reset bedtime." A new kind of therapy involving carefully timed exposure to bright lights (described below) may help these people.

However, Mamelak believes that in many cases, the sleep problems of owls stem primarily from social habits rather than a fundamental problem with the circadian system. Owls tend to be younger than larks; many are students or young adults just entering the work force who have had highly irregular sleep/wake habits during their school years and are finding it hard to adjust to having to get to work early in the morning. "They got a job and they have to be at work at eight or nine in the morning — and they've never *seen* that time. They do not know that 7:00 a.m. exists."

Reality and retraining often provide the solution for these people, he says. "An awful lot of owls have turned into larks when they got married and had children. They had to start getting up at seven o'clock in the morning and there was no way out. I have never failed to make an owl into a lark by just sitting on them and telling them they have to get up at seven o'clock. They can't tell me that this treatment is failing until they've done it seven days a week for six months. They're larks after that time, because they're getting up and going to work and that's the end of it. Life usually doesn't let them slip."

## IRREGULAR SLEEP/WAKE PATTERNS

For some people, the problem is not that their sleep/wake schedule has shifted to a later time than normal, it's that there's no regular sleep/wake schedule at all. Their sleeping and waking is spread all over the 24-hour day, which scrambles not only the sleep/wake rhythm, but all the other circadian rhythms as well. As a result, the patient is chronically sleepy and groggy and never feels refreshed by sleep.

In most cases, those who suffer from this problem are people who lack strong social time cues — the elderly, the unemployed, and people who are retired or who do freelance work. They often get into a vicious circle. Without social or work obligations to interfere, they tend to oversleep in the morning or take daytime naps if they have trouble falling asleep at night. Of course, by the time night rolls around again, they're too alert to sleep and a self-reinforcing irregular sleep/wake schedule is set in motion.

The prescription in these cases is a rigidly enforced regular sleep/wake schedule that involves a set late-evening bedtime, a regular wake-up time and no daytime napping. However, Hauri says that such patients can rarely normalize their sleep/wake pattern by themselves; they need constant reinforcement from others, and sometimes a stay in hospital, in order to do this.

Hauri says that in some severe cases, he recommends hiring a roommate to enforce regular sleep and wake-up times — but he doesn't say whether these enforcers get hazardous-duty pay.

## NON-24-HOUR SLEEP/WAKE SYNDROME

Let's call her Sally. She's 26, unmarried, a journalist — and she's just been fired for chronic oversleeping in the morning. Most nights, she lies in bed awake for 4 to 6 hours and once she does fall asleep, it's almost impossible for her to wake up on time the next morning. When she went to a sleep disorders clinic, the doctors instructed Sally to keep a sleep log for two weeks. Since she was unemployed, she simply allowed her sleep/wake schedule to free-run and discovered that each day, she went to sleep 4 to 6 hours later than the day before. Her insomnia disappeared — but, of course, her sleep/wake schedule was completely out of synch with a normal 24-hour day. She'd often stay up all night and sleep all day.

The doctors at the sleep clinic counseled Sally to go to sleep only when she felt sleepy and to sleep as long as she wanted to. She followed this regimen while writing a book. A one-month sleep log showed that she typically worked for 20 to 22 hours in a row, then relaxed for an hour or two and slept for 10 to 12 hours without interruption. It turned out that Sally has a biological day that is 36 to 38 hours long. She couldn't establish a regular late-evening to early-morning sleep pattern because this would require setting her biological clock back by about 12 hours every day — an impossible task.

Although she felt rested and alert on this extraordinary schedule, Sally didn't like its negative effect on her social life, so with the help of a drug to "speed up" her clock, she managed to settle into a more regular routine. For about three weeks of each month, she follows a 24-hour schedule, sleeping from midnight to 8:00 a.m., and during the final week, she lets herself free-run around the clock.

People with non-24-hour sleep/wake cycles are prone to episodic sleep loss and excessive daytime sleepiness at times when their sleep/wake pattern is out of synch with the outside world. When they are in synch, they can sleep well at night and remain alert during the day, but this harmony usually only lasts for a couple of weeks until they drift out of phase again. Unlike people with delayed sleep phase syndrome (who can maintain a stable albeit atypical daily sleep/wake schedule) people with non-24-hour cycles are unstable — their sleep/wake pattern is all over the place. Blind people, who do not perceive the light/dark cycle, and schizophrenics, who do not perceive social time-givers, are also prone to this syndrome. (At one time, scientists were uncertain whether blind people had circadian rhythms at all; it turns out they do, but they may free-run.)

## BACK TO BASICS: BRIGHT LIGHT RESETS OUR CLOCKS

It has long been known that the light/dark cycle is the most powerful environmental time-giver influencing circadian pacemakers in plants and animals, but its role in entraining the biological clocks of humans was debated for many years. In 1962, when Aschoff and Wever reported on the first free-running studies with humans, they concluded that the light/dark cycle was not as strong as social contacts and sleep/wake schedules in entraining their subjects to a 24-hour day. However, in the 1980s, experiments conducted by Charles Czeisler and colleagues at Montefiore Hospital in New York and Harvard Medical School proved otherwise. First, they put two subjects into a time-isolation lab and told them the lights would be turned on and off at any time. They found that the subjects' bed-rest/activity cycle, body temperature cycle and sleep/wake cycle (measured by polygraph) were all synchronized according to the arbitrary schedule of light and dark imposed by the experimenters.

At the time, they were unsure whether entrainment occurred because of the effect of the light/dark cycle in scheduling periods of sleeping and waking (i.e., because the subjects went to sleep when it was dark and woke up when it was light), or whether light actually had a direct physiological or biochemical effect on the biological clocks in the brain. (There was some support for the latter theory in the fact that blind people sometimes have great difficulty entraining to a 24-hour day even when a strict 24-hour sleep/wake schedule is imposed.)

In 1986, Czeisler and his colleagues at Brigham and Women's Hospital in Boston proved that light does have a direct effect on circadian clocks in the brain. They put a subject in front of a bank of bright lights between 8:00 p.m. and midnight for a week and within two days succeeded in setting her biological clock back by 6 hours. They were able to determine this by measuring shifts in the peaks of her core body temperature and secretion of the hormone cortisol. Both the magnitude of the phase shift and the rapidity with which it occurred surprised the researchers. The shift was so great that the researchers concluded that light had to be acting directly on the pacemaker, rather than through an intermediary process.

The subject, a 66-year-old woman, was carefully chosen. A major objective of the experiment was to show that light acted directly on the circadian pacemaker, not indirectly by altering the sleep/wake schedule. But it's difficult to do this because, in most people, the pacemaker is most sensitive to light in the middle of the night, a time when they're usually asleep; therefore, it's impossible to expose them to bright light at this time without waking them up — which, of course, affects the sleep/wake schedule and compromises the experiment.

The researchers wanted to find a way to dissociate what had been an inseparable link between the behavioral and the purely physiological ways in which the light/dark cycle might synchronize the circadian system. To do this, they found someone whose biological clock was maximally sensitive to light in the evening — at a time when she was normally awake but not usually exposed to bright light. They looked for their subject among the elderly because it's known that the circadian pacemaker runs faster as we age. The woman they selected had a normal sleep period (midnight to 6:00 a.m.) but a markedly advanced circadian cycle; in fact, her internal biological day was exceptionally short — just 23.7 hours — and her pacemaker was maximally sensitive to light in the midevening hours.

During "control" periods before and after the week of bright lights, the woman was exposed to normal levels of room lighting. Her sleep/wake schedule and social contacts remained the same during the control periods and the experimental period, to preclude the possibility that either of these two factors could entrain her circadian pacemaker instead of exposure to light.

The intensity of the light used in the experiment was about 7,000 to 12,000 lux, equivalent to being outdoors just after dawn and about a tenth of the typical brightness outside at noon. "We're not using an intensity of light that is blinding," said Czeisler. Before running the experiment, he sought the advice of a lighting expert on the potential hazards of exposing subjects to "bright" light. The man was amused. "I was talking about something in the 2,000-3,000 lux range, and he said, 'I always have to laugh when people say that's bright because if you were to lie outdoors at dusk and look up into the blue sky, you'd be getting about 8,000 lux of light, whereas at midday, it's about 100,000 lux.'"

The light used in the lab was, however, very much brighter than normal room lighting, which typically ranges from about 250 to 500 lux. "Five hundred lux would be a bright room and a candlelit dinner could be down in the 10-20 lux range," said Czeisler. "Most homes are probably well below the 500 range." This fact had not been appreciated by most physiologists studying circadian rhythms, he said. We think of ordinary room lighting as being quite bright but it's actually "closer to physiologic darkness than light. We spend quite a bit of time in almost total darkness."

In 1989, Czeisler and his colleagues reported in the journal *Science* the results of yet another series of experiments demonstrating that bright light exposure could be used to very rapidly reset the human circadian pacemaker forward or backward by any desired amount. In fact, they were able to induce shifts of up to nearly 11 hours — unprecedented in research with humans — by exposing subjects to 5 hours of bright lights on each of three successive days.

The timing of the exposure is critical, affecting both the magnitude and the direction of the phase change. The largest changes occurred in subjects who were exposed to bright light when their circadian temperature cycle was at its minimum. Normally this minimum occurs a few hours before waking, so the subjects were required to invert their normal sleep/wake cycle; however, by doing some control experiments, the researchers were able to demonstrate that it was indeed the bright light exposure, and not the inversion of the sleep/wake cycle, that was primarily responsible for resetting the circadian pacemaker.

The experiments showed that the pacemaker could be advanced to an earlier phase when the light exposure occurred late in the subjective night — that is, after the temperature minimum — while exposure earlier in the subjective night, before the temperature minimum, caused a phase delay. When exposure occurred during subjective day, only small circadian phase shifts were observed.

The researchers note that this is the first demonstration of strong circadian phase resetting in humans, or what is called "Type O" resetting. An accompanying article in *Science* described this as suddenly shifting a clock by 10 to 12 hours without moving the hands of the clock through the intervening positions. Previously, the only vertebrate in which Type O resetting had been observed was the house sparrow.

Czeisler and his colleagues also found that the amount and direction of the circadian shifts induced by the bright lights was modified by the timing of exposure to ordinary room light, "previously thought to be undetectable by the human pacemaker." They conclude that the human circadian pacemaker is far more sensitive to light than scientists have previously recognized and suggest that carefully timed exposure to a cycle of bright light, ordinary indoor lighting and darkness can facilitate human physiological adaptation to large phase shifts within three days.

How does light act on the biological clock? It's believed there is a "neural pathway" — a nerve connection — directly from the retina of the eye to the hypothalamus, the part of the brain where the circadian pacemaker is located, and that biochemical messages travel to the pacemaker along this pathway. The hormone melatonin, produced by the pineal gland, may also play a role. It's been known for some time that the secretion of melatonin increases at night and decreases during the day, and in 1980, Alfred Lewy, then at the U.S. National Institute of Mental Health, and his colleagues showed that exposing subjects to bright light at night could suppress the normal production of melatonin. In 1989, scientists at Massachusetts General Hospital reported finding that cells within the hypothalamus contain receptors for melatonin, providing "the first biochemical evidence that melatonin acts on the biological clock of human beings," according to one of the researchers, Steven Reppert.

Bright-light exposure has potential for treating a variety of circadian-related disorders, including depression, seasonal affective disorder (SAD), both delayed and advanced sleep phase syndrome and early awakening in the elderly. Czeisler says that bright-light exposure also "shows promise" for the treatment of sleep and circadian problems associated with shift work and jet lag, but more research is required before it can be widely used in these applications. He notes that critically timed bright-light exposure may bring about more rapid shifts than the "haphazard exposure" to the synchronizing cues that normally occur during, for example, transmeridian flight. "The timing of exposure to bright light and darkness can reset the circadian pacemaker to any desired phase within two or three days," whereas it usually takes a week or more to adjust to a phase shift of 6 hours or more. But it's important to get the timing just right: "It turns out that very small changes in the timing of the exposure to light will cause the pacemaker to be reset by quite widely varying amounts." A difference of as little as 1 to 1½ hours in the light exposure "can cause you to be reset to Hawaiian time rather than Italian time."

Bright-light therapy has already been used to treat patients suffering from seasonal affective disorder, which is characterized by bouts of depression, profound craving for carbohydrate foods, weight gain, excessive but nonrefreshing sleeping and daytime drowsiness. These symptoms typically appear in late fall or early winter and last until spring, when the patient becomes exuberantly happy and full of energy. This syndrome is linked to day length because it is far more prevalent in people living in northern latitudes than those who live nearer the equator. (Evidence of SAD can be found in the journal of 19th-century Arctic explorer Frederick Cook, who described his men as "sitting around sad and dejected, lost in dreams of melancholy . . . . All efforts to infuse bright hopes fail.") A survey by researchers at the University of California at Irvine indicated that the incidence of SAD in the northern United States is about 100 in 100,000 people, compared with fewer than six in 100,000 in the southern part of the country.

Why would these symptoms appear in people who live at high latitudes and not in those who live closer to the equator? It is suspected that SAD may be caused by excess production of melatonin. Remember that secretions of this hormone are highest at night. At high latitudes during the fall and winter, darkness takes up most, and sometimes all, of each 24-hour period; presumably, these longer nights cause elevated levels of melatonin to occur in our bodies — which, after all, evolved in temperate and subtropical regions where seasonal variations in the length of day and night are not nearly so pronounced. Studies have shown that large injected doses of melatonin can cause sleepiness and reduce alertness; this may explain why people suffering from SAD sleep so much and feel so drowsy during the winter months. Exposure to bright light, it is reasoned, counteracts this effect by suppressing melatonin and by, in effect, exposing people to a more normal distribution of day and night.

MIT researchers Richard and Judith Wurtman suggest that modern lifestyles increase vulnerability to SAD "by diminishing the amount of time we expose ourselves to light." (One study of elderly people in San Diego showed that the men were exposed to sunlight for only 75 minutes per 24 hours and the women for just 20 minutes.) Just as many office workers join health clubs to get some exercise, people with indoor jobs should perhaps consider arranging for adequate exposure to light to overcome the symptoms of SAD, the scientists suggest.

Several studies have now shown that exposure to bright light for several hours each morning can eliminate SAD symptoms within days. It is not certain which is more important, the duration of light exposure or its timing, but several researchers believe that morning exposure may be more effective because it advances the circadian cycle and reduces the amount of time patients are literally "in the dark" and thus subjected to higher melatonin levels. Lewy and his colleagues at Oregon Health Sciences University suggest that exposure to bright light in the morning advances the timing of circadian rhythms and exposure in the evening delays it. Thus, they say, this form of therapy could also be used to treat people suffering from delayed sleep phase syndrome and advanced sleep phase syndrome.

The former should first have their sleep period shifted by the chronotherapy treatment described earlier (moving their bedtime around the clock) and then sit in front of bright lights for an hour or two after waking up. This will shift their circadian cycle to an earlier hour and counteract their tendency to want to sleep at later and later times. These people should avoid bright lights in the evening. Exactly the opposite applies to people suffering from advanced sleep phase syndrome: they should be exposed to bright lights between about 8:00

and 10:00 p.m. and avoid bright lights in the morning. This will push their circadian cycle to a later time and help them stay awake until a normal late-evening bedtime.

Pierre Pham and Daniel Kripke at the University of California at San Diego have suggested that wearing "rose-colored glasses" might also help people suffering from sleep phase disorders. These colored glasses — which are actually goggles — filter out the green wavelengths of light thought to be most active in suppressing melatonin. The researchers suggest that goggles to filter out green light, if used in the morning, would act to delay the circadian cycle and, if used in the afternoon, would act to advance the cycle. "Use of rose-colored glasses in the afternoon might help people fall asleep at night and help them awaken in the morning."

# CHAPTER 6

# TROUBLE AT NIGHT; TROUBLE DURING THE DAY

*The medical, economic and social toll of sleep disorders is staggering, from the thousands of tired industrial shift workers who work when the brain is timed to sleep, to the accident victim who lost his fight to remain alert at the wheel, to the elderly grandfather placed in a nursing home because of nighttime wandering, to the sleepy child who once again fails the fifth grade, to the grieving couple who has lost their sleeping child to sudden infant death syndrome.*
THE ASSOCIATION OF PROFESSIONAL SLEEP SOCIETIES

It IS BARELY 8:00 A.M. AND already they're struggling to stay awake while riding the subway to work or, worse, piloting their cars through the morning rush. They drag through the day in a dopey haze, work abstractedly and inefficiently, sometimes drifting off to sleep during slow periods. Sometimes they are literally attacked by a sudden, irresistible urge to fall asleep at the most inappropriate times — in the middle of a business meeting, for example. Driving home in the afternoon without getting into an accident is a major accomplishment. After supper, they zonk out in front of the TV set, waking only to drag themselves off to bed. There they toss and turn for hours, despite the sleeping pills — or maybe because of them. They brood about the day's problems. They stare at the clock, becoming increasingly panicky about their inability to sleep. If they do manage to fall asleep, they wake up frequently during the night, or their sleep is disturbed and fragmented, often without their even knowing it. They snore loudly and gasp for breath.

They get up the next morning feeling sluggish, irritable and aching — feeling, in short, as if they've been run over by a truck — and the weary cycle begins again.

These are people who suffer from sleep disorders — maladies that disrupt sleep and make waking life a daily misery. There are millions of them, locked in a grim daily struggle with debilitating conditions that can literally destroy their lives. Because family, friends and employers often are not very sympathetic, the process of destruction can be quite merciless. Social and family life disintegrate and marriages break up. People afflicted with sleep disorders are regularly fired for sleeping on the job or for chronic lateness due to oversleeping. Promising careers are derailed. The tendency to fall asleep at inopportune times causes industrial accidents resulting in injuries and the loss of lives and property. An indeterminable number of those suffering from sleep disorders have killed themselves and others in traffic mishaps.

· · · · · · ·

Surveys indicate that one-third to one-half of adult populations in industrialized countries complain of poor sleep on a regular basis. A smaller but significant number experience chronic debilitating problems. "About 15 to 18 percent suffer from intractable sleep difficulties that are perceived to be impediments to their life," says Harvey Moldofsky, chief psychiatrist at Toronto Western Hospital. In a brochure describing the relatively new speciality of sleep disorders medicine, the Association of Professional Sleep Societies notes that millions of people "live much of their lives in a fog of unrelenting sleepiness and fatigue which knows no limits . . . . Drugs are prescribed and used in connection with sleep more than for any other therapeutic purpose."

It's hard to say whether the incidence of sleep disorders is actually increasing. They've no doubt been around as long as human beings have been — certainly, griping about poor sleep goes back thousands of years. But until recently it was rare for complaints about sleep to be taken seriously as a medical problem, and some of the more serious disorders have been discovered only in the past two or three decades. Many remain poorly understood and there are undoubtedly others we haven't even uncovered yet. But it does appear that sleep-related maladies are more diverse and probably more common than once thought — enough to give rise to an entirely new clinical discipline. At the same time, there's been an increase in public awareness that these disorders exist and that in many cases something can be done about them. The result is that it is no longer quite so likely for sufferers to be written off by family, friends, employers — and even by their doctors — as lazy, shiftless malingerers, hypochondriacs, neurotics or mentally retarded.

But there's much room for improvement, according to a task force of sleep experts commissioned by the Association of Professional Sleep Societies to investigate the state of teaching about sleep disorders in medical schools. In 1979, a survey revealed that U.S. medical schools offered at best only occasional courses on sleep disorders. An observational study by sleep researchers at Stanford University found that internists spent an average of only about 2 minutes with patients complaining of sleep problems — which included the time to write a prescription for sleeping pills. Things have improved in the past decade, but the task force concluded there are still relatively few physicians who "can recognize the signs and symptoms of sleep disorders and, above all, understand their implications. A major problem in America and throughout the world is that, outside of a very small group of specialists, such knowledgeable physicians do not now exist."

Fortunately, in the past two decades, there has been substantial growth in the number of labs where sleep disorders can be diagnosed and treated. The first sleep disorders clinic in the United States was established at Stanford University in 1969. Since then nearly 200 such clinics have been opened in North America. There are also sleep clinics in Europe, Australia, Japan, South America and Israel. The Association of Sleep Disorders Centers was established in 1975; its purpose is to accredit clinics in the United States and to promote professional education and the development of standards and guidelines for patient care.

Most sleep clinics are based in large urban hospitals or university medical schools, usually in conjunction with sleep-research programs. Medical experts from widely diverse fields are involved: psychologists and psychiatrists, internists, physiologists and specialists in disorders of the heart, lungs, brain, respiratory system and central nervous system, to name a few. Treatments include drugs, new technologies, psychological counseling and psychotherapy, behavior modification and relaxation techniques, biofeedback and lifestyle changes. As we saw in Chapter 4, chronotherapy, an entirely new form of treatment, has been developed to help people whose biological clocks and sleep/wake cycles are out of whack.

But before any of these treatments can be recommended, sleep experts have to ferret out the exact nature of the problem and what's causing it — and this frequently presents them with quite a challenge.

## DIAGNOSING SLEEP PROBLEMS:
## AN EXERCISE IN COMPLEXITY

Understanding abnormality implies a knowledge of what is "normal" — but when it comes to sleep, there's a high degree of individual variability to contend with. For example, sleep patterns and problems vary a great deal with age and sex. Disturbances of the sleep/wake cycle and the circadian system become more common as we grow older. It becomes increasingly difficult to stay asleep all night and awake all day; our ability to entrain to a regular 24-hour schedule diminishes and the incidence of sleep disorders and sleep-disrupting medical problems increases markedly. In a Finnish study of more than 31,000 people, the incidence of insomnia increased from about four percent among those 18 to 29 years old to more than 20 percent among people over 60. Other studies have suggested an even higher incidence (up to 40 percent) of insomnia among elderly people.

Numerous studies indicate that the incidence of poor sleep is higher among women than men. In a large U.S. survey conducted in 1964, involving more than one million people, 26 percent of female respondents complained of sleeping poorly, compared with only 13 percent of male respondents. Mortimer Mamelak, director of the Sleep Disorders Centre at Sunnybrook Medical Centre, says the reasons are complex, but he believes they're related mostly to social, not physiological, factors because "for practically all conditions, except gynecological disorders, women are hardier than men." One major cause of their sleep problems, he says, is the fact that so many of them have to get into bed at night with men who are in "a dead coma, snoring something fierce. I think sleep problems are more common among women than among men because women have to sleep with men who snore."

Sleep problems are also more common among the widowed, divorced and separated and among people with low incomes and low

socio-economic status. Life stress factors also cause significant variations in sleep habits from one individual to the next. Work and leisure
activities, the use of alcohol and drugs, travel, social and family
obligations — all these affect the ability to get a good night's sleep. In
some cases, a sleep problem is a symptom of another malady, sometimes a medical or psychiatric problem; in other cases, the disturbance
stems from a malfunction of the sleep/wake system itself.

To begin the process of sorting out the potential cause (or causes)
of a sleep problem, patients referred to a sleep clinic are first asked a
series of questions about their sleep habits, lifestyles and medical
problems. The questionnaire developed by the Stanford Sleep Disorders Clinic runs to 27 pages. Some typical questions are: What bothers
you most about your sleep? How long have you had trouble sleeping?
What is your bedroom like? What time do you go to bed and what
time do you wake up? What do you do in the hours before sleep? Do
you feel sad or depressed, worried about things? Do you disturb the
sleep of your bed partner? Do you depend on an alarm clock to wake
you up? Do you have vivid dreams or hallucinations while falling
asleep? Do you follow the same sleep pattern during the week and on
weekends? Do you snore loudly? Suffer chronic pain? Go to the
bathroom often at night? Do you fall asleep while having sexual
intercourse? Have you performed a complex action (such as driving
a car) without remembering it? Do you get "weak knees" when you
laugh?

Some of these questions might seem to have little to do with sleep,
but in fact the answers to these and many other questions provide
valuable clues to whether the sleep problem stems from underlying
physiological, medical or psychological factors, or some combination
of them. Often, helpful information about sleep behavior (e.g., heavy
snoring, sleepwalking) can also be obtained from bed partners, parents or roommates.

Patients are then usually asked to sleep for one or more nights or
to take several daytime naps in a lab specially designed for physiological monitoring; there, they are wired with electrodes that transmit
information on brain waves, heart rate, breathing patterns, leg movements, blood oxygen levels and so forth. In some cases, they may be
asked to wear an ambulatory monitoring device at home to record
heart rate, temperature, physical activity and respiratory data. When
disorders of the circadian system are suspected, patients may be

isolated from external time cues for a period of several days so their sleep/wake cycle can free-run.

## ENVIRONMENTAL FACTORS

Before discussing the psychological, physiological and medical problems associated with sleep disorders, it would be useful to examine some of the environmental factors that affect sleep, such as temperature, noise levels, exercise and the sleeping environment. These vary a great deal from one person to the next and individuals react differently to them. For example, some people are far more affected by noise than others. While one person might need absolute quiet to fall asleep, another might find dead silence to be quite alerting and prefer to drift off to sleep while watching TV or listening to music. Insomniacs sometimes develop an acute sensitivity to minor bedroom noises, like the ticking of a clock or the humming of a fan; they can even be disturbed by the sound of their own heartbeat.

The level of noise required to wake someone up is also quite variable; in one study of college students, wake-up thresholds ranged all the way from a whisper (15 decibels) to the noise level found in disco clubs (100 decibels). But loudness is not the only thing that determines whether a noise will wake someone up. When the noise occurs and how long it lasts are also significant; for example, you are more likely to be wakened during light sleep (Stages 1 and 2) than during deep (slow wave) sleep. The elderly, who have little SWS, are more easily awakened than younger people and some people who seem to have a predisposition toward lighter sleep may also experience more frequent sleep disruption caused by environmental noise.

The nature of the noise can be just as important as its loudness; a mother might sleep soundly through a storm but awaken immediately when her baby cries. Studies have shown that variable loud noises, such as those produced by passing trucks or overflying aircraft, can be very disruptive, even when the people affected don't remember being wakened or think they've gotten used to the noise. One survey showed that people living near Los Angeles International Airport (who believed they'd adjusted to aircraft noise) slept an average of 45 minutes less a night and had less deep sleep than people who lived in quieter locations.

One the most common and vexatious noise problems associated with sleeping is the snoring, sputtering and mutterings of a bed partner — a problem that is often bad enough to drive couples first to earplugs and then to separate bedrooms. (As we shall see later, loud snoring should not be ignored; it may be a symptom of a serious sleep disorder.)

Temperature and humidity are other environmental variables that affect sleep, as anyone who has ever tossed and turned through a hot, sticky summer night can attest. Studies have shown that temperatures over 24°C (75°F) seem to cause more movement during sleep, more awakenings and a decrease in REM and slow wave sleep. But contrary to the common belief that sleeping in a cold room is better for you, several studies suggest that cold may be even more disruptive than heat. Deborah Sewitch notes that most research on the effects of ambient temperature indicate that extremes of either hot or cold significantly increase awake time and decrease the ability to maintain sleep.

The effect of exercise on sleep is not clear. Various studies have produced contradictory results, although several suggest that people who exercise regularly and are aerobically fit do sleep better than people who are less fit. Moderate exercise in the late afternoon or early evening may improve sleep that night (and even if it doesn't have a direct effect on sleep, it might help by reducing tension); however, intense exercise may have a disrupting effect. Peter Hauri, director of the Dartmouth-Hitchcock Sleep Disorders Center in New Hampshire, recommends a regular program of moderate exercise at these times to enhance sleep. Early-morning and late-night exercising is less effective; late exercising in particular, especially if it's vigorous, may cause stimulation that makes falling asleep difficult.

· · · · · · ·

Sleep disorders are divided into two broad categories: *dyssomnias* and *parasomnias*. Dyssomnias, which are characterized by problems with the amount, quality or timing of sleep, include disorders like insomnia, excessive daytime sleepiness and disruption of the sleep/wake cycle. Parasomnias involve disturbances during sleep, such as sleepwalking and night terrors.

## I. Can't Fall Asleep
Most people think of insomnia primarily as a problem of falling asleep, but the concept also embraces frequent awakenings that disrupt and

fragment sleep, and waking up too early in the morning. Sleep doctors classify these complaints as disorders of initiating or maintaining sleep (DIMS).

Since individual sleep needs can vary a great deal, insomnia cannot be defined simply as the loss of a given number of hours of sleep each night. Some people get along quite well with comparatively little sleep at night, while others may sleep just as long or even longer than normal sleepers and still consider themselves insomniacs. These people have a strong perception that their sleep is inadequate and often complain of feeling inefficient, tired, anxious or sleepy during the day. (Some, however, don't experience daytime sleepiness; because of emotional problems, many seem to have a high level of arousal both at night and during the day.)

How accurate is the insomniac's perception of how much sleep is obtained? In many cases, not very: they often overestimate how long it takes them to fall asleep and underestimate how much sleep they get. In a Stanford University study in which a group of self-reported insomniacs was observed in the sleep lab, the subjects estimated it took them about an hour on average to fall asleep, whereas poly-graphic monitoring showed the real average was closer to 15 minutes. They also reported that they'd slept an average of only 4½ hours when, in reality, they'd slept closer to 6½ hours.

Despite these inaccuracies, however, the insomniac's perception of poor sleep is not all exaggeration. While many overestimate the amount of sleep lost, some studies have shown that poor sleepers do nevertheless get less sleep and take longer to fall asleep than normal sleepers. A major epidemiological survey done in the republic of San Marino indicated that it took poor sleepers an average of 30 minutes to fall asleep, compared with 10 minutes for good sleepers. They also got an average of two hours less sleep than good sleepers and woke up several times a night. Furthermore, if a person is a "long sleeper" by nature, he or she may in fact not be getting as much sleep as needed, even if six to eight hours of sleep a night is obtained.

Various surveys indicate that some 15 to 35 percent of the adult population in industrialized countries complain of poor sleep. In particular subgroups (e.g., shift workers and psychiatric patients), the reported incidence can be as high as 65 percent. Of all the complaints heard by general practitioners, insomnia is believed to rank third, after headaches and gastrointestinal problems. Mamelak says it's doubtful that insomnia was always as common as it is today; it is "virtually endemic to modern life." Evaluation of a large of number of chronic insomniacs suggests that most cases are caused primarily by stress or depression. (Depression can be a short-term response to a specific problem, which passes after the crisis is over, or it can be a chronic form of mental illness.) According to sleep consultant Richard Coleman, depression and other psychiatric problems account for about 35 percent of the cases, while the stresses associated with daily life account for another 15 percent. Another 30 percent can be attributed to underlying medical and physiological conditions, including respiratory problems and a disorder characterized by disturbing sensations in the legs. About 10 to 15 percent are due to a variety of other causes, including the use and abuse of alcohol and drugs, poor sleep habits and disturbances of the circadian system.

A small number of people suffer from child-onset insomnia, a condition that exists virtually from birth and that may be the result of neurological impairment affecting the sleep/wake system in the brain; their EEG readings are often quite unusual and their sleep tends to be extraordinarily sensitive to being disrupted by noise and stimulants such as caffeine. In about 10 percent of chronic cases, doctors can find no obvious cause for the insomnia.

When confronted with objective evidence that their sleep is normal or that they are in fact sleeping more than they think they are, some simply relax and stop worrying about their "insomnia." William Dement of the Stanford Sleep Disorders Clinic describes the case of a retired college professor who complained of severe insomnia and daytime fatigue lasting 40 years. When asked to keep a sleep diary, this man recorded fewer than 4 hours of sleep a night. However, overnight monitoring in the sleep lab showed that he actually slept about 8 hours. Later he wrote to Dement saying that he was not waking up in the middle of the night so much and was feeling less tired and depressed. Once he discovered he was getting a normal amount of sleep, he stopped fretting about it.

In other cases, behavioral techniques may change a patient's subjective impressions of how well he or she sleeps; Hauri cites one case of a man who felt his sleep improved after using self-hypnosis and meditation techniques, even though polygraphic evidence showed that he was sleeping just as well before this treatment as after it.

Treatment usually is not necessary in cases where no obvious cause of insomnia can be found and the patient does not feel overly anxious about a lack of sleep, particularly if he or she feels fine during the day. These people may be "short sleepers" who simply do not need as much sleep as the average person. Some short sleepers are persuaded that they're insomniacs by spouses who need more sleep.

In some situations in which no diagnosable cause of insomnia can be found, the patient remains convinced that something is wrong, insisting that the doctors have made a mistake and sometimes even threatening a malpractice suit. Coleman says some can become quite paranoid, accusing doctors of trying to trick them or manipulate their brain waves. He suggests this may be a kind of denial that enables these "pseudoinsomniacs" to avoid facing underlying psychological problems.

At one time, about half of those who complained of insomnia were labeled pseudoinsomniacs, but this has changed with the discovery of previously unknown sleep disorders and an increasingly sophisticated ability to detect sleep problems in the lab. Among those for whom no diagnosable cause of insomnia can be found may be people suffering from as yet undiscovered sleep disorders. "There are many sleep disorders that were unknown 10 years ago; others will be discovered in the future," Hauri notes.

## LIFE STRESS AND INSOMNIA

People who are naturally prone to anxiety and low self-esteem are particularly vulnerable to insomnia during times of stress, but even well-adjusted people will experience sleep problems when confronted with a crisis or major life changes. People who lack the resources to cope with life's stresses — for example, the elderly and the poor — are also more likely to experience insomnia than those who have a stronger social support system. Insomnia is most likely to be caused by emotional stress in younger people; in the elderly, the incidence of underlying medical or physiological causes increases substantially. Mamelak notes that the elderly are vulnerable on all counts. Not only do they suffer physical deterioration of their brains and circadian sleep/wake systems, but they're also more likely to have experienced painful psychological episodes simply by virtue of having lived longer. "Bereavements, loneliness, financial problems and poor health are all too often their lot. When these are combined with the loss of daily social routines, inactivity during the day, and perhaps a nap or two during the morning and afternoon to pass the time away, the stage is set for long stretches of wakefulness at night."

Of course, nearly everyone experiences a sleepless night now and then. The causes can range all over the emotional map, from over-excited anticipation of a long-awaited adventure* or tension before an important exam to the stress caused by death in the family, divorce or the loss of a job. The tag "psychophysiological" insomnia is attached to sleeplessness brought on primarily by the emotional and psychological wear and tear of daily life.

If the problem lasts less than about a month, and if a specific emotional cause is apparent, it is considered "transient and situational." Hypnotics (certain kinds of drugs to promote sleep) may be prescribed if sleeplessness persists more than a few nights, not only to provide the patient with needed rest but to forestall the possibility that anxiety over the insomnia itself will transform a temporary problem into a permanent one. Drugs can be useful as a temporary measure to get a patient through a short-term crisis, but they are counterproductive if used too frequently or for too long. They are not suitable for treating chronic forms of insomnia. "I spend most of my time taking people off medication," says Moldofsky. First-time patients in his sleep clinic have been known to dump large numbers of multihued sleeping pills on his desk when asked what they've been taking.

Unfortunately, for most people troubled with insomnia, the problem is a long-standing one. A 1979 Los Angeles survey revealed that of the nearly one-third of respondents who said they suffered from insomnia, fully 40 percent reported that the problem had persisted for more than five years and fewer than three percent said the problem was of less than one month's duration. In many cases, the problem had escalated from a temporary to a persistent one for a variety of psychological reasons. If the insomnia is symptomatic of deeper emotional problems, if the stress that originally caused it persists for a prolonged period or if the problems causing the stress cannot be resolved, chronic sleeplessness may result, particularly in people who already have a predisposition toward poor sleep.

---

* Coleman reports that insomnia is common among Olympic-level athletes the night before a big event, although they generally are excellent sleepers. On average, they lose about 1 to 3 hours of sleep the night before their performance. Some astronauts have commented that they had difficulty falling asleep the night before a space mission.

Hauri says that cases of persistent psychophysiological insomnia are often based on faulty habits and conditioning and are best treated with behavior modification techniques, relaxation training or psycho-therapy, rather than with hypnotics. Hypnotics should be used spar-ingly, if at all — no more than once or twice a week, Hauri says. Prolonged use can in itself disrupt sleep, and patients often develop a tolerance for the drugs, which prompts them to increase the dosage. Addiction can result and withdrawal can cause severe "rebound insomnia." Some of the drugs that are quickly removed from the body by metabolism can cause wakefulness and severe anxiety and some-times patients experience frightening dreams while on medication.

Insomnia can become stubbornly intractable, persisting long after the stress that precipitated it has disappeared. Some people develop an obsessional anxiety about not being able to fall asleep or an actual fear of insomnia — a classic case of the self-fulfilling prophecy. In people who hang the insomniac label on themselves, poor sleep habits established during a temporary bout of sleeplessness can settle in for the long haul. In effect, they have *learned* to be poor sleepers. Many insomniacs simply try too hard, with self-defeating results. If they become overly preoccupied with the need to fall asleep at night, tension increases as bedtime draws near. Often these people can drift off quite easily when they're not thinking about going to sleep — for example, while watching television — but perversely, the very deci-sion to go to bed precipitates wakefulness.

In these cases, the best treatment is to distract the patient's mind until he or she becomes tired enough to fall asleep. In tense or anxious people, relaxation or biofeedback techniques can be helpful; for milder cases, Hauri says, reading, watching TV or listening to the radio while lying in bed is recommended — but only if the insomniac gets up at a specified time the next morning. Otherwise, this technique may simply shift the sleep period and cause an unwanted reversal of the entire sleep/wake cycle.

One of the worst things to do when confronted with sleeplessness is to lie in bed brooding and becoming panicky about the loss of sleep. Under these circumstances, it is sometimes useful to short-circuit awareness of the passage of time by turning the clock to the wall. This type of experience can develop into a persistent form of sleeplessness known as "conditioned" insomnia, in which the sleep environment becomes linked in the patient's mind with wakefulness. Lying awake in bed, becoming increasingly angry and frustrated by an inability to sleep for whatever reason, can lead to a situation in which everything about the bedroom and the rituals of preparing for bed — getting undressed or brushing teeth, for example — triggers tension and alertness. This type of insomnia is not quite the same as that involving anticipatory anxiety. Here, wakefulness is associated not with the decision to go to sleep, but with the bedroom environment itself, and treatment requires a different approach — severing the mental link between wakefulness and lying in bed.

Unlike normal sleepers, who often find it difficult to fall asleep in a new or strange environment, people suffering from conditioned insomnia often find they sleep much better in unusual places, precisely because these places do not trigger deeply ingrained associations with wakefulness. They usually find they sleep better when traveling. At home, they might find themselves better able to sleep in the den or even curled up on the floor than in their own bed. Hauri tells the story of one chronic insomniac who found, much to his surprise, that he got his best night's sleep while on a hiking trip when he was forced to spend the night literally clinging to the rocks on a narrow mountain ledge. His conditioned insomnia was the legacy of a childhood spent lying in bed at night listening to his parents fighting and hurling death threats at each other. Not surprisingly, the mountain environment held no such painful associations and he found he had no trouble sleeping.

Camping out on precarious mountain ledges is perhaps a bit too drastic for most people to try, but a technique called stimulus-control behavior therapy can be used to break the mental link between the bedroom and sleeplessness. R. R. Bootzin, a behavioral therapist who developed this technique, recommends the following approach:

• Go to bed only when sleepy.

• Do not read or watch television in bed.

• If you can't sleep, get up and go to another room and don't return to bed until you're really sleepy. If you still can't fall sleep, get up again. Repeat this procedure as often as necessary throughout the night. It is crucial to train yourself to associate lying in bed with falling asleep quickly.

• Get up at a regular time in the morning *no matter how little sleep you got the night before.*

• Do not nap during the day.

During the first night on this regimen, patients usually get very little sleep, but by the second or third night they're so exhausted that they fall asleep quite readily. After a few weeks they again begin to associate the bedroom with falling asleep. However, many people find it hard to stick with the routine and generally require the support of a therapist.

Researchers at New York's Montefiore Medical Center have tested another technique, called sleep restriction therapy, which involves limiting the amount of time the insomniac is allowed to lie in bed each night. In the journal *Sleep*, Arthur J. Speilman and his colleagues suggest that excessive time in bed (TIB) is a significant factor that perpetuates insomnia even after the stress that originally caused it has disappeared. "Getting into bed early, staying in bed late and napping are short-sighted strategies that foster the fluctuations in the distribution and amounts of sleep and waking that are characteristic of the sleep of insomniacs. Repeatedly experiencing the irregularity and unpredictability of sleep heightens the insomniac's worried anticipation of the upcoming night's sleep." Restricting time in bed stabilizes sleep, making it more regular and predictable and thus helping to overcome the effects of anticipatory anxiety.

At the start of therapy, the insomniac's allowable time in bed was substantially reduced. For example, if a patient reported lying in bed for 8 hours each night, but actually sleeping an average of only 5 hours, his or her sleep schedule was altered to permit lying in bed for only 5 hours. (Regardless of the severity of their insomnia, none of the patients were prescribed fewer than 4½ hours in bed each night at the start of the eight-week experiment.) Since the morning awakening time was usually governed by the patient's work schedule, an appropriate bedtime change was made in the evening. The subjects were told not to nap or lie down during the day, but some of them did.

Each day, the patients reported when they went to bed, when they got up and an estimate of their total sleep time. This estimate took into account episodes of waking in the middle of the night so it reflected both difficulty in *falling* asleep and difficulty in *staying* asleep. If, during each five-day period, they reported actually sleeping at least 90 percent of the time they were lying in bed, they were allowed to increase their TIB by going to bed 15 minutes earlier at night. However, if their total reported sleep time was less than 85 percent of the time spent lying in bed, their time in bed was reduced. If the figure was between 85 and 90 percent, there was no change in the TIB. Because patient reports of total sleep time were used, the therapy was self-pacing; time in bed was increased only when a patient perceived an improvement in sleep and a reduction in nighttime wakefulness.

On the first night, the average TIB for the group was set at about 5½ hours, a reduction of more than 2 hours from the average amount of time the patients normally spent in bed. Initially, the subjects' total sleep time dropped below pretreatment levels — in short, they suffered a certain amount of sleep loss — and some found it quite a struggle to stay awake until the scheduled bedtime. The researchers suggest this sleep loss may be critical to the success of the therapy, perhaps because it consolidates the sleep period, or because it causes fatigue that lowers the insomniac's high level of arousal, or because it reduces the maladaptive conditioning caused by lying awake in bed.

By the second week, however, total sleep time was back up to pretreatment levels and it continued to rise throughout the test period. The actual increase in total sleep time was fairly modest — an average of about 23 minutes — but the ratio of total sleep time to time spent in bed improved from the outset and was 20 percent better by the last week of treatment. The researchers explain the significance of this: a number of studies have indicated that the problems of insomniacs may result less from the loss in total sleep time than from the fragmentation of sleep caused by repeated nighttime awakenings. They suggest that the efficacy of sleep-restriction therapy might therefore stem more from its effect in substantially reducing these disruptive awakenings than from the increase in total sleep time, which was modest.

In follow-up interviews, 30 of the 35 subjects who had lasted the entire eight weeks (and who had previously suffered from insomnia for an average of more than 15 years each) said their insomnia was better; the other five said it was no different. Two people dropped out before the end of the experiment because they improved so rapidly that they did not want to continue treatment. Another eight quit early because they became discouraged and found they could not follow the rigid schedule. Even though they'd been warned to anticipate an initial period of sleep loss and fatigue, some subjects became alarmed by the fact that they felt worse and worried that they wouldn't be able to perform at work, so they dropped out. When these figures were factored in, 71 percent of subjects reported an improvement in their insomnia while 29 percent reported no improvement using this form of therapy.

Whatever treatment is used, it is critical for the insomniac to develop a regular sleep period — about 7 to 8 hours beginning at the same time each night, including weekends, says Mamelak.* People trying to beat insomnia should also avoid daytime napping. Late-afternoon or early-evening exercise is a good idea, but heavy physical activity or mentally demanding work should not be done late in the evening. Alcohol and caffeine should also be avoided in the evening. Days should be active, both mentally and physically. It is particularly important for the elderly to have something useful to do during the day, Mamelak says, because "looking forward to the day is the best guarantee of a good night's sleep."

Perseverance is necessary to defeat poor sleep habits that have become firmly entrenched; it will often take several months for good sleep habits to take hold. If correction of poor sleep habits does not eliminate the insomnia, then underlying medical, physiological or psychiatric conditions are probably at the root of the problem.

## OTHER CAUSES OF INSOMNIA

More than one-third of people complaining of chronic insomnia suffer from depression or other psychiatric disorders, such as psychoses, mania, acute schizophrenia and extreme anxiety. In fact, sleep disturbances can be an early sign of the onset of psychiatric problems. People who have a fear of death or of losing control often engage in a prolonged and fussy ritual before going to bed. Sleep and psychiatric problems tend to reinforce each other, Hauri notes; when you're not sleeping, "everything looks worse, more hopeless and more threatening" and when life seems so bad, falling asleep becomes increasingly difficult.

The relationship between sleep and depression has been extensively studied, and researchers have found that the severity of insomnia often correlates with the severity of the depression. They've also

---

* Coleman notes that Alexandre Dumas, the author of *The Count of Monte Cristo*, was cured of insomnia by a doctor's "prescription" to eat an apple every morning at 7:00 a.m. under the Arc de Triomphe. The apple may not have done much for Dumas's sleep problem, but entraining his sleep/wake cycle to a regular day-night routine apparently did.

found that depression is often accompanied not only by problems in falling asleep and staying asleep, but by changes in the normal pattern of the sleep cycle as well. Unlike normal sleepers, many people suffering from depression and some other mental disorders tend to have reduced amounts of slow wave sleep and intense REM periods that appear earlier than normal, sometimes immediately on falling asleep. (This unusual pattern also occurs in people suffering from manic-depressive disorders; however, it is the manic phase that is usually associated with insomnia, while the depressive phase is often characterized by excessive sleeping.)

There appears to be an intimate link between REM sleep and depression. Antidepressant drugs are potent suppressors of REM sleep, and when patients go off them, they can experience a rebound effect involving increased REM sleep, excessive dreaming and nightmares. Researchers have found that deliberate REM deprivation (i.e., waking patients to prevent them from obtaining REM sleep) can produce the same antidepressant effect as drugs in patients suffering from "endogenous" depression (which is believed to result from an internal brain disorder, as distinguished from other kinds of depression related to psychiatric problems and external stresses). The antidepressant effect is not obtained when the patients are awakening from non-REM sleep. This finding provides one possible explanation for the fact that a night of total sleep loss often improves daytime mood and performance in endogenously depressed patients and in some people with other kinds of depression; perhaps this antidepressant effect stems from the fact that the sleep deprivation also causes REM deprivation. In some European hospitals, sleep deprivation is used therapeutically on newly diagnosed depressives to help them get through the few weeks it takes for antidepressant drugs to become effective. To date, there have been no reports that this treatment has been used clinically in North America.

Some researchers have investigated the effect of naps on depression. In some cases, the naps caused a recurrence of depression in "responders" (i.e., patients whose symptoms are improved by total sleep deprivation), but in other cases they did not. Since these tests involved naps of different lengths, occurring at various times of day and, in at least one study, including or not including REM sleep, further research is required to clarify the effects of these factors.

Hauri cites one case in which an unusual non-REM/REM pattern tipped doctors off to the fact that the patient was really suffering from unacknowledged depression. Psychological testing subsequently revealed that the 48-year-old woman, who had not been able to offer doctors any reason for the apparently sudden appearance of her severe insomnia, unconsciously felt useless and was simply waiting for old age and death to overtake her. After psychotherapy enabled her to confront her feelings, she became involved in charity work and her sleep improved dramatically. As this case demonstrates, insomnia can at times be the only overt symptom in patients who strongly repress their emotional problems.

When insomnia is associated with psychiatric problems, treatment usually focuses on them rather than on the sleeplessness itself. Coleman says that in counseling sessions he often forces patients to focus on these other problems by refusing to allow them to talk about their sleep difficulties at all. If psychotherapy or the use of antidepressant or antianxiety drugs successfully addresses underlying psychiatric causes, the insomnia usually clears up as well.

The same is true for medical conditions associated with sleep problems. Illness and disease are another major source of insomnia, particularly conditions that cause pain, such as arthritis, ulcers, angina and other diseases of the heart and circulatory system. Kidney disease, diabetes, hypoglycemia (low blood sugar), infections, endocrine and metabolic diseases can also cause sleep disturbances, as can mercury and arsenic poisoning. Some illnesses, such as diabetes and enlargement of the prostate gland, disrupt sleep by causing frequent nighttime awakening to go to the bathroom. In the elderly, poor sleep may also result from degenerative brain diseases; insomnia can be a component of the "sundown" syndrome, which is characterized by nighttime confusion and delirium.

Short, fragmented sleep is associated with weight loss, while weight gain is associated with long, uninterrupted sleep. Hauri notes that this phenomenon makes sense from an evolutionary point of view: "Starving animals ought to be awake and looking for food; satiated animals are safest when they hide and sleep. One wonders whether, in our weight-conscious society, some insomnia might be directly related to semistarvation diets." Evidence to support this view comes from the observation that insomnia is common among people suffering from anorexia nervosa, the eating disorder characterized by an obsession with thinness. Once anorexics start to gain weight, their sleep generally improves. Short sleep also occurs in people suffering from hyperthyroidism, which is associated with weight loss, while those suffering from hypothyroidism and weight gain tend to be long sleepers.

Treatment of a medical condition underlying a sleep problem can often result in an improvement in sleep; however, medical treatment can itself also cause sleep difficulties. For example, some of the sleep problems suffered by people with kidney disease may be partly related to dialysis treatments. Not surprisingly, many patients often experience sleep problems during a stay in the hospital. Patients in intensive care, for example, may lack normal time cues because they're in an environment in which the ambient light level remains nearly constant and they are monitored and cared for by nurses day and night.

## INSOMNIA AND DRUGS

Today, a wide range of drugs (prescribed and otherwise) are used for therapeutic and nontherapeutic purposes. Many of them affect both sleep and waking performance, often in complex ways, and combinations of drugs can be even more disruptive. Many drugs can cause either drowsiness or wakefulness as their primary, intended effects or as side effects. They can alter the normal pattern of sleep stages, reducing both deep sleep and REM sleep and upsetting the REM/NREM cycle. Some appear to cause frightening dreams.

Withdrawal from drugs in addicted users can also cause serious sleep disruptions; in particular, a sudden stoppage in the use of sleeping pills can cause severe rebound insomnia. Antihistamines can cause drowsiness and are often used as ersatz sleeping pills. Mamelak says their soporific qualities have not been fully studied, but some clinical tests suggest they may help alleviate mild to moderate insomnia for a few nights. The sleep effects of tranquilizers and "recreational" drugs such as cocaine and marijuana can be unpredictable and highly variable from one person to the next. Stimulants such as caffeine, amphetamines (often used in diet pills) and drugs used to treat depression and asthma can ultimately cause a "crash" characterized by overwhelming daytime sleepiness.

Two of the most widely used drugs in our society are caffeine and alcohol. Most people are aware that caffeine can keep them awake and it is frequently consumed deliberately for that purpose. But users are often unaware of just how much caffeine they consume, not only in coffee, but in tea, cola drinks and chocolate. Hauri describes a case of an overworked woman suffering from severe insomnia who was hospitalized three times in five years for "nervous exhaustion." During each hospital stay, she recovered from her insomnia, but the cure never lasted. After undergoing psychotherapy to treat depression, she was finally referred to a sleep clinic. She was asked the routine questions, including how much coffee she drank. The answer was shocking: when she kept a log for a week, she found she was drinking 20 to 25 cups of coffee a day! Withdrawal from caffeine was prescribed; it caused a bout of depression and lethargy for a few days, but within two weeks, the woman's insomnia had disappeared. It had been caused not by nervous exhaustion or depression, but by "undiagnosed caffeinism."

Individuals vary a great deal in their sensitivity to caffeine. Although studies have shown that insomniacs usually drink less coffee than normal sleepers, many show a very high sensitivity to the drug: even a single cup of chocolate or a cola drink can keep them awake. Caffeine can also disturb sleep in people who don't believe they're affected much by it. It can take virtually the whole day for caffeine to clear the body, so it certainly should be restricted in the evening, and people with a high sensitivity to caffeine should stop their consumption even earlier in the day or avoid it altogether.

The effect of nicotine in disturbing sleep is less well-known by the general public. Some studies indicate that the sleep of heavy smokers is more disturbed than that of nonsmokers and that sleep quality improves in smokers who quit.

It is a common misconception that a little nip of alcohol before bed will help you sleep. In fact, drinking before bedtime does little to enhance sleep and is far more likely to disrupt it. Alcohol does have a sedative effect and a nightcap might help tense people relax enough to fall asleep. However, even in moderate doses, alcohol often causes nighttime awakening several hours after sleep onset; this fragments sleep and reduces total sleep time and it can contribute to the development of chronic sleep problems. Those who feel they need a nightcap would be far better off with the traditional glass of warm milk (*not* hot chocolate). Milk contains tryptophan, an amino acid that is the precursor of serotonin, a brain chemical associated with sleep. Tryptophan is being studied as a possible drug treatment for insomnia.

Chronic alcoholism plays havoc with the sleep/wake system. The sleep of alcoholics is shallow and fragmented and excessive daytime sleepiness may occur. The delirium that often accompanies heavy drinking bouts may result from extreme sleep deprivation. Sleep disturbances can persist for a long time after an alcoholic stops drinking.

## RESTLESS LEGS

A 35-year-old man lies in bed, unable to fall asleep because of the strange creeping sensations in his legs. They're not painful, but they are disturbing enough to keep him awake and it's not long before he climbs out of bed to "walk off his legs" for 10 or 20 minutes. Night after night, he paces the floor, sometimes till 4:00 or 5:00 a.m. When he does finally fall asleep, his legs start twitching and jerking every 30 to 40 seconds for up to an hour at a time. Each jerk wakes him up for a few seconds and by morning he has awakened 300 to 400 times. Although he's not aware of the awakenings, he is aware of feeling tired and "washed out."

This man is suffering from two ailments: periodic involuntary movements in sleep (the leg jerks) and "restless legs" (the creeping sensations that keep him awake). Periodic involuntary movement is not the same thing as the occasional body jerks many people experience while falling asleep. Episodes are interspersed with normal sleep and can last from 5 minutes to 2 hours. The problem also affects bed partners who often spend the night being kicked. It's estimated that about 12 percent of insomniacs experience periodic leg movements, and the problem increases with age. This problem can occur in isolation or in association with a variety of medical and drug-related problems or with other sleep disorders. It is also a common problem experienced by kidney patients receiving dialysis treatment; often, these people complain of chronic fatigue, which may be misinterpreted as depression and treated inappropriately. The disorder is still not well understood and treatment is not very satisfactory, although some patients have been helped by certain drugs.

The restless legs syndrome, which occurs when the patient is awake and relaxing, involves unpleasant sensations that have been likened to having ants crawling around inside the legs. Mostly they occur in the calves but sometimes the thighs and feet are affected as well. Walking around seems to be the only way to get rid of them. In assessing patients in his sleep clinic, Moldofsky says that one of the "crazy questions" he asks is where they sit when they go to a movie; people who suffer from restless legs syndrome usually say they sit in an aisle seat near the back so that their fidgeting will not disturb other patrons and because they usually need to get up and walk around.

Exercise and muscle relaxation techniques practiced during the day may help some patients with restless legs. Drug treatments are currently being investigated and some good results have been reported.

The syndrome has been linked to a wide variety of medical conditions and diseases (including vitamin deficiency, caffeinism, anemia, inadequate circulation and many more). It can also be associated with excessive daytime sleepiness. It gets worse with age and is aggravated by sleep deprivation and pregnancy. In about one-third of the cases, other members of the family also have the problem.

## SLEEP APNEA: YOU CAN'T SLEEP WHEN YOU CAN'T BREATHE

Sleep apnea is a disorder in which sleep is fragmented by repeated interruptions in breathing during the night. Patients are usually unaware of this disruption in their sleep, however; the complaint that brings them into the sleep clinic is chronic daytime sleepiness. Consequently, this disorder will be discussed more fully in the next section.

## II. Can't Stay Awake

People who are excessively sleepy during the day or who cannot resist falling asleep at inappropriate times suffer from DOES (disorders of excessive sleepiness), aptly pronounced *doze*. Although DIMS and DOES can occur separately, they can also coexist, like opposite sides of a coin: someone who sleeps poorly at night is often excessively sleepy during the day.

Fewer people suffer from DOES (sometimes called hypersomnia) than from insomnia, but they often outnumber insomniac patients in sleep clinics. The reason is that these disorders are often more serious than insomnia — in fact, some can be life-threatening. DOES disorders are more likely than insomnia to be associated with underlying medical or physiological abnormalities and less likely to be caused by psychological or psychiatric problems.

A complaint of excessive daytime sleepiness (EDS) should not be dismissed lightly, especially if it's bad enough to drive someone to seek treatment. Far from being hypochondriacs, most sufferers are reluctant to run to the doctor. They tend to deny or underestimate the severity of their hypersomnia, often because they expect to be ridiculed for being lazy or penalized for sleeping on the job. Coleman describes one patient who stubbornly resisted his wife's attempts to get him to a doctor until the day he fell asleep in the middle of an exciting championship game involving his favorite football team. Missing this much-awaited game was a sign to him that he'd lost control of his ability to stay awake.

William Orr of the Sleep Disorders Center at Presbyterian Hospital in Oklahoma City comments that excessive sleepiness is not taken very seriously in our culture. Most people, many physicians included, think it can be cured simply by allowing more time for sleep. But in many cases, people with excessive daytime sleepiness appear to be getting adequate amounts of sleep at night, and in any event, their sleepiness is far too extreme to be dismissed as simple fatigue. Moreover, many of them are not just *sleepy* during the day — something most people experience from time to time, at least in a mild form — but they are often *asleep* during the day. These people have an unremitting daily struggle to stay awake and they are often in trouble for sleeping on the job. Some are literally attacked by an irresistible urge to sleep at unlikely and inappropriate times — for example, while eating or driving, or in the middle of conversations or meetings.

As with insomnia, a detailed sleep history is the first step in assessing a complaint of EDS. Sleepiness in the afternoon, especially after a heavy lunch, may not be cause for concern — it could be merely the circadian midafternoon dip in alertness that many people experience. Sleepiness during the normal circadian peaks — in the morning or midevening — is more worrying, particularly in people who seem to obtain adequate amounts of sleep at night.

Asking patients how they feel is strictly subjective, however, and they may not always be able or willing to accurately assess just how sleepy they are. Consequently, researchers have developed objective methods to assess pathological daytime sleepiness — for example, the Multiple Sleep Latency Test (MSLT). This involves having patients lie in bed and attempt to fall asleep three to six times during the day after having an adequate amount of sleep the night before. Polygraph readings are used to measure the amount of time it takes to fall asleep (known as sleep latency) during each attempt. In normal sleepers, sleep latencies average about 10 minutes, although they vary during the day because of circadian influences and, at times, normal sleepers may not fall asleep at all within the 20-minute period allowed for each attempt. Patients suffering from excessive daytime sleepiness are out in under 5 minutes on average, regardless of the time of day. In fact, sleep latencies of less than 5 minutes are generally considered to be pathological. If insufficient sleep, drugs, tumors, infections or other medical conditions are ruled out as the cause of excessive sleepiness, the most likely culprit will be either sleep apnea or narcolepsy, a disorder associated with abnormal REM sleep.

## SLEEP APNEA

A 45-year-old man stops breathing more than 500 times a night, which causes repeated "microwakes" lasting a few seconds each time. He's unaware this is happening and thinks he's slept normally, but in fact he has not had more than 3 minutes of uninterrupted sleep all night.

Chronically tired during the day, the man is not able to hold a job for more than two weeks at a time; he's always being fired for "laziness" because he keeps falling asleep at work. Obese and a heavy snorer, he is diagnosed as suffering from severe sleep apnea. The recommended treatment, throat surgery, is rejected as too extreme for a "mere sleep problem."

This man subsequently became an alcoholic, was jailed for armed robbery while trying to steal liquor and died in prison of "unknown causes." He was asleep at the time of his death. Peter Hauri cites this case as one of the more dramatic examples of the often tragic consequences of sleep apnea, one of the most dangerous of the sleep disorders because it is potentially life-threatening. Men suffer from sleep apnea 10 to 15 times more frequently than women and the incidence increases markedly with age.*

Apnea is characterized by repetitive pauses in breathing that can last from 10 seconds to 2 minutes. (The word *apnea* comes from the

---

* Apnea can occur in children in association with medical problems related to tonsils, adenoids and obesity. Scientists believe that apnea and other breathing abnormalities during sleep may be a significant contributing cause of sudden infant death syndrome (SIDS), a leading cause of death in infants that usually occurs during sleep. Babies at risk for SIDS are often monitored by a device that alerts parents when dangerous irregularities in breathing or heart function occur during sleep.

Greek, meaning "without breath." One of the most telltale symptoms of apnea is extremely loud snoring interspersed with gasping or choking noises as the apneic's respiratory system struggles to draw air into the lungs. In rare cases, the brain may even fail to alert the respiratory system to resume breathing, but in most cases the effort to resume breathing causes the sufferer to wake up repeatedly. Mamelak says that when the apneic's tongue falls back against his pharynx during sleep, a vacuum is created at the back of the throat that literally "zips his pharynx shut. The more he struggles to breathe, the stronger he's pulling on the zipper. The only way to open the back of the throat is to wake up."

The awakenings last only seconds but when they number in the hundreds, they add up to a virtually sleepless night. Remarkably, sufferers are usually unaware that they spend most of the night in a relentless struggle to take their next breath or that they have been awake most of the night. In fact, it is the apneic's bed partner, kept awake by the loud snoring, who is more likely to complain of a lack of sleep; the complaint that usually brings the apneic into the sleep clinic is an inability to stay awake during the day. (In many cases, patients are dragged to the doctor by worried and annoyed spouses who can no longer tolerate the deterioration in their relationship caused by the apneic's chronic sleepiness and their own fatigue.)

The apneas are often accompanied by restless body movements and night sweats. In addition, the patient also runs the risk of developing serious heart problems. The cessation in breathing causes a drop in blood oxygen levels, forcing the heart to labor all the harder to keep the blood oxygenated. High blood pressure and heartbeat irregularities are other frequent consequences of sleep apnea, and these cardiovascular problems usually get progressively worse unless the disorder is treated. Drinking alcohol before bedtime makes the symptoms worse. Obesity is frequently associated with apnea, and its presence should raise a suspicion of the disorder in patients showing other symptoms; however, not all apneics are overweight.

Daytime symptoms of apnea include frequent and prolonged but unrefreshing napping, severe morning headaches, depression and confusion, blackouts, impotence, amnesia and automatic behavior. (One patient, for example, reported having no absolutely no recollection of being at work or doing the company payroll during a two-week period.) The daytime sleepiness can cause industrial or traffic acci-

dents and in children may result in daytime lethargy and poor performance in school.

High blood pressure and sexual difficulties can also be symptoms
of apnea in men, and the apnea can exacerbate these conditions,
according to a study by psychologist Max Hirshkowitz and his
colleagues at Baylor College of Medicine and the Veterans Administration Medical Center in Houston. The researchers tested 285 men,
none of whom complained of the usual symptoms of disturbed sleep
or excessive sleepiness; they found that more than half of those who
had both high blood pressure or erectile difficulties also had sleep
apnea and that men with erectile problems were more likely to have
apnea than those who didn't, whether or not they had high blood
pressure. They also found that men whose blood pressure remained
high despite taking medication had more sleep apnea than cases in
which medication successfully controlled blood pressure; this raises
a concern that apnea may contribute directly to high blood pressure
problems and may even counteract the medication.

About one-tenth of adult men experience chronic erectile disorder;
the problem is common among men with high blood pressure, especially if they're on medication, and Hirshkowitz suggests this might
be an early warning sign of apnea. When he analyzed the medical
records of more than 1,000 men with the disorder, he found that "an
inordinate number" also had apnea. There may be a "strong association between high blood pressure, erectile disorders and sleep apnea,"
he says, but scientists don't know yet exactly how they're connected.

There are three different types of sleep apnea: central apneas;
obstructive or upper airway apneas; and mixed apneas, which are a
combination of the other two. With central apnea, respiratory effort
stops altogether; the diaphragm does not move at all. This form of
apnea, which is rare but potentially life-threatening, is sometimes
called Ondine's curse, after a nymph in German legend who cursed
a former lover by causing him to forget to breathe unless he consciously willed it. In one case, a woman's husband had to keep
nudging her awake at night. She said that after her husband died, her
cat, which slept on the bed, took to patting her on the face with its
paws to waken her whenever she stopped breathing.

In the case of upper airway apneas, which are more common, the
lack of respiration automatically triggers an effort to start breathing
again but a total or partial obstruction of the breathing passage

prevents the free flow of air. The obstruction can be caused by tonsils or adenoids, by fatty deposits or excess tissue that reduces the diameter of the airway or by abnormalities in the structure of the throat or jaw.

There are several treatments available for apnea, depending on the severity of the problem. Something as simple as sleeping on one's side rather than on the back may be enough to reduce the obstruction of the airway. (Some people have gone so far as to sew a marble or a sponge rubber ball to the back of their pajamas to prevent them from flopping over on their backs.) In obese patients, weight loss often helps; however, many people have trouble sticking to a weight-loss program even to avoid a serious medical problem like apnea.

The most common treatment is Continuous Positive Airway Pressure or CPAP, a highly effective technique involving the use of a device that gently pushes air through a nasal mask worn during sleep, which keeps the breathing passage open. "Blowing air down a person's nose during sleep essentially prevents the throat from shutting down," Mamelak said. A drug used in the treatment of depression has also proved effective. In severe cases, surgery may be necessary to increase the size of the breathing passage by removing soft tissue at the back of the throat or by rearranging the positions of the tongue and jaw. Removing tonsils or swollen adenoids is sometimes the solution. In emergency situations, a tracheotomy (cutting a hole in the throat) may be necessary. In other cases, drugs that act as respiratory stimulants can help. However, the use of alcohol or sleeping pills is definitely a mistake; they depress the respiratory system and exacerbate the apnea problem, possibly increasing the potential for death during sleep.

## NARCOLEPSY

A 52-year-old army officer, embarrassed by his tendency to fall asleep during meetings with superior officers, holds a set of keys in his hands so they will drop to the floor when he dozes off and wake him up. Once, while fishing, he abruptly fell asleep while hauling in his catch and toppled into the water. He often experiences hallucinations or sudden muscle paralysis as he's falling asleep.

While driving, a young man has to stop every half hour to walk around so he can stay awake. He frequently falls asleep at the wheel, once careering down an embankment. Needless to say, his friends refuse to ride with him.

These people are suffering from narcolepsy, a syndrome characterized by excessive daytime sleepiness accompanied by abnormal manifestations of REM sleep. Besides the sleepiness, the most
troublesome symptom is cataplexy, a loss of muscle tone that can be
severe enough to cause the sufferer to slump to the ground. Other
symptoms include paralysis and vivid, dreamlike hallucinations while
falling asleep or waking up. A survey of more than 900 narcoleptics
done by Stanford University and the American Narcolepsy Association showed the following breakdown: sleep attacks, 93 percent;
excessive daytime sleepiness, 91 percent; cataplexy, 77.5 percent;
sleep paralysis, 68 percent; frightening hallucinations, 62 percent.

Narcolepsy usually shows up first during the teenage years or early
twenties and it lasts a lifetime. There is no known cure, although drugs
help many patients. The disorder is not as rare as originally thought;
it affects about one in a thousand in the general population, about the
same incidence as multiple sclerosis. In some cases, it is genetically
transmitted. Unlike apnea, it affects men and women about equally.

The symptoms can range from mildly annoying to seriously debilitating. The primary symptom and the first to show up is excessive
daytime sleepiness (EDS). Even though narcoleptics usually sleep
from 8 to 12 hours at night, they still feel extremely drowsy all day
and they have periodic "sleep attacks" when they are overcome by an
abrupt and irresistible urge to fall asleep. These attacks can happen
as often as 15 to 20 times a day and usually last under 15 minutes,
although they can last as long as 2 to 3 hours.

Paradoxically, many narcoleptics suffer from insomnia and fragmented sleep at night, and in many cases, the disorder has been
preceded by years of insomnia and irregular sleep patterns. In the
Stanford-ANA study, 70 percent of the patients surveyed reported
disturbed nighttime sleep. Mamelak says that narcolepsy can be
viewed "as a condition in which a person for one reason or another is
unable to contain his sleep in an 8-hour period at night and it's drifting
around a 24-hour period."

Most narcoleptics also suffer from cataplectic attacks, which are
triggered by strong emotions such as anger, fear, amusement or
excitement; some people even experience cataplexy in the midst of
sexual intercourse. Laughter seems to be particularly at fault; in one
study, 94 percent of sufferers said this is what triggered their attacks.
Cataplexy usually shows up a few years after the onset of EDS, but

it can take as long as 30 years to manifest itself. Because of the embarrassment and inconvenience it causes — not to mention the potential danger — many sufferers find cataplexy even more trouble-some and annoying than the daytime sleepiness.

Cataplectic attacks can occur in conjunction with a sleep attack or separately, in which case the sufferer may remain conscious. They may involve nothing more than drooping eyelids or a sagging jaw, but they can also cause the arms to go limp and the legs to buckle, sending the sufferer tumbling to the floor. Many narcoleptics also experience vivid, terrifying hallucinations and sleep paralysis in the twilight zone between sleeping and waking. Sleep paralysis — a temporary inabil-ity to move while waking or falling asleep — occurs only rarely in normal sleepers, usually as a result of waking suddenly from a REM period and reaching consciousness before the body has overcome the muscle paralysis that is normal during REM sleep. In narcoleptics, sleep paralysis occurs much more frequently, and unlike normal sleepers, they experience it both while falling asleep and while waking up.

As if all this were not enough, some narcoleptics also exhibit automatic behavior, operating in a kind of "automatic pilot" mode without being able to remember afterward what they were doing. (Coleman describes one patient, a hospital repairman, who welded an entire set of tools to a hospital bed during one of his narcoleptic episodes. In another case, a farmer woke up to find himself sitting on his tractor ploughing a field in circles.)

During MSLT tests, narcoleptics usually fall asleep within a few minutes; in one study, for example, they lasted only about 3 minutes on average at 10:00 a.m. (typically a high point in the circadian cycle) compared with an average of 14 minutes for normal sleepers. But even more significantly, narcoleptics often enter a REM period almost immediately on falling asleep. In normal sleep, the first REM period does not normally occur until about 90 minutes after sleep onset (although it can occur earlier, even in nonnarcoleptics, under some circumstances.)

The causes of narcolepsy are not fully understood, but scientists believe that the disorder stems from some sort of imbalance between the REM/NREM system and the system that maintains wakefulness. In narcoleptics, wakefulness is weak and vulnerable to sudden intru-sions of REM sleep. The REM system is, in effect, always lurking about, ready to pounce. The other symptoms of narcolepsy are consistent with this idea; the loss of muscle control resembles the paralysis that occurs during normal REM sleep and the hallucinations are similar to the dreams that also characterize normal REM sleep.

Recently, researchers have found that more than 95 percent of people with narcolepsy and cataplexy have a "marker" in their blood. What this means is still unknown, but it may provide a clue about genetic predisposition to the disease.

There is no cure for narcolepsy. Most sufferers find that taking several 10- to 20-minute naps during the day helps. With increasing awareness on the part of employers that the narcoleptic's behavior stems from a sleep disorder and not from laziness or lack of motivation, napping during work hours is sometimes permitted.* In addition, narcoleptics are often prescribed stimulants and REM-suppressants to combat the sleepiness and the sleep attacks, usually in small doses to delay as much as possible the development of tolerance to the drugs, which reduces their effectiveness. Some narcoleptics use medication only when they absolutely have to stay awake — while driving a car, for example. The stimulants only delay the narcoleptic's need to sleep but do not eliminate it, says Mamelak, who compares the effect to "pushing water against the bathtub wall — sooner or later, it comes around behind you."

Other drugs are prescribed for the control of cataplexy. However, many narcoleptics who suffer from this ancillary symptom, embarrassed by their tendency to fall down in the midst of business or social situations, usually try very hard to keep their emotions under strict control and often go out of their way to avoid circumstances that are likely to trigger a cataplectic attack.

The drugs traditionally prescribed for narcoleptics are intended to reduce daytime symptoms like cataplexy and sleep attacks; moreover, they often produce unpleasant side effects and can become ineffective as patients develop tolerance to them. Mamelak and Broughton have tried a different approach — using an experimental drug called gamma-hydroxybutyrate to improve the quality of night sleep and help patients to sleep continuously and for longer periods of time. This has resulted in the marked reduction or complete disappearance of

---

* Increasing the public's awareness of this disorder is one of the major activities of groups like the Canadian Narcolepsy Association and the American Narcolepsy Association.

the entire range of narcoleptic symptoms, including debilitating occurrences of cataplexy, sleep attacks and extreme drowsiness during
the day. The drug, says Mamelak, "stabilizes [sleep] at night, so it's
no longer drifting." Patients using GHB have experienced few bad
side effects and did not develop a tolerance to the drug.

Unlike insomnia, which seems to be strictly a human malady,
narcolepsy can occur in other mammals. By careful breeding of dogs
who were found to have symptoms like those of narcoleptic humans,
researchers at Stanford University have established a colony of narcoleptic dogs used to study the disorder. One of these dogs, a poodle
called Vern, made an appearance on the Phil Donahue show with
William Dement of Stanford University. The excitement of being
offered a dog cookie was enough to cause Vern to slump to the floor.
He snoozed contentedly as the camera focused on his droopy eyes and
Donahue whispered into the microphone. In a few moments, an
obviously groggy Vern attempted to rouse himself, but his leg muscles
were not yet up to the challenge of supporting his small body and he
fell back to the floor. This elicited a sudden burst of laughter from the
audience which wakened Vern. He immediately bounced up and
started trotting back and forth across the stage as if nothing had
happened. His alertness was short-lived, however; within a few
minutes, the excitement got to him again and he collapsed to the floor
with his nose resting on his paws.

Another disorder of excessive sleepiness, known as idiopathic
hypersomnia, is different from either narcolepsy or apnea. Unlike
narcolepsy, it does not involve cataplexy, sleep paralysis, hallucinations or sleep-onset REM periods. Unlike apnea, it is not associated
with serious breathing problems during sleep. Its major symptoms are
very deep and prolonged sleep periods at night, extreme difficulty in
waking up and unrelenting drowsiness during the day. The urge to
sleep is *always* present, although, unlike narcoleptics, these
hypersomniacs are not subject to irresistible sleep attacks and can
usually manage to stay awake if they must — e.g., while at work or
driving. Generally they don't fall asleep in inappropriate circumstances — while eating or speaking, for example — but they can do
so while engaging in passive, sedentary activities (e.g., watching a
movie, listening to a lecture, reading and so on) or while walking.
They sometimes exhibit automatic behavior.

Because of their unrelenting sleepiness, these hypersomniacs often fall asleep early in the evening and sleep right through to the next morning. Sleep onset occurs rapidly and patients typically stay asleep for least 10 to 12 hours; some can easily sleep up to 20 hours at a time if left undisturbed. Polygraph studies indicate that they can experience as many as 14 sleep cycles a night, compared with four to six in normal sleepers, according to a study done by Czechoslovakian sleep researcher Bedrich Roth and his colleagues at Charles University in Prague.

Amazingly, these people still awaken feeling unrefreshed and sleepy. About 60 percent have extreme difficulty waking up at all; it can take them up to an hour just to get out of bed and from 2 to 4 hours to achieve full wakefulness (which presents obvious job-related difficulties.) Worse, on awakening, many of them experience a condition known as sleep drunkenness, characterized by extreme confusion, disorientation and poor coordination. (Polygraph evidence indicates that this phase features very brief episodes, or "microsleeps," of NREM sleep mixed in with wakefulness.) For these people, an alarm clock is useless; they just turn it off and go back to sleep, usually without even remembering having awakened. In most cases, only persistent effort by other family members is enough to get these hypersomniacs up in the morning.

Roth suggests that this disorder may stem from an excessive strength of the NREM sleep system, perhaps accompanied by weaknesses in the REM system and in the system that maintains wakefulness.

## OTHER CAUSES OF EXCESSIVE SLEEPINESS

Excessive daytime sleepiness, like insomnia, can be associated with a variety of medical conditions and diseases, including diabetes, hyperthyroidism, liver failure, nutritional deficiency and brain tumors. In women, excessive drowsiness can be associated with menstrual periods or premenstrual syndrome.

In other cases, myoclonus, drug and alcohol use, psychological problems or psychiatric disorders can be the cause of the sleepiness. Some people who are depressed or overwhelmed by life's problems attempt to escape into sleep. These tend to be passive personalities who have difficulty dealing with rejection and disappointment or facing up to feelings of anger or fear. Like insomnia, excessive sleeping can be a temporary thing — a transitory reaction to a life crisis like death or divorce — or it can become permanent, although this is comparatively rare. People who have trouble dealing with chronic stress or who have lost their sense of purpose may find themselves reacting to new challenges with listlessness, fatigue and episodes of excessive sleep. Tiredness becomes the bulwark of their defense against having to cope with life. Persistence of this behavior may in time lead to shifting of the sleep/wake cycle and desynchronization of the circadian system, causing further aggravation of sleep problems.

The use of alcohol and certain drugs — e.g., antidepressants, muscle relaxants, sleeping pills, even contraceptives in some cases — can cause daytime drowsiness, excessive sleeping at night and difficulty in waking up. Similar effects are caused by a sudden withdrawal from hypnotics, stimulants, tranquilizers, alcohol or caffeine, or by developing a tolerance to the dosages being used. These unpleasant effects can lead to the use of larger doses and contribute to the development of addiction.

Kleine-Levin syndrome is a rare disorder that affects primarily young men, although there have been some cases in females. It is characterized by periods lasting days to weeks during which sufferers sleep excessively (up to 18 hours a day) and wake up in an irritable or hostile mood. In severe cases, confusion, disorientation, delusions and hallucinations can also occur on awakening. Sufferers also overeat voraciously and may display uninhibited sexual exhibitionism toward both sexes. Between episodes, these patients appear to be completely normal and they usually do not remember their behavior during the episodes of hypersomnia. Drug therapy has proved effective in some cases and most patients get over it by age 40. The cause of this disorder is not known, but malfunctioning of portions of the brain is suspected.

Sleep researcher Peretz Lavie of Technion-Israel Institute of Technology has an intriguing theory that episodes of unusually prolonged sleep among women may have given rise to the "sleeping beauty" phenomenon featured in legends and fairy tales. Were these tales just products of imagination or were they rooted in reality? Lavie suggests the latter, citing documented cases from the late 19th century in which females between the ages of 11 and 32 slept for periods lasting from three to four days to as long as several months and, in one case, for years. The cause of this phenomenon is not known, but a scientist who studied these cases described it as a hysterical state, probably caused by violent emotions, fright, exhaustion and overwork. Lavie notes that, for unknown reasons, the syndrome appears to have vanished during the 20th century.

It should be noted, in conclusion, that not all people who sleep long hours are suffering from some bizarre disorder. They may simply be naturally "long sleepers" — people who just need more sleep than the average person.

It hardly comes as a surprise that excessive daytime sleepiness, whether caused by apnea, narcolepsy or other sleep disorders, makes life and work a daily struggle for many people. Marital and job-related problems are common among those who suffer from EDS and they are especially prone to accidents at home, on the road and in the workplace. Needless to say, they can create serious problems in jobs involving the operation of machinery or requiring prompt response to sudden, unexpected emergencies, or in situations where safety can be compromised by an inability to maintain high, constant levels of alertness or vigilance.

### III. Adventures in the Night

In May of 1987, a young man drove 23 kilometers (14 miles) from his home to the home of his parents-in-law, where he attacked them in their bed with a knife, killing his mother-in-law. He was acquitted of murder on the grounds that he was asleep during the entire incident and therefore not criminally responsible.

This case of "aggressive sleepwalking" belongs to a category of sleep disorders known as the parasomnias, which includes phenomena that occur during sleep or conditions that are exaggerated by sleep. The best-known are sleepwalking, bed-wetting and night terrors, a disturbance characterized by screaming, moaning, sweating and rapid breathing during sleep and an inchoate sense of dread and helplessness on awakening. Other parasomnias include head-banging, teeth-grinding, abnormal swallowing, painful erections, cluster headaches and sleep-related asthma. Clearly, these parasomnias are distressing to those who suffer them and their families; however, compared with the disorders already discussed, they affect a relatively small proportion of the total population (an estimated five percent in United States) and their overall impact on waking performance and work is not as widespread as that caused by insomnia and excessive daytime sleepiness. They will be discussed only briefly here.

A number of the parasomnias are fairly common in children — sleepwalking, for example, occurs in about 10 to 15 percent, compared with about five percent of adults. These disorders are usually outgrown by adolescence. If they occur in adults, they are considered more serious because they may be symptomatic of psychological problems, severe anxiety or difficulty in coping with life stress. In rare cases, sleepwalking, violent sleep behavior, night terrors or bedwetting may be manifestations of sleep-related epileptic seizures.

It has been theorized that some of the parasomnias — notably sleepwalking, night terrors and some cases of bed-wetting — may result from incomplete arousal from slow wave sleep. Support for this theory comes from observations that these problems occur most often in the early part of the night, usually within an hour after falling asleep, when slow wave sleep dominates; and that they occur most often in children, who have more and deeper slow wave sleep than adults. Hauri notes that in some patients (especially children) who are almost impossible to arouse at this time, brain-wave readings show a mixture of deep sleep and waking states. These people are, in a sense, awake and asleep at the same time, he says. The phenomenon is sometimes referred to as "night flying." Carlos Schenck of the Minnesota Regional Sleep Disorder Center in Minneapolis has described such people as being half awake and half asleep; their perceptual systems have contact with the outside world, but their judgment is suspended.

Sleepwalkers often engage in automatic behavior, including dressing, eating, going to the bathroom and even driving a car. (There have been some rather spectacular tales in the tabloids — for example, a man who does somersaults in his sleep and a family of six, sleepwalkers all, who reportedly spend their nights wandering around the house, raiding the refrigerator, rearranging the furniture and bumping into each other.)

But sometimes sleepwalking goes far beyond harmless ambling. Sleepwalkers have actually taken screens off windows, opened them and jumped out. In one remarkable case, an 11-year-old Illinois boy apparently hopped a train in his sleep; he was found walking at night almost 160 kilometers (100 miles) from home. Injuries among sleepwalkers are common — they stumble over furniture, break glass doors, fall down stairs, off ladders and into swimming pools — and some have killed themselves walking out of windows or over cliffs. During sleep the brain has no concept of "right or wrong, safe or not safe," notes Merrill Mitler of the Sleep Disorders Center at Scripps Clinic and Research Foundation in California.

In recent years, researchers have become particularly interested in violent sleepers, people who go on rampages while asleep and trash the house or do serious harm to themselves or others — and don't remember a thing in the morning. Among violent sleepers who have been studied by scientists, about 85 percent have injured themselves and 40 percent have injured their bed partners, according to Schenck. Some patients jump out of bed and run around in a frenzy, screaming and bumping into walls. One man dragged his wife around the bedroom by the hair. In 1985, a British man was acquitted of murder after strangling his wife while in the throes of a night terror involving defending himself against attack by two Japanese soldiers. Most of these people are not violent when awake and many can be successfully treated with drugs.

Violent sleep behavior can be associated with epileptic seizures, with psychiatric disorders, with nocturnal leg movements, with night terrors and with malfunctioning of the REM/non-REM sleep cycle. Scientists now believe that abnormalities in portions of the brain responsible for inhibiting movement during sleep may account for the violent behavior.

Contrary to what many people believe, this violent behavior and the more benign forms of sleepwalking usually do not involve the "acting out" of dreams. Vivid dreaming occurs during REM sleep, when the body's muscles are normally completely immobilized, and sleepwalking, as noted, probably follows incomplete arousal from non-REM sleep. In the murder case mentioned above, the man had been sleeping badly for some time because of personal problems, and on the day in question was physically exhausted from playing rugby, so it appears likely that he fell into a deep sleep. He remembered nothing between falling asleep in front of the TV in his home and waking up in a confused state beside the dead body of his mother-in-law. Those who engage in violent types of sleepwalking behavior generally do not report experiencing vivid dreams of being attacked or chased, but they sometimes report experiencing frightening sensations of moving objects, people or animals. For example, one woman said she felt a spider crawling over her face.

However, scientists were surprised recently to discover that in rare cases some people *do* act out their dreams. For some reason, these patients are not paralyzed during REM sleep, so they can get up to perform what's going on in their heads. The first case to be studied, diagnosed by Schenck in 1983, involved a 67-year-old man who ran himself into his bedroom dresser while dreaming he was a football player. In his dream, he was wearing pads; in reality, he ended up with a big gash on his forehead. In another case, a 19-year-old boy would spend his nights growling and hissing while he prowled and leaped around the house; in the morning he would recall vivid dreams about being a lion or tiger pursuing a zookeeper holding a piece of raw meat.

This phenomenon, which is known as REM behavior disorder, mainly affects men over the age of 50, although the reasons for this age/sex predominance are not known. Schenck, who has seen about 50 cases, says aging seems to be the causative factor in about 60 percent of the cases, while the other 40 percent have neurological disorders.

． ． ． ． ． ． ．

In this great smorgasbord of sleep problems, there is one category tucked away that is easily overshadowed by the many others that offer more bizarre and exotic fare. It is the category called "insufficient sleep" — in other words, sleep deprivation. As we have seen, many people feel sleepy because their circadian sleep/wake cycle has malfunctioned or because they have physiological sleep disorders. But there are millions of people today who function in a more or less constant state of daytime fatigue and sleepiness even without these problems. For them, juggling work, family life, social obligations and the myriad other hassles of getting through the day have taken a toll on their ability to let it all go at night.

Their lack of alertness is caused by something no more — and no less — complicated than the fact that busy lives and demanding work simply do not allow them to get enough sleep.

# SECTION 2:
# SLEEP AND WORK

# CHAPTER 7

# AN EPIDEMIC OF SLEEPINESS

*I was swimming up and down the aisles of the grocery store. There
was a friend in the water with me at the time and I said to my friend,
"Would you please go get a jar of peanut butter?"
He said, "What do you want peanut butter for? Where am I going to
get the peanut butter?"
I said, "Off the shelf, stupid. We're swimming in the grocery store."
So he went along with it — he went and got this imaginary jar of
peanut butter. And I said, "Okay, now there's a lot of Martians down
at the end of the aisle there. I'd like you to go spread the peanut butter
on the Martians, please, to get rid of them."
He looked at me rather strangely but he went down and spread the
imaginary peanut butter on the imaginary Martians.
And it worked. They disappeared.*

VICKI KEITH, MARATHON SWIMMER

T HIS IS VICKI KEITH'S FAVORITE
hallucination. It occurred during a record-setting swim that lasted
nearly 5½ days and ended only when she fell asleep in the water so
completely that friends watching over her could not waken her.

"When I was in the pool, I swam on my back with ice cubes on my
eyelids to keep me awake," Keith said. "I did doze off once in a while;
I did fall asleep underwater and they woke me up. At 120 hours, I was
hallucinating and it was my entire life. I didn't know anything else
was going on."

At one point, she fantasized that she was swimming in a grocery
store and when her mother asked her if she wanted to stop swimming,
"I thought she meant stopping in the grocery store. I was not aware

123

that I was swimming. At one point, I asked my parents, 'Would you please go and get the car so you can drive me down to the pool — I'm supposed to be swimming.'

"At 129 hours and 45 minutes, I fell asleep completely. I was floating on my back. They were yelling in my ear but they couldn't wake me up and that's when they pulled me out. They took me to the hospital and had me checked out. I was fine, except that I needed sleep. So I went back to my parents' place to sleep. My parents checked on me about one o'clock in the morning to be sure I was okay. I was lying in bed kicking my feet."

Sleep deprivation and the vivid hallucinations that accompany it are no strangers to Keith — they are the unavoidable byproduct of her marathon swims. But other people have set out specifically to deprive themselves of sleep for long periods of time. In 1959, New York disk jockey Peter Tripp went 200 hours without sleep to raise money for the March of Dimes, and in 1965, a 17-year-old San Diego high school student, Randy Gardner, broke the world record by staying awake for 264 hours — 11 days — as part of a science fair project. Both were monitored throughout their marathon by sleep researchers. The *Guinness Book of World Records* notes that a California man, "Ramblin' Rob" McDonald, endured 453 hours and 40 minutes — almost 19 days — in a rocking chair marathon in 1986.*

Surprisingly, sleep deprivation appears to cause no permanent or long-lasting ill effects in otherwise healthy people (although, as we shall see, it does cause severe short-term problems with mood and the ability to perform many kinds of mental and physical tasks). Perceptual illusions, intrusions of fantasy into wakefulness, waking dreams and mild hallucinations are not uncommon. Some people also exhibit temporary psychoticlike behavior. Tripp, for example, developed acute paranoia toward the end of his vigil and believed that unknown enemies were trying to slip drugs into his food to make him fall asleep, but he got over it quickly when he got some sleep. And Gardner experienced only mild hallucinations and no psychotic behavior.

Sleep-deprived people don't even have to make up for all the sleep they've lost; in most cases, a single extended sleep period lasting between about 10 and 15 hours puts them back to normal. Tripp slept

---

* Although *Guinness* doesn't specify whether McDonald was awake the whole time, presumably he couldn't have fallen asleep more than momentarily during this period without ceasing to rock the chair.

about 13 hours after his marathon and Gardner about 15; Keith slept for only about 10 hours the night after being pulled unconscious from the pool. "I got up about six o'clock the next morning, poured my mother a cup of coffee — I felt sorry for her — and went for a swim."

The ability of humans to bounce back so readily from extreme sleep loss is somewhat perplexing. If, as scientists believe, sleep is performing some essential function, why doesn't this sleep deprivation cause more serious or long-lasting damage? Some fascinating clues on this subject are provided by a series of intriguing experiments done with rats by sleep researcher Allan Rechtschaffen and his colleagues at the University of Chicago. They designed an apparatus that involved placing a pair of rats on a circular disk suspended over a shallow pan of water and rigged so it would start rotating whenever EEG readings on one of the rats indicated that it was falling asleep. The rotation wakened the rat and forced it to walk opposite to the disk rotation to avoid falling into the water; thus, it was forced to stay awake virtually all the time. (In some tests, however, the rat was deprived only of REM sleep.)

The second rat had things a bit easier; although it was subjected to exactly the same amount of disk rotation — during which it, too, was forced to walk and stay awake — it was free to rat-nap during the periods when the disk was stationary because its partner was awake. Otherwise, the environment of the two rats was identical.

Their fates, however, were not — far from it. The sleep-deprived rats developed a consistent set of symptoms, including a disheveled, scrawny appearance, brownish fur, ulcerated lesions on the tails and paws, weight loss in spite of markedly increased eating, increased expenditure of energy and a decrease in body temperature. All were dead within 11 to 32 days. (Some died and others were sacrificed when death seemed likely to occur in a day or two, in order to obtain tissues for postmortem analysis.)

Identical symptoms occurred when the rats were selectively deprived of REM sleep, except that the REM-deprived rats also became extremely sensitive to touch and so viciously aggressive that the researchers had to use steel mesh gloves to handle them. These rats died within 16 to 54 days.

None of the control rats died; in fact, they remained healthy and gave no indication that they could not continue to live under the experimental conditions.

Postmortem tests on the sleep-deprived rats did not reveal any anatomical abnormalities that could account for death. The researchers also ruled out factors such as the weight loss, dehydration, stress and excessive exercise. (The rats were forced to walk an average of less than a mile a day, whereas healthy rats will voluntarily run up to 30 miles a day on a running wheel.)

Perhaps the most significant findings relate to the changes in energy expenditure and regulation of body temperature that occurred in the sleep-deprived rats. They experienced an early rise in energy expenditure; in fact, their survival time could be predicted early in the experiment based on the rate at which energy use was growing. These rats continued to expend increasing amounts of energy throughout the experiment, which accounted for their weight loss despite increased food consumption. At about the midway point, core body temperature started to drop and the researchers suggest that excessive heat loss forced the rats to use increasing amounts of energy in an effort to protect body temperature. They attributed the loss of thermal regulation to sleep deprivation (possibly primarily to REM deprivation) and concluded that sleep may be necessary for effective thermoregulation — not only during sleep but during waking as well. However, it remains a mystery why the "complicated and time-consuming" state of sleep is needed to do this.

Carol Everson and other members of the same University of Chicago research group did a further study in which sleep-deprived rats were allowed recovery sleep. Those that had experienced the largest drops in body temperature died early in the recovery period, leading the researchers to conclude that sleep deprivation can go beyond a "point of no return." However, in the other rats, the symptoms of sleep deprivation were virtually completely reversed within 15 days and these rats still appeared normal 5 to 11 months later. The researchers attributed the reversal of the symptoms to recovery sleep, since rats in the other experiments, which were not allowed any recovery sleep, showed no such reversal spontaneously.

The rats' recovery sleep was characterized by an immediate increase in REM sleep far above normal levels. This surprised the researchers, and they suggested this indicates that REM sleep in particular was necessary to prevent most of the observed effects of sleep deprivation. There was no way of telling whether non-REM sleep was equally necessary.

. . . . . . .

Why don't the same things happen to sleep-deprived humans? Actually, we don't know that they wouldn't, if humans were subjected to conditions similar to those experienced by the rats. It's true that human sleep loss — to the extent it has so far been experienced in voluntary marathons or controlled sleep lab experiments — has not caused the debilitation seen in the rats, nor has it caused death. But then, keeping human subjects awake until they die is hardly approved procedure in such exercises.

But human studies provide some basis of comparison with the rat studies, and by drawing assumptions from these, Rechtschaffen and his colleagues argue that humans simply haven't been kept awake long enough to produce the same kind of devastating physiological effects experienced by the rats. They suggest that severe symptoms of sleep loss do not occur in humans as fast as they do in rats, estimating that rats respond anywhere from nearly twice as fast to more than 20 times as fast as humans do, depending on the factors considered.

Most controlled human studies of total sleep deprivation run about five days or less and the longest have been under two weeks; tests involving selective deprivation of REM sleep have been run for about 16 days or less. Rechtschaffen and his colleagues estimate that the duration of these human experiments would be equivalent to no more than the middle of the first quarter of the rats' survival time — a period during which the rats evinced almost no physiological effects from sleep loss. The researchers conclude that humans have not been totally deprived of sleep "anywhere near long enough" to produce effects as severe as those seen in rats.*

(Rechtschaffen notes that because we feel such pressure for sleep after as little as one night of sleep loss, we've perhaps been deceived into thinking that extreme effects of sleep deprivation should become apparent quickly. But this does not appear to be the case. He draws an analogy with hunger: missing a single meal may make you feel very hungry indeed, but it does most people little physiological harm.)

It appears doubtful, in fact, that it's even possible for humans to go

---

* Some people have had their REM sleep almost completely suppressed by drugs for up to a year or more without showing extreme physiological effects as the rats did. The significance of this is not clear — since scientists still don't know how essential REM sleep is to humans — but Rechtschaffen speculates this might represent a genuine difference in the response of the two species to REM deprivation.

totally without sleep for long periods of time. While there have been many anecdotal accounts and media stories about people who say they never sleep, none of the cases studied scientifically have stood up to detailed monitoring, according to Dinges. "There are many people who claim they don't sleep. Typically these are people with lifelong insomnia who have the strong impression they haven't slept. Yet when you hook them up, you find they do sleep, although the sleep may be abnormal."

Most sleep researchers have doubts of ever finding a healthy person who literally *never* sleeps and still leads a normal life. There have been cases of people with neurological damage who "basically don't sleep or sleep in very short episodes but most of these conditions are terminal," says Roger Broughton. "As far as we know, death is caused by the brain damage rather than the loss of sleep."

People who participate in scientifically supervised sleep-deprivation experiments (and in public marathons, for that matter) do not go completely without sleep, either — no matter how hard they or their watchdogs try to keep them awake. As the experiment described in Chapter 1 demonstrates, within 48 hours, the pressure for sleep starts to become relentless and, at times, irresistible. The urge to sleep is constantly on the prowl, ready to pounce upon wakefulness at any opportune moment, and after about two nights of total sleep deprivation, subjects start to experience *microsleeps* lasting a few seconds at a time. These are believed to be transient intrusions of light (Stage 1) sleep on wakefulness.

Microsleeps become longer and more frequent as sleep loss mounts. After about 10 days of deprivation, Peter Hauri notes, microsleeps and wakefulness are so entwined that scientists have a difficult time telling whether subjects are awake or asleep, even if they perform actions usually associated with wakefulness, such as walking.

The insidiousness of microsleeps was demonstrated in a study by S. E. Southmayd and colleagues at Kingston Psychiatric Hospital in Ontario. The researchers were investigating the effect of sleep deprivation in improving the mood of a depressed patient, a 44-year-old woman. Her mood had improved after 40 hours without sleep, but over the next 8 hours, she relapsed completely into depression. Although she appeared to have been awake for the entire 48 hours, EEG monitoring demonstrated that during the last 8 hours, she actually slept for about 11 minutes, mostly in stretches of less than 20 seconds at a time. But even this tiny amount of sleep appears to have been enough to counteract the effects of 40 hours of wakefulness and bring on a recurrence of her symptoms of depression. The microsleeps occurred despite the fact that the patient was working hard to stay awake and was constantly observed by nurses; in fact, the observers were unaware that sleep had occurred and the patient herself, while admitting to feeling drowsy at times, was convinced she had not slept.

Thus, it appears that *total* sleep deprivation never really occurs for very long in humans; after a point, the brain simply will not be denied any longer and it imposes sleep — if only for seconds at a time — despite all efforts to thwart it. Dinges says that no one has yet demonstrated that humans can be completely deprived of sleep for more than a day or two.

What happens to our ability to perform various mental and physical tasks when we're bedeviled by a brain utterly intent on going to sleep is a matter of great concern. Whatever long-term harm may or may not result from sleep deprivation, there's no doubt that the sleepiness it causes wreaks havoc with mood and performance in the short term. Nor does it take anything so extreme as a marathon swim or a rocking chair contest to bring us to this state; there is evidence that even a single night of lost sleep can cause impairment.

Many people today do not get enough sleep and/or do not feel adequately rested by the sleep they do get. For example, a 1975 study by Wilse Webb and H. W. Agnew of the University of Florida indicated that college students slept on average about 1½ hours less each day than their counterparts did in 1910. They suggested that reductions in sleep time have resulted from work schedules, increased socializing in the evening, television and, of course, the electric light.

In fact, a number of sleep researchers have suggested that most people in industrialized societies suffer from chronic partial sleep deprivation.* Mary Carskadon, for instance, believes that most people "probably need at least an hour more sleep every night than they're getting to be alert in the daytime." Roger Broughton suggests that perhaps as many as 90 percent of people in modern industrialized societies suffer from a chronic "sleep debt." "The vast majority require 6 to 8 hours; probably most people are getting something like 6 hours

---

* It should be noted here that British researcher James Horne argues that most normal sleepers could quite readily *reduce* their sleep time by about 1-1/2 to 2 hours a day. His theories will be discussed later.

of sleep, the minimum they need. Most people, if they regained their sleep debt, would perform better and feel better and probably be less accident-prone."

A study by psychologist Timothy Roehrs and his colleagues at Henry Ford Hospital in Detroit seems to bear this out. They studied 24 men, normal sleepers who were not nappers and did not complain of daytime sleepiness. Half were "alert" subjects who took an average of 16 minutes or more to fall asleep on the Multiple Sleep Latency Test and half were "sleepy" subjects who took 6 minutes or less to fall asleep. The alert subjects normally slept about 8 hours a night, the sleepy ones about 7 hours; otherwise they had similar sleep habits.

For six nights, the subjects increased their sleep time to 9 hours. Subsequent MSLT tests showed they'd all become more alert during the day. The "sleepy" group improved immediately and by the greatest amount, while the alert group improved gradually. However, the sleepy group didn't quite catch up to the others: at the end of the experiment, they fell asleep in 10 minutes (an improvement of 4 minutes on average), while the alert group fell asleep in 18 minutes (an improvement of 2 minutes).

Over the six days, both groups improved their performance in attention and vigilance tests, including one involving skills needed for driving. Roehrs concluded that people can "benefit from getting as much sleep as they can."[*] He said people should sleep until they're "slept out" and should be able to awaken spontaneously without an alarm clock. However, for many people, this is an almost unheard-of luxury. Work, family, chores and even leisure activities all steal time from sleep. Harvey Moldofsky recounts the story of one patient referred to a sleep clinic because he was having trouble staying awake in the evening. A battery of tests indicated no serious sleep disorders and when the man was questioned about his lifestyle, it was revealed that a change in his work schedule had forced him to get up earlier in the morning — in fact, he was getting up even earlier than necessary so he could find a parking spot at work — but he wasn't going to bed earlier at night.

"He'd been taking 5 to 5½ hours of sleep routinely. The problem is, he requires 8 hours of sleep," Moldofsky said. "He'd been seen by

---

[*]   Another study by Roger Godbout and Jacques Montplaisir of Hôpital du Sacré-Coeur in Montreal found that daytime napping in addition to regular nightly sleep improved performance on reaction-time tests.

all these doctors, we did all these expensive studies and I turned to him and said, 'You're not sleeping enough.' He said, 'I've stopped my alcohol, I've stopped my caffeine, but you're telling me that I'm going to have to go to bed earlier.' I said, 'Go to bed earlier.'"

When the man said he didn't want to go to bed earlier, complaining that he'd already given up watching Johnny Carson, Moldofsky prescribed a video recorder.

## HOW MUCH SLEEP DO WE NEED?

If it's true that millions of people are usually working in a sleep-deprived state (and a number of studies suggest that it is), then gaining a better understanding of what sleep loss does to our ability to function is a crucial first step in finding ways to combat the effects of sleepiness in the workplace.

How much sleep is enough? What is the minimum amount of sleep necessary to maintain alertness and performance? Can we train ourselves to sleep less?

These are key questions when it comes to understanding the impact of sleep on work performance, but, as usual, there are no simple answers. Since scientists don't even know exactly what it is that sleep does for us, it's hard for them to prescribe a magic number of hours of sleep guaranteed to ensure that we will feel rested, alert and up to facing the challenges of the day. There are many variables involved, including differences in individual physiology and in external circumstances.

Individuals vary in the amount of sleep they need; the cause of this is not known, but it may be at least partly genetic and therefore quite difficult to change. We also know that our need for sleep changes with age. As we saw in Chapter 3, infants and children typically sleep longer hours, and the elderly shorter hours, than young and middle-aged adults. (But these general rules of thumb do not always hold true; when William Dement recorded the sleep of his daughter for the first few months after she was born, he found she slept a surprising 5½ hours a day — very much less than the 16 to 18 hours that is normal for newborns.) Finally, changes in life circumstances can cause variations in sleep length; for example, pregnancy usually causes increased sleepiness and expectant mothers typically add a couple of hours a day to their normal sleep time.

It has been estimated that the vast majority of normal adult sleepers need between 6 and 9 hours of sleep each night — averaging between 7 and 8 hours — in order to feel alert and perform well the next day. But there is a small percentage of people who regularly sleep for longer or shorter periods of time; these people are considered healthy if they can function during the day without exhibiting symptoms of excessive sleepiness.

True long and short sleepers are quite rare; Richard Coleman says that many people who claim this distinction are just mistaken about how much sleep they actually get. Polygraph monitoring shows that many who claim to be long sleepers mistake the amount of time they lie in bed with actual sleep time, while many short sleepers (like many insomniacs) underestimate their nighttime sleep and are often found to nap during the day. A case in point is Thomas Edison, sleep's self-styled nemesis. He wrote in his diary: "I never found need of more than 4 or 5 hours' sleep in the 24." But those same diaries record that he was a frequent daytime napper and that, on many occasions, when he awoke after 4 or 5 hours of sleep, he turned over and went back to sleep.

However, there are several documented cases of people who regularly get less than three hours of sleep a night — and even some rare individuals who sleep less than an hour a night — and still seem to be able to function well during the day. It's possible that genetic factors may play a role in the development of these short sleep patterns. Are these short sleepers insomniacs (as friends and spouses often insist) or are they really getting as much sleep as they need to maintain alertness and performance while awake? Studies suggest that they may, in fact, be sleeping enough. For example, in 1978, Donald Stuss and Roger Broughton at the University of Ottawa studied a 57-year-old man who, for 25 years, had slept less than 2 hours a night without any "catch-up" sleep on weekends or holidays. He reported sleeping well and waking up rested. His short sleep pattern was confirmed during 12 days of continuous monitoring in the sleep lab.

Then the subject was asked to perform a series of vigilance, psychomotor, calculation and memory tasks after sleeping normally (i.e., about 1½ hours at night) and after sleeping for both shorter (three-quarters of an hour) and longer (2½ hours) periods of time. The subject's performance deteriorated in two of the six tests when he got less sleep and in *four* of the tests when he got more sleep than normal. The researchers noted that this man reported feeling groggy and lethargic after sleeping longer than normal, and his performance on one of the tests indicated a decrease in his willingness or motivation to respond.

This results of this study, which was the first to use performance testing to determine if a short sleeper could really function on so little sleep, suggest that "even extreme short sleepers may be obtaining their optimum sleep quota," the researchers concluded. They added that short sleepers should not worry about their sleep if they do not show symptoms of chronic sleep deprivation (i.e., excessive daytime sleepiness) and if they typically feel *worse* after oversleeping. These studies indicate that short sleep is not the same thing as insomnia. Some studies have also indicated that short sleepers may be psychologically healthier than long sleepers, but this is controversial.

As for long sleeping, it is actually very difficult for normal non-deprived sleepers to voluntarily extend their sleep by very much; even sleep-deprived people generally do not sleep for an excessively long time and they revert to normal sleep patterns quickly. Healthy long sleepers average about 9 to 10 hours of sleep a night; people who regularly sleep for much longer periods of time should be suspected of having an underlying sleep disorder or psychological problem, particularly if this excessive sleep is unrefreshing.

There is some evidence to suggest that for most people, sleeping either more or less than the average is not beneficial. French researchers studied more than 58,000 army draftees between 17 and 22 years old and found that those who slept between 7 and 9 hours experienced the least daytime sleepiness, whereas those who slept for longer or shorter periods at night had more daytime sleep epsiodes.

Some studies suggest there may even be an association between ill health and consistently sleeping more or less than 7 to 8 hours a night. For example, a study done by the American Cancer Society between 1959 and 1965 found that in some age groups, men who slept only about 4 hours a night were 10 times more likely to have died within those six years than those who had slept between 7 and 8 hours; those who slept more than 10 hours a night were twice as likely to have died than 7- to 8-hour sleepers. Even people whose sleep was only slightly off the average — between 6 and 7 hours or between 8 and 9 hours — had higher death rates. Short sleepers experienced more angina (chest pains), while long sleepers experienced more heart attacks and stroke, but it's not known whether sleep itself causes these conditions.

Peter Hauri notes that, while there is unquestionably a statistical relationship between sleep and mortality, this doesn't mean that forcing yourself to sleep between 7 and 8 hours will prolong your life. It may be that these studies were picking up an association between both short and long sleep and a higher incidence of underlying medical problems or sleep disorders that were the real causes of mortality.

## SLEEPINESS: WHAT IS IT, WHAT CAUSES IT?

One of the major reasons for the current scientific interest in sleep deprivation concerns the role that sleep loss plays in causing sleepiness and a lack of attention and alertness in the workplace, with attendant deficiencies in performance and increases in the risk to lives and property. This is no trivial academic pursuit if sleep researchers are right in their belief that most people in industrialized societies are at least partially sleep deprived — and therefore to some extent physiologically sleepy — most of the time. Thus, understanding the nature of sleepiness is not only relevant to the development of scientific theories about the function of sleep and to the treatment of sleep disorders, but it also has an important bearing on occupational health and safety.

David Dinges defines sleepiness as an increased pressure for sleep — "an increased probability that the brain will go to sleep against one's will. Sleepiness leads to sleep; you don't have sleep without sleepiness." He said the discovery of microsleeps enabled scientists to see that true physiological sleepiness is characterized by the involuntary imposition of light sleep on wakefulness. Later in this chapter, we will examine the various ways in which scientists measure sleepiness, but it is important to keep in mind here the distinction between *subjective* and *objective* measures of sleepiness. The former involve descriptive self-reports of how sleepy a person feels; the latter involve actually measuring the brain's increasing effort to impose sleep. For example, in one of most widely used objective measures, the Multiple Sleep Latency Test, EEG monitoring of brain waves is used to determine how long it takes subjects to fall asleep at various times of the day.

As to what causes sleepiness, scientists don't have all the answers. As we saw in Chapter 3, some theories suggest a biochemical mechanism — the idea that sleepiness is caused by a build-up of "hynotoxins" or "sleep factors" that are dissipated during sleep. This theory is in keeping with the idea that sleepiness is caused by prior sleep loss or the length of prior wakefulness. It's an idea that makes intuitive sense to most people: you get sleepy because you haven't had enough sleep or because you've been awake too long. Unfortunately, the situation isn't that simple. Many other factors are implicated in causing sleepiness: circadian rhythms, sleep disorders, age, physical and mental health, drug and alcohol use, environmental conditions and even sleep itself. In any given situation, sleepiness can be brought on or intensified by complex combinations of several of these factors. Its effect on our ability to perform various kinds of mental and physical tasks is equally complex.

In Chapter 4, we saw that the circadian system is one of the most important sources of sleepiness. Alertness and sleepiness vary throughout the day *regardless* of the amount of sleep we've had (or not had) or how long we've been awake. It also appears that circadian variations in body temperature seem to play a critical role in when we choose to go to sleep and how long we sleep.

Dinges grumbles that nature has been unkind to scientists in its "temporal confounding" of circadian factors and prior wakefulness, which makes it difficult to determine their respective contributions to sleepiness and often impossible to separate their relative influence in everyday life. He gives the example of night-shift workers who may feel sleepy on the job both because they're working during their circadian trough *and* because they're sleep deprived from trying unsuccessfully to sleep well during their daytime circadian peak.

However, sleep loss can exacerbate and ultimately overwhelm circadian effects. In a rested person, circadian ups and downs in sleepiness can be fairly pronounced during the day, but Dinges says they are much less in evidence when sleep loss causes the brain to start "pushing for sleep. Once the brain gets intensely sleepy, [it] will simply go to sleep at any time, any phase — it doesn't matter."

The use of drugs and alcohol also figures into the complex interaction between circadian factors and sleep loss in causing sleepiness. Alcohol taken during the circadian troughs (i.e., at noon or late in the evening) has a more potent effect than when taken during the circadian peaks (i.e., in the morning or early evening.) A study by Timothy Roehrs and his colleagues, which was the first to compare the effects of caffeine and alcohol on daytime sleepiness, demonstrated that alcohol and sleep loss are a particularly dangerous combination. The study involved people who were asked to consume alcohol and caffeine on mornings after obtaining first 5, then 8 and finally 11 hours of sleep the night before. One group of subjects got enough alcohol to bring their blood levels nearly up to the legal level of intoxication; the others got an amount of caffeine equivalent to that contained in three cups of coffee.

The researchers administered the Multiple Sleep Latency Test to measure changes in the subjects' level of daytime sleepiness; subjects were asked to try falling asleep during four 20-minute periods at 10:00 a.m., noon, 2:00 p.m. and 4:00 p.m. (The time it takes to fall asleep is known as *sleep latency*.) The findings for the second day of the tests included the following:

• Alcohol drinkers who had had only 5 hours' sleep were the sleepiest, especially during the 2:00 p.m. circadian trough, when they fell asleep in under 3½ minutes (which is within the range of "pathological" sleepiness caused by sleep disorders). During the 10:00 a.m. circadian peak, they fell asleep in 10 to 12 minutes — still somewhat low by normal standards. The caffeine drinkers didn't fall asleep at all at 10:00 a.m. (Normal sleepers who haven't consumed alcohol or caffeine usually take 15 to 20 minutes to fall asleep at 10:00 a.m.) Average sleep latencies for the whole day were under 8 minutes for the alcohol drinkers, compared with more than 15 minutes for the caffeine drinkers.

• Alcohol drinkers who had had 8 hours of sleep weren't much better off than those who had had only 5 hours. Their average sleep latency was just over 8 minutes, compared with more than 16 minutes for caffeine drinkers who had slept 8 hours. During the 2:00 p.m. trough, they fell asleep in under 7 minutes, compared with nearly 16 minutes for the caffeine drinkers.

• Only when the alcohol drinkers got 11 hours of sleep the night before did their daytime sleep latencies approach more normal levels. The average for the day was about 13½ minutes (ranging from about 10½ minutes during the circadian trough to nearly 16 minutes during the 10:00 a.m. peak). Caffeine drinkers averaged more than 18 minutes for the day.

In short, it appears that the alcohol drinkers required 11 hours of sleep the night before to counteract excessive daytime sleepiness caused by drinking alcohol. Conversely, caffeine was found to increase alertness in subjects allowed only 5 hours of sleep. "Sleep-deprived people who drink alcohol have slowed reaction time and increased lapses in attention, making it hazardous to drive or operate machinery," Roehrs commented. "Unfortunately, the times when people don't sleep well — after shift-work schedule changes or when under stress, for instance — are also the times they tend to consume more alcohol to aid sleep or relaxation."

## SLEEP CAUSES SLEEPINESS

Another cause of sleepiness — perhaps a surprising one to most people — is sleep itself, or, more specifically, waking up. Paradoxically, people often feel sleepier (and perform less effectively) just after waking up than they do just before going to sleep, says Dinges. The phenomenon of awakening extremely sleepy and confused is called postdormital disorientation or, more commonly, *sleep inertia*.* It usually doesn't last long — typically only a few minutes, although it can linger for up to half an hour or even longer, depending on the time of awakening, the amount of prior sleep loss and other circumstances.

Studies done by researchers at the Defence and Civil Institute of Environmental Medicine in Toronto suggest that sleep inertia is actually quite similar to Stage 1 sleep; Bob Angus notes that subjects may look as if they're awake, but in fact they're not fully awake physiologically. The sleepiness associated with sleep inertia can be even more intense than that experienced during circadian troughs or during periods of actual sleep deprivation; consequently, mental acuity and physical reflexes can be greatly degraded and subjects often do poorly on a wide variety of tests, including those designed to assess reaction time, decision-making ability, memory, vigilance, arithmetic problem solving and sensory discrimination.

Sleep inertia is strongly linked to awakening from slow wave sleep. This is why awakening within the first three hours after falling asleep — when SWS dominates the early sleep cycles — is likely to result in grogginess and confusion. It can be extremely difficult to even rouse subjects from slow wave sleep, and almost invariably, they suffer longer periods of sleep inertia than subjects awakened at times of lighter sleep. Sleep inertia is also likely to be more pronounced

---

* The Associated Press reported that actress Shirley Jones was planning to sue a radio station for invasion of privacy after she was called between 6:00 a.m. and 7:00 a.m. Jones's suit claimed that the station made a habit of waking celebrities to see what embarrassing or confused things they might say.

following afternoon naps, which are known to contain more SWS than morning or evening naps.

The severity of the sleep inertia is affected not only by awakening from the slow wave stage of sleep, but also by the amount and depth of SWS, the circadian timing of awakening and the amount of prior sleep deprivation. Prior sleep loss aggravates sleep inertia because it causes subsequent sleep to be deeper (i.e., to have more SWS) than usual. "As time goes by, there's more pressure for sleep, the sleep gets deeper and you get more sleep inertia," says Dinges.

Although sleep inertia can occur even in well-rested subjects wakened near the daily circadian peak in alertness, the most severe cases occur in people abruptly wakened during the circadian trough from only a few hours' sleep after being sleep deprived for more than 24 hours. In one study, Dinges found that when subjects were wakened from a 2-hour nap after 42 to 54 hours of wakefulness, their performance was 70 percent below prenap levels and they experienced disorientation, hallucinations and amnesia — symptoms similar to those associated with the disorders of arousal (e.g., sleepwalking).

Slow wave sleep may also be implicated in a seemingly paradoxical situation — the fact that *oversleeping* can cause sleepiness, or at least subjective feelings of sleepiness. In 1969, G. Globus of the University of California reported the results of a survey in which young adults complained of feeling "worn out" after sleeping for 10 hours or more without prior sleep loss. A subsequent study by John Taub of St. Louis University and his colleagues indicated that oversleeping negatively affected performance on various types of tasks; he and a colleague, Ralph Berger, dubbed this the "Rip Van Winkle effect."

Broughton suggests that the grogginess following oversleeping may be related to a 12-hour rhythm of slow wave sleep. Remember that a normal sleep period consists of four to six 90-minute REM/NREM cycles in which the first two are dominated by slow wave sleep, and that awakening during those first cycles is often accompanied by extreme sleep inertia. Studies have shown that when sleep is extended beyond normal, a second "pulse" of slow wave sleep occurs approximately 12½ hours after the first. In effect, then, the sleeper appears to be "starting over" with the early SWS-dominated sleep cycles, without awakening in between. Thus, it appears that awakening after extended sleep can be essentially equivalent to awakening during the first two sleep cycles, in terms of the sleep inertia effects.*

Broughton has argued that the sleepiness caused by oversleeping is actually a qualitatively different kind of sleepiness from that caused by sleep loss (just as REM and NREM are different kinds of sleep). "When people are sleep deprived, they usually get hyperreactive, overresponsive and jittery and some types of performance are decreased. If they sleep too much, they feel differently. They describe themselves as thick-headed, groggy, slow — sometimes they feel sort of drunken — and different performance parameters deteriorate."

In a scientific paper on the subject, he argued that the "underlying physiological state of the brain is quite different" in each case and drew two conclusions: that tests used to measure one kind of sleepiness should be used with caution in measuring the other kind and that searching for a single best measure of sleepiness may not be very useful.

Is there a difference in mood and performance when you oversleep to recover from a period of prior sleep loss, rather than simply extending your habitual sleep period? Some studies have suggested that mood and performance can deteriorate for a time immediately after recovery oversleeping. However, a study by Mary Carskadon and colleagues at Brown University and Stanford University raises questions about this — and whether oversleeping really does cause impairment of performance. These researchers compared the effects of oversleeping (12 hours) in subjects who had first slept normally (8½ hours) the night before oversleeping and then slept for a reduced amount of time (6½ hours) the night before oversleeping. They tested the volunteers for several factors: subjective and objective sleepiness, mood and performance on tasks involving vigilance, word memory, verbal reasoning, manual dexterity and searching ability. On only one test for subjective sleepiness did the volunteers show signs of deterioration after oversleeping; on all other tests — including the objective test (MSLT) and *other* subjective tests for sleepiness — they showed either improvement or no change after oversleeping.

Carskadon said the subjects who overslept after getting a regular night's sleep "perceived themselves as somewhat sleepy, [but] the

---

* However, Horne suggests that this slow wave sleep may instead represent a "paying off" of a SWS "debt" that builds up as a result of increased REM sleep and brief periods of wakefulness during the extended sleep period.

ones who were sleep deprived and overslept showed absolutely no symptoms from oversleeping, and *objectively*, they all got less sleepy. We found no effect on performance and no real effect on several measures of mood." The researchers concluded that while these findings allow for the possibility that some people may well feel "worn out" after oversleeping, most of the tests indicated that one night of oversleeping, with or without prior sleep loss, "is more likely to improve daytime well-being than to cause discomfort." Timothy Roehrs' study of extended sleep cited earlier in this chapter is consistent with this.

## ENVIRONMENTAL FACTORS AND SLEEPINESS

When you ask people what makes them sleepy, the odds are they won't say "circadian rhythms" or even "sleep deprivation." They're more likely to finger "a boring lecture, a ride through Kansas, a hot room, a big meal," says Dinges. "They'll attribute it to the environment." But do these environmental factors actually *cause* sleepiness, or do they merely *expose* it in certain contexts? Dinges says this cannot yet be determined; however, he notes that, while people often attribute feelings of sleepiness to things like boredom, uninteresting tasks and hot rooms, these environmental factors are not invariably associated with sleepiness.

In fact, Carskadon and Dement, in their 1982 paper describing the Multiple Sleep Latency Test, argue that a subject who is truly alert "does not feel or appear to be sleepy when placed in a low-stimulus environment." However, they say, a low-stimulus environment will " unmask" sleepiness in someone suffering from physiological (i.e., objective) sleepiness. In other words, a sleepy person will not appear to be (or behave as if) sleepy while in a stimulating environment, but sleepiness will quickly manifest itself when that same person is put into a nonstimulating environment.

A classic example of this occurs when a sleep-deprived person gets into a car after being in a high-stimulus environment. "Two minutes down the road, and you can't stay awake anymore," Dinges says. Robert Conn, a cardiology resident at Toronto's Hospital for Sick Children, agrees. "If you were to pick the one most frightening thing about my residency, it would be driving home. I'd leave the hospital wide awake and fall asleep on the way home. It doesn't matter what you do — you roll down the windows in the middle of winter, have the radio up, and you cannot keep your eyes open. When I did my cardiac surgery training, I made sure I got an apartment within a block of the hospital because I knew that I wouldn't be able to drive home."

Dinges says that the marked — and apparently sudden — increase in subjective feelings of sleepiness in situations like this are often mistakenly attributed to environmental factors "because it is not clear why we feel so sleepy when 30 minutes earlier we felt more alert. The more the brain becomes inherently sleepy, biologically sleepy, the more dependent it becomes upon the environment. It can be propped up with social interaction or it can be immediately put to sleep with a boring stimulus."

In sleep-deprivation studies, Dinges has found that subjects prefer to engage in game playing, an activity that provides intense social interaction, competitiveness and some motor activity. His subjects were still able to play Monopoly after 52 hours of sleep deprivation, while their performance on a simple reaction-time task deteriorated after 24 hours without sleep. This suggests that the *effort* required to remain awake is greatly reduced when the environment provides enjoyable social stimulation.

Motivation and incentives to perform can sometimes override negative environmental factors, but usually only for a short time. In the end, Dinges says, the level of stimulation provided by the environment determines whether and when sleepiness will manifest itself, affecting behavior and performance. Thus, interaction with the environment may ultimately determine the extent to which most people will be incapacitated by sleepiness. He adds that when we're "propped up" by environmental stimulation, we're usually not aware of the extent to which sleep loss has diminished our capacity to function; the fact that our subjective feelings of sleepiness can change so rapidly and unexpectedly when the context changes makes it difficult to predict whether we'll be able to stay awake or how alert we're likely to be later on.

This clearly has important implications in the workplace, particularly when workers suffering from sleepiness caused by sleep loss or circadian factors are engaged in work that is essentially boring. Modification of work schedules could help in some cases, says Carskadon. For example, active rather than passive tasks should be scheduled for the circadian trough in the afternoon. As she wryly points out, you should "not have conferences in the middle of the afternoon unless the conferences aren't important."

In a number of occupations, however, tedium is unavoidable — for example, maintaining constant vigilance over automated equipment. Dinges says that the need to identify on-the-job sleepiness and its operational consequences in these situations is especially acute, particularly when human error can have serious consequences, such as in nuclear power plants and aboard aircraft.

Being physiologically sleepy doesn't mean we will inevitably perform badly on the job, but it makes us more vulnerable to doing so, says Carskadon. Humans are "good coping machines and most of us function pretty well, even in the face of this vulnerability," she says. But when the situation is compounded by sleep loss, alcohol, a low-stimulus environment, redundant tasks or circadian influences, "all of a sudden we do something stupid and blame it on something other than sleep."

# No Sleep for the Cooks

In 1988, a group of Canadian chefs won gold medals at the Culinary Olympics in Frankfurt, West Germany — their reward for months of hard work, nearly two weeks with virtually no sleep and perseverance in the face of misadventure.

The six chefs created about 90 dishes to present at the competition; the entries included meal plates, restaurant platters, hors d'oeuvres, desserts and show pieces sculpted out of sugar and chocolate. Many were at least partially prepared during intense late-night cooking sessions over a week or so before the team left Toronto for Frankfurt, according to the group leader, Edourd Colonerus, Master Chef of Campbell's Soup Co. Canada. "The last 10 days before we left for Frankfurt, it was on high gear. Each one of us had to do his own job and then another 10 or 12 hours for the competition. We met about five o'clock down at the Convention Centre and we worked sometimes until two or three o'clock in the morning.

"The last two days, there was no sleep whatsoever because we had to get everything packed properly. We had nearly five tonnes (4.5 tons) of food and equipment with us, so there was a lot of logistics. I went home in the morning about six o'clock, got my suitcase, changed and went back, because then we had to load the truck to bring the stuff to the airport."

Pearson International Airport in Toronto was the scene of the pastry chef's first setback. The group had arranged with the airline to allow the chocolate sculpture, a basket, to be taken on the aircraft. "When we went through security, the guy dropped the box and tipped it over to put onto the belt. He didn't even wait until we explained," said Colonerus. "So the chocolate basket was already in a thousand pieces before we left. It was a total write-off."

After a 4-hour delay, the plane left for Frankfurt. Colonerus said there was too much noise and activity on the aircraft for them to get much sleep, and when they got to Frankfurt, everything had to be unloaded from the plane, checked through customs and loaded on a truck to be taken to the hotel. "Then we had to look after all our boxes because we had to unpack. So, except for dozing off in the airplane, we actually went another day and a night straight through without sleep — plus the jet lag. We left here on a Thursday, we got to

Frankfurt on a Friday. We went to bed Saturday morning at 3:00 a.m. European time."

They were up again at 6:00 a.m. to go to the market for more supplies. "We went straight back to work on Saturday. We worked until two in the morning, went to bed until six, which was Sunday morning, and then we worked straight through until Tuesday morning at 10 o'clock, without any sleep." They got some sleep on Tuesday and then were awake from 6:00 a.m. Wednesday through to Friday at 3:00 a.m.

The judging took place on Thursday morning. By 6:00 a.m., they were loading their dishes into a truck to carry them to where the judging would be done. Some items that were too fragile to be put in the truck were to be moved by car instead; among them was a new chocolate basket prepared by the pastry chef, which sat on the front seat of the car. Unfortunately, one of their assistants, a woman who was carrying a shoulder purse, bent down to put something into the car and her purse came swinging around and "knocked out a thousand pieces of our chocolate basket again," Colonerus said. "So there was our showpiece, 10 minutes before the judging.

"When I saw the team was about to break down and probably start arguing, I chased everybody out. I said, 'Go over there and look after your things; set them up properly and make sure nothing happens.' Then I sat down with my pastry chef. He was in shock. He wanted to redo a chocolate basket. I said, 'You need a whole day to do that. We exhibit at eight o'clock. We don't have the time.'"

Fortunately, there was a backup showpiece — a chocolate sculpture of a horse. It did not quite fit the theme of the rest of the dishes, but it was their only choice.

Once the dishes were set up and the judging was under way, "most people just collapsed," Colonerus said. He went to the hotel to get some sleep, but he was called back almost immediately to deal with a problem concerning the team's registration cards. By the time that was sorted out, he had just enough time to rush to the hotel to change for the awards ceremony.

One by one, the members of the Canadian team were called up to receive gold medals — all except the pastry chef. But Colonerus refused to believe his pastry chef hadn't won at least a silver or bronze medal, so he spoke to the organizers. They discovered that the pastry chef's name was not in the computer. His cards had not been properly registered, so his marks were not in the computer. They hastily called the judges back and "as soon as we got to the table, the judge said, 'I marked this one already for a gold medal,'" Colonerus said.

So all six members of the group got individual gold medals and they won the team gold as well. More than 1,000 individual chefs, 135 national teams and 154 regional teams had entered the competition, Colonerus said.

Not surprisingly, stamina is much-valued trait in chefs who compete internationally. "These guys are chosen by how much pressure they can stand and, if something happens, if they can jump in and think quickly," said Colonerus. "If they tire out after a couple of hours, it's a drag on all the others." He normally sleeps only about 4 or 5 hours a night and wakes up on schedule without an alarm clock. He can also nap for 10 minutes and then "go full speed ahead," he added.

Colonerus got back from Frankfurt on a Sunday night. At 6:30 on Monday morning, "I was back at work as if nothing had happened."

. . . . . . . . . . . . . . . . . . . . . . . . . . . . . .

CHAPTER 8

# SLEEPINESS AND PERFORMANCE

*English is a terrible language when it comes to the word* tired.
SLEEP RESEARCHER HARVEY MOLDOFSKY

M ANY PEOPLE USE WORDS
like *tiredness, fatigue* and *exhaustion* interchangeably with *sleepiness*, but
they're not necessarily the same thing. "*Tired* could be used to mean
irresistibly sleepy — you can't stay awake," says Moldofsky. "Tiredness is also physical exhaustion, as though you've labored heavily in
the woods chopping down trees; you're physically tired but not sleepy.
Then there's mental fatigue. It's not that you're sleepy; it's not that
you're physically fatigued, because you've done nothing all day except
think and write and read, and yet you think, 'Oh, I'm tired.' Tiredness
could also reflect the lack of motivation found in people who are bored
or who suffer from a chronic mental illness such as depression or
schizophrenia."

Individual personality factors, willpower and motivation (e.g., the
desire to pass an exam, to get a promotion, to set a world record) are
also important variables affecting how tired people will report feeling.
These factors enable an individual to override the pressure to sleep,
at least for a short time, and this makes it even more difficult to predict
the effect of sleepiness on performance in any given situation. The
combination of sleep loss with strenuous mental or physical work
causes even further blurring of the meaning of fatigue and sleepiness
ratings, Dinges adds.

Thus, one of the great difficulties in determining the effect of sleepiness on performance has been to find reliable ways to *measure* both sleepiness and performance. Emotional state — whether you're feeling happy, angry, irritated, cheerful or tense — also fits into this equation, and so researchers have also developed measures of mood. While many of these tests are suitable for use only in a controlled laboratory environment, scientists are also trying to develop variants that are of short duration, inexpensive to administer and suitable for use in real work environments. They hope these tests can be used to provide a reliable assessment of the effects of sleep loss on job performance.

Tests measuring subjective sleepiness and fatigue were described in Chapter 1. They were the source of the "damn fool questions" asked by the computer, such as whether we felt "alert, wide awake," "foggy, slowed down" or "losing the struggle to remain awake" and whether we were "extremely peppy" or "ready to drop." We were also given a mood scale ranging from "carefree, cheerful" to "dull, drowsy, defiant."

To some degree, both sleepiness and mood — or at least the extent to which they are overtly manifested — are in the eye of the beholder; for example, one study showed that observers tend to rate sleep-deprived subjects as being sleepier than the subjects thought themselves to be. Subjective sleepiness ratings will also be influenced by how interesting or tedious they find the tasks they're given to do; in the experiment described in Chapter 1, for instance, a greater degree of subjective sleepiness was felt during the boring, repetitive tests than during the more intellectually stimulating computerized war game. Rest breaks also affect subjective sleepiness ratings; several studies have shown that subjects almost always report feeling less sleepy and in a better mood just after a rest break than during the middle or near the end of a work session. Rest breaks can, in fact, be quite alerting if they include social interaction; this is the main reason that, in the experiment described in Chapter 1, the researchers and support staff minimized their contact with the subjects when they were outside the testing rooms as much as possible.

As for mood, Dinges notes that the extent to which feelings of irritability, anger and unhappiness will be expressed depends on the context in which sleep loss occurs. Sleep-deprived subjects are more likely to express these negative feelings if, for example, they feel deceived, or lack food or other creature comforts or if the tasks demanded of them are too onerous and the rewards too small. These feelings might not even be expressed in sleep lab experiments, in which subjects are often paid for their participation and are usually cooperative, highly motivated and well treated, Dinges says. In the workplace, sleepy people might be more likely to express resentment and anger if they feel they're not being well treated.

It would seem, therefore, that *objective* measures of sleepiness should provide more reliable estimates of how sleepy subjects really are and, in particular, how much sleepiness affects their ability to function. But as usual, life is never that simple in the sleep lab. Take the Multiple Sleep Latency Test, for example. Sleep latency — how long it takes you to fall asleep — is a very sensitive indicator of how sleepy you are, and as we saw in previous chapters, this test has proved very useful in studying variations in sleepiness caused by circadian factors and excessive daytime sleepiness resulting from sleep disorders.

Subjects taking the MSLT lie in bed in a quiet, dark room and are instructed to "try to go to sleep" every 2 hours during the day. If they do go to sleep, they are wakened almost immediately; if they fail to fall asleep within 20 minutes, the attempt is terminated. Surprisingly, most normal sleepers do fall asleep within 20 minutes in these circumstances, even if they have not been sleep deprived, and many fall asleep within 5 to 10 minutes, which is almost as fast as people suffering from sleep disorders. What does this mean? It means, Dinges says, that this test is very good for determining how vulnerable subjects are to falling asleep in an environment deliberately designed to promote sleep, but it does not measure how well subjects are able to *resist* falling asleep in such an environment. Nor does it measure how vulnerable those same subjects are to falling asleep — or how well they can resist sleep — in more stimulating environments.

Studies have shown that when subjects in sleep latency tests are asked to "try to stay awake," they do in fact stay awake longer than people asked to "try to go to sleep," even in an environment conducive to falling asleep. Dinges concludes that a sleepy person, *when encouraged to do so,* will fall asleep much more rapidly than a nonsleepy person is able to, but the sleepy person's ability to *resist* falling asleep "may remain relatively intact for some time longer," depending on circadian, psychological and environmental factors. Clearly, the ability to resist sleep, in both stimulating and nonstimulating work environments, is an important factor to consider in assessing the effects of sleepiness in impairing performance in the workplace. Thus, he says, traditional sleep latency tests must be used with caution in efforts to determine the occupational impact of sleepiness.

The ability to resist sleep in nonstimulating circumstances also has an important bearing on the operation of vehicles of all kinds, because this is an activity that often demands sustained vigilance in a monotonous environment. The peak incidence of single-vehicle traffic accidents (which are more likely than multivehicle accidents to result from lapses in attention) during the circadian sleepiness troughs is testament to this fact, and sleep loss only worsens the circadian effects.

## MEASURING THE EFFECT OF SLEEP LOSS ON PERFORMANCE

Unfortunately, measuring performance after sleep loss is as complicated as measuring sleepiness. Many different factors come into play: memory, motor skills, verbal and mathematical reasoning, reaction time, vigilance, the ability to recognize and respond to signals — to name just a few. The sensitivity of different types of tasks to sleep loss varies, depending on the duration and complexity of the task, how interesting or tedious it is and whether subjects are given feedback on their performance.

These factors can also affect the subjects' motivation — i.e., their *willingness* to perform, as opposed to their actual *ability* to perform. Motivation and willpower are often sufficient to overcome sleepiness for a time, if the task is interesting enough. Boring, repetitive tasks, which are the first to elicit performance deficits under conditions of sleep deprivation, generally do not inspire the kind of motivation needed to offset the effects of extreme fatigue.

In the past three decades, sleep researchers have devoted considerable effort to the development of tests that can accurately measure the effects of sleep loss and sleepiness on performance. Their objective is a difficult one: to find tests capable of detecting changes in performance caused by minute fluctuations in the brain's state of alertness and sleepiness — fluctuations that can occur over periods as brief as thousandths of a second. And they're looking for tests that are practical for use in field studies in real work situations — in particular, tests that are sensitive to moderate sleep loss (e.g., a single night of lost or reduced sleep), which is far more common in the workplace than the extreme sleep deprivation often studied in the lab.

Performance tests used in controlled laboratory studies are often long and boring, yet require sustained attention for extended periods of time; these types of tests have been found to be the most sensitive to sleep loss. In early studies, sleep researcher Robert Wilkinson of the Medical Research Council Applied Psychology Unit in Cambridge, England, found that if subjects were given interesting tasks to do, they showed no impairment in performance for up to 42 hours without sleep. He also found that on most tasks, impairment following one night of sleep loss could not be detected during the first five minutes of a test, but it became evident if the tests lasted for at least 15 minutes and preferably up to an hour. He developed an auditory vigilance test, in which subjects repond to a series of short tones presented over a 1-hour period, that has been widely used in sleep-deprivation studies.

However, such tests generally are not feasible for use outside the laboratory, and more recent research has focused on finding tests that are shorter but still sensitive to the effects of sleep loss on performance. Some simple 10-minute reaction-time tests have been found to be quite sensitive. However, Ron Heslegrave and Bob Angus at the Defence and Civil Institute of Environmental Medicine argue in one of their scientific papers that even 10-minute tests are too long to be used in the workplace and that they may produce inaccurate estimates of how much the ability to perform has been degraded by sleep loss. On the one hand, if subjects can readily distinguish these tests from their normal work and/or find the tests interesting, they may make a special effort to perform well. On the other hand, if they find the tests disruptive and uninteresting, the deterioration in their ability to perform their normal work may be falsely exaggerated. Therefore, minimizing the length of the tests may make their inclusion in real work situations "both more practical and a more accurate reflection of performance levels," the researchers conclude.

Several studies have now shown that tests much shorter than half an hour, and shorter even than 10 minutes, can be sensitive to moderate sleep loss. For example, a study done by Daniel J. Mullaney and his colleagues at the University of California at San Diego found that when subjects were required to work continuously at 3-minute tasks and subjective sleepiness ratings repeated every 10 minutes during 42 hours of sleep deprivation, their performance deteriorated and they experienced episodes of hallucination and disorientation within 18 hours — earlier than had usually been the case in previous sleep-deprivation experiments. (However, these results may have been somewhat exaggerated by the monotony of the tests.)

In their study, Heslegrave and Angus found that even 1-minute tests involving reaction-time, logical reasoning and subtraction tasks are just as sensitive to sleep loss as 10-minute variants of the same tests, as long as subjects do them in the middle of long sessions involving continuous, mentally demanding work with only brief rest breaks in between. (This was the protocol used in the experiment described in Chapter 1.) They say that a continuous, highly demanding workload can minimize motivational factors that might cause performance ability to be overestimated; if performance testing is intermittent and infrequent, subjects may be able to expend extra effort in short-term bursts by drawing on reserves they don't need in the interim periods (particularly if the workload demands during these interim periods are low) to perform especially well during the test periods.

The timing of performance testing is an important factor too. Are the tests done at a time when the subject is suffering from postawakening sleep inertia or several hours after awakening? Are the tests done during circadian troughs or peaks? Are they done after a rest break or in the middle of a testing session? Heslegrave and Angus found that tests done just after a rest break are less sensitive to sleep loss than tests done after subjects were well into a continuous work session. Consequently, they say, tests done before such work sessions, or in isolation from them, may not provide valid estimates of the effects of sleep loss on subsequent work.

They concluded that if short-duration tests are embedded within longer sessions involving a high workload of mentally demanding tasks, they can be sensitive indicators of the effects of sleep loss on performance. They also incorporated a 4-minute "eyes-closed" period into their experiments to determine if subjects could resist the temptation to fall asleep. This test is more practical than the MSLT, since it's usually not feasible to administer a 20-minute MSLT in a real work setting.

As we have seen, scientists believe that lapses in alertness and performance occur when the sleepy brain imposes microsleeps lasting a few seconds. These lapses appear to be a feature of extreme drowsiness, Dinges notes, but even before they cause observable effects on performance, the brain experiences "fragmented wakefulness" —

fluctuations in alertness occurring over periods of thousandths of a second. Dinges says that as long as a task makes relatively high and unrelenting demands, "the brain can be 'caught' going to sleep." He adds that if someone is unable to do a simple 10-minute reaction-time task without showing a significant drop in performance, then performance of more complex tasks might also be at risk in a low-stimulus environment.

## SLEEP LOSS AND PERFORMANCE

Sorting out the complex interplay of subjective and objective sleepiness, mood, circadian rhythms and performance has proved to be a formidable task for scientists. They attempt to address these questions by conducting controlled laboratory studies with sleep-deprived volunteer subjects. The first sleep-deprivation experiment involving humans was done in 1896, but scientific study of the phenomenon began in earnest in the 1920s in the lab of sleep research pioneer Nathaniel Kleitman. Since then, hundreds of sleep-deprivation experiments have been done in labs all over the world.

Many of these studies involve total sleep deprivation ranging from about two to five days (and sometimes longer), but a number of researchers have also explored the effects on performance of reducing total sleep time or of fragmenting sleep into smaller periods by repeatedly waking subjects. More recently, researchers have studied the effects of multiple sleep episodes, known as ultrashort sleep/wake schedules, and have begun to explore the potential of napping for improving or maintaining performance in work situations. These studies will be examined in the next chapters.

What do these sleep-deprivation studies tell us about the effect of sleep loss on performance? In Kleitman's early tests, student subjects were asked to maintain their normal daily routine except for lying awake in bed all night (an onerous task in the days before all-night radio and TV, cassette players or stereos). During the first night, subjects could often stay awake; they did not feel exceptionally tired or sleepy and were able to read or study without too much difficulty, except for increased drowsiness between 3:00 and 6:00 a.m. The next day, the subjects were able to function well as long as they kept active.

But during the second night without sleep, the situation changed dramatically. Subjects could not stay awake all the time, and sleepiness made reading or studying almost impossible. Kleitman observed that during the circadian trough in the middle of the second night, "the desire for sleep was almost overpowering." In the morning, sleepiness abated somewhat and subjects were able to do laboratory work, but they could not attend lectures or take notes without running the risk of falling asleep. One subject could not count his pulse for more than a minute at a time; he lost track of the numbers and dozed off.

Kleitman found the third and fourth nights similar to the second and concluded that, after about 62 to 65 hours without sleep, subjects are as sleepy as they're going to get. He noted that those who remained awake this long experienced "wavelike" peaks and troughs in sleepiness and the greatest sleepiness occurred about the same time each night.

We know now, of course, that these waves of sleepiness are caused by circadian influences. Laboratory experiments have shown that the effects of sleep loss and circadian influences appear to be additive — sleep-deprived subjects feel sleepiest during the circadian troughs and most alert near the circadian peak. Dinges says this additive effect is what accounts for the extreme, virtually irresistible sleepiness typically experienced about 40 hours or so into sleep-deprivation experiments. This phenomenon usually occurs in the middle of the second night of the experiment, when subjects have to contend with increased sleepiness in the circadian trough on top of the sleepiness caused by nearly two full days of sleep loss. During this period, Dinges says, subjects are likely to experience the greatest increase in sleepiness from their normal well-rested condition than at any subsequent time in the experiment, even if it continues for another nine days.

Sleep loss also enhances the sleepiness normally felt during the midafternoon circadian trough, says Mary Carskadon. Even well-rested people will often get sleepy in the afternoon, but "it gets worse if you don't get enough sleep."

Dinges says that without the use of stimulants, subjects are unable to remain continuously alert after the circadian trough of the second full 24-hour period of sleeplessness; at this stage, the brain starts to impose sleep in the form of microsleep episodes. Thus, it appears to be impossible to totally deprive humans of sleep for more than about 48 hours.

In addition to increased sleepiness and microsleeps, other typical symptoms of sleep deprivation can include increased appetite and sex drive, increased sensitivity to pain, drooping eyelids, dryness or itchiness of the eyes, seeing double and hand tremors.

Loss of motivation — a just-don't-care-anymore attitude — is also very common. In fact, motivation is one of the first things to go and it can be as serious a consequence of sleep loss as deterioration in the actual ability to perform. Under these circumstances, errors of omission can be a particular hazard. These are the types of errors most commonly made by overtired interns and residents, says Robert Conn, a cardiology resident and former president of the Canadian Association of Internes and Residents. "It's not so much errors of commission, where you actually do something wrong, but people forget to do things. You forget to check on a lab value, you forget to look at an X-ray. That's a combination of being tired and just the amount of work you have to do."

As mentioned earlier, sleep deprivation may cause psychoticlike behavior in some susceptible individuals, particularly those with a history of psychiatric problems. Many people suffering from mental illness also suffer from sleep problems, and sleep loss may precipitate psychotic symptoms in schizophrenics. And sleep deprivation has been used, in combination with social isolation and emotional and physical trauma, as an instrument of torture dating back at least as far as the Spanish Inquisition.

However, controlled laboratory studies have shown unequivocally that neither sleep deprivation nor deprivation of REM sleep in particular precipitates serious or permanent mental disorders in otherwise normal people. Although REM deprivation does appear to bring out psychotic symptoms in schizophrenics, it seems to cause no more than some anxiety, irritability and difficulty in concentration in normal subjects. And as mentioned in Chapter 5, it can actually reduce symptoms of depression in some patients.

William Dement notes that the 11-day marathon by student Randy Gardner in 1965 did a great deal to undermine the widespread public belief that sleep loss can drive people mad. Gardner experienced only mild hallucinations and exhibited no paranoid symptoms or emotional distress. In fact, at the end of his 264-hour ordeal, he acquitted himself in "impeccable fashion" during a press conference attended by reporters from all over the U.S. A decade later, Gardner showed no lasting mental or physical ill effects from the experiment. In his book *Some Must Watch While Some Must Sleep*, Dement commented that even

Gardner's psychomotor skills appeared to remain remarkably intact; on the last night of the experiment, they spent hours in an arcade playing a baseball game, and Gardner won every one of the approximately 100 games they played.

The high stimulation and intense social interaction provided by these games undoubtedly accounted, at least in part, for Gardner's ability to play so well despite being awake for more than 260 hours. Studies in which subjects have been carefully monitored while doing a wide variety of physical and mental tasks show, however, that even much shorter periods of sleep loss do cause significant deterioration in the ability to perform. Sleep researcher Paul Naitoh of the Naval Health Research Center in San Diego has concluded that the upper limit for working continuously at tasks that make both physical and mental demands is about two to three days without sleep.

Angus and his colleagues at DCIEM found that the performance of sleep-deprived subjects required to do continuous, mentally demanding work dropped to less than 40 percent of their peak ability after about 42 hours without sleep. Their performance on various tests — serial reaction time, vigilance and subtraction tasks — all follow a similar pattern. At the beginning of the experiment, subjects are alert and perform at a high level; in fact, their performance may actually show a short-lived improvement as they learn the tasks and become more proficient. In the circadian trough of the first night of sleep loss — about 18 hours into the experiment — their performance shows a dramatic drop to less than 70 percent of peak. This tends to level out during the subsequent day and may even rise somewhat during circadian peaks. However, this is still about one-third or so below the levels of performance the subjects can achieve when well rested.

But it is during the circadian trough of the second night that performance drops precipitously. After 42 hours of sleep loss — by early morning after the second night without sleep — performance was down 60 percent or more from peak levels. This drop was greater than that found in previous studies, the researchers note, and they suggest that these results are likely to indicate more accurately the reduction in performance that can be expected during sustained operations.

As we have seen, in most sleep-deprivation studies, performance is measured using relatively simple and unstimulating reaction-time or vigilance tests. British researcher James Horne, in a paper published in the journal *Sleep*, says that these tests have been used because they are the most sensitive to sleepiness and are easy to score. But he contends that they are more a measure of the motivation to perform (i.e., interest in the task) than of inherent capacity to perform, and he questions whether they enlighten us about what effect sleep and sleep loss have on higher mental function. (In Chapter 3, we discussed Horne's theory that in humans and other advanced mammals, sleep primarily restores the cerebral cortex, which is responsible for complex thought processes.)

Some sleep-deprivation studies have used more complex tests such as IQ tests, reading comprehension and decision-making. These tests generally do not show a performance drop until the second night of lost sleep; they are more stimulating than reaction-time or vigilance tests, and sleep-deprived subjects can usually do well at them by concentrating harder because they involve *convergent* thinking — the ability to "home in" on solutions and use well-established mental skills. Real-life examples of such behavior include doing a multiple-choice test, making something with your hands or handling an anticipated type of emergency with practiced, preprogrammed procedures.

However, Horne argues that even one sleepless night can affect our most creative kind of thinking, known as *divergent* thinking, which involves spontaneity, flexibility and originality. This type of thinking is used in creative pursuits such as writing or painting and is required to respond in innovative ways in an emergency. Horne says that our ability to try different approaches to a problem or to generate new or unusual ideas is undermined by the loss of only a single night's sleep; the mind gets into a rut and sticks to known ways of doing things. These findings have important implications for people who may be required to think creatively in an emergency after being awake all night. He also commented that studying all night might be fine for a multiple-choice exam, but not very good for an exam that calls for creative responses, such as essay writing or analysis.

Horne says that no one has previously studied the effect of sleep loss on divergent thinking because the tests take a long time to do and are tedious to score. He adapted several short-duration exercises from longer versions of tests designed to measure creative thinking. In one, subjects are given a picture of a person doing an apparently meaningless act and are asked to write down all the questions that come to mind that might help explain the situation and to list as many possible causes and consequences of the event as they can think of. Other tests involved listing as many possible uses of a cardboard box as they could think of and describing the consequences of some unimaginable event (i.e., What if clouds had strings attached to them hanging down to earth?) Still other tests involved completing drawings of partially drawn abstract figures and incorporating pages of small circles into as many different, simple pictures as possible.

These tests were rated on four factors: *flexibility* (producing a variety of ideas, shifting approaches or using different strategies); *originality* (producing ideas that were not commonplace or obvious); *elaboration* (the ability to embellish ideas) and *fluency* (the number of ideas produced). The students were also given a test involving manipulation of colored beads and pegs and a word-fluency test in which they were asked to think up as many four-letter words and as many "any-length" words as they could, starting with given letters of the alphabet.

Twenty-four student volunteers were divided into two groups. Both groups first took the tests while fully rested and had comparable scores. Then, half the group took the tests again after obtaining a normal night's sleep while the other half took it after 32 hours without sleep. The objective was to determine whether a single night of lost sleep impaired the students' divergent-thinking ability and whether this impairment was caused by a decline in their motivation to perform or by an actual decrease in their ability to think divergently.

Horne said that 32 hours without sleep had a substantial impact on most aspects of divergent thinking measured in the experiment. In all cases, the sleep-deprived subjects performed worse than the rested subjects — in most cases, markedly so. For example, their ratings for flexibility, originality, fluency and elaboration were only one-third to two-thirds those of the well-rested subjects. On the word-fluency tests, they were able to think up nearly as many four-letter words as the rested subjects, but only three-quarters as many any-length words. On the bead-and-peg test, which requires flexibility in thinking style, they exhibited *perseveration* — a tendency to persist in using previously successful strategies to solve new problems that required a different approach. This phenomenon also occurred in word tests: sleep-deprived subjects often wrote down the same word repeatedly, then crossed it out, Horne noted.

To assess the role of motivation and incentive in affecting performance, Horne encouraged a competitive atmosphere among the subjects on one of the word tests and offered an attractive monetary reward for each word they thought up. On the any-length word test, the rested subjects increased their average word count by one-third when rewarded, while the sleep-deprived subjects barely increased their word count at all, despite the incentives. Moreover, their performance on short-duration, stimulating tasks — the ones least likely to cause a loss of interest and motivation — was also affected by sleep loss, despite their best efforts to perform well.

Horne concluded that divergent and flexible thinking is impaired by a single night of sleep loss and that, at best, this can be only partly attributed to changes in motivation. Something "more fundamental" occurs with this kind of thinking during sleep loss, he suggests.

Horne also conducted one test of convergent thinking — an anagram test — and found no significant differences in performance between the two groups. This is consistent with other findings indicating that convergent thinking is not affected until the second night of lost sleep.

A study by researchers Carlyle Smith and Megan Whittaker of Trent University in Peterborough, Ontario, indicates that sleep may play an active role in learning over a period of several days and "it may well be involved in the process of integrating newly acquired material with that already in memory." They asked 56 subjects to spend 1½ hours learning the rules and practicing simple examples of a logic game. Then the group was divided into six groups. Five groups were sleep deprived at various times ranging from the night of training to three nights later; the sixth group was not sleep deprived at all.

A week later, all the subjects were asked to play the logic game. The researchers found that the ability to effectively apply the rules of the game learned a week earlier was inferior in subjects who had been sleep deprived the night of training and between 48 and 72 hours after training. They concluded that "sleep in humans is involved with the ability to apply a set of rules to complex problems."

In two subsequent studies, Smith and Ann Pirolli found evidence that REM sleep was the most important in learning the complex logic task. Subjects selectively deprived of REM sleep performed significantly more poorly than subjects who were not sleep deprived or who were deprived only of non-REM sleep.

Surprisingly, the researchers also found that interrupting REM during the first two sleep cycles of the night caused just as much of a drop in performance as interrupting it during the last two sleep cycles — about 30 percent below that of subjects who were not sleep deprived. Remember that the first two cycles are almost completely dominated by slow wave sleep and usually contain little REM, while the last two cycles normally contain large amounts of REM. In fact, it's been shown that REM in the last two cycles often increases after a person has been involved in learning something. Consequently, Smith and Pirolli theorized that depriving subjects of the last two REM periods would have a much more devastating effect on their learning than depriving them of the first two periods. But this didn't happen, and so they suggest that "for certain kinds of material, the entire night of REM sleep, including all the REM periods, is important for efficient learning/memory processing."

Another surprise was the discovery that simply delaying the normal sleep period for several hours also had a marked negative effect on learning, even if little or no REM sleep was actually lost. This displacement of sleep was just as devastating as staying up all night, said Smith. "Not only do you have to have the normal amount of REM sleep, you have to have it when your body normally thinks you're going to have it. If you don't do that, you pay." One implication of these findings, he said, is that students shouldn't stay up all night cramming for exams; in fact, even staying up for as little as 2 hours past their normal bedtime could seriously affect how well they retain the information they learned that day.

The Trent experiments showed no significant differences among REM-deprived, non-REM-deprived and control subjects in the performance of a simple word-association task, and other studies also suggest that less complex learning tasks may not be as affected by selective REM deprivation. However, one study did find that REM-deprived subjects were more likely to feel agitated and aggressive while SWS-deprived subjects tended to be withdrawn and physically uncomfortable. Consequently, Hauri suggests that REM sleep might be related to psychological recovery while SWS may be more related to physiological and metabolic recovery.

## RECOVERY SLEEP

Several studies have shown that the amount of recovery sleep required to restore performance to optimum levels increases the longer someone has been awake. For example, a study by Wilkinson found that the performance levels of subjects who had been awake for one night could be restored by just 2 hours of sleep, but after two nights of sleep loss, they required 5 hours of recovery sleep. Similarly, a study by Roger Rosa and his colleagues found that after 48 hours of continuous work, subjects required 4 hours of sleep to recover to their original levels of performance, while subjects who had worked 64 hours without sleep required 8 hours of recovery sleep.

But, as mentioned earlier, it's not necessary to sleep for extraordinarily long periods of time in order to recover from even extreme sleep deprivation. Sleep-deprived subjects typically extend their first sleep period, but even in extreme cases, this usually lasts no more than 10 to 15 hours. After that, their sleep duration quickly returns to normal and they appear to be fully recovered with no lingering ill effects (although a study by Wilkinson indicates that vigilance performance may be degraded on the first morning after extended recovery sleep).

Why is it that the amount of recovery sleep needed is less than the total amount of sleep lost? Scientists are intrigued by the possibility that this phenomenon may be telling us something about the importance of the different stages of sleep — in particular, slow wave sleep. Many studies have shown that the amount of slow wave sleep that occurs in a sleep period is very sensitive to prior sleep loss. After a period of sleep deprivation, recovery sleep is characterized by an increase in slow wave sleep; in fact, nearly *all* the slow wave sleep that was lost is "made up" during recovery sleep. In contrast, only about half of the lost REM sleep is made up, and the lighter stages of sleep may not be recovered at all. In one study, for example, four subjects were kept awake for eight days and then allowed three nights of recovery sleep amounting to 12 hours on the first night and 9 hours each on the subsequent two. This restored their performance to normal, even though they made up only about 12 percent of the sleep they'd lost. They recovered all their slow wave sleep but only one-third to two-thirds of their REM sleep.

It has also been shown that even if sleep is only reduced rather than completely eliminated, normal amounts of slow wave sleep are still preserved at the expense of the other sleep stages. For example, one study showed that subjects who got only 3 hours of sleep a night for a week obtained the same amount of slow wave sleep as they would have during seven full nights of sleep. Slow wave sleep is also preserved in situations where nighttime sleep is replaced or augmented by naps; one study found that subjects who took 10 1-hour naps over a 40-hour period got just as much slow wave sleep as they would have during the normal night's sleep that the naps replaced. Moreover, taking an afternoon nap has been shown to reduce slow wave sleep by an equivalent amount during subsequent nighttime sleep.

Sleep researchers Andrew Tilley, Frank Donohoe and Sharon Hensby of the University of Queensland, Australia, did an experiment indicating that "there may be a 'need' for a set amount of slow wave sleep per day." They reduced the amount of slow wave sleep subjects got at night and then "paid back" the debt in various amounts during daytime naps. They wanted to see if this repayment of the SWS debt affected how much slow wave sleep the subjects would get during subsequent recovery sleep at night — and they found that the sleep system operates like a finely tuned budget in which SWS debts are faithfully paid. "It appears that the sleep system is programmed to obtain a more or less fixed amount of SWS per day, with any shortfall being carried over into the next night's sleep. The SWS debt can be reduced by an afternoon nap."

Other lines of evidence support the idea that slow wave sleep is preserved. For example, it has been found that short sleepers get nearly the same amount of slow wave sleep (and REM sleep) as normal sleepers and they also get about as much slow wave sleep as long sleepers. Long sleepers get about half again as much REM sleep as short sleepers.

What does all this tell us about our need for slow wave sleep? As mentioned in Chapter 3, scientists still don't fully understand the functions of the different stages of sleep; Moldofsky notes that the EEG readings that distinguish the different stages are "just squiggles on a piece of paper. These are just signals coming from the scalp; this doesn't tell us what's really going on in the body." However, the fact that slow wave sleep is preserved by the sleep system and that slow wave sleep debt is preferentially made up during recovery sleep certainly suggests that slow wave sleep plays a particularly important role. Some researchers believe that it is the most physiologically restorative sleep stage and is critically important in restoring and maintaining performance.

Horne argues, in fact, that slow wave sleep may be almost completely obligatory while REM may be partly optional. This, he says, accounts for the fact that people can reduce their sleep to about 5 hours or so, but no more without impairing their performance ability. Remember that most slow wave sleep is highly concentrated in the first two or three of the 90-minute sleep cycles; by the third cycle, REM sleep starts to increase and it dominates the last two cycles, while slow wave sleep virtually disappears. Therefore, after about 4½ to 5 hours, we have obtained nearly all our slow wave sleep for the night and about half of the REM sleep, Horne says. This constitutes what he calls "core sleep." He suggests the last two cycles of the night, consisting mostly of REM sleep and light (Stage 2) sleep, are mostly optional — more a matter of habit than necessity.

In fact, a number of researchers have speculated that the latter, REM-dominated cycles of the sleep period may not be entirely necessary, but rather may reflect individual variations in the need for the psychological restoration presumed to be supplied by REM sleep. Remember that it is primarily in the amount of REM sleep that long and short sleepers differ. It appears, however, that REM sleep is far from completely dispensable even in normal and short sleepers. Subjects selectively deprived of REM sleep try very hard to obtain it during the experiments and to make up for it when they resume sleeping normally — a phenomenon known as REM rebound.

In his book *Why We Sleep*, Horne summarizes his conclusions about core and optional sleep. He contends that normal sleepers who get 7 to 8 hours of sleep a night can quite readily decrease their sleep to about 5½ to 6 hours a night. This is done by reducing optional sleep (i.e., the latter two sleep cycles of the night). If sleep reduction is done gradually over a period of several weeks, the average sleeper can reduce his or her sleep by about 1½ to 2 hours "on a more or less permanent basis" without suffering from excessive daytime sleepiness or reduced psychological performance, Horne says.

He notes that the sleepiness that occurs after this sleep reduction would be what he calls *optional sleepiness* and this would diminish after several days of reduced sleep, leading to what would appear to be "full adaptation to sleep reduction."

However, he concludes by saying that he's not advocating that people cut their sleep to, say, 6 hours a night — "only that it can be done." In one of his experiments, he found that subjects who reduced their sleep did not seem to make productive use of the extra time, but in fact wasted most of it; their normal day's work was spread out over the available time. He adds that optional sleep should not be regarded as a waste of time because it provides many people with relaxation that they cannot get while awake. Sleeping less because of work pressures is all right for a few nights, he says, but it's not a good long-term strategy because it causes the loss of valuable relaxation. His advice: if you're content and enjoy being awake, then reduce your sleep time, but if your waking hours are a struggle and are full of stress, you should maintain your regular sleep.

Horne's views about obligatory and optional sleep differ from those of other sleep researchers who contend that most people in modern industrial societies suffer from chronic partial sleep deprivation. These other researchers simply do not believe that most people can function well indefinitely on only 5 hours of sleep a night. Mary Carskadon comments, "I agree there is some optional sleep. I guess where we differ is that I think the obligatory component is bigger than he does."

## REDUCING THE IMPACT OF SLEEP LOSS ON PERFORMANCE

Is there a way to reduce the negative impact of sleep loss on performance? Several groups of researchers have looked at this question and have, in particular, examined the role that physical conditioning and exercise might play in maintaining alertness and performance in a sleep-deprived condition. The results have been contradictory: some studies have shown good effects, others bad effects and still others no effect at all.

One of the latter was a study done by Bob Angus and his colleagues at DCIEM. They asked sleep-deprived subjects to spend every third hour of the experiment walking on a treadmill and compared their results with other subjects who spent that hour watching TV, reading or playing cards. No differences were found between the two groups, either in the performance of mental tasks or in their subjective sensations of mood. In another experiment, subjects were asked to perform a single episode of hard physical exercise in the middle of the second night of sleep loss; again, their performance on mental tasks was no better than subjects who did not do the exercise. "It appears that a brief burst of exercise did not improve cognitive performance in sleep-deprived people who have been expending intense mental effort," the scientists concluded. They also compared subjects with high and average levels of general fitness and found no differences in their ability to perform various mental tasks (although it is likely there would be differences in performing more physically demanding tasks).

Another study by A. Lubin and his colleagues at the U.S. Naval Health Research Center in San Diego indicated that exercise might greatly exacerbate the deterioration in performance caused by sleep loss. On the other hand, Andrew Tilley and Philip Bohle of the University of Queensland in Australia found that performance on a reaction-time test was improved in high school students who did the test every two hours while participating in an all-night disco-dancing marathon. This exercise was virtually continuous and described as light to moderate. The researchers found that performance on the reaction-time test was better during the dance marathon than when the students spent a sleepless night in quiet, relaxing activities. It was particularly beneficial in maintaining performance during the circadian trough between 4:00 and 6:00 a.m.

Tilley and Bohle suggest that the timing of the exercise might be more important than the fact that it was being done continuously. They say that exercising immediately before testing will improve performance by reducing drowsiness, although only transiently. If exercising is done well before testing, particularly if it is intense and prolonged, then performance will likely be impaired by increased drowsiness or fatigue.

In any event, doing continuous exercise (especially disco dancing) clearly is not feasible as a method of maintaining alertness and performance in the workplace. William Dement notes that while vigorous exercise can help keep sleep-deprived people awake, as sleep loss increases, almost continuous muscular activity is required for wakefulness and people cannot sustain this level of exercise indefinitely.

Is taking a rest break any better as a method of alleviating the effects of sleep loss on performance? The researchers at DCIEM looked at this too. They compared two groups of subjects who engaged in continuous work for 30 hours. Following this, one group continued working but the other group spent most of the next 12 hours reading, watching TV, playing games or resting (but not sleeping). No differences were found in the performance of the two groups. The group that was allowed to rest reported feeling just as fatigued as the group that worked continuously, and their performance levels showed the sharp drop during the second night of sleep loss that is expected in sleep-deprived subjects performing continuous mental work. Thus, reducing an individual's workload or the level of mental activity during sleep deprivation does not appear to have long-term benefits.

However, rest breaks do produce a short-lived improvement; mood and performance are "consistently better immediately after breaks than an hour into the work sessions. The breaks seem to have a short-lasting positive influence on the subjects and may provide a means by which temporary increases in performance can be effected during sustained operations," the DCIEM researchers say.

Nevertheless, they conclude that "the most obvious intervention for counteracting the effects of sleep loss is sleep itself." But it's often impossible for people in modern society to get 7 to 8 hours of sleep in one continuous stretch at night, especially if they have to work shifts or when they're required to work for long hours for an extended period. This brings us to the potential of napping for maintaining or restoring alertness and performance in the workplace.

"Maybe," says Angus, "the only thing that helps the loss of sleep is to get a little bit of it."

CHAPTER 9

# A LITTLE BIT OF SLEEP

$I$N 1975, A YOUNG ITALIAN DOCTOR, while working on the thesis for his medical degree at the University of Bologna, found himself at sea — literally. Deciding to combine his medical studies on biological rhythms with his love of sailing, Claudio Stampi participated in an around-the-world yacht race to study sailors who undertake this grueling challenge. These yachtsmen cross many time zones during a race, though less rapidly than people who fly, and Stampi was curious about the effect of "boat lag" on their biological clocks.

During the course of his study, he became intrigued by another aspect of the races. He discovered that many competitors, especially those who sail solo, adopted an unusually fragmented sleep pattern that involved taking very short naps — as little as 10 minutes at a time — in order to cope with extraordinary demands on their energies during races that cover thousands of kilometers of open ocean and take from two to seven weeks to complete.

Stampi's curiosity was aroused. Was there a relationship between the sailors' race results and the sleep patterns they adopted? How quickly and easily did they adapt to taking short naps at sea? How long could they function effectively while following this unusual sleep pattern? Did the sailors nap regularly when they weren't racing? If not, could they train themselves to sleep this way before the race? Did the sailors have personality characteristics that correlated with the particular sleep patterns they adopted during the race? If so, would it be possible to use such correlations to develop a method of predicting and prescribing optimum nap strategies for individuals?

Such a technique, Stampi reasoned, might have important practical implications far beyond improving the performance of competitive sailors. Most people, after all, haven't the slightest intention of sailing

168

solo across the ocean, but many do have jobs that can be nearly as arduous at times, demanding long stretches of continuous work and high levels of alertness, vigilance and performance. Some of the more dramatic examples include astronauts, deep-sea divers, polar explorers and mountain climbers, but the requirement to fight off fatigue while performing demanding work efficiently for prolonged periods of time is not unique to these esoteric pursuits: it is also an occupational hazard of police and firefighters, air traffic controllers, aerospace workers, pilots, doctors, athletes, search-and-rescue workers, soldiers, shift workers, executives and professionals.

David Dinges notes that in many cases these high-demand jobs first cause people to lose sleep, then require them to work for long periods with high levels of efficiency, accuracy and motivation. The attitude that mental or physical "toughness" can carry them through is common, Dinges says, but though this may motivate someone to try harder to persevere, there's little evidence that these factors can prevent sleepiness or its behavioral consequences. He concludes that "there appears to be no substitute for sleep itself."

Research on the restorative effects of napping is still in its infancy; although the earliest documented napping study dates back to 1934, only during the 1980s has the impact of napping on performance been seriously studied by sleep researchers. Stampi's studies on solo sailors, which he started in 1980, were the first field studies of napping patterns in civilians who had voluntarily undertaken continuous work for a prolonged period of time and they will be discussed in more detail later in this chapter.

First, however, it's necessary to set the stage by examining the research that has been done on partial sleep loss and its effect on performance. While many studies in the past have focused on the effects of total sleep deprivation — mainly in an attempt to answer fundamental questions about the function of sleep — researchers have more recently become interested in the effects of reduced sleep and in the potential application of "ultrashort" sleep/wake schedules and planned napping to combat sleepiness on the job. Scientists suggest that in some work environments, particularly high-demand jobs involving continuous or prolonged work periods, these ultrashort sleep schedules could be an important way to combat the deterioration of performance and mood caused by sleep loss — as long as naps are carefully scheduled, tailored as much as possible to individual sleep needs and designed to minimize the negative effects of sleep inertia.

This trend is being affected by two things. The first is the simple fact that millions of people today simply cannot sleep in the old-fashioned way — i.e., for 8 hours in a row, at night, every 24 hours. This is taking a major toll not only on their ability to work productively and safely, but on their personal lives and their mental and physical health as well. "It's hard for people to sleep well regularly," says Roger Broughton, and this has stimulated increasing scientific interest in "finding solutions to getting enough sleep in very irregular, unusual jobs." In fact, Paul Naitoh proposes that occupations demanding irregular or prolonged work ought to have "sleep managers" to establish humane work/sleep schedules to make work safer and more productive.

The second factor driving the scientific interest in ultrashort sleep/wake patterns is a growing conviction on the part of at least some sleep researchers that the human sleep/wake system may be much more adaptable (or to use the terminology of science, more "plastic") than generally believed. Broughton is one proponent of this view: "Sleep is in fact a very flexible system, much more flexible than most people appreciate. We tend to sleep at very fixed hours, but many people can train themselves to sleep on very unusual, very different schedules."

In the previous chapter, we briefly considered the question, How much sleep do we need? In this chapter, we will examine that same question from a different perspective: How *little* sleep do we need?

## PARTIAL SLEEP LOSS AND PERFORMANCE

In our society, partial sleep loss is more of a problem than total sleep loss. It's relatively rare for people to go more than a day or so without getting any sleep at all, even under the most extreme work conditions, but it is very common for people to regularly curtail their sleep to meet work demands, often by substantial amounts over extended periods of time. This partial sleep loss is often coupled with recovery oversleeping, especially on weekends or holidays.

How much sleep is enough to "get by" on? As usual, there are individual variations, but a number of scientists suggest that about half the sleep you'd get in a normal night is needed to function the next day. "Sleeping down to roughly 50 percent of what you need to be fully alert during the day will maintain performance — not necessarily mood, but performance — for acute periods of time," Dinges says. "You may not feel very good doing it, but you'll be able to do it. But that'll start to deteriorate over time. It's not the absolute hours you get; it's relative to what you need to be alert." Thus, a person who normally sleeps 8 hours might be able to manage on 4 hours for a few days, whereas a 10-hour sleeper might need a minimum of 5 hours to maintain the same levels of performance.

For one day, you might be able to get by with a little less sleep — say, 3 hours — but the cumulative effects of sleep loss will catch up with you quickly: by the second night, about 5 hours will be needed to maintain performance over a longer period. A number of studies suggest that for the majority of people, 4 to 5 hours seems to be a kind of minimum "sleep barrier," below which it becomes extremely difficult to maintain alertness, mood and performance for any sustained period of time.

Some of the first studies to explore the question of the minimal amount of needed sleep were done by Robert Wilkinson and his colleagues at the Medical Research Council Applied Psychology Unit in Cambridge, England. In one, subjects were allowed varying amounts of sleep on two consecutive nights, ranging from no sleep at all to 7½ hours. Those who had 2 hours of sleep or less the first night showed impaired performance on vigilance and arithmetic tasks the next day, while those who had 3 hours or more maintained their normal level of performance. By the end of the second night, the cumulative sleep loss caused even those who had had 5 hours of sleep each night to show impaired performance. A follow-up study showed that performance was degraded in subjects allowed only 4 hours of sleep a night over four nights, compared with subjects allowed 6 and 7½ hours of sleep each night.

Similar results were obtained in studies done by researchers at the U.S. Naval Health Research Center (NHRC) in San Diego and the University of California. In these cases, however, subjects were asked to reduce their sleep very gradually over a period of months. They were able to function quite well with moderate sleep reduction, but their performance and mood began to deteriorate below the 5-hour mark. One of the studies, done by D. J. Mullaney and his colleagues, involved four couples, three of whom normally slept 8 hours a night and one who normally slept 6½ hours a night. They were asked to reduce their sleep time by half an hour every three weeks; when they reached 6 hours a night, they started to experience difficulty getting up in the morning and by the time they were down to about 5 hours, they began having problems with daytime sleepiness and performance. (However, when they were allowed to go back to sleeping normally, those who had been 8-hour sleepers continued to sleep 1 to 2½ hours less than they had before. The 6½-hour sleepers reverted to their regular sleeping pattern.

Horne says that a gradual reduction in sleep time appears to cause much less daytime sleepiness than a sudden drop. He did a study in which volunteers, normally 7½- to 8½-hour sleepers, were asked to sleep 7 hours a night for the first week, 6½ hours a night for the next three weeks and 6 hours a night for the next two weeks. They were compared with a matched control group that did not reduce their sleep. The sleep-reduced subjects had some difficulty waking up in the mornings, but had no problem with daytime sleepiness after the first couple of days after each reduction in sleep. Both groups performed the same on vigilance tasks.

The reduced-sleep group said they felt they could continue sleeping less with little difficulty, but they did not appear to put the extra time to particularly good use. In fact, Horne comments, most found that "they tended to spend more of the day wasting time."

In another sleep-reduction study done by the J. K. Friedmann and colleagues at the Naval Research Center and the University of California, it was found that both long sleepers and short sleepers ended up getting about 5 hours of sleep a night. The long sleepers, who normally slept 9 hours a night, were able to cut 4 hours off their sleep period, but the short sleepers, who usually got about 6 hours of sleep a night, could cut only 1 hour. A study by Horne and A. Minard found that after long sleepers were deprived for sleep for 36 hours, their recovery sleep was no longer than their regular sleep, whereas normal and short sleepers overslept for periods of one-quarter to one-third longer than normal under the same conditions. Horne argues that long sleepers, who are getting quite a bit of optional sleep, are able to absorb the need for increased slow wave sleep after sleep loss within their normal sleep period. Short sleepers, who normally get little optional sleep, must extend their sleep period in order to meet the demand for increased SWS after sleep deprivation.

Joel Herscovitch of the University of Ottawa, in collaboration with Roger Broughton, did a study in which subjects slept for about 4½ hours a night for five nights, and then were allowed two nights of recovery sleep lasting about 10½ hours the first night and 9 hours the second. This sleep pattern is similar to that followed by people who reduce their sleep during the work week and make up for it by sleeping late on weekends.

The subjects did poorly on reaction time and vigilance tests and reported an increase in subjective sleepiness and a decrease in ratings of mood and energy after reduced sleep. For the most part, these measures returned to normal after recovery sleep; in fact, subjects experienced a large rebound in alertness and energy ratings immediately after recovery sleep and energy ratings actually increased to a level higher than they'd been before the experiment began, when the subjects were sleeping normal hours. This result was different from that reported in other studies of extended sleep in which subjects who overslept *without prior sleep loss* reported feeling groggy and worn out. Herscovitch and Broughton suggested that subjects who have gone without sleep beforehand may attach a self-perceived positive benefit to such oversleeping, in contrast to the negative feelings reported by subjects who have not been deprived and do not need the extra sleep.

The researchers note that while some previous studies showed that individuals may be able to adapt to and tolerate reductions in total sleep time over an extended period, the results of their study indicate that over the short term, partial sleep loss causes a significant drop in performance and a negative effect on subjective ratings of mood and sleepiness. They suggest that these short-term disruptions may be caused as much by circadian factors as by actual sleep loss, since both shortening and lengthening the sleep period alters the normal circadian timing of sleep/wake patterns. Over longer periods of partial sleep-deprivation, the sleep-loss effects would become more dominant.

But regardless of the underlying mechanisms, they say their study indicates "that a schedule that approximates a typical work week for many individuals, undersleeping on weekdays and oversleeping on weekends, may produce definite performance deficits."

One thing seems clear, however: even though you may not be able to perform at your peak when you get too little sleep, you're virtually always in better shape with even a small amount of sleep than if you try to work with no sleep at all. Wilse Webb of the University of Florida found that subjects who were given 2-hour naps did better than subjects who got no sleep (although not as well as subjects who got 4-hour naps). This principle was also demonstrated in a field study by Diana Haslam of the British Army Personnel Research Establishment. The subjects, who were soldiers involved in a nine-day exercise, were divided into three groups: one was given no sleep; the second, 1½ hours of sleep; and the third, 3 hours of sleep each night. All 22 of those who were totally sleep deprived withdrew from the exercise after the fourth night, whereas 20 of the 22 who were allowed 3 hours of sleep a night completed the exercise. Twelve of the 23 soldiers who were allowed 1½ hours of sleep a night also lasted the nine days; however, they were deemed to be "combat effective" for only six of those days, while those who had slept 3 hours a night were considered combat effective for the entire test period.

This study and others like it have shown unequivocally that a little bit of sleep is usually better than none. But perhaps this is not the real issue. Perhaps we should be asking instead: is a little bit of sleep enough?

## Ultrashort sleep/wake schedules

Most of the early studies on partial sleep-deprivation and its effect on performance involved simply reducing the normal nocturnal sleep period, but they still involved only a single period of continuous sleep within each 24-hour period. In recent years, many studies have focused instead on other sleep strategies involving numerous short sleep periods. These include schedules combining naps with a certain amount of "core" or "anchor" sleep and ultrashort sleep/wake patterns, in which several naps, each lasting under 2 to 3 hours, are distributed throughout a 24-hour period.

Many sleep researchers define a nap as a sleep period less than half that of a person's normal nightly sleep period. By this definition, naps could be as long as 4 or 5 hours, but many recent studies have focused on shorter periods, ranging from about 2 to 4 hours to as little as 1 to 4 minutes. Naps shorter than 2 hours are often labeled ultrashort sleep periods. In many of the studies that will be discussed here, naps are sleep episodes taken *in place of,* rather than *in addition to,* a normal nocturnal sleep period.

Dinges says that napping has been largely ignored by sleep researchers, who have tended to view it as the preserve of children and the elderly or as a peculiarity of the unstructured lifestyles of university students, who nap a lot, usually because they don't get enough sleep at night. Moreover, doctors who treat people with sleep disorders view napping in a negative light. Involuntary naps are indicative of excessive daytime sleepiness, the prime symptom of several sleep disorders. People with insomnia or delayed phase sleep syndrome are usually advised to avoid daytime napping because it can cause continuing disruption of nocturnal sleep and the circadian system.

However, as Dinges points out, many healthy adults nap regularly, especially those who have irregular work schedules, such as shift workers, flight crews and truck drivers. In these groups, and in college students, napping does not indicate a sleep disorder, he says. Unlike people with sleep disorders, who often fall asleep unwillingly, napping in these groups seems to be voluntary — occurring most often to compensate for prior sleep loss caused by work schedules or in anticipation of future work-related sleep loss.

A perfect example of just such a napping strategy is provided by Joyce Schoones, a nurse who was once a transplant coordinator at Toronto General Hospital. Her job with the transplant program required her to be available at any time of the day or night to go anywhere in North America to coordinate the collection of kidneys, livers, hearts and lungs from donors to be used in transplant operations. She often worked 12- to 18-hour shifts while on duty, and when she was on call, she'd often be wakened in the middle of the night and sent scurrying off to the airport. Schoones had the knack for napping on planes, in operating rooms while waiting for doctors to remove organs, in racing ambulances (sometimes with sirens screaming) and in the midst of office chaos. "You get sleep where you can," she said. "I'd sleep in a chair in the office. It's hustle and bustle, people are eating their lunches and 'The Young and the Restless' is on the television and I'm out like a light. I can nap anywhere, anytime; I sleep for 15 minutes and I'm up like new. I don't think anyone who wasn't able to do that could do the job."

## HUMANS MAY BE NATURAL NAPPERS

Most people consider it normal to sleep once in every 24 hours, usually at night. This pattern, known as *monophasic* sleep, is the most dominant in human cultures, certainly in modern industrialized societies. However, a number of sleep researchers are now questioning whether monophasic sleep is really a physiological necessity. Broughton, for example, argues that it is primarily a social response to the requirements of early agricultural and industrial economic systems. The economic systems of today — driven by the global interconnectedness made possible by advanced communications, transportation and computer technologies — are pushing us toward a 24-hour lifestyle, yet we still cling to archaic concepts about appropriate sleep/wake patterns. Monophasic sleep, Broughton says, "was oversold as normal." In fact, he contends, humans have a natural propensity for *polyphasic* sleep — that is, sleeping more than once every 24 hours. In particular, there is tendency for humans to feel pressure for sleep twice a day, a *biphasic* pattern.

Several lines of evidence support the idea that biphasic sleep comes naturally to humans. One is the approximately 12-hour cycle in which maximum sleepiness occurs in the middle of the night and in midafternoon. This cycle occurs even in well-rested people, although it is more pronounced in people suffering from sleep loss or sleep disorders. Then there are the "siesta cultures," which formally permit a regular afternoon sleep period, although in some countries, this tradition is disappearing for economic reasons. (Ironically, this comes at a time when sleep researchers are suggesting that daytime napping might have a role to play in maintaining alertness on the job.) Broughton adds that there's evidence that some primitive human tribes are nappers, which also implies that polyphasic sleep comes naturally to humans.

Further evidence is provided by scientific studies. Many free-running experiments have shown that subjects who are allowed to sleep at will typically split their sleep into a major period, which coincides with the circadian nadir in the middle of the night, and a minor period (nap) at the time of the circadian temperature peak in the midafternoon.

Most animals are polyphasic sleepers, and it has been speculated that at one time primitive humans may have had a similar sleep/wake pattern, perhaps because their fate was so closely tied to their ability to hunt animals for food. "Many of the animals you were going to be hunting had morning and evening activity [and] a midday downtime," Mary Carskadon comments, suggesting that this pattern might have been related to climate: "Humans evolved in a climate where it makes sense to get out of the midday sun." One can speculate that since it takes a lot of energy to be active during the hottest part of the day and since most of the animals weren't active at that time anyway, it made sense for humans to adopt a biphasic sleep/wake pattern that was efficient in terms of conserving energy and maximizing the hunt for food. "Probably the earlier gathering and hunting style would be more likely to be associated with polyphasic sleep," Broughton suggests.

Harvard sleep researcher Martin Moore-Ede has suggested that the development of monophasic sleep was an important step forward for humanity. While many mammals alternate periods of waking and sleeping throughout the day, humans and primates have the ability to sustain wakefulness all day and this might have been "one of the most significant evolutionary adaptations which permitted the development of the human intellect." He notes that it's difficult to envisage how we could have accomplished our creative and intellectual achievements without being able to "sustain concentrated thought uninterrupted by repeated bouts of sleep."

Dinges says it's difficult to say whether either the monophasic or the polyphasic sleep pattern can be considered "more natural" than the other in humans. "Both are possible. The monophasic pattern is powerful because if you don't sleep at all, you have a lot of trouble, so there is a strong requirement for at least one sleep period every 24 hours. But the sleep/wake system appears to be structured such that we can also obtain sleep in other ways and one of the ways we can obtain it is with a biphasic sleep pattern."

It's far less common to find humans who regularly sleep more than twice in every 24 hours, so it's more difficult to determine how well suited we are to a pattern of multiple short sleep episodes. Dinges says "there are apocryphal stories of people like Winston Churchill or Thomas Edison who ostensibly lived their lives in these napping regimes but they've never really been cleanly documented." There's also an anecdotal report that Leonardo da Vinci slept for only 15 minutes every 4 hours, for a total of 1½ hours in every 24. "There are all sorts of claims," says Dinges. These stories seem to imply that "great geniuses aren't subject to the same laws of biology the rest of us are, that they've discovered another way to sleep. I think it's true that inventors, scientists and artists are sometimes more likely to muck around with their sleep/wake system, and probably find that polyphasic or biphasic sleep works pretty well, but so do a lot of other people. I don't think there's anything special about genius and polyphasic sleep."

Broughton notes that many people have adapted to polyphasic patterns in the sleep lab. "There are many unusual schedules in the lab that people have been asked to follow. Most people adapt quite readily to very short naps." In some experiments, subjects have followed highly fragmented schedules; in one experiment, they followed a pattern of 7 minutes of sleep followed by 13 minutes awake every 20 minutes. In another, they were wakened from sleep after every minute and after every 4 minutes.

However, these studies did not examine the effects of these polyphasic sleep patterns on performance; therefore, there has been a lack of information about the feasibility of adopting ultrashort sleep/wake patterns in real work situations. This is one reason why Stampi's study of solo sailors is so interesting. He found that the sailors seemed to adjust quite readily to a highly fragmented polyphasic sleep schedule for periods of up to two months.

Stampi says there's also anecdotal evidence from one man who successfully followed a napping schedule — Leonardo da Vinci's purported regimen of 15 minutes of sleep every 4 hours — for 6 months. This man's experience brings to mind the infamous maxim about being careful what you wish for because you might get it. After a difficult first two weeks, he adapted to the schedule, didn't feel sleepy and had a lot of extra time. But after six months he suddenly quit — not, he told curious scientists, because he had any difficulty maintaining the schedule but because he found he had *too much* time on his hands."He was starting to feel alone," says Stampi. "When he was awake at night, he said, 'Why am I here? I don't need all this time.'" The man told Stampi that while da Vinci was obviously able to put the extra time to good use, "I am not so much a genius."

Stampi is among those who think that polyphasic sleep may be a natural ability that's masked in most people by the monophasic sleep pattern imposed by modern life. "It is too early to say we could substitute all our activities by a napping schedule. What I can say is that I believe human beings would not find it so difficult because we probably have this in our heritage. Most animal species have a fragmented sleep/wake pattern and we probably have in our biological heritage the capacity to return to a polyphasic sleep/work pattern."

## NAPS: HOW MANY, HOW LONG, AND WHEN?

We saw earlier that a reduced, continuous sleep period is better than no sleep at all. The same can be said of naps; even a single nap in a 24-hour period is an improvement over no sleep, although naps lasting only a few hours are rarely as recuperative as a full night's sleep. A nap's restorative power depends on several factors, including how long it is, when it occurs and how much sleep has been lost beforehand. The amount of time that elapses between the nap and the work period is also important, as is the nature of the work and when it occurs.

With these complexities in mind, a number of research groups are currently investigating napping strategies, addressing such questions as: Can naps be effective in maintaining high levels of alertness and performance during demanding continuous work situations? What is the shortest nap duration that can maintain or restore performance? What is the ideal nap duration? When should naps be taken and how often? Should they occur after a period of sleep loss, in order to *recover* alertness and function, or before a large sleep debt accumulates, in order to *prevent* the deterioration in mood and performance that sleep deprivation inevitably causes? How long after waking from a nap should someone be required to start working? Do these factors vary from person to person, and if so, can a sleep strategy be devised for each individual? How can these strategies be applied in the workplace, and how much will they cost? Under what work circumstances is napping appropriate and when is it not?

They hope the answers to these questions will one day allow napping strategies to be applied in the workplace, particularly in high-demand jobs where people are often required to work long hours, sometimes virtually continuously, over extended periods of time. As Broughton notes, it's usually precisely when normal sleep is most disrupted that the need for high levels of performance is most critical. Stampi says napping is a feasible and promising way to maintain efficiency in continuous work situations.

## NAP DURATION AND PERFORMANCE

How short can a nap be and still be recuperative? This is a critical question if practical napping strategies are to be devised for use in work situations, particularly those involving continuous operations or extended work periods when only brief periods can be set aside for sleeping.

There are many anecdotal tales about people who claim to be revitalized by very short naps. The most remarkable story, though perhaps apocryphal, concerns the artist Salvador Dali who, it is claimed, would fall asleep in a chair holding a spoon in his hand. The spoon would slip from his fingers and hit a tin plate that he'd placed beside the chair — and the resulting clatter would wake him up. Dali claimed to be revived by the amount of sleep he obtained in the moments it took the spoon to fall from his hand to the floor.

However, there's no scientific support for the idea that such incredibly brief sleep episodes have much restorative power. In fact, all the available evidence suggests that very frequent interruptions of sleep cause problems with alertness and waking performance. For instance:

• People suffering from sleep apnea experience hundreds of microwakes (arousals lasting a few seconds) each night because of breathing difficulties. As a result, they often have problems with severe daytime sleepiness. Similarly, people who suffer from restless legs syndrome and periodic leg movements at night suffer from fragmented sleep and increased daytime sleepiness.

• In a study of five sisters, three of whom had narcolepsy, Mortimer Mamelak found that the sleep of the three afflicted sisters was significantly more fragmented than that of their sisters and they all suffered from excessive daytime sleepiness.

• Patients who wake up unrefreshed and complaining of widespread, diffuse pain and chronic fatigue are believed to suffer from a sleep anomaly involving a state of arousal that persists throughout NREM sleep.

• The elderly, whose sleep is more fragmented than that of younger people, often have problems with excessive daytime sleepiness.

• People whose sleep has been frequently interrupted by aircraft overflights suffer a decline in daytime performance on a complex monitoring task.

One laboratory study also provides evidence that fragmenting naps reduces their recuperative power. Researchers at Henry Ford Hospital in Detroit, Michigan, gave a group of subjects naps of 15, 30, 60 and 120 minutes after they were initially sleep deprived. All the naps were uninterrupted except for the 120-minute nap, during which the first hour was undisturbed, but the second hour was interrupted by frequent arousals. The researchers found that all the naps lasting between 15 and 60 minutes increased alertness, but the 120-minute nap provided no further benefit, which indicates that fragmentation of the last hour of that nap had effectively halted its recuperative effect.

Mary Carskadon and William Dement and, more recently, Michael Bonnet of the Pettis Veterans Adminstration Hospital in Loma Linda, California, have advanced the theory that *continuity* of sleep is more important in restoring performance than the *amount* of sleep (or of specific sleep stages) obtained. In other words, interruptions of sleep take a greater toll on performance than reductions in total sleep, or reductions in slow wave sleep specifically. "Sleep continuity is the essential component in allowing sleep to be restorative," says Bonnet in a scientific paper co-authored with colleague Ralph Downey. They note that subjects who were frequently aroused during sleep became confused and disoriented, were unable to do simple tasks and at times reported being unable to understand English, even though they knew they were being spoken to and were required to respond.

Bonnet concludes from his studies that sleep periods must exceed 10 minutes in order to be restorative. For example, in one study, he and his colleagues found that patients with mild apnea who were able to sleep for uninterrupted periods of 20 to 85 minutes had far less trouble with daytime sleepiness than apneics with more severe conditions, who rarely got 10 minutes of sleep without interruption.

In other experiments, the researchers compared the performance of subjects whose sleep was frequently disrupted. First, the subjects were totally deprived of sleep for 64 hours and their performance was tested. Then they followed three different regimens. In the first case, their sleep over two nights was disrupted every minute. In the second case, it was disrupted every 10 minutes. In the third case, they were allowed to sleep undisturbed for 2½ hours and then kept awake the rest of the night.

Not surprisingly, those who went without sleep had the worst performance record doing an arithmetic problem. Those whose sleep was interrupted every minute did little better; after the second night, their impairment was similar to that of the sleep-deprived subjects. Those who got 2½ hours of uninterrupted sleep each night showed the least impairment. The performance of those whose sleep was disrupted every 10 minutes was intermediate between the 2½-hour and 1-minute groups — even though the subjects in the 10-minute group actually accumulated more total sleep time than those in the 2½-hour group.

In a follow-up experiment, Downey and Bonnet examined how rapidly performance deteriorated in these various conditions. They found that detrimental effects occurred early and grew very rapidly when sleep was disrupted every minute or every 10 minutes. For example, by the first night, those who were wakened every minute took three times as long as rested subjects to answer a simple addition question, while those who were wakened every 10 minutes actually took four times as long. But by the second night, the 1-minute group was taking more than seven times as long to answer the question, while the 10-minute group continued to take four times as long. The performance of the subjects who got 2½-hour naps was more stable; their response time was about twice that of the control group on the first night and only a little longer on the second night.

The researchers concluded that the sleep continuity theory best explained their results. From these and other studies they conducted, they also concluded that the drop in performance was caused by the disruption of sleep, not by differences in the total amount of sleep obtained, which were relatively minor between the different sleep conditions. Nor did differences in the amount of slow wave sleep obtained affect performance; subjects who were deprived of SWS did just as well as those who were not (an aspect that was examined because SWS is thought to be the most physiologically restorative stage of sleep). The researchers concluded that periodic, frequent disruptions of sleep represented the single most important factor in reducing its capacity to restore performance.

Bonnet has suggested that 10 minutes is the lower limit for sleep to be restorative, but some other studies suggest that uninterrupted sleep of as little as 3 to 5 minutes may also have some restorative effect. In one study, subjects who were were wakened every 4 minutes did not experience excessive daytime sleepiness, compared with subjects wakened every minute. Another study by the research group at Henry Ford Hospital suggests that the point at which sleep becomes so fragmented that it no longer sustains alertness "lies somewhere between 30 and 65 arousals per 90 minutes"(which amounts to one arousal approximately every 1½ to 3 minutes). They found that uninterrupted sleep episodes of 3 minutes had some restorative effect, while sleep episodes of 5 minutes were just as restorative as undisturbed sleep. The researchers say these findings must be viewed with caution because the sleep interruptions occurred during naps lasting only 100 minutes; the same results might not occur when sleep is interrupted with the same frequency throughout a full 8-hour sleep period. (Indeed, Bonnet's and Downey's experiments involved two full nights of sleep disruption and they showed impairment with disruptions less than 10 minutes apart.)

The Detroit researchers concluded that there's a direct, linear relationship between the rate of sleep fragmentation and daytime sleepiness, at least when sleep is interrupted every 1½ to 4½ minutes. "As the arousal rate increases, the restorative capacity of sleep is diminished." But whether this relationship holds over a full night's sleep is unknown, they said.

These experiments suggest that the absolute lower limit for sleep to be recuperative is perhaps about 5 minutes and more likely closer to 10. But these studies were concerned mainly with studying the effects of extreme fragmentation caused by sleep disorders. They do not necessarily tell us what would be the *best* nap length to use as a hedge against sleepiness and loss of performance in the workplace. Stampi says that scientists don't yet know the ideal duration of short sleep episodes, but his study of solo sailors suggests that naps might be most recuperative if they are fairly short. He speculates that each individual might have an ideal nap duration somewhere between about 10 minutes and 1½ hours.

## SHORT NAPPERS WIN RACES

In his study of sailors who participate in long-range solo races, Stampi found that his subjects, spurred on by their extremely competitive natures and the lure of large prizes, were highly motivated to find an efficient sleep strategy. For most of them, this involved "fragmenting their sleep to incredibly short durations" — in some cases, as little as 10 or 15 minutes at a time — for days and weeks on end.

He set out to discover whether there was a relationship between the degree of sleep fragmentation and race performance — in particular, whether those who took the shortest naps achieved better race results. Sleeping for short periods has obvious advantages because it permits a sailor to maintain course and monitor conditions more frequently. However, if sleep is reduced or disrupted too much to be restful, the resulting sleepiness and sleep inertia could have a negative effect on race performance that could more than offset the advantages of being on watch for longer periods of time.

During a long solo race, the demands on a sailor's energies, both physical and mental, are constant and relentless. In addition to handling the boat, competitors are continually assessing weather and sea conditions and revising their course to sustain maximum speed and gain a competitive edge over opponents. "And that's not even counting the storms and the risk of colliding with ships, which is quite high," said Stampi. "There is not much visibility and it's not easy for a big ship to see a very small sailing boat in the ocean." Under normal visibility conditions, a sailor should check the horizon every 15 minutes to prevent collisions. During sleep, the yacht may also go off course or its speed may not be optimal.

Today, Stampi says, the human being is the limiting factor in these races. The boats are constantly being upgraded with new technologies to increase speed and performance and the success of these efforts is reflected in race results: in 1960, Sir Francis Chichester took 38 days to win the first Observer Single-handed Transatlantic Race (OSTAR), while in 1984 it was won in 16 days. Unlike the yachts, however, human physiology cannot be technologically upgraded every year — it remains pretty much as it has been for millions of years.

In 1980, Stampi arranged to study the sleep patterns of 54 sailors participating in the 5,500-km (3,000-nautical-mile) OSTAR. He repeated the study in 1982 with 29 sailors in the 3,500-km (1,900 nautical miles) Round Britain Race (RBR) and again in 1983 with 16 sailors in the 8,000-km (4,300 nautical miles) Mini-Transit race (MT). The OSTAR and MT were solo races; the RBR involved crews of two. The OSTAR was nonstop, while the MT involved one stopover and the RBR four stopovers. The winner of the OSTAR — who was also the oldest competitor at 67 — completed the course in 17 days, compared with 49 days for the last-place finisher. The MT was won in 31 days, with the last competitor taking 40 days, and the best and worst times in the RBR were eight and 20 days respectively, excluding stopover times. The ages of the competitors ranged from 20 to 67 years, with most being in their 30s. Only four of the 99 subjects were women.

The subjects were interviewed before and after the race about their normal sleep patterns and any sleep problems they might have; they were also asked to describe the sleep patterns they planned to follow during the race and the pattern they actually adopted. Stampi said the interviewers were careful to avoid giving the subjects any advice about which sleep strategies to adopt. The racers were also asked to keep detailed sleep logs during the race, in which they were to record the exact moment when they began and ended each sleep period; or, if that wasn't possible, to write a daily summary estimating the minimum and maximum duration of their sleep periods and the total amount of sleep obtained every 24 hours.

During the race, Stampi daily collected satellite data on the position and speed of each yacht and this information was later compared with the subjects' reports of their sleep patterns. Race results, based on the speed of the yachts, were used as the measure of performance.

A clear relationship between nap duration and race performance emerged from these studies. "There was a very high correlation between shorter sleep episodes and race results," said Stampi. "The best results are obtained by those sleeping between 10 to 20 minutes and one hour. Then you have a big decrease in performance; if your sleep episode duration is three hours, that's too much."

In summary, he found that:

• Most of the sailors (e.g., two-thirds of the OSTAR competitors) adopted a sleep pattern involving naps of two hours or less. In fact, the most favored nap length was one hour, adopted by fully one-third of those who participated in the OSTAR. Nearly 17 percent of the competitors in all the races, including the winners, took much shorter naps of between 10 and 30 minutes.

• The most experienced and competitive sailors adopted the shorter nap times. Seven of the 10 sailors classified as the most experienced racers had mean nap times of 20 minutes to 1 hour. Stampi said that ability to use one's energy wisely is crucial to winning solo races, and this means adopting a sleep/wake strategy that maximizes performance. As sailors gain race experience, they learn by trial and error that they can reduce the length of their sleep periods and still perform well. "You learn you can adapt your body to sleep episodes that are shorter each time. The more you do races, the more you understand you can reduce your sleep duration."

The exact duration of the naps seemed to be very important to the yachtsmen, he said. Most of the sailors (who generally were able to wake up spontaneously at scheduled times without an alarm) tried to limit their nap length to the period of time that experience had taught them would most restore them and cause the least amount of drowsiness and impairment on waking up. In fact, they deliberately avoided sleeping for longer periods of time, even when conditions permitted, because this tended to produce unwanted drowsiness on awakening.

• Those who adopted the shortest nap times were the most successful. The best results were obtained by those who napped for 1 hour or less and there was a sharp drop in performance among sailors who took naps of more than 2 hours. Those who slept "normally" (i.e., 6 to 8 hours at night) were not successful competitors. These sailors either were not interested in race success or simply couldn't adjust to taking short naps, Stampi said.

• The sailors did not reduce the total amount of time they slept in every 24 hours by very much, compared with the amount of sleep they usually got at home. They averaged about 6.3 hours of sleep in every 24 hours, compared with about 7.5 hours at home. However, some individuals got as little as 3 hours of sleep in 24 hours, while quite a large number (28 percent in the OSTAR race) managed fully 8 hours of total sleep time (TST). However, the sailors who had a longer total sleep time did not perform well in the race; those who slept 6 hours or more showed a huge decrease in performance.

"The shortest TSTs predicted the best race performance results," Stampi said. Those who slept between 3 and 5½ hours performed the best, with the highest race speeds being obtained by those who slept for a total of 4½ hours in 24. (Relatively few actually slept for 4½ hours or less; nearly half of the individuals in this short-sleeping group slept 5 hours in every 24.) Stampi said about two-thirds of those in the group with TSTs of 5 hours or less were also those who took the shorter naps. Thus, he said, it is the combination of short total sleep time each day and the short duration of the individual naps that had the best effect on sailing performance.

Many of the sailors appeared to adapt quickly and easily to the napping pattern, even though most were not regular nappers at home. However, a few days of adjustment to the new sleep schedule were required, during which most of the sailors experienced greater fatigue than they did in the last few days of the race — even after they'd been sailing for more than 5,000 kilometers (2,700 nautical miles). Stampi found that a few of the sailors "trained" for several weeks before the race by taking several short naps each day. Most believed that such training is useful, but only 10 percent of the sailors found they could manage to do it during the busy precompetition period.

Nearly half of the sailors felt that the naps should be regularly timed and that sleep schedules should be followed closely, although only a quarter found they could actually do this at sea, because of the unpredictable demands of the race. Only a small number of the yachtsmen (about seven percent) said they followed no regular pattern of sleep duration or timing, but slept whenever they could.

Stampi concluded that for each individual there may a nap duration that is best — one that produces the maximum benefits in terms of recuperation from fatigue and improvement in performance and the least amount of sleep inertia. This appears to be a stable individual characteristic and adjusting one's sleep pattern to this "ideal" nap duration is important to ensure that the naps will have a restorative rather than a negative effect on performance.

Summing up the results of the study, he said that the sailors tried to satisfy their need to stay awake and on watch as much as possible not by greatly reducing their total amount of sleep but by fragmenting it. He suggests that people who can adapt to taking short naps between about 10 to 20 minutes and 1 hour may be able to maintain performance while sleeping for only about 4½ to 5½ hours in total every 24 hours. If they are highly motivated and/or under extreme work demands, such people may have little difficulty maintaining efficiency while following an ultrashort sleep/wake pattern for comparatively long periods of time.

Just how long an ultrashort sleep schedule can be followed is not known at present. Scientific opinion varies considerably. Angus, for example, says, "I think we're always talking about exceptional circumstances. Nobody is talking about napping for the rest of your life." Naitoh, on the other hand, does not find it inconceivable that a napping-only regime could be followed almost indefinitely. "If you continue on with short sleep periods replacing all the standard long sleep, perhaps our body adapts to that peculiar kind of sleep pattern." Stampi believes that his study of sailors indicates that ultrashort sleep schedules can certainly be followed for weeks and perhaps for months at a time, but he says it's still too early to say if polyphasic sleep could be followed for years or a lifetime. "For the very long term, monophasic sleep could be better."

## NAPPING AS A SUBSTITUTE FOR CONTINUOUS SLEEP

Nevertheless, the fact that the sailors who performed best were able to follow napping-only sleep patterns for up to two months without any apparent ill effects suggests that it may be possible to substitute napping for continuous sleep periods for extended periods of time — particularly in the high-demand work situations in which the ability to fragment sleep while maintaining performance would be most useful.

Naitoh says these observations represented a major breakthrough for sleep-management theory. For a long time, sleep researchers believed that sleep had to be continuous for a substantial period of time in order to be recuperative; therefore, sleep managers "were discouraged from recommending very short sleep to workers because fragmented sleep is believed to have little or no recuperative power."

However, the evidence for the restorative effects of multiple short naps on performance is still somewhat equivocal. For example, a number of studies have been done in which subjects who obtained a given amount of sleep in a continuous period were compared with subjects given the same amount of sleep distributed over several naps. Some found that the continuous sleepers did better than the nappers, others that the nappers did better, and still others that there were no significant differences in performance between the two groups. In a paper summarizing these findings, Bob Angus and his colleagues conclude that while both single and multiple naps can reverse the deterioration in performance caused by sleep loss, it is not yet clear whether one of these sleep patterns does so more effectively than the other. (It should be noted also that other factors come into play here — including the amount of prior sleep loss and the timing of the naps relative to the performance tests, which will be discussed later in this chapter.)

Stampi and Broughton recently started a series of laboratory studies comparing the effects of several different napping strategies. Volunteers were subjected to four different sleep patterns over periods of four days. In the first three experiments, subjects were allowed 4 hours of "anchor" sleep from 1:00 a.m. to 5:00 a.m. and another 4 hours of sleep in the form of naps distributed regularly throughout the remaining 20 hours of the day. In the first test, the naps were 80 minutes long; in the second, 50 minutes long and in the third, 20 minutes long. Between naps, the subjects did a battery of performance tests.

"In this study people are getting a fixed amount of reduced sleep at night, 4 hours, and then they take the rest of their sleep in naps of different durations at different times of day," Broughton said. "We want to find out whether one nap duration or one nap time, independent of whatever duration, has the greatest recuperative effect."

Stampi said it's not known whether anchor sleep is really needed; since the sailors in his study who did without long periods of continuous sleep ended their races in good shape, he speculates that a long single sleep episode each night can be dispensed with, at least for a while. To test this idea, in the final phase of the experiment, subjects were allowed only to nap for 12 days. The nap length was selected according to that which produced the best performance in the earlier three sessions. Between the four test sessions, the subjects left the sleep lab for two weeks and followed a normal sleep/wake pattern to "wash out" the effects of each of the experimental sleep patterns before starting the next round.

During the experiment, Stampi also investigated whether certain physiological and personality factors might help scientists determine ideal nap durations for individuals. The subjects were given the morningness/eveningness test and their circadian body temperature cycle was also monitored.

In the first series of tests, he found that the subjects performed best on the regimen involving anchor sleep plus 80-minute naps. Surprisingly, though, their performance was almost as good when they combined anchor sleep with 20-minute naps. The worst performance occurred on the anchor sleep/50-minute nap regimen. Stampi theorizes that this resulted from sleep-inertia effects; 50 minutes provided enough time to enter slow wave sleep but not enough time to return to lighter stages of sleep. During 20-minute naps, subjects rarely reached the slow wave sleep stage, and during 80-minute naps they were able to emerge from it into light sleep before awakening.

In the second phase of the test, Stampi had his subjects adopt a napping-only sleep pattern involving 20 minutes of sleep and 40 minutes of wakefulness every hour. Thus, they were technically allowed to sleep for a total of 8 hours in every 24; however, since they often found it difficult to fall asleep in 20 minutes, particularly during circadian peaks, they only got about 3½ to 4 hours of sleep on average each day. The first week on this regimen was difficult, Stampi said, but after that "surprisingly, they seemed to adapt and their overall performance seemed to be quite reasonable."

The subjects found that awakening from naps in the circadian troughs was extremely difficult, probably because of sleep inertia. Stampi said some of them devised an interesting strategy to cope with this — what he described as "anchor wakefulness." The subjects found that if they simply skipped the naps in the trough altogether, they were able to wake up more easily after the next nap.

Stampi chose to study the effects of 20-minute naps because the results from the first set of experiments involving 20-minute naps were unexpected and intriguing. But he acknowledges that a 20/40 minute sleep/wake pattern would not be feasible in the workplace. "The problem with the 20-minute condition is not the napping, but that you have a very limited wakefulness duration. Forty minutes is not enough for most types of jobs. It was a study of the lower limit of the scale."

However, he hopes this research will lead to "a practical strategy. The next studies will involve a combination of nap durations. We're preparing a methodology that allows us to decide for each individual which are the best times of day for an 80-minute nap, for a 50-minute nap and a 20-minute nap — or an average nap duration. So you may get two or three 80-minute naps, a number of 20s and so forth."

## CIRCADIAN TIMING AND LENGTH OF PRIOR SLEEP LOSS

The length of a nap isn't the only factor that determines its recuperative value. Factors such as circadian timing of the nap, the amount of prior sleep loss and the effects of sleep inertia are also significant, and they comprise a complex tangle of interacting variables that makes it difficult for scientists to offer a tidy nap "prescription" that can be applied in the workplace.

Take the question of circadian timing, for example. Is it better to have a nap during the midafternoon circadian trough? During the trough in the middle of the night? Or is better to nap during the circadian peaks in midmorning or early evening? Unfortunately, research results on this question have been somewhat contradictory.

Some studies have shown that naps taken during a circadian peak are more restorative than naps taken during a trough. For example, Naitoh and his colleagues found that a 2-hour nap taken during the rising phase of the circadian cycle (noon to 2:00 p.m.) was more recuperative than a 2-hour nap taken during the 4:00 a.m. to 6:00 a.m. trough, even though the afternoon nap followed a longer period of sleep-deprivation — i.e., 53 hours compared with only 45 hours of deprivation before the early-morning nap. Other researchers have also reported differences in performance apparently caused by the circadian timing of naps.

On the other hand, there are several studies that have shown no significant differences in performance attributable to the circadian placement of naps. For example, Angus and his colleagues have found that both evening and morning naps were of benefit following periods of sleep loss of 40 and 46 hours respectively, which implies that at least for this amount of sleep loss, the restorative effects of naps may override the influence of circadian differences. They also found that sleep inertia negatively affected performance immediately after both evening and morning naps. Studies by Dinges and his colleagues (discussed later) suggest that in sleep-deprived subjects, naps improve performance (but not mood) no matter when they are taken. Thus, the question of whether there is an optimum circadian timing for naps remains unresolved.

Further complication (as if it were needed) is provided by two other interrelated factors: the amount of prior sleep loss and the severity of sleep inertia. Dinges says that circadian ups and downs are much less obvious in subjects who are sleep deprived than in those who are well rested. "In our studies, we were interested in what happens when you only get a few hours' sleep or a nap during a prolonged period of wakefulness, so we had subjects in a severely sleep-deprived condition. In those cases, we have no evidence that the circadian phase of the nap makes any difference."

Many studies indicate that prior sleep loss is undoubtedly a critical variable affecting the restorative effects of naps. It has been shown, for example, that the longer subjects have been awake, the more recovery sleep they need to return their performance to the levels achieved when they are fully rested. One study found that if subjects were deprived of sleep for 48 hours, a 4-hour nap would restore performance. However, after 64 hours of sleep loss, they required a full 8 hours of recovery sleep. Another study found that 4 hours of sleep restored performance to 70 percent of normal levels in subjects who had been sleep deprived for 36 hours, but the same amount of sleep restored performance only to the 40 percent level in subjects who had been sleep deprived for 44 hours.

The researchers at DCIEM found that the amount of prior sleep loss has a bearing on how a nap will affect subsequent performance. Specifically, they say that when sleep loss is less severe, naps may serve to *maintain* performance and when it is more severe, naps may serve to *restore* performance. They compared two groups of subjects who were given naps after 40 hours and 46 hours of sleep loss. The first group was given a 2-hour nap between 10:00 p.m. and midnight as they were going into their second night of sleep deprivation. Usually, there would be a dramatic drop in performance during the circadian trough in the middle of the second night; however, in this case, the nap helped the subjects to perform tasks on the third day about as well as they had on the second day — at about 70 percent of their baseline performance at the start of the experiment. In comparison, the performance of subjects who did not receive the evening nap dropped to 40 percent of their starting performance levels. Thus, the nap *maintained* performance and prevented the major drop that would normally have occurred during the second night of sleep loss.

The second group of subjects were given a nap between 4:00 a.m. and 6:00 a.m. on the second night — after 46 hours without sleep and right in the middle of the circadian trough. Their performance had already started to drop by this time, as expected, and the nap restored performance to the levels of the previous day. Thus, it provided *recuperation*, even after performance had started to deteriorate during the circadian trough of the second night of sleep loss.

There's little doubt that napping helps sleep-deprived subjects maintain or improve their performance over what they can achieve if they get no sleep at all. However, Dinges cautions, "let's be quite clear that they were still significantly below their baseline performance. The nap helped performance — it kept it at 70 percent of baseline, relative to no sleep, where it went to 40 percent of baseline. So, yes, it helped considerably, but it didn't restore fully their ability to function." Nor do these naps appear to do much to restore mood, Dinges and his colleagues have found in their studies. Nevertheless, although longer or more frequent sleep periods appear to be necessary to produce optimal benefits, they say it is "striking" how much benefit can be derived from obtaining only 2 hours of sleep in more than two days of wakefulness.

## SLEEP INERTIA: THE DOWNSIDE OF NAPPING

As sleep loss accumulates, the probability of waking up from a nap with severe sleep inertia increases. This is because prolonged sleep loss causes subsequent sleep periods, including naps, to contain increased amounts of slow wave sleep. A dozen studies have shown that awakening from slow wave sleep causes impairment of a wide range of performance measures, including reaction time, vigilance, memory, sensory discrimination and arithmetical problem solving. Dinges notes that the worst drowsiness and confusion follow abrupt awakening from a short nap that occurs after a long period of prior wakefulness (i.e., in excess of 24 hours). How long the sleep inertia lasts depends on the actual amount of prior sleep loss, but performance can be degraded for anywhere from a few minutes to an hour or perhaps more.

Thus, napping can be a two-edged sword, and one of keys to developing an effective napping strategy is to find a sleep pattern that provides the maximum recuperation with the minimum amount of sleep inertia. This is especially important in situations involving multiple naps, because if each sleep episode is accompanied by a lengthy and/or severe bout of sleep inertia, this could completely cancel out the benefits of napping.

"If wakening can be relatively slow and there's no performance demand immediately on awakening, then sleep inertia is not a major issue," Dinges says. Unfortunately, however, in some work situations where napping might prove helpful, there's no guarantee that people will be able to wake up leisurely and get their act together before being required to work. Understandably, then, napping must be employed with caution in situations where someone might be required to cope with urgent work demands or an emergency immediately on awakening. For example, a five-day simulation of a moon mission conducted by researchers with the U.S. National Aeronautics and Space Administration found that subjects who were abruptly wakened did poorly on performance tasks for up to 12 minutes afterward.

Naitoh says that fighter pilots aboard aircraft carriers are not allowed to doze in the cockpits of their jets while on alert status or on standby duty. Even with commercial pilots on scheduled flights, if napping occurs "after a very heavy work schedule, if the guy is sleep deprived — you know, nodding on the take-off apron — that napping is very dangerous because when he wakes up, he's completely disoriented." He also said napping may not be appropriate for forest fire fighters who work almost continuously and often have to drive unstable four-wheel-drive vehicles over rough terrain. He cautions against napping in this case. "In many cases, they wake up and grab the gears and they always make a mistake and the vehicle tumbles."

Dinges argues that the best way to minimize the potentially damaging effects of sleep inertia during a period of sustained work is to "start napping early. Don't wait until you're so massively sleepy that the naps are basically short periods of incredibly deep sleep." In short, make a down payment on your sleep debt before it grows too large.

## PROPHYLACTIC NAPPING

Martin Orne, a colleague of Dinges, coined the term "prophylactic nap" to describe a nap taken in *advance* of a period of sustained work to prevent the buildup of sleepiness and the deterioration of performance caused by sleep loss. Based on a series of sleep-deprivation studies, these researchers have concluded that it's crucial to prevent or at least postpone the development of a sleep debt as long as possible. In one test, subjects were given a single 2-hour nap at one of five times during a 56-hour period in which they were not otherwise permitted to sleep. These naps occurred at 12-hour intervals and were preceded by periods of wakefulness lasting 6, 18, 30, 42 and 54 hours. Some naps occurred during the circadian peak, others during the trough.

The researchers found that the naps taken earlier in the experiment — after only 6 or 18 hours of wakefulness — had a stronger and more long-lasting positive effect on performance than naps taken after 30, 42 or 54 hours of wakefulness. Differences in performance between the early-nap and late-nap groups were substantial, and the benefits of the early naps extended beyond 24 hours after they occurred, even though they were shorter and consisted of lighter sleep than the later naps.

Although severe sleep inertia occurred after each of the naps in this study, when subjects were tested at least 20 minutes after they had awakened and started moving around, there was no longer any sign of the disorientation or confusion that often accompanies abrupt awakening from naps.

Although both early and late naps occurred at peaks and troughs in the circadian cycle, the circadian factor did not affect performance. The researchers concluded that "napping prior to a night of sleep loss is more important for meeting subsequent performance demands than is the circadian placement of the nap."

They found these results surprising and unexpected. The earlier naps contain lighter sleep than later naps (which have a greater amount of slow wave sleep because more sleep loss has accumulated), and sleep researchers have generally assumed that SWS sleep is more restorative than light sleep. Theoretically, then, the later naps should provide more benefit. However, the researchers say that while it might be generally true that slow wave sleep is more restorative than light sleep, the situation appears to be different when someone attempts to "pay off" a large SWS debt with only a short nap. In situations where someone has been sleep deprived for more than 24 hours and then gets only a short amount of recovery sleep, the accumulated slow wave sleep debt is not fully discharged by the nap and thus, longer and more severe sleep inertia occurs on awakening.

They conclude that warding off sleepiness or the accumulation of a sleep debt during prolonged work by napping early "is as beneficial as attempting to pay it off later by napping deeply." Napping during periods of prolonged sleep deprivation may serve to "prevent sleepiness more readily than it permits recovery from it."

This study also produced another particularly interesting finding: while a nap improved subjects' performance, it did not do much for mood. The two appeared to become decoupled, so that even though the subjects' ability to perform the tasks was better after the nap, they still reported feeling fatigued and sleepy, regardless of the timing of the naps. This suggests that self-reported measures of mood, and particularly measures of subjective sleepiness, are not very sensitive indicators of the effects of naps in situations involving sustained work (although why this should be the case is unclear). The implications of this for on-the-job monitoring of performance will be discussed later.

The researchers conclude that naps can help performance if someone must work for 24 hours or longer, even if the nap is taken early in the period of wakefulness, before a sleep debt has accumulated, and *"even if the subject is not aware of any benefit."*

Most people who find themselves in a situation involving prolonged, demanding work know that they can't go more than a couple of days without sleep, but they have a tendency to keep at it until they drop. If, instead, they plan their sleep ahead of time and take short early naps — even though they don't think they need to sleep that early — they may be able extend their staying power by at least several more days. "I think you should be concerned about how lousy you might feel, how many people you might offend because you feel lousy, but in terms of [working] you'll probably do okay," Angus says.

## STORING SLEEP

Scientists have long debated whether it's possible to "store" sleep — that is, to sleep in advance of a period of prolonged sleep loss in order to maintain performance during that period without having further sleep. Dinges says it appears that within a short time frame, sleep can to some extent be stored. His studies showed that an early nap, taken before the subjects are sleep deprived at all, helped performance more than 24 hours hours later. "You don't see the benefits of [the nap] until the subjects get into the sleep-deprivation zone. In other words, performance doesn't differ between that group and the no-nap group until after about 2:00 a.m. the following morning. It's sort of sitting on the shelf unused, at least according to the performance aspect of things, but then suddenly we start seeing the benefit hours later. So to that extent, sleep does seem to be stored. Within a 24-hour period, in my view, you can certainly can store sleep."

It seems less likely that oversleeping ahead of time can maintain performance for several days or longer without further sleep. A small number of the sailors in Stampi's study (about 7 percent) claimed to be capable of what he terms "sleep accumulation" — sleeping in excess ahead of time so they could later stay awake for three to four days without sleep. But this strategy did not produce the best race results; although three sailors classified as sleep accumulators did better than sailors who took naps lasting 2 to 3 hours, they did not do as well as those who took naps of 1 hour or less. However, there has been no laboratory verification that long-term sleep storage is possible, and Stampi's findings suggest, in any event, that it may be at best a rare talent.

Naitoh says it's probably not a good idea to take a longer-than-normal sleep period in anticipation of having to reduce sleep in the future. Such oversleeping may cause grogginess and reduction in performance on awakening (the "Rip Van Winkle effect"). But prophylactic napping is not the same thing as early oversleeping: "It's extra sleep away from major sleep periods. There's a time between major sleep and prophylactic napping and the time between is absolutely crucial."

In other words, the preferred method for maintaining performance throughout a period of extended sleep loss is not to sleep for 12 or more hours beforehand, but to take a short nap early in the work period and to continue taking naps periodically throughout it so that you never go too long without getting any sleep at all.

# CHAPTER 10

# CAUGHT NAPPING?

*A short sleep or nap on a work site enhances safety and productivity of workers under irregular or prolonged work schedules. Society should support new work ethics where yawning and sleeping at the work site are looked upon favorably.*

SLEEP RESEARCHER PAUL NAITOH

ALTHOUGH SCIENTISTS HAVE not yet resolved all the questions regarding the best nap strategies, their experiments have begun to provide some intriguing and instructive insights into the complex relationship between sleep and work and the role that napping may one day play in helping people in a wide range of occupations cope with chronic fatigue and sleepiness on the job.

In summary, the research to date suggests that:

• Napping can help to maintain or restore performance, especially when sustained high levels of performance are required at a time when there is little or no opportunity for normal nocturnal sleep.

• When faced with a high-demand workload, many people may be capable of substituting a series of short naps for single, long sleep episodes for relatively long periods of time (i.e., at least several weeks). However, it is not known how long an ultrashort sleep/wake schedule can be followed; some scientists think it is suitable primarily for acute periods of high-demand work while others think it could be carried on almost indefinitely.

• Naps as short as 10 minutes in length can have a restorative effect on performance. Naps of 2 hours or less may have the optimum positive effect, but more research is needed to establish this. In any event, optimum nap lengths probably differ from one person to the next, and techniques for assessing these individual differences are being developed.

• Naps should be taken before a large amount of sleep loss accumulates, in order to prevent a deterioration in performance and minimize the debilitating effects of sleep inertia. These early naps can have long-term positive effects on performance and may be more beneficial than naps taken after a substantial amount of sleep has been lost. However, even a late nap is better than no sleep at all, although allowance must be made for the effects of sleep inertia.

• Because of sleep inertia, napping should be used with caution in work situations where people may be faced with urgent and critical performance demands immediately on awakening. There are work situations in which the use of napping is not appropriate. Moreover, workplace napping, even if scheduled, may not be appropriate for people suffering from sleep disorders or other persistent sleep problems.

• It is uncertain whether the beneficial effect of a nap is influenced by the time of day it is taken (i.e., its placement in the circadian cycle).

· · · · · · ·

Translating these laboratory findings into the real work world may take some time. Much basic research remains to be done to understand the effects of napping on alertness and performance and particularly to devise economic and practical methods of implementing napping in the workplace. The types of performance measures used in many sleep-lab experiments often are not representative of real work situations. It must also be kept in mind that the negative effects of sleepiness and the positive effects of naps can be greatly influenced by the nature of the work involved. As the experiment described in Chapter 1 shows, tasks that are boring and repetitive become difficult or impossible to do much more quickly than tasks that are varied, interesting and intellectually challenging. In fact, some studies have shown that performance of stimulating tasks often shows no obvious impairment for up to 42 hours without sleep.

However, David Dinges and his colleagues argue that we can no longer afford to allow these complexities to prevent us from putting what we have learned to practical use. All humans get sleepy and eventually fall asleep: "this is an internally timed process that happens every day whether we consent to it or not," the researchers observe in one of their scientific papers. If we resist sleep, our ability to perform will invariably be affected, and no one can resist it indefinitely. Describing sleep as "perhaps the most pervasive behavioral control in nature," they say that sleepiness is among the most powerful factors influencing performance in sustained work situations, even when the people involved are highly skilled, dedicated and motivated.

These realities must be faced in a world increasingly dependent on people being able to function around the clock for indefinite periods of time, they contend. Sleep loss and chronobiological variability are "two of the most pervasive limitors of human ability. To ignore them is to court disaster."

Broughton says that sleep scientists hope their research will enable them to provide "rational guidelines" on sleep scheduling for those workers who can schedule their sleep. In some situations, people can't do this and are forced to sleep whenever they can, but in many cases, workers do have choices, and they should sleep as efficiently as possible. "Sleep will be most recuperative if it makes allowances for the underlying biological laws," he said. For example, we know that there are times of "privileged ability to sleep. If it's very unlikely that sleep will occur at a particular time of day, or even if it does occur, that it will have a significant effect on performance or well-being, why try and sleep then? There's no sense in trying to sleep at 8:00 p.m. when, in many people, the body just will not sleep."

Sleep researchers say it's even more important that employers and society develop new attitudes toward the relationship of sleep and work. "Some companies look at it very poorly if you nap on the job, even if it's a situation where napping may be advantageous to meet the performance demands of the job," says Broughton. Napping is regarded as a symptom of disinterest and lack of motivation or as an indication of a lack of productivity. "But in many situations where there's no immediate danger, if you have a nap it improves your performance later much more than trying to continuously fight against sleepiness."

Harvey Moldofsky comments that sleep doctors who in the past have tended to discourage daytime napping because of concerns about its effect on people with sleep disorders may have to start rethinking some of their views on the subject in light of recent research about the benefits of napping. "There might be a role for napping if we're going to deal with automation."

Paul Naitoh, who advocates the adoption of work-related sleep-management programs and the appointment of professional sleep managers, says it's important to distinguish between napping *on the job* (i.e., surreptitious, unapproved napping) and sleeping *at the work site* (i.e., planned, approved napping). "Sneaking in a nap is napping on the job," he says. "Sleeping openly is not sneaking a nap, it's napping at the work site." The former can cause problems; the latter can help to solve them. He believes that ultrashort sleep periods — naps of 5 to 10 minutes — can improve safety and increase productivity and are the most likely to find favor with managers, who will find it easier to approve brief naps taken right at the work site rather than naps of an hour or more taken somewhere away from the work site in the middle of the work period.

"Napping at the work site has to be encouraged and the company has to make a policy on this issue," according to Naitoh. But he says several important questions must be answered before such workplace napping can be implemented. For example, What is the optimum timing and length of naps for the type of work in question? How long will the performance benefits last? Should the naps be taken in chairs or on cots? Should cots be placed right in the work area or in a more secluded place? And — perhaps the thorniest question of all — who should decide when a worker needs a nap and by what means should this decision be made?

## MEASURING SLEEPINESS AND PERFORMANCE ON THE JOB

Perhaps one of the biggest potential stumbling blocks in introducing workplace napping concerns on-the-job monitoring of workers for sleepiness and performance. Someone must make decisions about when workers should take naps. Should it be the workers themselves? Should the decision be based on how sleepy they feel, or on how well they're doing their jobs? How do you determine how sleepy someone is and what effect that's having on performance?

We saw earlier that a distinction must be made between objective measures of sleepiness (i.e., how sleepy the brain is physiologically) and subjective measure of sleepiness (i.e., how sleepy people say they feel). These are not necessarily the same thing. In a stimulating environment, people may not behave as if they're sleepy, even though their brains may in fact be biologically very sleepy. Their true state of sleepiness can be masked by environmental/social factors and then suddenly manifest itself if the level of external stimulation drops.

Moreover, people may not always be able to judge accurately their ability to perform certain tasks based on their subjective feelings of sleepiness. Several studies have shown that when subjects are partially sleep deprived, their reports of how sleepy they feel do not correlate very well with how well they perform a variety of tasks. For example, Dinges and his colleagues found that subjects who received a 2-hour nap during a period of 54 hours of wakefulness did not report even brief improvements in mood or self-ratings of sleepiness after the nap. Dinges says this occurs because the nap does not fully restore the missed sleep. A 2-hour nap is only a small fraction of the time spent in wakefulness during the experiment (whereas sleep normally consumes roughly a third of a person's day), so it "pales in comparision to the on-going sleep debt. If you get 2 hours of sleep out of 54 hours, that's not enough and you feel awful."

The 2-hour nap *does* improve performance — *but the subjects are usually unaware of this.* In another study, these researchers measured eight different types of tasks and 24 aspects of self-reported mood and they found that the enhancement in performance after the nap was not reflected in any of the mood measures — and subjective sleepiness was among the least improved.

This situation is a complete reversal of what occurs with people who are *not* sleep deprived when they nap — that is, when they take naps *in addition* to regular sleep. In these cases, Dinges says, most of the research evidence indicates that mood is improved, but performance generally is not — possibly because performance hasn't been degraded because of sleep loss in the first place.

He adds that people suffering from sleep inertia are also poor judges of how well they're performing. "You report you're doing very well and in fact you're doing very poorly."

"Sleep-deprived individuals cannot be a good judge of performance; that's one of the dangerous things about sleep deprivation," Naitoh said. "There's not much awareness of how poorly they are performing, particularly under emergency conditions."

It should be noted that at least one study has shown a strong correlation between subjective sleepiness and performance on reaction time, vigilance and addition tasks in subjects who received a

2-hour nap during 40 hours of wakefulness. Nevertheless, it does appear open to question whether subjective feelings of sleepiness provide the best basis on which to make decisions about when workers should nap, because these feelings may not always reflect how well they're actually performing their work.

Clearly, objective measures would be better, but they pose some practical and economic problems. As Stampi says, "Subjective measures are easy to find; everybody has subjective measures. Objective measures are more complicated; you need tests, you need instruments." Objective tests can also be time-consuming and intrusive, which will not endear them to managers concerned about on-the-job productivity. This is the main reason that many sleep researchers have put such a premium on finding effective measures of sleepiness and performance that are short, simple, unobtrusive and that require minimal gadgetry. For example, a simple device worn around the wrist can be used to monitor hand movements. In many work situations, total inactivity of the hands can be taken as an indication that the person is asleep or close to it.

In some cases — for example, jobs that require the use of computers — the machine could be programmed to monitor performance and to administer periodic performance tests. There is also the possibility that in the future, physiological monitoring of brain waves, heart rate and other biological parameters could provide objective measures of a worker's state of alertness. Angus and his colleagues at DCIEM are studying how well these physiological measures correlate with performance. If a reliable relationship between these two sets of data can be established in the lab, then it should be possible to make only the physiological measurements in the field and use them to assess or predict the ability of someone to continue working. "If you get a strong correlation in the lab, then you feel reasonably happy when you go out in the field and get only the physiological measures back, that the information gives an indication of whether or not an operator is in good shape," Angus said. "When he falls asleep on the job, you can measure that, but you'd like to be able to have some kind of predictive power before that." The objective is to develop a way of predicting, on an individual basis, when people should nap and when they should wake up in order to maintain a certain level of efficiency on the job.

Angus says it should be technically feasible to develop a monitoring device in the form of a cap that could be worn on the head. "That would be almost ideal for on-the-job application, especially in the military where people are wearing protective devices on their heads anyway. All helmets could have a cloth liner with thin-film superconductors."

These superconductors would be used to measure not the brain's electrical activity, like an EEG, but its biomagnetic activity. Neural currents flowing through the brain produce magnetic fields. The signals are "quite small, but they are detectable," says Max Burbank, president of CTF Systems Inc., a British Columbia company that's developing a very sensitive measuring device in collaboration with psychology professor Hal Weinberg of Simon Fraser University. The device, called a SQUID (Superconducting Quantum Interference Detector) magnetometer, is "the magnetic analogue of electroencephalography," Burbank said.

There are two major objectives. The first is to design a helmetlike device capable of monitoring all magnetic brain activity simultaneously. This requires about 60 sensors positioned all around the head. The second is to design a device that can be used without special shielding against external magnetic signals. Because the brain's signals are so small and the outside environment is typically filled with competing magnetic "noise," the challenge is to develop sensors that "only see that activity very close to where the sensors are located," Burbank said. "You make an instrument that is very nearsighted, myopic." These two characteristics will greatly increase the potential for using this device in clinical and research programs and for evaluating and improving work performance. Part of the funding for the research has come from Transport Canada, the federal transportation department, which is interested in the possibility of using the SQUID technology to assess people studying to be air traffic controllers and to improve their training program.

"The instrument is used to establish which parts of the brain are used in the analysis of information," says Weinberg. In the case of an air traffic controller, "one of the questions that comes up is what parts of the brain are involved in processing the different kinds of information that controllers have to process and what the effects of different kinds of workloads are on this process." The researchers hope to be able to use SQUID to assess how the ATC training programs actually influence the trainees and how these programs might be improved.

It might even be possible to individually tailor the training, Weinberg said. "Different individuals approach the same thing in different ways. For example, let's say you have to have somebody do some tracking on a radar screen. There are particular parts of the brain that are involved in this tracking and by looking at the way in which [they] respond to tracking, we might get some understanding of how to best modify the training program so as to make it specific to a particular individual."

Weinberg acknowledges that it's possible some people might be wary of such brain monitoring, thinking it to be a kind of "Big Brother" situation, but he says this is not their intention. In fact, their goal is to "get some understanding of how to change the training so as to make it best fit the individual. Our approach is not to throw the individual out, but to modify the system so as to make the maximum capability of the talent that's available." He notes that about half the people taking ATC training flunk the course. "If we can reduce that, what we're actually doing is helping people get through the training program and become effective air traffic controllers. It's not monitoring them as they're doing their job; it's finding a way to help them become better air traffic controllers."

Weinberg said the SQUID device is even better than an EEG in determining whether someone is asleep or awake and says this technology has great potential in sleep research, particularly as it relates to work performance. He added that a primary objective of their study is "to see the way sleep deprivation and workload impact on an individual's capability to process information and to see whether you might identify the capability of different individuals with respect to their ability to withstand sleep deprivation or stresses related to workload."

Weinberg foresees the technology being applied in simulator training in many fields — aviation and nuclear plant operation are two candidates that immediately come to mind — and it's conceivable that biomagnetic helmets could even be used on the job in the future. However, a breakthrough in superconductivity is required before that can happen. The current technology is too cumbersome and expensive for use in the field because the superconductors must be cooled to extremely low temperatures using liquid helium. "Right now you need a room this size and a device that's like a big hair dryer on top of your head," Angus says. If the promised revolution in higher-temperature superconductors materializes, this is one technology that will benefit greatly from it.

. . . . . . .

Naitoh suggests that all these sleep studies will one day make it possible to develop a "computerized behavioral model" to administer a workplace sleep-management program. First, it would be necessary to establish a "minimum performance threshold" below which a worker's performance would no longer be considered acceptable. Next would be to apply what is known from napping studies about the predictable decline in performance that occurs with continuing partial sleep loss over a period of several days. Naps can then be scheduled to occur before the workers' performance is predicted to drop below the acceptable threshold. EEG measurements, as well as other physiological parameters such as eye movements, heart rate and mood measures would all form part of the data base that would be used to predict when napping should start.

Deciding when napping should end would involve other factors — not the least of which would be a sudden need to have the sleeping worker on the job. The recommended duration of the nap must also take into account a number of other factors. Individual differences in sleep habits and requirements must be considered — e.g., whether someone is naturally a short sleeper or a long sleeper or an owl or a lark. The amount of prior sleep loss is important: how long has it been since the last sleep period and how long did that sleep period last? Finally, the nature of the job itself must be factored in. The decision when to wake sleeping workers will be difficult and requires further research, Naitoh says.

But he concludes that judicious timing of naps should permit workers to stay above the threshold of acceptable performance almost indefinitely, even under conditions of continuing partial sleep loss.

## AUTOMATED PERFORMANCE MONITORING: A NEW LABOR/MANAGEMENT PROBLEM?

The greatest challenge in introducing such measures will be sociological, not technological. Dinges says that something like brain-wave monitoring might be particularly difficult to implement, primarily because many people won't stand for it. But he says that monitoring performance makes more sense anyway. "What matters on the job, ultimately, finally and inevitably, is performance, and it is performance that will be evaluated. I could see a computer system that monitors performance variability." Such a system could feed that information back to the worker — and also to the manager.

Automated feedback could also be used in vehicles, he says. "It's easy for me to see a situation where you get feedback from your automobile. It might say" (and here his voice takes on the monotone of HAL, the computer in the movie *2001*) "'Dave, you've strayed over the center line a couple of times and your speed is quite variable. I recommend that you stay over in your lane.'" It would even be possible in some cases for the machine to take corrective action without even bothering to discuss it with the human being. "It's the language part of machines that annoys most of us. We don't want the damned thing talking to us. But there isn't any reason why the computer couldn't just make the correction based on what you've done. Somebody's speeding, so what the microprocessor does is slow the vehicle."

Dinges acknowledges that many people will resist this, at least initially, but he believes it to be inevitable. "You have to look at it pragmatically. It doesn't matter what people think; there's no way to stop it. If there's anything we have learned after World War II, it's that you cannot stop the onslaught of technology. And you cannot stop the role of computers in interacting with people in the future." In any event, he thinks people will come around, as they did with microcomputers. "The plain truth is that people ultimately like it, once they see what it can do for them."

And yet, even if it's true that people will eventually "come around," there will likely be a difficult period of adjustment, just as there was with microcomputers. And much will depend on workers' perceptions of why performance monitoring is being done, how it is done and what the consequences will be. The introduction of microcomputers into offices in the 1970s caused most resentment among employees who felt they were being watched and controlled by a machine. Will they be any happier with a system in which they are monitored by a machine whose purpose is to tell them — or worse, to tell their boss — that they're too tired to do their job?

"It depends on the job," Stampi suggests. If workers are informed about the problems caused by sleep loss, and know that their ability to evaluate their own performance may not always be reliable, they might even be grateful to have an objective system of measuring performance that would tell them, "Go to bed before you do something wrong." Stampi believes this is more likely to be accepted in occupations where lives or public safety are involved than in situations where the system is intended primarily to increase worker productivity for the financial benefit of the employer. "If you're dealing with air traffic controllers who could endanger the lives of passengers, or nuclear power plant operators, they will be grateful to have something that will help them to evaluate whenever it's time to have a break."

Dinges agrees that automated performance monitoring will mainly be used in situations "where a human error can be catastrophic for both the worker and/or the industry" and says that it should be set up to help workers do their job better, not to punish them.

In fact, Stampi suggests that the monitoring system should not be arbitrary; instead, it should only suggest that it's time for the worker to get some sleep and allow the worker to make up his or her own mind whether to follow that advice. However, it's interesting to speculate whether legal problems might arise if a worker decided to stay on the job against the recommendation of the monitoring system and was thereafter involved in an accident that caused loss of life or property.

Dinges says that "behavioral impositions" are the kinds that workers resent most. They might even object to the implementation of a system of workplace napping, not because they have anything against napping, but because they object to their employers "telling them what to do when, or what's good for them. Do you want to be told when you should sleep and wake? Most people take the view that the boss can tell them what they do on the job, in terms of their work performance, but that's it." Thus, the issue of workplace napping will "become a bargaining chip, along with their dental plans and everything else."

This is one reason why automated monitoring of performance is most likely to occur first in situations where workers are under strong forms of management control, such as in the military and in industries closely regulated by the government. It's no coincidence that many of the studies on the application of ultrashort sleep/wake schedules have been funded by the military. "Much of the nap research has been driven by the military and the other institutions that would like to find out how capable their people will be in emergency situations," says Angus.

"They have captive audiences, so they can certainly do it," adds Dinges. He says governments are also willing to explore the use of automated performance monitoring in fields where public health or safety is at risk, such as nuclear power plant operations and air traffic control. "If automation makes any impact, it will come first in the federal sector."

But trying to introduce such a system into the private sector could create a host of new labor/management problems. There's bound to be resistance to the idea and even suspicion on the part of both employers and employees. Employers will be concerned about the costs of implementing workplace napping and the potential effects on worker productivity; workers will be concerned about increased on-the-job monitoring of performance and potential effects on pay, job security and promotions.

Introducing ultrashort sleep schedules in the workplace is not impossible; in Japan, scheduled napping among night-shift workers is already extensively practiced — perhaps not surprising in a culture in which workaholism is endemic. But it may take more time for these practices to gain widespread acceptance elsewhere in the industrial world. "I think it's too early," Broughton said. "People are just now getting interested in the recuperative effects of naps and the overall gains and losses of different schedules."

Alison Smiley, president of Human Factors North Inc., a Toronto company that does shift-work consulting, has recommended workplace napping, but she says the idea is often greeted with reluctance by both managers and workers. "There's a feeling that if you're sleeping you shouldn't be getting paid. It's okay to eat; we accept that that's a necessary function and we have to have food. But sleep — you ought to be able to grit your teeth and get through it."

Stampi agrees that introducing ultrashort sleep schedules into the workplace will "not be easy. I think it will take a long time before society will accept this because everything is so structured into the 9-to-5 schedule." Even the introduction of shift work has not changed the fundamental monophasic nature of our sleep/work pattern: "The 9-to-5 has been shifted to whatever — 10:00 p.m. to 4:00 a.m. — but the idea is still the same: a continuous period of work and another continuous period of sleep. Our system has been like that for ages, for thousands of years probably."

But Paul Naitoh says that many people who work irregular or long shifts are doing it "not because it is good for them but because it is good for society. The least a sleep manager can do is to make their work more bearable, safe and productive by proper sleep management."

Dinges comments that many human factors experts "worry about the quality of the seating and the instrument panels and these kinds of things" but pay virtually no attention to sleep management because they think nothing can be done about it. They tend to take the view that "people will just have to tough it out," he says. "But one thing we've learned is that you can't tough it out."

CHAPTER 11

# TOUGHING IT OUT

$$I$$
N 1987, HARVARD SLEEP RESEARCH-
er Martin Moore-Ede gave a speech at the founding conference of the
International Space University, an organization devoted to the even-
tual establishment of an international university "campus" aboard
a space station orbiting several hundred kilometers above the earth.
ISU is an ambitious project originally conceived by students and now
supported by governments, industries and universities around the
world, who envisage a time when space will be permanently inhabited
by humans living, working and learning up there as they do down
here on earth.

But space is not like earth; in fact, it could hardly be more hostile
to our survival. It's an environment the human body has never before
encountered in its entire evolutionary history, and Moore-Ede cau-
tioned his audience not to forget this in their quest to cross the new
frontier. He urged them to temper their enthusiasm with an awareness
that "the design specs of the most sophisticated piece of equipment
[the human being] are not intended for space flight. We must take
into account the overriding influence of design decisions made millions of years ago. Human error, human incapacity, is the limiting
factor, not technology."

It's true that space is an extreme environment that makes extraordinary demands on human physiology, but what Moore-Ede said can
just as easily be applied to much of what we do down here on earth.
Machines are designed for continuous operation, but the human body
"isn't designed like any piece of hardware," he says. It has a "periodic
feature; it's designed to be switched off at night — for 6 to 8 hours
continuously at night." Today, the work demands that millions impose
on themselves, or have imposed on them by economic necessity, often

213

exceed the "design tolerance" of our physiological sleep/wake system. The signs are everywhere:

• For economic or safety reasons, many industries and essential services operate around the clock; hospitals, nuclear power plants, fire and police departments don't simply shut down for the night. Moreover, many other types of businesses and services have adopted 24-hour operations to tap into the emerging overnight economy generated by the millions of consumers who are active between midnight and dawn. Recreation and entertainment industries, data-processing services, brokerage firms, grocery stores, even hairdressing salons now stay open all night.

• Many people work very long hours for days or weeks at a time. Work weeks of 60 to 100 hours are not uncommon and, in some cases, the people working these long hours — pilots, doctors and emergency workers, for example — hold the lives of other people in their hands. Often, these demanding workloads cannot be eased simply by assigning others to the job because a certain person, or a small group of people, may have critically needed skills or leadership responsibilities and thus may frequently be required to work unusually long hours to meet deadlines or cope with emergencies. Such was the case at the Kennedy Space Center during the month prior to the *Challenger* space shuttle accident, a period during which workers had to deal with numerous technical problems and an unprecedented spate of launch delays.

• Some jobs are monotonous and lacking in stimulation but still require high vigilance and sharp reactions, especially when an emergency occurs. Examples include monitoring automatic equipment in an industrial or power plant or in the cockpit of an aircraft. In other cases, the job requires workers to maintain for long periods of time the high level of alertness needed to respond to and cope with a steady diet of demanding but unpredictable crises. Examples include doctors and emergency-response workers, such as firefighters, police officers and ambulance attendants.

• Executives, managers and professionals are increasingly required to put in long hours on the job and to travel a great deal. Global communications and transportation systems — and the business they generate — not only permit people to work anytime, anywhere, but have spawned a work culture that requires them to do so to get ahead. The rapid development of technologies such as cellular phones, portable fax machines and laptop computers has made work hours more flexible for many, but they have also extended work hours and blurred the distinction between work and leisure. Many people almost literally cannot leave the office.

During the past decade, sleep problems in the workplace have become a matter of much greater concern to workers, employers and political leaders than they were two or three decades ago. Partly, this reflects increasing knowledge and awareness about the impact of sleep-related problems on health and performance, but there's more to it than that. David Dinges offers four major reasons for the growing concern:

• **Automation:** Sophisticated automated systems permit around-the-clock operation of complex industrial systems such as nuclear power stations and chemical and manufacturing plants, but monitoring these technical systems and being prepared to intervene when something goes wrong imposes onerous demands for vigilance and alertness on human workers. Unfortunately, continuous monitoring of automated equipment is one of the things the human brain does least well. Nothing puts the brain to sleep faster than watching machines do boring things.

• **Sleep loss:** Shift work, jet lag and chronic partial sleep deprivation are more widespread in today's working world. "We have many more people suffering from occupationally induced sleep loss than we used to have," says Dinges.

• **Sleep disorders:** Improved understanding and diagnosis of sleep disorders has created an awareness that "we have many more people with sleep disorders that affect daytime ability to function than we ever thought possible."

• **Consequences:** "This is possibly the most important one," says Dinges. "Because of the kinds of technology and materials we now deal with, the consequences of a human error are more severe now than they were 30 years ago." For example, an airplane crash in the 1950s might have killed perhaps 40 or 50 people; today, if a fully loaded jumbo jet goes down over a major city or collides with a similar aircraft, the death toll could easily exceed a thousand people. In the 1950s, a train derailment might involve the loss of a load of coal or sand; today, it could just as easily release a cloud of deadly chlorine gas or a flood of toxic chemicals. In the 1950s, an accident at a hydroelectric plant might electrocute a worker, shut down the plant and black out a city, "but you didn't kill millions of people," says Dinges. "You screw up at a nuclear power plant now and you risk a vapor cloud over major metropolitan areas. We live in a world where the margin of error is narrower."

In previous chapters, we saw that three major factors influence our state of alertness and our ability to perform on the job — the circadian cycle, sleep disorders and sleep loss. When it comes to shift work and jet lag, disruption of the circadian system plays a major role. In situations involving prolonged and/or continuous work, cumulative partial sleep loss is usually the major problem. However, in any given work situation, circadian factors and sleep deprivation can interact in complex ways and the existence of clinical sleep disorders will inevitably exacerbate the problem.

These work scenarios will be examined first and then will be applied more specifically to several different occupations in which sleep-related problems can have serious consequences for economic productivity and public health and safety.

## SLEEP DISORDERS AND WORK

Sleep disorders — most notably insomnia, apnea, narcolepsy and disorders of the sleep/wake schedule — are often a source of serious trouble on the job because they reduce alertness and ability to function during the work period. At best, workers suffering from these disorders may feel sleepy and slow-witted while working; at worst, they may be prone to falling asleep involuntarily on the job, even in critical situations. Moreover, these disorders not only affect job performance directly, but they can also have a devastating indirect effect by contributing to chronic psychological and emotional problems and by disrupting family and social life.

Chronic insomniacs and people suffering from delayed sleep phase syndrome often have trouble getting started in the morning; consequently, their job performance may suffer badly, particularly in the early part of the day. A study by Swiss sleep researcher Dietrich Schneider-Helmert found that chronic insomniacs did not perform as well in the morning as normal sleepers on a word test, an addition problem or a logical reasoning task. Later in the day, their performance improved, but they still reported feeling sleepier all day than did normal sleepers.

One study found that good sleepers tend to be busier, more active and more involved with other people and with work than insomniacs; they also tend to spend more time at work than insomniacs. However, another study (which used slightly different criteria for selecting insomniacs) found the opposite — that insomniacs spent more time at work and less time at home than good sleepers. This study also found that insomniacs reported thinking more about the present and less about the future than good sleepers and more about their families, work, illnesses and passive relaxation (i.e., watching TV), compared with good sleepers, whose thoughts focused more on their environment, general problems and active relaxation, such as sports activities.

As we saw in Chapter 5, the extreme sleep fragmentation caused by sleep apnea causes excessive daytime sleepiness that severely affects performance. However, sleep loss itself is not the only problem; when the apneic stops breathing during sleep, this causes a drop in blood oxygen levels, which reduces the amount of oxygen reaching the brain. A study by researchers at Yale University indicates that apneics may have significant problems during the day with attention, concentration and memory because of oxygen deprivation of the brain at night. On various performance tests, apneics performed significantly worse than two other groups — subjects who were normal sleepers *and* subjects with sleep disorders (other than apnea) that also cause excessive daytime sleepiness. Robert Watson, who headed the study, said that the performance deficits were of the kind that could interfere with activities like driving a car, operating a computer terminal or working on an assembly line. The subjects who had had apnea the longest showed the greatest deficit, which, he said, underscores the need for prompt diagnosis and treatment.

Fortunately, many apneics can now be successfully treated and, once their sleep quality improves, many are once again able to function well during the day. Increased efforts are being made to detect and treat the disorder. For example, scientists at the University of Wisconsin medical school recently embarked on a five-year program of screening 800 state employees for sleep-disordered breathing problems, including apnea. The study, the most elaborate examination of sleep-disordered breathing to date, is funded by a $6.5-million grant from the U.S. National Heart, Lung and Blood Institute; the purpose is to examine the prevalence of the problems, the risk factors involved and the health consequences, which can include high blood pressure, heart disease and psychological problems. It will involve overnight monitoring of each of the subjects in the sleep lab every 3½ years. The researchers expect the study to last beyond the initial five-year phase and they hope to develop ways of predicting who may be at risk for sleep-disordered breathing.

Narcolepsy can have an even more devastating effect on work and daily life than sleep apnea. The disorder, characterized not only by excessive daytime sleepiness but also by irresistible sleep attacks, cataplexy and hallucinations, can be much harder to control and it can seriously affect education, work, driving and recreation, according to Roger Broughton and colleagues in Japan and Czechoslovakia who did a "life-effects" survey of 180 narcoleptics in three countries. About four out of five of the narcoleptics were working at the time of the survey (compared with nearly everyone in a control sample of normal sleepers) but they attributed a higher incidence of job-related problems to their narcolepsy symptoms compared with normal sleepers who attributed similar work problems to daytime sleepiness.

For example, more than three-quarters of the working narcoleptics attributed reduced work performance to their symptoms and nearly half said their earnings were decreased. In comparison, only about nine percent of the working normal sleepers attributed reduced work performance to sleepiness and only slightly more than one percent felt that sleepiness had resulted in decreased earnings.

Nearly half of the working narcoleptics feared losing their jobs because of their disorder, while nearly eight out of 10 felt they'd been denied promotion. One-fifth of the total sample of narcoleptics said they'd actually been dismissed from a job because of their disorder. None of the normal sleepers attributed similar occupational problems to daytime sleepiness.

About 95 percent of the working narcoleptics said sleep attacks caused them problems on the job. About one-third or more also attributed job difficulties to poor concentration and poor memory, compared with only about nine and 11 percent of the working normal sleepers who reported similar problems caused by sleepiness. (In this and other studies, about half of narcoleptics report memory problems, mainly for recent events. They also experience amnesic episodes involving automatic behavior.)

Narcoleptics seem to be able to rally their resources to do short, stimulating tasks, but have great difficulty maintaining alertness while doing long, monotonous tasks, according to another study by Victoria

Valley and Roger Broughton at the University of Ottawa. However, the effort to fight off sleepiness even for short periods appears to exact a considerable toll; for example, two of the most drowsy narcoleptics in their study had cataplectic attacks immediately after doing the short tests.

The researchers noted that although some studies suggest narcoleptics might do best in a stimulating work environment, their results "imply that more moderate levels of stimulation and the ability to schedule breaks or naps might permit better overall levels of performance and feelings of well-being." This study also indicates that narcoleptics' subjective feelings of sleepiness do not correlate with how well they perform, a phenomenon that also occurs in people suffering from partial sleep loss.

In the studies done by Broughton and his Japanese and Czecho-slovakian colleagues, narcoleptics also reported more severe problems with interpersonal relationships and personality changes than normal sleepers. Narcoleptics told the researchers that they often assumed a placid and withdrawn emotional state to avoid cataplexy. "I now lack confidence. It makes life such a struggle," one patient wrote. Other narcoleptics said that people around them often refused to consider them ill and thought of them instead as being bored, lazy or drunk. Sometimes they told jokes deliberately to provoke cataleptic attacks (which frequently accompany laughter).

Mortimer Mamelak says that many narcoleptics "just drop out of work. A lot of them turn into shift workers. They can be alert at night perhaps easier than other people; they get a little nap and then they're alert for a while. And on the night shift, there aren't too many people around, so they can sleep longer." Unfortunately, however, shift work is bad for narcoleptics because it causes further fragmentation of their sleep and upset of their circadian rhythms, which aggravates their symptoms, as do jet lag and irregular sleep habits. In fact, disturbances of regular nightly sleep may play a role in precipitating the disorder, Broughton and Mamelak say. Researchers have found that narcolepsy is more likely to develop in people whose sleep is chronically disrupted by shift work or irregular sleep/wake schedules and some studies have shown that as many as half to three-quarters of narcoleptics have a history of severe sleep deprivation or irregular sleep habits, which often occurred many years before the onset of the disorder.

Narcoleptics reported a much higher incidence of occupational, household and driving accidents compared with the control group. Nearly half of the narcoleptics attributed accidents in the home or at work to their symptoms, compared with less than two percent of the normal sleepers who attributed accidents to sleepiness. These accidents are often quite serious. One patient fell asleep in the bathtub several times and nearly drowned. Another slid off a roof while repairing it.

Not surprisingly, the narcoleptics have major problems with driving. Less than half of the narcoleptics in the same study were still driving, compared with nearly two-thirds of those in the control group. Of the narcoleptics still driving, two-thirds reported falling asleep at the wheel (compared with only six percent of the drivers in the control group) and more than one-quarter reported experiencing cataplexy while driving. Two-thirds of the narcoleptic drivers reported frequent near-accidents (compared with none in the control group) and more than one-third said their symptoms actually led to an accident (compared with about five percent of normal sleepers who attributed accidents to sleepiness).

These figures may actually underestimate the incidence of these problems in North America because the sample included patients from Czechoslovakia, which has stringent laws prohibiting narcoleptics from driving. Most people diagnosed with the disorder there lose their licenses quickly.

A survey of patients with sleep disorders who were involved in traffic accidents, done by Michael Aldrich and his colleagues at the University of Michigan, suggests that narcoleptics are more prone than apneics to automobile accidents associated with sleepiness. They found that seven out of 17 narcoleptics studied (41 percent) had sleep-related accidents, compared with 12 out of 66 apneics studied (18 percent). The narcoleptics also reported an average of about 22 near-accidents, compared with an average of about seven reported by the apneics.

When they compared the sleep characteristics of narcoleptics who had had accidents with those who had not, they found that those who had accidents had significantly greater amounts of light (Stage 1) sleep and a greater tendency to have lowered blood oxygen levels during sleep. Other measurements indicated that narcoleptics who had had accidents experienced greater disruption of their nighttime sleep than those who hadn't. (Interestingly, the narcoleptics who had

not had accidents reported *higher* subjective levels of daytime sleepiness than those who'd had accidents; perhaps this caused them to be
more cautious about driving.)

The researchers concluded that narcoleptics whose nighttime sleep
is disrupted and who experience lowered blood oxygen levels at night
"appear to be at particularly high risk for involvement in sleepiness-
related automobile accidents and should be appropriately advised."
(They also noted that apneics who had accidents likewise had a
greater tendency toward disrupted sleep and low oxygen levels than
apneics who didn't have accidents.)

Once narcolepsy develops, these serious life effects and socio-economic problems are likely to persist, Broughton and his colleagues
concluded. The fact that there were relatively few differences in the
incidence of work and education problems and accidents associated
with narcolepsy in three widely separate geographic regions suggests
that these life effects are integral aspects of the disease and not
attributable to cultural or genetic differences. This is reinforced by
the finding that factors such as age, sex, duration of the condition and
the presence or absence of treatment did not significantly affect the
results, the researchers say. Traditional drug treatments for narcolepsy may help alleviate the symptoms and provide some improvement in the quality of life, but excessive daytime sleepiness is
extremely stubborn in narcoleptics and the treatments "certainly do
not normalize them in any sense of the word."

Another study by some of these researchers found that people
suffering from idiopathic hypersomnia experience very similar life
effects and socio-economic problems.

· · · · · · ·

These studies show that the direct effects of sleep disorders on daily
life can be quite devastating, but the secondary effects — psychological problems, marital and family disruption — can be equally bad and
these may have an indirect negative effect on work performance.
Some studies have shown that the effort to perform adequately at
work often wears these people out so much that they have few
resources left to deal with their families or a social life. "It's stressful
to strive to perform as well as before the sleep problems started," says
Schneider-Helmert, who suggests that the hypochondria and depression commonly found in insomniacs may be more a consequence of

their sleep problems than the cause of them. He notes that chronic insomniacs usually feel so exhausted after work that they give up on leisure activities and social engagements.

Similar findings came from a study of apneics and their wives by Rosalind Cartwright and Sara Knight, researchers at Chicago's Rush-Prestbyterian-St. Luke's Medical Center, who suggest that for apneics, marriage is usually an added burden, not a source of support. They found that both the women and the men in their study expressed the greatest dissatisfaction with marriage and family relationships and the least dissatisfaction with their work. They concluded that while apneics seem to derive satisfaction from their work, they have little energy left over to cope with marital and family responsibilities, especially child-rearing.

By the time they're seen in a sleep clinic, many apneics no longer share a bed with their partners and their social and family life has been severely curtailed because of their inability to stay awake in the evening. In a study of 10 wives of apneics, Cartwright and Knight found that these women reacted to their husbands' snoring and chronic daytime sleepiness with anger, disappointment, loneliness, frustration and irritation. They were unhappy with the marital relationship, the lack of time spent together in social and leisure activities, the lack of joint problem-solving and poor emotional communication. Child-rearing was a source of major dissatisfaction for the wives. The husbands in the study expressed similar dissatisfactions, particularly with the family unit and with their role as parents. Those who were still married were more exhausted, depressed and socially isolated than those who were divorced.

The researchers suggest that a support group is needed for the spouses of apneics, along the lines of the Al-Anon group that helps relatives of alcoholics. Apnea, they say, "creates extended stress on the marital and family unit, interfering as it does with both shared social and sleeping arrangements. The attendant marriage problems need to be recognized while the patient's sleep disorder is being brought under control."

## I. Shift Work: Circadian Chaos

It's difficult to determine exactly how many people today work shifts, but sleep researchers typically cite a figure of roughly one-fifth to one-quarter of all workers in the industrialized world. According to a 1985 survey by the U.S. Department of Labor, about 16 percent of the American work force — an estimated 11.6 million people — were working shifts, but other estimates have ranged as high as 20 to 30 million people, depending on how shift work is defined.

Shift work has existed in some form for much of human history; soldiers and sailors, for example, have had to stand night watch for centuries. But its wholesale introduction into industry and business occurred only a little more than a century ago and was made possible in large part by (of course) Thomas Edison's invention of the light bulb. Until that time, workers labored only during daylight, although the workday could extend to 14 hours during the summer.

Industrialists soon realized, however, that productivity and profits could be increased by running their plants around the clock. This was especially true in capital-intensive operations, such as iron foundries and steel mills, where repeated shutting down and starting up of the equipment is inefficient and expensive. By the late 1800s, such industries were commonly running 24 hours a day, seven days a week, usually on 12-hour shifts. In the early 1900s, Henry Ford introduced shift work into the auto industry and during the First and Second World Wars, many more people joined the ranks of shift workers to support the war effort.

After the end of the Second World War, shift work grew at a rate of nearly one percent a year, and today, 24-hour operations are commonplace not only in the steel and auto industries, but in the chemical, paper, aerospace, energy, plastics and food industries and in the manufacturing of a wide range of consumer products. The cost of the automated equipment in these plants is so great that industries cannot afford to run them for only 40 hours a week (which amounts to only about one-quarter of the 168 hours available each week). "Generally speaking, shift work is a great advantage to employers who need to match production with demand, accommodate the nature of certain production processes and reduce the cost of capital per employee," notes Earl Mellor, an economist with the U.S. Bureau of Labor Statistics. "However . . . shift work often does not benefit workers or their families."

Nevertheless, "shift work's not going to go away," says Moore-Ede. "The more automated we get, the more locked into it we are. Facilities requiring people to work around the clock are not going to go away; in fact, it's growing rather rapidly right now and we're a long way off from people not being needed. It's going to be quite a number of years before we can truly have automated factories, so we've got to use people for the next 20 or 30 years."

In addition, a number of service industries also depend on extensive shift work. In the past, these consisted mostly of essential services, such as hospitals, police and fire departments and other emergency services and the transportation industry. According to the 1985 survey by the U.S. Bureau of Labor Statistics, the people most likely to be working shifts were in protective services (61 percent), food services (43 percent) and health services (36 percent). About one-quarter of laborers, fabricators and people in retail sales were shift workers and 10 percent or less of those in managerial, professional, administrative support and clerical jobs were on shifts.

Recently, there has been an increasing trend toward 24-hour operations in consumer-oriented services, such as grocery stores, radio stations, bars and nightclubs, brokerage firms, postal and courier operations — even hairdressing salons. Even some traditional 9-to-5 white-collar activities are going on a 24-hour schedule; for example, intensive data-processing operations are increasingly being done overnight to maximize the use of expensive mainframe computers.

This trend reflects the growing economic impact of the millions of people who are awake and in the mood to do business at all hours of the day and night. "It's a 24-hour world," agrees Dinges — although he says there's a "lovely kind of irony" in the fact that the U.S. Post Office in Philadelphia and the Philadelphia Stock Exchange announced they were going to around-the-clock operations on the very day that the nearby Peach Bottom nuclear reactor was shut down by the U.S. Nuclear Regulatory Commission because its operators had been found asleep on the job.

Clearly, economics has been the prime driver behind the introduction and growth of shift work in industrialized societies; the objective is to run businesses as efficiently, productively and profitably as possible. But what many people have failed to appreciate until quite recently is that shift-work schedules introduced without regard to the realities of human physiology have many hidden costs, including worker dissatisfaction, health problems and disability, absenteeism, excessive overtime, morale problems and family and marital difficulties. Moreover, lack of alertness on the job caused by sleep loss and circadian disturbances — both of which are inherent features of shift work — reduces productivity and the quality of the product, increases the chances of operator error, reduces safety and results in expensive accidents.

These problems would exist to some extent with any kind of shift work, but many of the schedules in use today are particularly bad, having been handed down from earlier times when the scientific understanding of circadian factors was scant and confined, such as it was, to academic circles. Richard Coleman comments in his book *Wide Awake at 3 a.m.* that in most of the companies he has examined, the shift-work schedule was not designed specifically for that company by anyone who actually works there, but had either been copied from another operation or inherited from generation to generation with scarcely a second thought.

Coleman is one of a number of sleep researchers who now offer consulting services on shift-work scheduling. Two firms in the Boston area — Circadian Technologies Inc., headed by Moore-Ede, and the Center for Design of Industrial Schedules, headed by Charles Czeisler of Brigham and Women's Hospital — have also been extensively involved in redesigning shift-work schedules in accordance with circadian principles. In Canada, sleep and shift-work consulting are done by Jon Shearer and Associates of Ottawa and Human Factors North Inc. of Toronto, headed by Alison Smiley. Scores of companies and institutions have used chronobiological consultants, including police forces, hospitals and health-care workers, athletes, utilities, corporations, government agencies and professional associations.

## SHIFT WORK DISRUPTS CIRCADIAN RHYTHMS

The major problem with shift work is that it's a remarkably efficient device for scrambling circadian rhythms, notably the sleep/wake cycle. In fact, many of the most common shift-work schedules could not do a better job of this if they'd been deliberately designed for the purpose. Two of their worst features are weekly rotation and phase advancement — that is, rotation in a counterclockwise direction (e.g., from day shift to night shift to evening shift).

Rotation of shifts on a weekly basis is extremely disruptive. Because it takes the circadian sleep/wake system a minimum of several days to adjust to an 8-hour schedule change, it barely gets a chance to settle down when another change is forced on it. This process, repeated month after month, year after year, guarantees virtually continuous disturbance of the circadian system. Typically there's only two or three days off between shift changes (and sometimes only one) and workers often revert to a normal daytime sleep/wake pattern during these breaks, which further exacerbates desynchronization of their circadian systems.

The fact that such large time shifts are involved is an added complication. The circadian system can readily adjust to a change of only an hour or two a day; a sudden 8-hour shift produces about as much circadian disturbance as flying from the middle of North America to Europe. No wonder this phenomenon has been dubbed "blue-collar jet lag." In fact, working a week of days, a week of nights and a week of evening shifts is comparable to taking a whirlwind tour around the world in three weeks — but without the pleasures of visiting London or Tokyo or Rio.

To make matters worse, shifts often rotate in a counterclockwise direction — a phase-*advance* situation that works against the natural propensity of the human circadian system toward phase *delay*. To expect shift workers to advance their clocks by 8 hours every week is a prescription for chronic circadian chaos.

It's not surprising, then, that more than 60 percent of people who work shifts complain of sleep disturbances, compared with about 20 percent of regular day workers. Problems with insomnia, chronic fatigue and sleepiness on the job are common occupational hazards, particularly for people on night shifts. When workers first go on the night shift after being on days, they usually have trouble staying awake during the circadian trough in the middle of the night. Their biological clocks say it's time to be asleep and, all too often, that's precisely what they are. Swedish researchers who took EEG readings on shift workers at a paper mill over a 48-hour period found that one-fifth of them fell asleep, mostly involuntarily, between about 2:00 and 4:00 a.m. for an average of about three-quarters of an hour. These naps were taken sitting up in chairs and were described by the workers as "dozing off," although the EEG readings indicated that their sleep contained a substantial amount (32 percent) of deep sleep. These naps coincided with periods of decreased workload, times when workers gave high ratings of work monotony and subjective sleepiness. The researchers concluded that the sleepiness was caused primarily by circadian factors and that "sleepiness during night work often reaches a level where reasonable wakefulness cannot be maintained."

In a laboratory study, researchers at Deaconess Hospital in St. Louis, Missouri, used the Multiple Sleep Latency Test to measure the sleepiness of subjects who followed a simulated night-shift schedule. They found the subjects to be profoundly sleepy between 2:00 and 7:00 a.m., particularly on the first two or three nights of the shift, no matter how much sleep they'd got before the shift or whether they'd taken sleeping pills to help them sleep. Subjects in their 20s overcame the sleepiness a night or two sooner than the middle-aged subjects.

When night workers get off their shift in the morning, they have exactly the opposite problem: just as it's time for them to go to bed, their circadian system is climbing toward its daytime peak of alertness and is not the least inclined to let them sleep. (Jon Shearer suggested to one policeman that he delay his sleep period from morning to afternoon after a night shift. The man now spends mornings on the golf course and reports a marked improvement in his sleep.) To further complicate matters, they also have to deal with higher levels of light and noise during the day, and perhaps also with disturbances caused by family members. Family and social responsibilities and the normal routine chores of day-to-day living also cut into the time allowed for sleeping during the day. Studies indicate that most shift workers average only about 5 to 6 hours of sleep during the day, unless they stay on their shifts for longer than a week at a time.

The researchers at Deaconess Hospital investigated whether sleeping pills help night-shift workers sleep better during the day. In their laboratory study using a simulated night-shift schedule, they found that the use of sleeping pills did increase daytime sleep by about 50 minutes on average. However, this extra sleep did not improve alertness on the job; the subjects were still very sleepy in the middle of the night. The researchers concluded that shift workers might find it helpful to take a sleeping pill for the first day or two after a shift change and this might help improve the quality of their time off; however, they added that taking an evening nap might be just as beneficial.

Moving from the evening shift to the day shift also causes trouble for the circadian system. Evening workers are awake at the time (e.g., 10:00 or 11:00 p.m.) when most day workers normally go to sleep;

they go to bed later, about 2:00 or 3:00 a.m., and wake up later (about midmorning) than regular day workers. But when they move to the day shift, suddenly they need to advance their sleep period to 11:00 p.m. and get up at 7:00 a.m. This is very difficult — it's like asking someone who works regular days to go to sleep at 8:00 p.m.

In fact, shift workers in this situation face exactly the same problem as someone who has delayed sleep phase syndrome. As we saw previously, it's virtually impossible for people with DSPS to advance their sleep period in a counterclockwise direction to, say, 11:00 p.m. from 3:00 a.m. People with DSPS are regarded as having a sleep disorder, and doctors go to elaborate lengths to correct their sleep/wake cycle by delaying their sleep periods in a clockwise direction — and yet, every day, millions of workers are forced into precisely the same dilemma by shift schedules that rotate in a counterclockwise direction.

In rare cases, shift workers encounter a sleep/work schedule not based on the 24-hour day at all. One notable example is an 18-hour schedule followed by men on board U.S. Navy nuclear submarines. Most submarines operate with three watch sections, so that each man is on watch for 6 hours and off duty for 12. A Navy spokesman said the reason for this is that "there's only a limited number of spaces for crew on board and it just works out that 6 hours of work, 6 hours of sleep and 6 hours of training, study and free time becomes a do-able schedule." He added that "at one time studies were done to try find out if there were detrimental effects, and to my knowledge no detrimental effects were ever demonstrated."

Nevertheless, sleep researchers believe that an 18-hour "day" can cause circadian desynchronization. Moore-Ede and his colleagues have commented that the high turnover rate among submariners is indicative of the stress this schedule causes; as many as one-third to one-half of the crew leave after each 90-day tour of duty and only a small number last for more than two or three tours. This means that a substantial proportion of each crew consists of new trainees working on a schedule that disrupts their sleep — clearly a cause for concern when, as Moore-Ede points out, these are men with "fingers directly on the nuclear button."

Of all the shifts, afternoons or evenings are perhaps the best from a strictly circadian point of view. Workers may not get to sleep until late, perhaps around 2:00 or 3:00 a.m., but they can also sleep late in the morning. And since there's a circadian peak in the early evening, they're likely to feel quite alert on the job, at least during the early part of their shift. However, afternoon or evening shifts are not popular with workers because they usually have a terribly disruptive effect on family and social life. "Night shift kills the body; afternoon shift kills the family," says Shearer.

Permanent assignment to one shift would overcome some of these problems, but few people like working nights all the time. In any event, such a schedule wouldn't cause circadian problems to disappear; evening and night workers have a tendency to adopt a "normal" sleep/wake schedule on days off and holidays, which is another source of circadian desynchronization and problems with alertness on the job.

It's natural for shift workers to want to spend time with family and friends on days off and holidays, but, with their sleep/wake system in disarray, they often cannot enjoy these breaks because they lack the energy and enthusiasm to participate in social activities. "Shift work turns you into a couch potato very quickly," says Jon Shearer. "You don't have the energy to talk to the people you love. Children suffer; spouses suffer." In fact, many shift workers spend a good portion of their time off trying to make up for lost sleep. For example, a surgical nurse who works nine nights in a row and then gets five days off says she usually spends the first two days off just catching up on her sleep. She's thinking about looking for another job to escape the night work. Smiley says that shift workers should work fewer hours than day workers because "they spend a lot of time off recovering from the effects of the shift" — but, in fact, shift workers usually work longer hours.

Another major health consequence of shift work is an increase in digestive problems, particularly among night workers who often eat at a time when the circadian system has turned off the digestive juices for the night. The fact that they frequently eat junk food washed down with coffee or caffeine-containing soft drinks doesn't help matters any. The excessive caffeine further disrupts sleep and bad eating habits can lead to stomach and gastrointestinal problems. Moore-Ede notes that shift workers are more prone than day workers to ulcers and constipation and they are also vulnerable to obesity because they eat both during the day and at night.

He says the worst medical problems occur in workers who cannot afford to switch to day jobs for financial reasons. Cardiovascular problems may develop after years on shift work — people whose schedules are extremely disruptive are more prone to heart attacks than day workers — and conditions like diabetes and epilepsy may get out of control when someone leads an irregular life.

It's not known whether shift work actually shortens lives in humans. Some animal studies suggest that long-term exposure to rotating schedules reduces lifespan, but it's difficult to translate these studies into human terms because, unlike experimental animals, humans who find shift work intolerable can choose to get out. One study comparing 4,000 shift workers with 4,000 day workers and 500 former shift workers found no significant differences in mortality over a 10-year period; however, it should be kept in mind that a number of people in this study had voluntarily left shift work for medical reasons. If they'd had to remain, perhaps the results would have been different.

## SHIFT WORK, SLEEP LOSS AND PERFORMANCE

Mismatches between the circadian cycle and the external world are most severe during the first few days on a new shift schedule, because the biological clocks are still set to the old schedule. Weekly rotation, especially in the counterclockwise direction, makes it virtually impossible for the circadian system ever to synchronize properly with the external world. The result is that shift workers often do not get enough sleep; one study found that only 15 percent of night-shift workers got 7 to 8 hours of sleep, compared with 50 percent of regular day workers. Furthermore, what sleep shift workers do get is often not very restful; these problems increase the temptation to use alcohol or sleeping pills as sedatives, but of course this only makes matters worse.

In many cases, these problems are further exacerbated by overtime and irregular shift schedules caused by having to cover for ill or vacationing co-workers or to respond to sudden emergencies. Coleman estimates that shift workers work an average of 400 more hours a year than day workers — equivalent to 10 extra 40-hour work weeks. Two occupations particularly prone to these problems are nursing and police work. Dinges says that nursing has "one of the most chaotic systems imaginable . . . virtually every kind of shift you can imagine." The long working hours and lack of control over shift schedules are often cited by hospital nurses as a major source of discontent and they have contributed to increasingly militant labor union actions. Paula Greenwood Callens, president of a nurses' union local in Toronto, says that although she loves her work, she hates night shifts. "I don't know anybody who doesn't. The scheduling is awful." Her complaint is echoed by many nurses. When columnist Ann Landers printed a letter from a nurse who signed it "Tired and Disgusted," she received a flood of mail from other nurses all over the country voicing similar complaints. A 1988 survey of job-related stress among health-care professionals found that nurses reported greater levels of stress than doctors and pharmacists.

Nurses also complain of overwork because of cutbacks in the number of nursing assistants and orderlies; for example, one nurse said she'd spent most of her afternoon shift moving furniture because there are no longer any orderlies on the floor during that shift. These problems, along with complaints about pay and lack of decision-making authority, are causing nurses to leave the profession in droves. The numbers graduating from nursing schools are also down. As a result, hospitals all over North America are facing a severe shortage of nursing staff, which has been particularly felt in emergency rooms and critical care wards, and have taken to hunting far afield; for example, U.S. hospitals have been recruiting in Canada and Canadian hospitals are going to Britain.

· · · · · · ·

Because many shift workers are chronically sleep deprived, they experience even higher levels of sleepiness at work than would be expected as a result of circadian factors alone. Certainly it's clear that shift workers have a much harder time than regular day workers staying awake on the job. In a study done with William Dement, Richard Coleman compared episodes of falling asleep at work among 907 workers at eight industrial plants (manufacturing, utility, petro-chemical, oil and paper companies). Seven of the plants had shift schedules and one operated on straight days. The researchers found that on average, more than half of the shift workers reported falling asleep on the night shift and about one-fifth reported falling asleep on day and evening shifts. This is compared with only eight percent of permanent day workers who reported falling asleep at work. Thus, it appears that poor adaptation of the circadian system to rotating schedules causes excessive sleepiness on all shifts, but especially on the night shift.

This study also provided some interesting insights into the debilitating effects of rapid shift rotation in a counterclockwise direction. In one plant where workers remained on a shift for three months at a time, the incidence of falling asleep during the day and evening shifts (11 and 16 percent respectively) was lower than in plants with a weekly rotation rate; however, 59 percent of the night workers reported falling asleep on the job, even when they rotated only every three months — a higher rate than for some of the other plants on weekly rotation schedules. Sleep diaries revealed that these night workers reverted to a regular sleep/wake schedule on days off, which disrupted their circadian cycles.

In plants that followed a phase-delay schedule (days to evenings to nights), workers on day and evening shifts reported a much lower incidence of falling asleep on the job than workers in plants who followed phase-advance schedules (days to nights to evenings). Again, the incidence of falling asleep was higher among night workers in both cases, but less of a problem in a phase-delay schedule than in a phase-advance schedule.

In another study of schedules at an electrical utility company, Coleman found that 60 percent of the employees fell asleep on the job at least once a week, that 69 percent believed the shift schedule impaired their work performance and that 36 percent took sick days in order to cope with fatigue. Half of the supervisors said they'd observed operating errors or near accidents that were attributable to worker fatigue.

As we saw in Chapter 4, performance during the circadian trough can be badly degraded, particularly when sleep loss is also involved. Vigilance, psychomotor ability, reaction time, verbal and arithmetic skills — all can be affected by lapses in attention caused by micro-sleeps imposed by a sleepy brain. Studies have shown that during the circadian trough between about 3:00 a.m. and 6:00 a.m. people make more errors in reading gas meters and responding to warning alarms and take more time to answer phone calls. Workers whose brains are shifting back and forth between sleep and wakefulness may engage in automatic behavior, performing routine tasks with little awareness of what they're doing. For example, computer operators have been known to run expensive data-analysis programs many times over without realizing it. In this condition, workers often cannot respond well to unexpected events such as alarm signals.

Night workers may also experience "night-shift paralysis," a kind of sleep paralysis in which they manage to maintain wakefulness while under great pressure to sleep. Their muscles become so rigid that they literally cannot move; in fact, it takes a lot of effort even for other people to move them. They may be incapacitated for up to several minutes, even though they remain conscious (and aware of their inability to move) and can see and hear. Many report feeling sleepier than usual during these episodes, which typically occur when the person is sedentary. The problem can be insidious; some people have reported that their muscles may have been immobilized before they became aware of it.

Although it appears to be rare, night-shift paralysis gives cause for concern because it has been reported by nurses, naval officers and air traffic controllers. About 12 percent of nurses and six percent of air traffic controllers said they had experienced the condition in surveys conducted by sleep researchers Simon Folkard and Ruth Condon of the University of Sussex in England. These studies indicated that the incidence of night-shift paralysis is highest around 5:00 a.m., in the middle of the circadian trough, and that it gets much worse with successive night shifts.

Jon Shearer suggests that night-shift paralysis might be an even more serious problem than the Folkard study indicates. "I think Folkard is too tight on his definition of sleep paralysis. Ask any group of shift workers if they've had the experience of knowing that they should move but just don't feel like it." He remembers a case in which he was studying police officers working night shifts. "It's 4:30 in the morning and we're sitting at a stop light. I watched the light turn twice. Finally, on the third green, I said, 'How come you didn't go on the first green?' And he said, 'I just didn't feel like it.' That floored me." Shearer says that if instead of Folkard's strict definition of sleep paralysis — an actual inability to move — this less severe type of paralysis is considered, "the statistics will frighten you." Both he and Smiley are emphatic that shift workers should not be required to work more than three consecutive nights.

Increasing automation in many manufacturing and industrial plants is compounding the problem caused by on-the-job sleepiness. Instead of actually doing things and moving around, many shift workers spend their time watching computers, dials and gauges or television monitors. Coleman tells of visiting one paper mill where workers spent their entire shift watching an image of burning wood chips on a TV screen.

Moore-Ede said that automation is a response to situations in which work demands are so high that people cannot perform well; but if the result is to remove all stimulation and social interaction and reduce the workload, particularly at night, you end up with inattentive and sleepy workers. "Basically, there's overshoot right now in the design of technological systems." As an example, he cites the increasing automation of control rooms in nuclear power plants. "Instead of having someone in a control room with several people running around all night because you had a lot of manual, hands-on activities to do, now you put this one person in a comfortable chair in a darkened room with a computer display screen. It's so well automated that you rarely ask him to do anything except for watching it, and he has no social interaction with anyone else. You absolutely set him up."

In one survey of nuclear power plant operators, Czeisler found that half reported falling asleep on the job. In August 1988, the U.S. Nuclear Regulatory Commission shut down the Peach Bottom nuclear reactor in Pennsylvania after operators were found sleeping on duty. The company was fined $1.25 million for failing to report and deal with inattentive operators and 33 operators were also fined from $500 to $1,000 each for sleeping or inattention to duty. (The company was given permission to restart the reactor in April 1989.)

It comes as no surprise to sleep researchers that many serious nuclear accidents have occurred on the night shift. For example, in March 1979, a near meltdown occurred at the Three Mile Island nuclear plant in Pennsylvania. The incident began just after 4:00 a.m. and involved a crew on a weekly rotation schedule that had been on the overnight shift for only a few nights. "Between the hours of 4:00 and 6:00 a.m., shift workers failed to recognize the loss of core coolant water resulting from a stuck valve," according to a report called *Catastrophes, Sleep and Public Policy* prepared by a group of top U.S. sleep researchers for the Association of Professional Sleep Societies. "Although a mechanical problem precipitated the incident, it was chiefly this human error of omission and the subsequent flawed corrective action that caused the near meltdown of the reactor later that morning." The report notes that the Chernobyl nuclear accident, which occurred in April 1986, began at 1:23 a.m. and was also the result of human error.

There have been other less serious, though equally worrying, incidents at nuclear plants. In 1985, the Davis-Besse reactor in Ohio was automatically shut down after the total loss of coolant water at 1:35 a.m. The incident became even more critical when a control-room operator pushed the wrong buttons, but corrective action then stabilized the situation. In another 1985 incident, operators at a reactor in California were slow to regain control of the plant when the control system lost electrical power at 4:14 a.m.

## ON-CALL SLEEPING

Automation provides increased opportunities for on-call duty among night workers — a situation in which they can sleep except when called to deal with an off-nominal situation or emergency. On-call sleeping is common in several service fields — medicine, emergency response, firefighting, for example — and it is spreading to other occupations, according to Swedish sleep researchers Lars Torsvall and Torbjörn Åkerstedt of the Karolinska Institute and the National Institute for Psychosocial Factors and Health. However, when they studied on-call sleeping among ship's engineers in the merchant marine — the first study of its kind — they got disquieting results.

While sleeping on call, the engineers got about 1½ hours less sleep than normal each night. Their sleep was interrupted by an average of two alarms a night, each of which took an average of about half an hour to deal with. Not only was the total amount of sleep time reduced, but also both REM sleep and slow wave sleep were reduced — including slow wave sleep obtained during the first sleep cycle, even though it was undisturbed by alarms. The engineers also experienced an increased heart rate during on-call sleep and, in a questionnaire, reported reduced sleep quality and increased sleepiness the day after on-call sleep.

The reduction in slow wave sleep — which resulted in lighter sleep overall — was rather surprising. SWS normally dominates during the early part of the sleep period and should not have been so affected by the relatively small reduction in total sleep time. Moreover, this early sleep was not interrupted by alarms. But in the questionnaire the engineers reported feelings of uneasiness and the researchers suggest that apprehension about being summoned by an alarm acted as a stressor that prevented the normal development of deep sleep.

They conclude that on-call sleep is affected "beyond the mere sleep time lost while being out of bed (and while falling asleep again)." Indirect effects, possibly caused by apprehension, also disturb on-call sleep.

Shearer, who calls this "anticipatory sleep," says that it's extremely fragmented "because you're checking the environment all the time and you've got all these random arousals. It's fitful, shallow sleep." Firefighters and medical emergency pilots often say they have trouble sleeping well on call. "Firemen will tell you that the sleep they get in the fire hall is just terrible because they're waiting for the bell to go off," Shearer said. He adds that any parent who has been concerned about a sick child or has waited for a teenager to get in from a date is also well acquainted with the problem.

## COPING WITH SHIFT WORK

Most people working rotating or night shifts are not very happy about their schedules. Although about 28 percent of U.S. shift workers say they prefer shift work because of the extra pay, longer breaks, greater flexibility in handling family and child-care responsibilities and having time off in the middle of the week, the majority say they'd prefer to work straight days, Monday through Friday. Coleman says that when he asks workers who designed their shift schedules, a typical response is: a person who doesn't work shifts. Although these workers certainly won't refuse extra pay, they nevertheless try to get the day shift. And even though they're paid a 30 to 40 percent premium, they are report more dissatisfaction with their jobs than day workers do. (Managers "always consider shift workers to be bitchers," notes one sleep expert.)

The negative elements of shift work were brought to light during hearings by a U.S. Congressional committee that investigated shift-work scheduling in 1983.

A police officer said that he found his weekly rotation schedule "the single most distasteful aspect of my career, greater even than the frustration of seeing justice sometimes denied, of witnessing various cases of human suffering and the very real personal danger my job involves." He said that his children didn't know whether he was coming or going and that disputes with his wife over his work schedule "robbed us of a closeness we might otherwise have had."

Fatigue and anxiety were common problems, and it was impossible to maintain a regular pattern of meals and exercise. His sleep was often curtailed by the other demands of daily life — such as child care and doctor's appointments — as well as by the need to testify in court. As a result, he was often "forced to go 24 to 36 hours without sleeping and the fatigue and loss of alertness and reflexes has been a source of concern to me, considering the life-and-death nature of police work."

Another shift worker from a manufacturing plant gave a textbook litany of the problems associated with shift work, including sleep disturbances, digestive upset, family problems and disintegration of leisure activities. Some of his observations: "I have actually seen workers go to sleep standing up while operating a piece of equipment. . . . Even driving home is a task in itself, particularly when I worked the midnight shift; several times I caught myself dozing and running off the side of the highway. . . . I used to hunt, fish and enjoy sport activities; that all stopped. I lost interest in everything. . . ." Serious morale problems occurred at work: "I could see such a difference in my friends at work. People would go to the break area and no one would talk to each other; and if they did, it was something negative about their work. . . . It was a constant battle between production workers and management. . . ."

Initially, this worker thought he would adjust to the schedule, but "the longer I stayed, the worse it became." The problems with morale, productivity, absenteeism and accidents finally got so bad that the company abolished the weekly rotating shifts. "If I had to go back to [it] tomorrow, tomorrow would be my last day to work."

· · · · · · ·

Individuals vary in their susceptibility to the problems caused by shift work. It's clear, for example, that younger people are more adaptable to unusual or irregular sleep/wake schedules than middle-aged or older people. And there is some evidence to suggest that people who are owls or who follow flexible sleeping habits may be more suited to shift work than larks or people who require a rigid sleep/wake routine.

Some researchers have in fact suggested that workers could be assessed physiologically and chronobiologically for their adaptability to shift work. In what he believes to be the first study of its kind, Shearer is collaborating with Northern Telecom Electronics Ltd., an Ottawa high-tech company, to explore the usefulness of "chronotype" tests in assessing the ability of newly hired workers to cope with shift work. Along with undergoing several other tests and interviews, the workers will fill out questionnaires designed to help the researchers evaluate how flexible they are in their sleeping habits, how much of a regular routine they require in their lives and the extent to which they can overcome drowsiness and continue working while feeling fatigued.

Alison Smiley says that chronotype tests are "not foolproof by any means" but they could be useful in warning workers about potential problems with shift work. "I would suggest screening, not in the sense of eliminating people but in the sense of informing people that they are likely to have a lot of difficulty and they may want to rethink it before they get heavily involved."

It has been suggested that the use of such screening might be considered discriminatory, particularly in the United States. However, Harvey Moldofsky says he sees no reason why it should be regarded this way. "After all, when you hire someone to lift heavy weights, you're not going to take someone who is a 90-pound weakling. There are particular skills that are required for a particular job and this would be a 'skill' — that a person is more flexibile in terms of their sleep/wake behavior."

However, there's little doubt that many, perhaps most, workers find adjustment to shift work extremely difficult. Studies by the International Labor Organization suggest that only about a third of workers can adapt easily to night work. Shearer says the ILO has recommended that night work should be kept to a minimum, that workers should be retired early from shift work and that shift workers should have extended time off. "Many people cannot tolerate shift work," says Mamelak. "It's a big, big problem. There's no question that the extraordinary irregularity makes for sleep problems." And contrary to a common belief, it never gets any easier. The human body does not grow accustomed to shift work, says Moore-Ede. The older you get, the more difficult it becomes because rotating schedules exacerbate the deterioration in sleep quality and the increase in digestive problems that aging normally brings.

If someone has trouble adjusting to shift work, the most obvious course of action is to get off it and take a day job. This is in fact what sleep specialists usually recommend to such individuals, and in many cases, it's undoubtedly the best solution. There is evidence that people with a low tolerance for shift work have more serious medical problems when forced to continue working shifts than people who have a greater natural tolerance.

Unfortunately, it's not always possible for a shift worker to switch to day work. There may be few day jobs available, particularly for people who lack advanced education or special skills. Low wage earners in particular may have few alternatives; a study by the province of Quebec's bureau of statistics found that more than half of the people in the province who earn less than $5 an hour work evenings or nights. And even educated or skilled workers may find their choices limited if they work in an industry dominated by shift work; this applies not only to the traditional blue-collar industries, but increasingly in some white-collar occupations such as data processing.

In any case, advising individual workers to leave shift work won't make shift work go away, so someone has to do it. In fact, some tens of millions of people have to do it. Coleman says that scientists have not always appreciated the magnitude of the problem but now they're devoting greater effort to finding ways to alleviate the stress of shift work for those who have no alternative.

In a booklet called *Shiftwork and Your Health*, Moore-Ede makes a number of suggestions that individuals can follow to improve their adjustment to shift work:

• Try to keep as regular a sleep schedule as possible. Sleep at the same time each day while on each shift and avoid random napping. (He also advises following a regular meal schedule and eating only light snacks like fruit, soup and toast at night, in order to avoid digestive problems.)

• A couple of days before starting a night shift, go to bed a bit later at night and wake up later in the morning. This phase delay will give your circadian system a head start in adjusting to the new shift.

• Use light and dark to reset your biological clocks as rapidly as possible. The bedroom should be very dark when you're sleeping and when you wake up, make the room you're in as bright as possible.

• Ensure that you have a quiet place to sleep during the day.

• Avoid caffeine for at least 3 hours before going to bed.

Exposure to bright light also has potential as a method to help workers cope with rotating shift schedules. As we saw in Chapter 5,

Charles Czeisler and his colleagues have demonstrated that if the exposure is carefully timed, it's possible to shift the circadian cycle to a new schedule quite rapidly.

Alfred Lewy of the Oregon Health Sciences University suggests the technique might be most effective if used at home rather than in the workplace. Michael Terman, a Columbia University psychiatry professor, has said that recent research indicates that briefly exposing night-shift workers to intense light in the early evening before they go to work may reduce the effects of the circadian trough in middle of the night and improve sleep during the day.

Jon Shearer has embarked on a study using 110 volunteer night-shift workers, including police officers, air traffic controllers, nurses and paper-mill workers, who have rigged in their bedrooms a special lighting system that mimics sunrise. A timer is set so that about half an hour before the worker is scheduled to get up a bedside light is gradually turned up to a maximum of about 2,000 to 2,500 lux. "The response has been just amazing," Shearer said. "A number of them have said that it's surprising how waking up with the light on has not only changed their outlook, but they seem to have more energy. The period of grogginess is reduced and they seem to be ready to go at the world." They also report that the middle-of-the-night "fight with sleep is lessened, although it's still there."

Czeisler says that bright lights may well prove to be very helpful, but "only if they're properly used," with a full understanding of "when they should be on and when they should be off."* The effects are not instantaneous, and if the timing of the exposure to the lights is off, the effect could be exactly opposite to that intended. "It will not be the type of system where you can simply switch on a light and be at your peak phase at one time and switch off the light and be at your trough phase at a different time."

Czeizler added that the introduction of lighting was what has caused the problem in the first place — since it permits people to work long and irregular hours and "completely disrupts the timing of when they sleep and wake." He warned that a scheme of using timed bright

---

* Sleep researchers caution that you should never look directly into a light, particularly a high-intensity point source, such as an incandescent bulb. Czeisler's experiments involved the use of large banks of fluorescent lights shielded to prevent exposing subjects to extra ultraviolet radiation.

lights "could be abused. Like any technology, it can be used appropriately or inappropriately."

## NEW SHIFT-WORK SCHEMES

While measures such as those discussed above may help individual workers adjust to rotating shifts, they cannot make up for poorly designed schedules that fly in the face of circadian reality. In the past decade, sleep researchers have been successful in implementing new shift-work schedules based on sound circadian principles in dozens of companies and industries around the world.

As logical as this sounds, suggestions that existing shift-work schedules be examined and redesigned is not always greeted with enthusiasm by either employees or employers, even when they're not happy with the way things are. There's often a great reluctance to examine the negative effects of shift work because it raises the touchy issue of human error, says Dinges. "Human error continues to account for 60 percent of the problems in almost every industry, despite all the automation." Hospitals, police departments and the nuclear and transportation industries — to name just a few examples — are not keen on shift-work studies because "it opens up a huge can of worms," he says. "It's hard to get at data like this. How do you get them to open up their books? It's a major breakthrough just to get a federal agency to acknowledge that they've got a problem, that something has to be done."

And Coleman notes that when innovations in long-standing shift-work schedules are proposed, workers are often most concerned about how a new schedule will affect their time off and their paychecks and give relatively little thought, at least at the outset, to how it might improve their health, sleep patterns and alertness on the job. It's not until a new schedule is implemented that its positive features can be fully appreciated by workers — particularly its effect on making them feel better.

Nevertheless, there have been successes. One of the first occurred at a potash mine and processing plant operated by Great Salt Lake Minerals and Chemicals of Ogden, Utah, where workers had been on a shift schedule involving weekly counterclockwise rotation for nine months of the year. They had only one day off between the week of evenings and the week of days, which, as we have seen, is a particularly difficult phase-advance situation. While on rotation, 29 percent of the workers reported falling asleep at work and a quarter of the workers said they were never able to adjust to a schedule before being rotated again. During the other three months of the year, the workers were on straight days and Coleman says the contrast may have been a contributing factor to their discontent with the shift-work schedule.

In 1980, Czeisler, Moore-Ede and Coleman implemented two new schedules on a trial basis at GSL. For one group of 33 workers, only the direction of rotation was changed, from counterclockwise to clockwise. For the second group of 52 workers, not only the direction was changed, but the rate of rotation was slowed down — they changed every three weeks instead of weekly. (The researchers also suggested eliminating the abrupt 8-hour change between shifts with a "slow-drift rotation" that would help their biological clocks to adjust: for the first three days of the new shift, the workers would start work each day about 2½ hours later than the day before. But the workers and their families didn't like this idea and it was dropped.)

In order to make the schedule change work, management also introduced changes in the nature of the work to make it more challenging to workers. Production manager Preston Richey said that for years they'd been trying to make the work simpler but this "assembly-line mentality" had caused boredom and "stupid mistakes."

Nine months later, the results were analyzed. The workers overwhelmingly favored the phase-delay rotation to the phase-advance rotation. Complaints that the schedule rotated too fast dropped among all workers on phase-delay; the complaints among those on the three-week schedule dropped from 90 to 20 percent, but even among those who were still rotating weekly, complaints dropped from 90 to about 60 percent. Nearly all the workers on the 21-day phase-delay schedule pronounced themselves satisfied with the schedule and they also reported improvements in their health. The turnover in workers dropped by about 20 percent. Moreover, there were significant improvements in productivity: the amount of potash mined increased by more than 20 percent and the amount processed increased by nearly 14 percent.

One worker, testifying at a U.S. Congressional committee hearing said that this new shift system had improved morale as well as productivity and was very much favored by workers. "Some said that it seemed like they had a lot more time to do the things they wanted to do, instead of just 'eat, sleep and go to work. . . .' They have a chance to get used to a shift and can get by on a lot less sleep, which gives more free time."

Summarizing the results of the Utah study in the journal *Science,* the researchers concluded that phase-delay shift schedules with an extended period between rotations are the ones most compatible with the human circadian system — but they added that any specific shift-work schedule must take the nature of the work and the needs of the workers into account.

In 1986, Czeisler used these circadian principles to devise a new work schedule for police officers in Philadelphia, as part of a project for the U.S. Fraternal Order of Police, a national police union. About half the police officers surveyed said they were having sleep problems as a result of their eight-day counterclockwise rotation and Czeisler found that those working nights had four times as many accidents as their colleagues working days. The new schedule, which involved an 18-day clockwise rotation alternating four days on and two days off, resulted in major improvements in sleep quality and daytime alertness and reduced use of sleeping pills and alcohol. There was a decline of 25 to 30 percent in sleeping on the job and a 40 percent drop in on-the-job car accidents. And there was a five-fold increase in family satisfaction with the work schedule. A similar schedule change in a Swedish police department resulted in a significant lowering of the risk factors associated with coronary heart disease.

A somewhat different philosophy of shift work is prevalent in Europe, where workers are often rotated through night shifts very fast. For example, a typical schedule is two day shifts, two afternoon shifts, two night shifts and then three days off. The idea is to get workers through the shift changes too fast for their circadian systems to start adjusting to each new "time zone," which is what happens with a weekly rotation.

Shearer argues that this very rapid rotation is preferable to much longer rotations, which he says do not allow realistically for the fact that most people revert to a "normal" diurnal schedule on their days off. This means they experience continuing circadian upheaval despite being on a shift rotation intended to allow their clocks to adjust. "If you put people on, say, 14 or 21 consecutive nights, with days off interspersed, that's fine if you've got an incredibly disciplined person who on days off will remain nocturnal. I tend not to see that as a reality. If you've got a family and social aspects of your world that make demands on you, you're not going to do that."

## THE REEMERGENCE OF THE 12-HOUR SHIFT

In the late 1800s and early 1900s, 12-hour shifts were common. They fell out of favor for several decades, but now they're staging a comeback. The difference is that 100 years ago, workers worked an 84-hour work week — 12 hours a day, seven days in a row. During the shift changeover, one worker got a day off (the only one in the entire month) and the other worked a 24-hour shift. Obviously, such a schedule would not be tolerated today, but a number of around-the-clock industries follow a schedule involving 12-hour workdays and a shortened work week, so that the total hours worked are typically about 40 to 42 hours a week. Coleman says that by 1984 some 60,000 workers in the United States, mostly those in the chemical and petrochemical industries, were on 12-hour shifts. Nursing staff in hospitals were also increasingly working 12-hour shifts.

The appeal of the 12-hour shift lies not in the extended work period itself, but in the fact that it gives the worker more time off. For example, in one common scheme, workers get fully half of each four-week period off (although not all at once) and, in every second week, they work only two days.

A variant of this system — which involves assigning workers permanently to two 12-hour shifts on Saturday and Sunday — has been successfully implemented in at least half a dozen Canadian plants in recent years. Workers receive pay for 40 to 42 hours of work, and retain all benefits, for a two-day, 24-hour work "week" and they get all five weekdays off. (In one plant, all workers are given the opportunity to work one of these 24-hour weeks each month; during the other three weeks, they work a regular 40-hour week.) The schedule permits continuous use of capital-intensive equipment and costs about the same as paying regular shift workers for overtime shifts while reducing absenteeism resulting from the fatigue that overtime causes.

The weekend workers report great satisfaction with the schedule. For example, a young single mother says it saves her $100 a week in child-care costs. "It would kill me to have to go back to a Monday-to-Friday week," she said. Other workers have been able to use the time off to further their education and upgrade their skills. None of the weekend workers have asked to go back to Monday-to-Friday shifts. "Everyone on the weekend shift appears to be content, and most would be disappointed if they had to go back to their old shifts," said one worker. There was initially some concern that weekend workers would take a second job — the system "was not designed so that people could kill themselves working two jobs," said one union official — but this hasn't happened.

All in all, then, the 12-hour schedule seems to have found favor with workers and management alike. The only loser, it appears, is the circadian system, which is being asked to cope with frequent, abrupt 12-hour phase shifts. Certainly rotating 12-hour shifts tax its adaptive capacity; Coleman says most people on these shifts simply "tough it out." Not surprisingly, younger people are more willing (and able) than older workers to accept the physiological cost of 12-hour shifts in exchange for more time off; poor quality sleep and the constant lack of alertness make it a poor bargain for many middle-aged workers.

Roger Rosa and Michael Colligan of the U.S. National Institute for Occupational Safety and Health in Cincinnati did a study of control-room operators in which they compared the effects of a schedule of 12-hour days on a four-day week with the one the workers had previously followed, which involved 8-hour shifts on a five- to seven-day rotation. Fifty workers were studied, 48 of them under 35 years old. For the most part, the researchers found that overall sleep quality was about normal for shift workers. Under both schedules, night-shift work resulted in poorer sleep quality than day-shift work. There was relatively little difference between night-shift workers on the two schedules, with two exceptions: the 12-hour workers took fewer naps and their sleep was disrupted by awakenings more than any other group. One surprising finding was that the night-shift workers under both schedules slept *longer* than the day-shift workers and those on the 12-hour night shift got the greatest total amount of sleep of all. This is in contrast to other studies that have indicated night-shift workers usually get less sleep than day-shift workers.

Rosa and Colligan did find, however, that workers on the 12-hour shifts seem to accumulate a sleep debt and become increasingly fatigued over the four-day work week. Their total sleep time dropped by about 45 minutes between the first and fourth days of the shift; they also fell asleep faster, took fewer naps and rated their sleep as being deeper — all of which suggests they were experiencing increasing levels of sleep deprivation and sleepiness. The researchers noted that the workers appeared to be sacrificing sleep in order to fit nonwork activities into their workdays.

In a previous laboratory study, these researchers found that a 12-hour/4-day week "was more detrimental to performance and feelings of alertness and fatigue" than an 8-hour/6-day week. They noted that 12-hour schedules "might necessitate tolerance of more fatigue in order to derive other benefits from the longer day" — such as increased production or worker preferences. But they add that this raises the question of "how much fatigue is allowable before the safety or health of the worker is compromised."

The report *Catastrophes, Sleep and Public Policy* notes that console operators at the Kennedy Space Center had been on duty for 11 hours on their third day of working 12-hour night (8:00 p.m. to 8:00 a.m.) shifts when they inadvertently drained more than 8,200 kilograms (18,000 pounds) of liquid oxygen from a space shuttle's fuel tanks just five minutes before the scheduled liftoff. These workers misinterpreted information concerning a valve failure and, instead of manually overriding the automatic system to close the next valve, pressed the Continue button that caused vent and drain valves to open prematurely. Fortunately, this resulted in a warning signal that caused the launch to be stopped just 31 seconds before liftoff.

It was not until after the hold had occurred that anyone realized a significant amount of the shuttle's fuel had been drained; if the launch had gone ahead, the ability of the shuttle to reach orbit would have been "significantly impacted" according to experts who investigated the incident. They cited operator fatigue as one of the major contributing factors. This mistake, which occurred at a time when workers at the space center were under extreme pressure and putting in an unusual amount of overtime, happened less than a month before the *Challenger* explosion on January 28, 1986.

Coleman and his associates have found that a 12-hour schedule can work if the rotation period between day and night shifts is slow and if no more than two to three shifts are worked without a break. They devised a four-week rotation schedule complemented with brighter lighting in the control room to entrain circadian rhythms and instruction for the workers on how to avoid desynchronization of the sleep/wake cycle on their days off. Worker satisfaction with the shift schedule jumped from 32 to 56 percent and their satisfaction with the days-off pattern went from nine to 74 percent. They reported improved sleep quality and a substantial increase in alertness (from 13 to 39 percent). Their families were also happier; their positive ratings of the schedule jumped from 35 to 64 percent. Finally, absenteeism dropped and overtime was substantially reduced from 108.5 to 39.4 hours for every 1,000 hours worked.

## NAPPING AND SHIFT WORK

We saw earlier that shift workers, especially those on night shifts, are prone to falling asleep because of excessive sleepiness caused by circadian desynchronization and accumulating sleep loss. Clearly, involuntary napping on the job is not a good thing. However, scheduled and permitted napping may be. As we saw in the previous chapter, laboratory experiments have shown that strategically timed naps can have a long-lasting positive effect on performance and alertness. Applying these laboratory findings to the real world is complicated, however. Could napping actually help nurses, police officers or nuclear plant operators? "Possibly," says Dinges, but he cautions that scientists don't yet know "how all of the things we've learned about sleep and chronobiology apply to given work scenarios."

Still, some evidence suggests that shift workers can benefit from napping. For example, a study by Mikko Harma and Juhani Ilmarien of the Institute of Occupational Health in Finland found that night-shift workers who took daytime naps were more alert than non-nappers during most of their shift and particularly at the end of the shift, when all workers were most tired.

The study compared 82 nappers with 64 nonnappers. The naps were taken between 10:00 a.m. and 9:00 p.m. and lasted from about half an hour to nearly 5 hours, averaging about 2 hours. Both the nappers and the nonnappers were given alertness and short-term memory tests between 8:00 p.m. and 8:00 a.m. The researchers found that the nappers were more alert from about 10:00 p.m. through to the end of the shift and the difference between the two groups was greatest during the circadian trough from about 4:00 a.m. to 8:00 a.m. There were no differences between the two groups on the short-term memory tests.

Two Japanese university researchers, Kazuya Matsumoto and Yusuke Morita, investigated the benefits of napping on the night shift and concluded that nighttime naps appear to compensate for the sleep loss caused during night duty. In a paper published in the journal *Sleep*, they say that "naps during night duty are widely practiced in Japan, possibly more frequently than in other countries, [but] the physiological effects of such naps are not yet well known." They took EEG recordings on 16 male security guards who work 24-hour shifts every other day and take a 3½-hour nap during their 24 hours on duty, from about 3:00 a.m. to 6:30 a.m. On the alternate days off, they can sleep as long as they want to.

At the start of the study, the guards spent three holiday nights in the lab, where their sleep was recorded from 11:00 p.m. until they woke up, to establish a "control" measurement. Then their sleep was recorded when they napped during their 24-hour shift and again during daytime sleep on the day following their shift, from 11:00 a.m. until waking.

Consistent with other studies, this one showed that daytime sleep after night work was shorter than normal nighttime sleep. On days after their shifts, the guards slept for only about 4 hours (compared with 8 hours during their "control" night in the lab). Moreover, their daytime sleep was disturbed by a greater number of awakenings and more shifts between different sleep stages — factors that contribute to subjective feelings of poor sleep. This poor daytime sleep was probably caused by the fact that the circadian peaks in alertness occur during the day, the researchers said.

Thus, this study confirmed other findings that night work leads to sleep loss. To test whether nighttime napping can make up for this sleep loss, the researchers compared the sleep obtained by eight of the younger guards with that of five night-shift nurses who did not nap during their duty hours. The nurses got about 5 hours of sleep during the day, compared with 7½ hours of sleep obtained on a control night. In contrast, the combination of daytime sleep and nighttime napping gave the guards a total of about 7½ hours of sleep, only an hour less than their average of 8½ hours on the control night. Moreover, the nurses got markedly less REM and slow wave sleep than the guards.

These findings suggest that the guards' nighttime naps compensated for sleep loss caused by night duty, compared with the nurses who were awake all night. They also suggest that "a short nighttime nap could be effective for fatigue recovery," the researchers noted.

## II. Jet Lag: Shift Work with Wings

Jet lag is aptly named because it is truly a consequence of the speed and range of modern aircraft. When people crossed the oceans by sailing ships, although they certainly had their share of problems, the symptoms caused by jet lag were not among them. It wasn't until the beginning of the 1960s, with the advent of mass commercial air travel, that the problem first became widespread enough to attract the attention of scientists and the public.

Once again, our biological clocks are the root of the problem. When you fly overnight from New York to London, arriving at, say, 8:00 a.m. London time, your biological clock is still on New York time — 3:00 a.m. Consequently, you may find yourself driving a car in rush-hour traffic or having to cope with an important business meeting or playing a championship tennis match at a time when you are physiologically in the middle of the circadian trough and probably sleep deprived as well. In 1953, the U.S. loss of the Aswan Dam project in Egypt to the Soviet Union was blamed at least partly on jet lag; then U.S. secretary of state John Foster Dulles and his associates were fatigued when they began negotiations with the Egyptian representatives shortly after their long flight. Later, Dulles advised diplomats to avoid doing important business too soon after long-distance travel.

The physiological effects of the mismatch between your internal biological clocks and external time can linger for as long as two weeks, depending on individual physiology and how many time zones you've crossed. As your circadian rhythms struggle to resynchronize to the new time zone, you'll feel tired, achy, disoriented and generally out of sorts.

Sleep disturbances are among the most common and obvious symptoms of jet lag. Because your body wants to sleep at the "wrong" times, you'll suffer from insomnia at night and excessive sleepiness during the day; these bouts of alternating alertness and sleepiness may become unpredictable after a few days as the circadian system gradually adjusts to the new time zone. Sleep researcher Anthony Nicholson of Britain's Royal Air Force Institute of Aviation Medicine says that there may be a delayed effect in sleep disturbances after an eastbound flight crossing more than five time zones. Sleep may be satisfactory the first night at the destination, but disturbances show up on subsequent nights. In one study, he found that subjects slept for 7.6 hours the first night, but total sleep time steadily declined over the next four nights to 7.3 hours. Moreover, the time it took subjects to fall asleep doubled on the second night (from about 15 minutes to nearly 32 minutes) and remained high at the end of five days (35½ minutes). The amount of slow wave sleep also declined, from about 65 minutes to less than 51 minutes. These findings indicate a drop in the quality of sleep. Nicholson said that the fact that changes in sleep patterns lasted beyond five nights after eastbound flights suggests the existence of persistent sleep disturbance.

Because the circadian rhythms of eating and digestion are also deranged by long-distance travel, appetite may be variable and often inappropriate to local meal times at the destination, and digestive and gastrointestinal problems, such as upset stomach, diarrhea or constipation, will be common.

Reduced physical and mental efficiency is also a side effect of jet lag; problems include lapses in concentration, short attention span, confusion, irritability and a distorted sense of time and distance. It's easy to make silly mistakes. (Wiley Post, who flew around the world in eight days in 1931, actually took off on one leg of the flight without any fuel; he also fell asleep in the middle of answering reporters' questions. Before the flight, he tried to break himself of the habit of sleeping regularly and said he found this more difficult than flying a plane.)

German sleep researchers Karl Klein and Hans Wegman found that on the first day after a flight crossing six time zones, a person's performance on psychomotor tasks was degraded in the late afternoon and early evening after a westbound flight and in the morning and afternoon after an eastbound flight. These effects lasted for three to five days. The researchers note that motivation and extra effort can sometimes overcome circadian effects on performance, but said that these periods of degraded performance represented the times of day when it would be most difficult to do so.

The amount of disruption increases with the number of time zones crossed. A shift of one or two time zones usually doesn't create much of a problem, but most people begin to feel effects after crossing five or six time zones, the typical length of overnight transatlantic flights. Virtually everyone has serious trouble with flights that cross 12 times zones or more. (Ironically, however, if you cross all 24 time zones rapidly without stopping, you'll end up back where you started without having reset your biological clocks and you won't be jet lagged at all.)

Eastbound travel causes the worst jet lag because it forces you to set your clocks (mechanical and biological) ahead, thereby shortening your day. This is equivalent to a phase advance. Westbound travel requires you to set your clocks back, which extends the day, which is equivalent to a phase delay. (North/south travel within the same time zone has no effect on circadian rhythms, although it does, of course, cause fatigue.) As we have seen, adjusting to a phase delay is much easier for the human circadian system. In fact, a study by Klein and Wegman indicates that resynchronization of circadian rhythms occurs about 50 percent faster after westbound flight than after eastbound flight. They assessed a number of psycho-physiological factors, including heart rate, biochemistry and psychomotor skills and reaction time, in subjects who flew 6-hour transatlantic flights in both directions. Reentrainment of their circadian rhythms occurred at a more rapid rate — an average of 88 minutes a day — after the westbound flight than after the eastbound flight, which averaged only 56 minutes a day.

However, what is perhaps more significant than this average rate of reentrainment is the fact that some rhythms adjust faster than others. For example, in the eastbound direction, heart rate reentrained at a average rate of 60 minutes a day, psychomotor performance at 38 minutes a day, reaction time at 74 minutes a day and body temperature at 39 minutes a day. Moreover, reentrainment does not occur at the same rate every day; it goes faster at first and then slows down. A rough rule of thumb, according to Klein and Wegman, is every 48 hours the circadian system shifts about half the remaining distance to full resynchronization. For example, if you've crossed six time zones, you'll shift 50 percent (3 hours) by the second day, 75 percent (4½ hours) by the fourth day and about 88 percent (5¼ hours) by the sixth day and so forth. This process is also affected by the number of time zones crossed.

The net result is that for a period of time (up to two weeks or more) after a flight, different rhythms become decoupled — i.e., they lose their normal relationship to one another. In short, your circadian system is completely scrambled; you are not only out of synch with the external world, you are also *internally* desynchronized. (And if you return home before this process has sorted itself out, you'll rescramble everything all over again.)

Individuals can vary considerably in their rate of resynchronization. In another study, Klein and Wegman studied psychomotor performance in 14 subjects after a 6-hour westbound trip. (Psychomotor skills are those used in rather complex mental/physical activities such as driving, flying an aircraft, operating a computer terminal or competing in a sports event.) They found that adjustment took from 60 to 210 minutes a day; some of the subjects took as little as one and a half days, but most took three to six days. In the eastbound direction, resynchronization was typically slower, ranging from 31 minutes a day to 125 minutes a day. Most subjects took between three and 11 days to adjust, but three of them took fully 14 to 18 days to shift their psychomotor rhythm — which put them into the category of those who "adapt only with considerable difficulty," the researchers said.

Personality and age also affect how rapidly someone will adjust to a new time zone. As with shift work, "evening" types and younger people are more adaptable than "morning" types and older people. The tendency toward internal desynchronization of circadian rhythms is greater in older people and it has been speculated that there may be a threshold, about 40 years of age, after which this tendency increases markedly.

Another way in which individuals differ in their adjustment to new time zones concerns the direction in which the circadian rhythms shift in order to resynchronize with the new environment. In some cases, rhythms will go the "wrong" way around the clock. For example, after an eastward flight across nine time zones, the body temperature cycle in some people will resynchronize by advancing 9 hours, while in others, it will resynchronize by a 15-hour delay. This indicates the strength of the body's preference for phase-delay over phase-advance strategies in coping with time shifts; when it cannot adjust to a shorter day, it drifts (free-runs) in the opposite direction until it "catches up" to local time — a phenomenon similar to the chronotherapy technique, described in Chapter 4, used to treat people with sleep phase delay syndrome.

It has been suggested, in fact, that the body temperature rhythm in most people may shift the "wrong" way around (i.e., phase delay) after eastbound flight and the "right" way around (also phase delay) after westbound flight. One study found that two-thirds of the subjects on an eastbound flight across six time zones adjusted their rhythms via an 18-hour phase delay, rather than a 6-hour phase advance.

Moreover, within an individual, not all rhythms need shift in the same direction; it has been shown that some people experience what is known as "reentrainment by partition" — which means that some rhythms resynchronize in one direction and others go the opposite way around. The likelihood of this split occurring appears to be greater after eastbound flight than after westbound flight and seems to increase with the number of time zones crossed.

Traveling also often causes fatigue and sleep loss independently of its effect on the circadian system. Stress before a trip, the loss of sleep on overnight flights and insomnia at the destination all conspire to rob the traveler of much-needed sleep, and this greatly compounds the problems caused by the circadian effects of travel. It is wise to make an attempt to catch up on sleep loss and regularize your sleep/wake pattern as soon as possible after arriving at your destination.

There are circumstances in which people not only don't want to hasten adjustment to the new time zone, but in fact would like to *prevent* it from happening altogether if possible. Say, for example, that you'll be returning home in only a few days. The trip won't be long enough to permit your circadian rhythms to adjust to the new time zone before they're scrambled again by the trip home. The best strategy in this case is to try to maintain the home-base schedule as much as possible by minimizing exposure to social and environmental time cues at the destination. This strategy may be appropriate (and possible) only in special circumstances. For example, former U.S. president Lyndon Johnson is reported to have maintained Washington time on Air Force One while meeting with Vietnamese officials.

Pilots often try to maintain their home-base schedule when they're on quick turnaround flights. In these cases, Klein and Wegman say, it's important that the schedule permit them enough time to get sufficient rest between flights and that they be provided with sleeping quarters shielded from light and noise during local daytime hours.

In most cases, however, people want to adjust as quickly as possible to the new time zone. There are a number of things you can do before, during and after your flight to minimize jet lag and hasten this adjustment.

## COPING WITH JET LAG

You can start shifting your circadian rhythms gradually before you leave on your trip. If you're headed west, you should go to bed and wake up later each day, which will move your sleep/wake schedule in the direction suitable for your destination. The opposite pattern would be appropriate for eastbound flights, but your circadian system may make it more difficult for you to advance the time you go to sleep at night. This technique does present some practical problems, however, since full adjustment to the destination time zone would require about a 1-hour shift each day for each time zone you'll be crossing. Some people might find it possible to make a 2- or 3-hour adjustment for a transcontinental flight, but shifting at-home sleep/wake patterns by the 5 to 6 hours needed for a transatlantic trip might be quite difficult.

When you get to your destination, you should expose your circadian system to strong social and environmental time cues to get it on track as quickly as possible. For example, if you arrive, groggy and disoriented, on the morning after an eastbound overnight flight, don't hide out in a darkened hotel room, sleeping away the day and ordering meals at odd hours from room service. Instead, stay awake, get outside in the sunlight and be active (although it's best to avoid scheduling important work at this time) and eat meals at the proper local times. Go to bed early that night and try to get a few more hours of sleep than usual, using a mild, short-acting hypnotic if necessary. These techniques will help reset your clocks faster. Klein and Wegman found that when subjects were kept in relative isolation in their hotel rooms, they took about 50 percent longer to resynchronize their psychomotor performance rhythm than subjects who were allowed to go outdoors every second day. They attributed this more rapid adjustment to the "higher degree of social contact."

If you're flying westbound, try to take a flight that arrives close to your usual at-home bedtime and go to sleep as soon as possible, even though this will be early according to local time.

More recently, some scientists have suggested that strategic manipulation of diet and light can also be used to assist rapid adjustment of the circadian system.

It's best to avoid rich, heavy foods, especially on overnight flights; your digestive system, largely shut down for the night, will deal more easily with light snacks. Foods with a high fat content, such as gravies, sauces and whipped cream, should particularly be avoided because they slow digestion. Dehydration is a major problem because the pressurized air in aircraft cabins is very dry (sometimes less than five percent relative humidity); therefore, passengers should drink lots of fluids, preferably water or fruit juices. Alcohol and caffeinated drinks just make the dehydration problem worse.

It has been suggested that jet lag can be minimized by following a particular pattern of eating before and during the flight and by carefully controlling the times when caffeine is consumed. However, a number of sleep researchers question the efficacy of such plans. Moldofsky, for one, said he's not aware of any scientific evidence to support the idea that any particular food or sequence of meals can work as a treatment for jet lag. Experiments have been done with animals to test the effect of various pharmacological agents (such as caffeine, alcohol and other drugs) in resetting biological clocks.

Some people do take hypnotics to help them sleep during the flight, but this is usually not a good idea. The combined effects of the pills, sleep loss and circadian dysrhythmia can be unpredictable, especially if combined with even moderate amounts of alcohol. There have been several reported cases of travelers who experienced temporary amnesia after taking a hypnotic in flight and also drinking alcohol. One case involved a man who had had only one glass of wine on a transatlantic flight; he disembarked in Frankfurt, cleared customs, boarded a plane to Munich, was met and taken to his hotel and then to lunch — and later remembered none of it. In another case, a woman went to an airline counter to report a missing bag and found, much to her surprise, that she'd been there before and had already filled out all the forms.

Exposure to bright light may also help people adjust more quickly to a new time zone. We saw in Chapter 4 that some studies suggest exposure to bright light either in the morning or the afternoon can be used to shift the circadian rhythms of people with delayed sleep phase syndrome or advanced sleep phase syndrome. Jet-lagged people are in the same boat, in essence, and Alfred Lewy and his colleagues of the Oregon Health Sciences University have suggested that after an eastbound flight of 6 hours or less, travelers should get out in the sun in the morning, and after a westbound flight the light exposure should occur in the late afternoon.

People who cross six time zones or more should time their light exposure for midday local time, because according to their internal clocks, it will either be morning or evening; at the same time, eastbound travelers should avoid light during the local morning, and westbound travelers should avoid it during the local evening. Lewy has found that subjects who were shifted eastbound across nine time zones resynchronized their rhythms within a week if exposed to 2 or 3 hours of midday sun, while avoiding light in the morning. Those who were not exposed to sunlight took twice as long to adjust. Since this is the more difficult adjustment for biological clocks to make, he believes that midday exposure and light avoidance in the evening would work for westbound travelers.

Richard Kronauer, a member of the team of researchers who collaborated with Charles Czeisler, provides the example of a trip from the eastern United States to Sydney, Australia, a 14-hour time difference. If a traveler went to work right away, exposing himself only to indoor lighting, it would take about 10 days for his biological clock to adjust. If, instead, he exposed himself to bright outdoor light, he should be reset to Australian time in just two days.*

Czeisler has successfully used bright-light exposure to shift a jet-lagged traveler's circadian rhythm by 10 hours in three days. The experiment was performed on Michael Long, a writer for *National Geographic* magazine, who described the experience in the December 1987 issue. Long flew from Tokyo to Boston wearing goggles to shield his eyes from exposure to light, and was put into Czeisler's time-isolation lab where, for the next three days, he was subjected to carefully timed exposure to light for several hours each day, alternating with periods of darkness and rest. At the end of three days, he emerged with his biological clock adjusted to Boston time; under normal circumstances it would have taken him another week to adjust. Of course, it would hardly be practical to put millions of travelers into time-isolation labs, but Czeisler envisages a time when airports might be equipped with special light rooms.

---

* A word of caution: scientists warn that you should never look directly at the sun or into an artificial light source, such as sun lamp, as this could cause serious eye damage. And if you expose your body to bright sunlight, you should take care to protect yourself from ultraviolet radiation, which can cause skin cancer.

Something of the sort may well be needed if aviation technology continues to evolve toward ever-faster aircraft. We already have supersonic planes that cut transatlantic flight times almost in half compared with conventional jets. If commercial hypersonic planes (which are only a step removed from spacecraft) are developed, a transatlantic crossing might take only 15 minutes. This would be a godsend for people who want to go somewhere and return almost immediately; their circadian system would barely be ruffled. But for travelers planning to stay in the new time zone for any length of time, being zapped between continents nearly as fast as the starship *Enterprise* beams people around will cause even more severe circadian shock than they currently experience. Inevitably, techniques that offer the promise of rapid adjustment to new time zones will become increasingly popular.

· · · · · · ·

In this age of frequent travel, many people are affected by jet lag, but in some occupations the consequences can be quite serious — a business executive might muff a multimillion-dollar deal, an athlete might lose a medal or a championship, a pilot might make a mistake resulting in the loss of an aircraft and the death of passengers. Many people have learned the hard way that if they're traveling for a specific event, such as a sports competition or a business meeting, they should try to arrive at least a day or so early. Where once they blithely plunged into the thick of things with no more than a quick shower and a change of clothing to revive them, most are now aware that it's wiser to give their circadian system at least 24 to 48 hours to adjust to the new time zone. But as we have seen, even 48 hours may not be enough. In the next chapter, we will examine more closely the effects of jet lag — as well as sleep loss and extended work hours — on a variety of different occupations.

CHAPTER 12

# ASLEEP IN THE FAST LANE

A GROUP OF GERMAN SCIEN-
tists once did an experiment to test driving performance at night. They
wired a subject with electrodes to measure brain waves and eye
blinking and then sent him off on a drive that took nearly 3½ hours
in the middle of the night. For about half the time, he was driving on
a monotonous stretch of expressway.

When the scientists examined the tape-recorded data afterward,
they found something rather alarming: for a 20-minute period while
driving on the Autobahn, the driver did not blink his eyes at all,
indicating that his eyes were either completely closed or completely
open for the entire time. Moreover, the EEG readings indicated that
for at least part of that 20-minute period, the driver's brain was asleep.
Since the driver did not have an accident, the researchers concluded
that the man had been speeding along the expressway at about 113
kilometers per hour (70 miles per hour) essentially on automatic pilot,
with his eyes open and his brain asleep.

This is possibly the most literal example to be found of someone
"asleep in the fast lane," but many people today are doing pretty much
the same thing in a figurative sense. Increasingly, the human being is
evaluated by the standard of the machine; the watch words are
*productivity*, *efficiency* and, most important of all, *tirelessness* — the
ability to keep on going at all hours of the day or night. The essence
of this type of work ethic was succinctly captured by James Beggs, a
former administrator of the U.S. National Aeronautics and Space
Administration, who, in commenting on an unprecedented spate of
resignations from the astronaut corps in 1987, lamented that NASA
was losing some of its most skilled and experienced people — people
"who still have a lot of tread left on them."

The symbolism of the machine extends to the issue of sleep, which is viewed by fast-trackers mainly as unproductive "downtime." Asked how he copes with the demands on his time, one executive shrugs and says that he "just" cuts his sleep time. This attitude is especially prevalent in the "Right Stuff" occupations — medicine, law, aviation, business and investment, sports and, of course, the space program — where the attitude seems to be: if you can't take a licking and keep on ticking, you don't belong here in the first place. John Lauber of the U.S. National Transportation Safety Board comments that many people today have the mistaken notion that overcoming the effects of a lack of sleep is merely a matter of motivation.

"An active, mentally demanding 16- to 18-hour day has become the expected norm in our society," says Mortimer Mamelak. "Many people have to be alert and going at top speed for immensely long hours. For every person who wants to sleep more, there is another trying to do with even less. . . . Too many of us are overtired and overstimulated when we finally get to bed and we then allow too little time for sleep."

This is a lifestyle that gives new meaning to the word *timeless*. Consider the statistics: in the United States, leisure time has decreased by 37 percent in the past 15 years, from about 26½ to 16½ hours a week, and the average work week has increased to 46.8 hours from 40.6 hours. Professionals and owners of small businesses put in even longer hours — an average of 52.2 hours and 57.3 hours a week respectively. Work weeks of 60 to 80 hours are common in business, finance and the professions.

In Japan, workaholism is so firmly entrenched that companies have to prod their employees to take their holidays; on average, they take only half, and according to one government survey, one-third of Japanese workers never take a break of more than three consecutive days. One Tokyo real estate firm has started paying a premium for each day of paid vacation their employees actually take. (This relentlessness starts early; most Japanese students spend virtually all their "free" time, including summer holidays, in extracurricular tutoring or attending summer "cram" schools.)

Paradoxical as it sounds, the Japanese Ministry of International Trade and Industry runs a Leisure Development Center. Each summer, the government mounts a major campaign to get workers to take a vacation. "Let's get absent-minded," one poster exhorted workers. One year, the slogan of the goof-off campaign was "To Take a

Vacation Is Proof of Your Competence." According to one official, the government is trying to persuade workers that taking a time off is "not a bad thing," but changing the prevailing mentality is a formidable task. Even taking a weekend off causes some Japanese workers to retire to their beds complaining of sharp pains in the neck and shoulders — until Monday rolls around and they can get back to the office. This "holiday disease" is uniquely Japanese, according to psychiatrist Tooru Sekiya, who said the families of these men live separate lives without them. Paul Naitoh of the U.S. Naval Research Health Center, who is himself Japanese, says there are few insomniacs in Japan because "they push themselves 16 hours a day, so they collapse."

The government is currently promoting a five-day work week; one Labor ministry official wrote a song urging workers to frolic like Bambi in the woods. In 1987, less than seven percent of Japanese companies closed on Saturdays, but others have been moving toward the five-day work week. And, according to some observers, younger Japanese workers have not been bitten quite as hard by the work bug as their predecessors and appear more willing to take time off.

Still, workaholism hardly seems in imminent danger of disappearing — in Japan or elsewhere in the industrialized world. In April 1989, *Fortune* magazine ran a story about "The Workaholic Generation" in which it profiled baby-boom managers in the United States, who typically get into the office by 6:30 or 7:00 a.m., regularly put in 60- to 90-hour work weeks, work at home in the evenings and on weekends and travel as much as 70 percent of the time. *The New York Times* ran a front-page story entitled "Sleep? Why? There's No Money in It," about a study done by Michigan State University economists Jeff Biddle and Daniel Hamermesh for the National Bureau of Economics Research, which found that sleep time decreases as time on the job becomes more lucrative. "Higher wages reduce sleep," said Hamermesh. The study, which involved more than 700 people keeping minute-by-minute diaries, found that a wage increase of 25 percent resulted in a one-percent drop in sleep time and that every extra hour of work reduces sleep by 10 minutes. (The authors note that economists and other social scientists almost entirely ignore sleep in their analyses of how people spend their time, even though sleep takes up more of many people's time than any other activity, including work.)

Perhaps more telling than all the statistics are the ads that appear in business magazines and newspapers with increasing frequency. Those who sell the new portable technologies know that they're not really selling hardware; they're selling a style of working. They're selling control over time — a commodity that has perhaps already outstripped sex and money as a bargaining chip with today's fast-trackers. Cellular phones are advertised as the "tireless wireless," and one cellular company tells potential customers that they'll soon realize they've "almost literally 'found time.'" A computer company pitches a high-powered portable computer to the "confirmed workaholic" whose workday does not end when the overnight cleaning staff arrives at the office door; this worker just packs up his or her portable computer and heads off for several more hours of "peak productivity" at home. A telephone company shows us "Liz" eating sushi at her marble-topped desk, chopsticks in one hand, telephone in the other, discussing business with partners in five different cities; teleconferencing, we're told, lets these people make decisions any-where, anytime. A weary businessman in a darkened hotel room gratefully abandons a computer printout for a mushroom omelet and coffee delivered by a room service waiter at 3:30 in the morning. This is typical of hotel ads aimed at executives, which offer not only gourmet food at any time of the day or night but also business services such as rental cars and typists.

The reasons for the prevalence of this work-till-you-drop syndrome in today's industrial society are complex and varied, reflecting both personal and psychological factors, as well as wider social and eco-nomic trends. In broad terms, five factors have contributed to the rapid growth and entrenchment of the workaholic lifestyle in indus-trialized countries in the past three decades: economic conditions, the changing psychological/cultural role of work, the equating of great wealth and material possessions with success, the impact of new technologies, and the changing roles of women and men in the work force and at home. These trends, which will be discussed here only briefly, provide the backdrop against which to examine the impact of sleep problems on a number of specific high-demand occupations.

• **Economic trends**: Rapid expansion of the economy occurred in most of the industrialized world during the 1960s and the 1970s, coincident with the entry into the work force of the baby boom generation — more numerous and better educated than any previous generation. Perhaps nowhere was this phenomenon more pronounced than in the high-tech industries, particularly electronics and microcomputers, which experienced an explosive growth in the late 70s and gave rise to the cult of the brash, youthful entrepreneur. Silicon Valley became the quintessence of the high-tech fast track, where success was measured in how many millions you'd made before the age of 30. In the 1980s, the locus of this almost religious frenzy of workaholism spread to the investment field, corporate law and the world of the business entrepreneur. Indeed, it is the success of the electronics industry — specifically, the global computer-communications systems it spawned — that accelerated the transformation of business investment into an around-the-clock, around-the-world occupation, a trend reflected in the emergence of 24-hour operations in stock markets and brokerage firms.

Paradoxically, the economic retrenchment of the "lean and mean" 1980s has had an equally powerful effect in fostering workaholism. The recession in 1981-82 and the stock-market crash in 1987 tumbled many people who had been riding high on the crest of the technological tidal wave. Suddenly, they found that there was no longer an assured demand for their services. Mergers, takeovers, budget-cutting and staff reductions — combined with the huge size of the baby boom cohort and the influx of women into the workforce — have left many white-collar workers and professionals feeling insecure and less cavalier about the potential for job-hopping. Where once the corporate culture was dominated by the idea that if you were not moving up, you were a loser, now articles in business magazines and newspapers are giving workers advice on how to come to terms with being "plateaued" by a lack of opportunities for upward mobility.

University of Montreal psychologist Ethel Roskies, who has studied the factors that cause job insecurity, says that the transformation of traditionally secure managerial jobs into insecure ones has been one of the most radical changes in the workplace in recent years. Managers and professionals are being forced to face the same kind of job insecurity that has more traditionally been the lot of blue-collar workers, she says.

One result of this insecurity is the pressure to work even harder. In order to remain competitive, down-sized companies are demanding more of their employees' time, as fewer workers are expected to do more work. According to executive-search consultants, the job market has become more competitive just as many workers are expressing the wish to get off the treadmill and lead more balanced lives.

Another consequence of this insecurity is that company loyalty is reduced; employees start thinking first of what's best for them and are more willing to strike out on their own if the opportunity presents itself. Self-employment has increased substantially in the past 15 years, mostly in service industries such as retailing and business services. Statistics Canada figures showed that between 1975 and 1986, the number of self-employed workers rose by 54 percent, more than 2½ times the increase in the number of paid employees during the same period. This trend has increased workaholism; running your own business requires full-time commitment and, of necessity, the self-employed tend to work longer hours than many people who are employed by others.

• **Changes in the psychological and cultural role of work**: Work is increasingly tied to personal identity and self-esteem. For many people today, work defines who they are; it marks their place in society. A cover story in *Psychology Today* magazine notes that the job has become the "center of excitement" and describes work as "our intoxicant," a source of psychological gratification in "the age of the enhanced self." A survey on social attitudes commissioned by Chivas Regal, the Scotch manufacturer, found that respondents (U.S. workers between the ages of 25 and 49 working outside the home) cited three factors as most important in their choice of jobs: about one-third ranked money first, but the other two-thirds mentioned either independence in the workplace or personal gratification as being the most important factor.

Many of the people who work long, hard hours — particularly those in business and the professions — do not describe themselves as unhappy or under pressure. In fact, they are typically quoted saying that this fast-paced lifestyle gives them an incomparable psychological "high" and makes them feel alive. *Fortune* cites one woman executive saying that work should be given another name, because the term suggests drudgery rather than the enjoyment and stimulation it provides. The article notes that many of these overachievers are characterized by a competitive spirit similar to that found in sports, and they are seeking a unique identity in the world. They want, in the words of one man, to be "a phenomenon."*

Like any other drug, however, work leaves addicts hungry for ever-larger fixes. Human beings have a need for challenge, but we're usually engaged in "a tricky balancing act" between achievement and our capacity to perform, according to social psychologist Gilbert Brim, who has written a book called *Losing and Winning: The Nature of Ambition in Everyday Life*. We choose challenges that are tough enough to keep us on our toes, but not so tough as to provide a steady diet of failure — a phenomenon that has been dubbed the level of "just manageable difficulty." In practice, Brim says, this means working at about 80 percent of capacity. Pushing too far beyond this level causes stress and burnout; falling too far below it causes boredom and stagnation.

It's also part of human nature to move on to more demanding work after mastering a job. One long-term study showed that successful executives become increasingly work oriented, while those who are less successful turn more of their attention to family, social and recreational activities. But being on the vertical-mobility fast track exacts a toll — the spiral of rising expectations eventually pushes people into work that demands 90 to 100 percent of their capacity. They have, in the words of the famous Peter Principle, risen to the level of their incompetence, and failures start to outnumber successes.

• **The growth of materialism and the equation of money and possessions with success**: The preoccupation with earning and spending that characterizes the 1980s is reflected in the swelling ranks of students in M.B.A. programs and the observation of university educators that students these days are concerned not so much with getting an education in the broad sense of the word, but in acquiring marketable skills that will gain them entrée into the careers offering the best prospects for fast and huge financial rewards. In 1985, the siren song of Wall Street attracted 28 percent of the graduating class of Harvard Business School (compared with one percent in 1949). These days, some M.B.A.'s are pulling in annual earnings exceeding $200,000 just a few years after getting out of school.

---

* It was noted, however, that all this striving for professional achievement might be at least partly rooted in an attempt to exert control over lives that have fallen prey to failings and insecurities on the personal front.

These people live in an intense, predatory environment in which the dominant mindset is that your worth in dollars serves to calibrate your worth as a person. Some analysts see phenomena like stock scams and insider trading scandals — often perpetrated by people who are extremely well-off by any normal standard — as the most extreme manifestation of this mindset.

• **The impact of new technologies**: Technology has always transformed the way people work, but the rate of change has arguably been more dramatic in the past two decades than at any time in human history. The introduction of the desktop microcomputer into the office in the late 1970s and early 1980s was followed by the rapid growth in the use of pagers, cellular phones, fax machines and most especially the portable computer equipped with a modem.*

What these new technologies are doing is altering the time/space coordinates of our lives. They're doing for work what the VCR did for — or to — television. Just as the VCR allows us to time-shift television viewing, portable technologies enable us to time-shift — and place-shift — the rest of our lives. Executives can, in any given 24-hour period, wheel and deal all the way around the world. For example, a Tokyo-based executive dictates messages to his New York office at night (New York time). The notes are typed up during the day in New York and faxed back to him so he receives them the next morning in Tokyo. Another executive involved in international trade says his fax machine enables him to conduct business in Asia, Africa, Latin America and the U.S. all in a single day.

These gadgets have, moreover, broken down the boundaries of the

---

* In fact, the spread of modem-equipped personal microcomputers has created an extensive subculture of people who use their computers not only for work, but also for a new kind of social contact that is paradoxically both arm's-length and intimate. The emergence of electronic bulletin boards is a particularly notable example of this trend; as their name implies, these microcomputer-based boards provide a means for people all over the world to exchange public and private messages, to exchange ideas and information, to debate issues and to seek advice on everything from computers and microwave ovens to bicycle helmets and running shoes. (They have even resulted in a few marriages.) Most major North American cities now have dozens, sometimes even hundreds, of local bulletin boards, many of which are tied into regional, national and international networks — and they are as much abuzz at three o'clock in the morning as they are at three o'clock in the afternoon.

traditional office, both physically and temporally, by making it possible for people to work in cars, on planes, in hotel rooms — even, paradoxically, while on "vacation." These days, high-powered executives can do business from boats, ski lodges, cottage retreats, even while golfing or watching baseball games.* With features like voice mail, call forwarding, call following, hands-free dialing and many more, you can stay in touch with your boss, secretary, clients, co-workers, mother, kids — probably even your dog if you want to. And if you go to another city, no problem: your calls will literally hunt you down. You don't have to tell anyone where you're going, or even *that* you've gone. Pretty soon, astronauts will be taking them on the space shuttle.

The machines do have off switches, of course. The fact is that most people who use them don't want them switched off. When Bell Cellular Inc. ran an ad depicting a businessman being pursued through the woods by a phone-equipped car, it was "very well received," said president Robert Latham. "There's a group of people who want to be in touch." Ultimately, then, we must look to the human psyche — not the gadgetry — to find the driving force behind the mobile techno-work craze.

Its cachet as a status symbol is clear — typified in an ad run by a car manufacturer to pitch one of its upscale vehicles to the "mobile executive" who, we're told, needs immediate access to information at all times. Declaring that a car must meet the needs of people with a "career on the move," the ad shows us this mobile person standing beside the car with cellular phone at the ear, portable computer at the fingertips and portable fax machine lurking at the ready on the hood nearby.

Nor is there any need to "drop the ball" (as one article put it) if you're on a plane, 30,000 feet over the ocean. Many aircraft now have phones that operate on air-to-ground communications and British Airways announced recently that it's installed Skyphones on two of its aircraft, reportedly the first to use satellite communications to relay calls all over the world. You can dial any of 190 countries for $9.50 a minute. The airline says that passengers may soon be able to receive incoming phone calls and faxes during their flight and may be allowed

---

* After Toronto's new SkyDome stadium was built, Bell Cellular Inc. decided to install transmission equipment inside the ballpark so that cellular users don't have to suffer telephone withdrawal when the retractable dome is closed.

to use their own portable phones. An international consortium has announced that it will soon be offering a full range of inflight telecommunications services to more than 350 airlines that will allow executives "to maintain contact and conduct business almost as if they were at the office."

For some workers, all this electronic gadgetry can be quite liberating. Since it permits people to work when they feel most alert — even if that happens to be in the middle of the night — computer technology has the potential to release owls and other phase-delayed "misfits" from the lark-inspired tyranny of the 9-to-5 office routine. "Even though there are more distractions at home, it's easier to work at the best time," says Mary Carskadon, who believes that the trend toward flexible work hours and working at home will make napping increasingly feasible as a method of coping with long work hours.

Working at home will also give many people — particularly single parents — more flexibility in handling family responsibilities, although it won't eliminate child-care problems, since watching children and doing work that demands undivided attention won't mix any better at home than they do at the office. Most professional women who work at home require full-time child care, according to Kathleen Christensen, who has written a book called *Women and Home-Based Work.*

"Telecommuting" will also free many workers from spending long, draining and unproductive hours in gridlocked traffic — something that would also have a salutary effect on the environment. (Smog-bound California has already brought in air pollution legislation aimed at reducing work-related car usage.) Telecommuting is still comparatively rare — according to one estimate, only about 20,000 people in the United States were doing it full-time in 1988 — but it's predicted that millions will be doing it on a full- or part-time basis by the turn of the century.

Despite these advantages, however, the new technologies probably will result in people working longer hours and they will undoubtedly cause further blurring of the lines between work and leisure time. These electronic goodies do more than merely *permit* people to work anywhere, anytime — they have fostered a work ethic that says they ought to. One woman stockbroker who gave up trading because it meant following the markets around the clock says that trying to be "a little bit of a trader" was like being "a little bit pregnant."

"There's a feeding frenzy for information," says William Allen, president of a Toronto investment firm, Allenvest Group Ltd. The investment world, he says, is particularly afflicted with "dumbophobia" — the fear of not knowing. "They're traumatized that somewhere in the world, something of modest importance is going on and they don't know about it. It's becoming an enormous racket, purveying the ultimate wisdom without which you can't even brush your teeth, never mind do your job."

Given this level of competitiveness, many people feel under pressure to be available at all times. "I'm never out of the office" is a comment frequently heard from plugged-in executives and professionals. Whether this is a boast or a complaint — or a little of both — is not always clear, but one thing that often seems to be missing is any real appreciation that human physiology simply doesn't have the same staying power as the machines.

University of Texas professor James Quick suggests only half jokingly that these devices perhaps ought to have warning labels that they can be dangerous to your health. "The risk in being able to work around the clock anywhere in the world is that you'll do just that," he told *Psychology Today*. "You may get a lot done, but you also may be dead sooner."

• **Women, men and work**: With the rise of feminism in the 1970s, women were told they could "have it all" — work, marriage and family. But after two decades of trying to play Superwoman, many women have come to the disconcerting realization that, as one battle-weary participant put it, "having it all means doing it all." Numerous studies have shown that while women struggle for job and pay equality with men — with all the demands on their energies that that entails — they continue to bear a disproportionate responsibility for housework and child care. In fact, many women, whether married or not, put in what amounts to a second full workday looking after the home and children. (One study cited the case of a judge who reduced compensation to a bereaved family by refusing to accept their claim about how much work the woman of the house had done, both in the home and working at a part-time job outside. He remarked that there weren't enough hours in the day for anyone to do that much work.)

A 1987 Harris poll found that although men are doing more around the house than they used to, women still do most of the cleaning, cooking and caring for children, even though most of them work just as many hours outside the home as men. The unequal burden of marriage on women was cited as the major source of pressure on U.S. families. Similarly, a study by researchers at two Texas universities characterized marriage as a "weakened and declining institution" because women are not getting as much out of it as they once did; for most, marriage means an increased workload rather than the historical bartering of homemaking services for financial security. A 1988 *Time* magazine poll found that 73 percent of women complained of having too little leisure time, compared with 51 percent of men.

Economists Jeff Biddle and Daniel Hamermesh found a difference in the behavior of men and women who work longer hours when they are paid more. Men do this by reducing their sleep time, while women steal time from leisure activities, not from sleep. Hamermesh speculates that this may be because the women are already operating too close to their biological limit for sleep. When they compared working women and men with similar characteristics and lifestyles, the researchers found that the women slept, on average, about five percent less than the men, which probably reflects the fact that women continue to carry the major burden of work in the home, Hamermesh said. Their study showed that men's sleep time was "essentially unaffected" by the presence of young children in the family, but "young mothers' sleep is substantially reduced by the care devoted to young children."

All indications are that this situation is common everywhere, regardless of economic or political ideology. Studies in the Soviet Union indicate that most women there work full-time and put in another 40-hour week on family work, according to an article by Jeff Sallot, Moscow bureau chief for the Toronto *Globe and Mail.* He quotes a woman who ridiculed (wearily) the suggestion that women in their 30s are more sexually active than other age groups. In a letter to a Soviet magazine, she asks what kind of sex she could possibly have on her mind after working 8 hours a day, lining up in shopping queues during her lunch hour and after work, and doing a "second shift" of domestic work in the evening. Her husband sulks, she adds, "but sees no need to help me."

Single mothers are even more hard-pressed because of continuing day-care shortages. Here, too, women's burden is disproportionate; despite changes in child-custody arrangements, they still comprise the majority of single parents and their careers are, for the most part, far more affected by child-care problems than those of men. Single parenthood often causes extraordinary difficulties for women in getting an education or training and in finding and keeping a job and a home, and their situation is often made all the more desperate by difficulties in collecting court-awarded child-support payments from ex-husbands. Even for women who are economically self-sufficient, child care represents a major claim on their time and energies that unquestionably affects their competitiveness with men in the workplace. One indication of this is the trend among professional women to hire full-time nannies, and sometimes not just one during the day but another for evenings or weekends.

Women put in a "double day" involving paid work, housework and child-rearing, which causes a kind of stress rarely experienced by men, according to Sylvia Gold, president of the Canadian Advisory Council on the Status of Women. She was commenting on a study that concluded that the stress caused by the combination of these duties may be the leading health hazard for women. Economic recession also hits women harder, the report noted; it intensifies their domestic role, forcing them to spend more time "bargain-hunting, preparing food, cleaning and repairing clothes and looking after children."

Because of the persistence of the double standard in business and the professions, many women have stopped trying to "have it all" and are struggling to find new, female-oriented work styles. It isn't easy, especially in professions still dominated by men.

Women lawyers face subtle pressure to emulate the male ideal of success, which means that they must work long hours and not take time off, even for maternity leave, says Toronto lawyer Carole Curtis, a family law specialist with an interest in women's issues. "The male model of success in our profession is partnership in a large firm — long hours of work at a very high pace. It's also based on having a wife — on having somebody else to have your children, somebody else to cook your meals, somebody else to buy your pork chops. If you look at highly successful men, one of the reasons that they're free to work 12-hour days and bring work home on the weekend is that they have a personal manager at home.

"It's tremendously liberating to have your life planned and organized like that. All of us had it as children because we had mothers, and men have it as adults, but women do not have that freedom. A disproportionate number of highly motivated, highly successful women are unmarried or childless in comparison to the same level of achievers who are men."

Felice Schwartz, president of Catalyst, an organization that specializes in leadership development of women, writes in the *Harvard Business Review* that, by age 40, 90 percent of executive men have children, compared with only 35 percent of executive women. She says that the male corporate culture perceives women who are as competitive and aggressive as men ("career-primary women") to be unfeminine, while those who struggle for a balance between work and family are viewed as lacking in professional commitment. In fact, women who do try the balancing act run the risk of being derailed onto the middle-management "mommy track" leading nowhere. Some women may not mind being "plateaued" in this way, but for others who do want to get ahead in their careers, their reward for carrying a triple workload is to place third in the pecking order, behind men and single women. *

Ironically, some men — though still very few — are finding out what it's like to be bumped off the fast track by the same tug-of-war between career and family life that has exhausted women for the past two decades. Because most married women are now working outside the home, ** men are under increasing pressure to share household and child-care responsibilities, and they find it harder to justify to their wives spending extra time at work when both spouses are bringing in a paycheck. Some couples have even gone so far as to work out job-sharing arrangements with their employers (putting themselves into the sociological niche known as "part-time urban professional parents" or puppies). Men are also more likely than at any time in the past to have shared or sole custody of children after divorce. Consequently, many of them are, for the first time, facing the problem of explaining to the boss why they can't work late at the office or take an out-of-town business trip because they have to pick up their

---

* Many women, tired of the unequal battle in male-dominated corporations, opt to start their own companies. Studies have shown that in recent years women have started small businesses at a greater rate than men and they've generally had greater staying power. But the price they pay is working longer hours than most salaried employees.

** In Canada, more than 70 percent of married women between the ages of 20 and 44 work outside the home, including half the women with children still living with them. Men are the sole breadwinners in only seven percent of Canadian families, compared with 70 percent three decades ago.

children at the day-care center or take them to the dentist.

Employers are inclined to welcome such requests from men even less than they do from women. At the most senior levels, business executives and managers belong largely to the prebaby-boom generation. The article in *Fortune* said that fewer than a dozen baby boomers (the oldest of whom are in their early to mid-40s) have as yet made it to the pinnacle of large corporations. There is evidence that despite the profound social changes of the past two decades, many older senior executives remain entrenched in the view that men go to work and wives stay at home and take care of the house and kids. These executives typically overestimate by a considerable margin the number of their employees whose family life fits this traditional pattern; during a seminar at Harvard University, their estimates ranged from 40 to 70 percent, whereas the real figure was a mere 10 percent.

An article on "the new executive father" in *The Globe and Mail*'s *Report on Business Magazine* noted that the demands that family responsibilities now put on men are viewed with "mixed emotion" even by enlightened managers because intensified business competition has made "bottom-line realities" tougher than ever. As one executive father put it, leaving work at 3:00 p.m. to attend a child's school play still does not meet with executive approval, but more fathers are doing it anyway. In order to spend more time with his children, this man reduced his work week from more than 60 hours to between 40 and 50 hours.

But men who do this are finding what women have known all along — you pay a professional price if you're not willing to put in long hours on the job. For example, one U.S. study of 1,100 single fathers found that four to five percent said they'd been fired as a result of child-care problems and another eight percent said they had quit their jobs. About one-third said they'd had to reduce travel or miss work and 42 percent said they'd had to arrive at work late and leave early. Fathers who share custody were less likely to be fired or quit, but they missed work just about as much.

Some studies have suggested that men sometimes experience even more stress than women do in the same circumstances because their identities are still more closely tied to their work and because in the male-oriented business world a preoccupation with the needs of children over those of the job is still widely considered to be unmanly. Men, says Schwartz, continue to regard parenting as "fundamentally female" and a career as "fundamentally male." Since many still perceive women as "the rearers of their children," they find it appropriate for a woman to renounce her career in favor of raising a family.

However, such behavior is rarely acceptable in male employees. One man who cited family reasons for turning down a job requiring a lot of travel was asked by his boss why he didn't have his wife "under control." The lack of applicants for paternity leave (in the rare situations in which it's available) is further evidence of an awareness that family obligations and professional advancement don't mix. Why a man would want to stay home with children is beyond the comprehension of most male bosses, according to one business consultant who specializes in flexible work schedules.

Like single mothers, single fathers find child care time-consuming and energy draining. One man, a university professor, commented that after spending the early evening with his kids and putting them to bed, he has a hard time resuming his research because he is just "too damn tired."

In a 1987 cover story on relations between the sexes, *Time* magazine noted that women who are "staggering under the burden of trying to be all things to all people" are now asking men to do the same. "Can this work, or will it merely leave everybody frazzled?" Just six months later, the magazine ran another cover story entitled: "The Rat Race, How America Is Running Itself Ragged." It quoted Arlie Hochschild, author of a book on working couples, saying that many of the people she interviewed "talked about sleep the way a hungry person talks about food."

Certainly, a lot of people on the fast track in business and the professions are frazzled and worse: alcohol and drug abuse are common occupational hazards and burnout occurs frequently.* Psychologists report seeing "victims of success": people not yet 40 who have found the achievement of success and wealth to be disconcertingly disappointing — as in the case of one man who started treatment

---

* An extreme example concerns a senior civil servant who resigned after pleading guilty in court to a charge of assault following an incident on board an aircraft in which he grabbed a stewardess by the wrists several times and used abusive and obscene language. The man's lawyer described him as a workaholic who had had only a few hours' sleep the night before the 9-hour flight; he was on medication for high blood pressure and had also taken several sleeping pills. The combination of fatigue, medication and a few drinks had led to the man's "antisocial behavior," the lawyer said.

for depression just two months after achieving a lifelong dream of being worth $1 million. The money, he found, improved his bank balance but not his self-esteem.

Insomnia is one of the first warning signs of stress. Studies have shown that people sleep significantly less than normal, and report needing more sleep, during periods of high stress. Persistent sleep disturbance is a major feature of burnout caused by chronic stress. A Swedish researcher, Gunilla Burell of the University of Uppsala, evaluated 33 insomniacs and found that they all showed a considerable tendency to be Type A personalities — people who exhibit hard-driving, time-pressured behavior, extreme competitiveness and easily aroused anger and hostility. The level of Type A behavior among the insomniac patients exceeded that found in nonpatients and was even somewhat higher than that found among heart patients. (Coronary heart disease has been found to be correlated with Type A behavior.) The insomniacs expressed anger and resentment related to past events or chronic problems with other people and they often put excessive demands on themselves and others.

Curiously, however, the sleep problems of white-collar workaholics seem to command relatively little attention from sleep researchers, compared with those of shift workers and people who work in high-stress life-and-death occupations. This probably stems from several factors: the latter groups (particularly shift workers) include very large numbers of workers; their sleep problems are more directly tied to the nature of the work and are arguably more profound; and, finally, the consequences of human error in many of these occupations can be catastrophic. But there may also be a perception that professionals and business executives have far more personal control over their work lives than many other workers — that their workaholism is more a matter of choice than necessity — and that, in any event, they are well rewarded for their work, financially and intellectually. "Forget about executives and all these people who have fantasies that they're really making the difference in the world," says David Dinges dismissively. "They wear better suits, they make better money, but they don't work particularly long hours. If they hang around the office, it's usually because their personal lives are in a wreck."

Still, fatigue and sleep-related problems among executives, managers and professionals can have far-reaching social and economic consequences. In North America, job-related stress costs tens of billions of dollars a year in health care and lost productivity, according to some estimates. And it's not hard to find cases in which fatigue and overwork in the white-collar world affect us all. Politics and the law provide some disquieting instances in which important social, political and economic decisions have been made by people enduring a considerable amount of sleep deprivation. For example:

• In December 1987, the U.S. Congress passed a $604-billion omnibus appropriation bill in a one-week blitz during which senators and representatives were making multibillion-dollar decisions in a daze of 18-hour workdays. Similar circumstances occur right down to the level of municipal government: during one 3:00 a.m. vote, bleary-eyed councillers in Metropolitan Toronto set the pay of the area's six mayors at exactly zero. Later, according to one weary participant, they were "still trying to figure out what happened." In a letter to a local newspaper, a citizen suggested that it was hardly reassuring for taxpayers to see the officials running their billion-dollar municipal corporation making decisions in such a condition.

• In December 1987, the final text of the Canada-U.S. free trade agreement, a pact with multibillion-dollar implications for both countries, was hammered out during a weekend bargaining session that stretched over three days and late into two consecutive nights.* The agreement, which met with strong opposition in Canada, became the focal point of a bitterly fought election in the fall of 1988, and in December, newly reelected Prime Minister Brian Mulroney suspended the rules of the House of Commons to extend sittings up to midnight each night in an effort to get the implementing legislation passed before the Christmas break. He was accused of trying to "legislate by exhaustion" by the opposition.

• In June 1987, Mulroney and the leaders of Canada's 10 provinces met for 19 hours continuously to work out the legal language of a new constitutional agreement between the federal and provincial governments. Some of the most crucial aspects of the agreement were negotiated in the wee hours of the morning, a period described in subsequent news reports as being very tense. One official was quoted

---

* It was not long afterward that Patricia Carney, Canada's International Trade minister at the time of the negotiations, resigned for reasons of poor health and exhaustion after serving in several high-profile portfolios. "I am worn out," she told the media, adding that she'd "crammed a whole political career into eight years."

as saying, "I would have shot every constitutional lawyer in the world in the middle of the night." One of the most controversial provisions of the agreement — a section dealing with the province of Quebec's status as a "distinct society" within the Canadian federation — was finally settled between about 2:00 and 3:00 a.m. after many long hours of haggling. This provision subsequently became a major source of national discord, and by the end of 1989 the agreement appeared to be unraveling. These issues "should not have been decided in the middle of the night," said one opponent.

• Officials of the Toronto Stock Exchange had to handle a major crisis stemming from the collapse of a large Canadian investment firm just a few months after the stock-market crash of October 1987. One official enduring a series of 12-hour workdays wearily noted that they'd come through the "October meltdown" in a tired condition, only to face this new crisis. Management experts commented that the situation demonstrated certain classic features of a crisis — including the need for rapid decision-making on the basis of incomplete information by people who were becoming ever more fatigued.

Fatigue and sleeplessness are also an integral part of many labor/management negotiations. Some negotiatiors, in fact, believe that mediators often deliberately employ around-the-clock bargaining sessions to test the resolve of both sides in a dispute. In 1987, in the midst of yet another strike in Canada's perennially troubled postal service, a union negotiator commented that government mediator William Kelly "probably figures that by five o'clock in the morning, [his ideas] will sound better." But Kelly, who settled many tough strikes in 22 years as a top-ranked mediator, was later quoted in *The Globe and Mail* saying he didn't consciously aim to wear negotiators down, although this might have been a secondary benefit. It was just that when things finally start to move, "you don't quit," he said.

The legal system is another venue in which important decisions are often made in a context of overwork and fatigue. In both Canada and the United States, the courts are overloaded at all levels, which causes long delays and burnout among judges and lawyers. For example, in December 1988, Mr. Justice Gerald Le Dain resigned from the Supreme Court of Canada as a result of nervous strain. During his tenure in the mid-1980s, the Court was called upon to decide a number of thorny cases relating to the new Canadian Constitution and the

Charter of Rights and Freedoms and it was said that the seriousness of his decisions constantly worried Le Dain. "He slept with his decisions, he ate with them and he went on vacation with them," commented one observer.

Lawyers, too, often find themselves caught up in trials that are not only time-consuming and demanding, but emotionally draining as well. One particularly noteworthy example is a long (145-day), controversial and highly charged trial that occurred in Hamilton, Ontario, in 1987, in which the parents of two young girls were charged with satanic ritual child abuse. Afterward, lawyer John Harper, who represented the Children's Aid Society, ended up in the intensive care ward with a heart attack at the age of 39. For five months, he'd spent his days in court and most of each night preparing for the next day, surviving on coffee, cigarettes and a few hours of what he called "skim sleeping."

Toronto lawyer Michael Hartrick, who was involved in the same case, was also exhausted by the length and the emotional wear and tear of the trial and by a 90-minute daily commute to Hamilton. He too worked nights and weekends, juggling the demands of the trial with the needs of his other clients. Normally a sound sleeper, Hartrick found himself waking up abruptly night after night after only a few hours of sleep with an overpowering sensation of being in the middle of the court case. Usually, he could not get back to sleep.

"Lawyers who do demanding intellectual work late at night often don't sleep," comments Mamelak. In fact, anyone who does mentally demanding work just before bed — teachers, researchers, writers, executives — is likely to share this problem. "I've seen a lot of people for whom alcoholism started this way," says Mamelak. "They're wound up and they start to drink at night in order to sleep."

## DIFFICULT COMBINATIONS

In some occupations, many of the elements discussed — shift work, jet lag, excessively long work hours, high performance demands, sleep disruption and high risks associated with human error — come together to create unusual amounts of stress, often for extended periods of time. Examples from four different fields will be considered: medicine (interns and residents); transportation (truckers, train operators, seamen, pilots and air traffic controllers); sports; and the space program (ground crews and astronauts/cosmonauts).

## I. Medicine

The resident rubbed his face wearily and suddenly stopped speaking in midsentence. Blinking, he asked journalist Mike Wallace of "60 Minutes" to repeat the question he'd just asked. The doctor was coming off a 36-hour hospital shift, during which he'd slept for only 3 hours, and he looked it: his drawn, morose face bore little resemblance to the fresh, cheerful countenance with which he'd started the shift.

Wallace observed that it was disquieting to think of being treated by a doctor who was so tired that he couldn't keep a few questions straight in his mind. The comments of other residents on the show were also disquieting: they described patients as the bane of their existence and expressed resentment at patients for taking up their time, for not being appreciative and especially for not getting well. (Patients were sometimes called GOMER, for "get out of my emergency room." ) These doctors described feelings of depression and cynicism; one said that what bothered him about death was the paperwork — which elicited a weary laugh from the others in the room. Another doctor said he sometimes experienced hallucinations from sleep deprivation and added that, after about 24 hours without sleep, "you start to cry."

These are not isolated cases; variations on the theme can be found at just about any teaching hospital in North America, where medical school graduates train prior to obtaining their licenses. The training program is intended to provide young doctors with the supervised practical experience they need before they can assume independent responsibility for patient care. Internships usually last one or two years, after which a doctor can become a general practitioner. Residencies, which are required for specialities such as surgery, internal medicine, pediatrics or obstetrics and gynecology, can take another eight or 10 years.

Throughout North America, these residents and interns (often referred to as house staff) are required to put in extremely long hours — typically 90 to 100 hours or more a week. Every three or four days, on average, they spend 36 hours (two full days and a night) on call in the hospital, responding to whatever emergencies arise. Although residents and interns are allowed to sleep while on call, in practice they rarely get more than a couple of hours' sleep and often they get none at all.

"It depends on the service that you're on," says Robert Conn, a resident at the Hospital for Sick Children in Toronto, who is specializing in children's heart surgery, and a former president of the Canadian Association of Internes and Residents. "For example, on some of the internal medicine services, you will be up for that entire 36 hours, actively working all of the time. In some of the surgical specialities, you can be in the operating room for the majority of that 36 hours. In some of the other services, you may sleep the whole night." He estimated that most interns and residents spend at least 80 percent of the 36 hours awake. And even if they do sleep, they may not be very rested. As we saw in Chapter 11, on-call sleeping is often shallow and restless because the sleeper anticipates being wakened.

In Ontario, residents and interns are not allowed to work 36-hour shifts more than once every third day, averaged over a three-month period; in practice, this means there can be occasions when they work 36-hour shifts every second day. One survey found that the average work week across all specialities was about 95 hours, but work weeks exceeding 100 hours are not uncommon, said Conn. Entering his 10th year as a resident, he said he can now sleep "anywhere anytime" — even standing up. He said it's common for doctors to nap briefly during periods of inactivity in the operating room; in open heart surgery, for example, there are times when the patient is rewarming while on by-pass equipment "so there's 25 minutes of just standing waiting. That's a perfect time to catch 5 minutes of sleep."

The long work hours, plus frequent schedule changes that make for a disruptive, irregular work pattern involving rapid alternations between day and night shifts, means that both chronic and acute sleep deprivation are built into the system. This work schedule, part of a long-standing tradition in medical training, is one that in most industrial or business settings would be illegal under labor laws in most jurisdictions. Nevertheless, it's standard procedure in a field that involves the expenditure of billions of dollars of public funds and the well-being of millions of people each year.

Amazingly, residents and interns today actually work fewer hours than they did two or three decades ago, when shifts every other night were common.

However, increasing demand on hospital services, combined with budget restrictions and shortages of nursing and support staff, have increased the workload and stress associated with residency. Writing in the *New England Journal of Medicine*, Dr. Timothy McCall says that today residents have more and sicker patients to treat than ever before; a greater amount of factual knowledge is required and aggressive medical treatment is more routine than in the past. Conn noted that the Ontario government, in trying to reduce the number of doctors in the province, is cutting back on the number of residents and interns; however, "the size of the hospitals and the number of beds aren't being reduced that much, so the amount of work per person is going up."

In recent years, this system has become increasingly controversial since a New York grand jury found that the long working hours of residents had contributed to the death of a young woman in a New York City teaching hospital. In 1987, a special committee set up by the state to investigate the working conditions of residents recommended that they should not work for more than 12 consecutive hours in the emergency department or, "as a matter of course," for more than 24 consecutive hours in other departments. They also said that residents' work week should not exceed an average of 80 hours a week over a four-week period. "By ordinary standards, an 80-hour work week is excessive; by existing standards for residents, it is a significant reform."

New York State subsequently limited the work hours of postgraduate trainees (*and* attending physicians) to no more than 12 consecutive hours on each assignment to an emergency department with more than 15,000 visits a year. Otherwise, trainees are not permitted to work more than 80 hours a week averaged over a four-week period, or to be scheduled for shifts exceeding 24 consecutive hours.

Some critics of the traditional system say it is maintained more because an antiquated macho work ethic of "toughing it out" still prevails in the profession rather than because this is the ideal way to train doctors or care for patients. (Conn notes that when residents retail stories about their on-call shifts, they complain about the long hours, but "it's complaining with a bragging element.")

Many medical education experts say that the grueling workload is necessary to ensure that future doctors are adequately trained in all aspects of medicine. They say patients would not be satisfied being cared for by a doctor who has never had any personal experience with the medical condition he or she is being called on to treat. They also cite continuity of care as an important factor, saying that patients are better served by doctors who know their personal medical histories. One senior doctor interviewed on "60 Minutes" said that illnesses aren't like "snapshots"; instead, they evolve over several hours or days, and doctors must learn how to deal with the "total problem."

Moreover, errors can occur if cases are shifted among different doctors too often, says Norman Levinsky of Boston University Medical Center, who noted in *The New England Journal of Medicine* that mistakes can be attributed to faulty information transfer as least as often as to fatigue resulting from being on call all night. He said there's no evidence to support claims that inadequate supervision of residents and interns and long work weeks are major causes of poor patient care, a view echoed by Robert Glickman of Columbia University's College of Physicians and Surgeons, who wrote that "isolated, individual lapses" do not provide support for such claims.*

However, critics of the current system — including many interns and residents — argue that tired doctors neither learn well nor provide optimum care to patients. They cite studies showing that sleep-deprived residents and interns exhibit deficiencies in mental functions, psychomotor performance, mood and behavior. Their mathematical skills and their ability to recognize abnormal heart rhythms from electrocardiograms have been shown to be impaired, and they experience difficulty in thinking and problems with short-term memory.

Conn noted that it is primarily the routine tasks, particularly paperwork, that are the hardest to cope with while fatigued. "If there's something life-threatening or something that requires a lot of attention, somehow you get the adrenaline surge and you're able to do it. But charting, recording what it is you've done, is the hardest." Yet record-keeping is extremely important, both for patient care and for legal reasons. Fortunately, he said, "there are quite a few checks in the system."

The long work hours also affect doctors' moods and emotions. A survey of more than 600 medical students found that one-third reported symptoms of anxiety greater than levels experienced in the normal population. Long work hours and little personal time were

---

* They say that residents' fatigue can be reduced by measures other than reducing their work hours — notably increasing nonmedical staff and support facilities to assume many routine and technical tasks now assigned to residents because they're a cheap source of labor.

two of the major reasons cited for this anxiety. Other studies have shown that residents and interns frequently exhibit symptoms of depression, irritability, depersonalization, cynicism and chronic anger. "You hate to think that you're not being a good doctor, but there are times when you're so tired that you can come to view the patient as the enemy," says Conn. "Especially when you've done everything you possibly can to make them better and they're still not getting better. The nurse is calling you to say they're getting worse and you're exhausted and you can't think of anything else to do. There's some resentment. It's like, 'If you don't want to get better, okay.'"

Conn said fatigue also makes doctors irritable when they're forced to switch suddenly from dealing with a life-and-death situation to a less serious problem. "You're with a family trying to bring them to some understanding that their son has just died, as well as asking for organ donations. I don't care who you are, that takes a toll. Twenty minutes later you get a phone call from a nurse asking about somebody's bowel movements and suppositories. To her, that's really important — and to the patient too — but I'm absolutely exhausted and I've just dealt with something that's really stressful." In such circumstances, he said, it's difficult to maintain a sense of balance and to treat each problem with respect "without thinking, 'What the heck are they bothering me with this for?' "

Far from being rewarded for getting to know patients, residents are effectively punished for it, McCall says. They try to get their work done as fast as possible and to avoid time-consuming activities, such as talking with patients any longer than necessary, because this delays their departure from the hospital or cuts into what little sleep they get on call. (As one doctor put it, they have "no patience with their patients.") McCall said they can be ruthless in protecting their sleep; if called to examine a patient, they may resist going personally and instead give orders over the phone. He added that many residents try to lighten their workload by manipulating attending physicians to discharge patients as rapidly as possible.

He contends that the overwork fosters arrogance in doctors, an attitude that the world "owes them" for what they've endured. Patients complain frequently about lack of communication and the failure of doctors to spend enough time with them; these "bad habits," learned in residency, fuel the current malpractice crisis in the United

States, McCall said. Similar concerns were expressed in a 1988 report of the New York Academy of Medicine, which concluded that medical schools must train doctors to be "more skilled in doctor-patient relationships."

Conn, who has trained both in Canada and the United States, said U.S. medical students place a higher priority on the status and financial rewards of becoming a doctor than Canadian students, who know they're going into a system based on government-supported medicare. But even in Canada, the grueling workload in residency causes lingering resentment, and Conn suggested this may have played a role in a bitter showdown between doctors and the Ontario government over extra-billing.* "There was a lot of doctor-bashing going on," Conn said. "There's a real resentment that builds up because doctors are working long hours; they really do care about their patients and then you hear people say that doctors are fat cats and they don't care."

Another question in dispute is whether residents and interns can learn anything while in a state of extreme fatigue. McCall says there's no scientific support for the idea that working long hours improves either medical education or the quality of patient care. "Residents are so drained . . . that they are rarely in the best state of mind to learn from their experiences." They have little time to read or study and often fail to attend conferences. Even when they do, they may not get much out of it — except for an opportunity to grab a few minutes of much-needed sleep "the minute the slide projector comes on," says Conn, who described one conference at which he estimated that "40 percent of the room was asleep."

Conn agrees with proponents of the current system that having too many doctors looking after a patient is not ideal: "When you have one person responsible, they worry about those patients 24 hours a day, and the quality of care is much better. And certainly there are some things that you learn by following one patient through from beginning to end. But there's no question that when you're exhausted your ability to learn, or more appropriately, your ability to be *interested* in learning, is really reduced."

---

\* Extra-billing refers to the practice by some doctors, mostly specialists, of billing patients directly for more than the amount covered by medicare according to guidelines set by the Ontario Medical Association.

This is one situation in which regularly scheduled ultrashort napping might be put to good use, Claudio Stampi suggests. Residents might, for example, try to schedule naps of about 10 to 30 minutes every four hours throughout their shift, including at the beginning of the work period, to prevent the accumulation of a large sleep debt. The nap duration would depend on the individual. Stampi suggests that if a nap must be missed because of an emergency, it should not be postponed but should be eliminated altogether and the next nap should be taken at its originally scheduled time. "You adapt to accept the napping at regular intervals; everything in your body is geared to receive sleep. You would confuse your biological rhythms if you delay the nap, so it's better just to skip it and go to the next one."

## II. Transportation

Operating a vehicle is one of the most sensitive measures of alertness. Not coincidentally, it is also one of the most dangerous things to do while sleepy. It's impossible to tell exactly how much of the death and property loss that results from transportation accidents is caused by sleepiness and fatigue, but circumstantial evidence suggests the toll must be considerable. It has been estimated that as many as 13 percent of the more than 50,000 deaths caused each year by automobile accidents in the United States may be attributable to falling asleep at the wheel. Each year, these and other transportation-related accidents result in medical expenses, insurance costs, property loss and lost wages running into the tens of billions of dollars; according to one estimate, a single major air accident can cost an airline as much as half a billion dollars.

Between 65 and 90 percent of these accidents are caused by human error, according to John Lauber of the U.S. National Transportation Safety Board (NTSB). But in a speech at the annual meeting of the Association of Professional Sleep Societies in June 1988, he said that the real challenge for accident investigators is "to get behind the mere fact of human error" and to discover the "why" of human error. Investigators now routinely examine lifestyle issues — including sleep/wake patterns — to discover what may have affected the performance of a pilot or train engineer, ship's captain or truck driver. While they do find some "horror stories," the findings are more commonly "ambiguous, inconclusive and . . . downright misleading.

The true incidence of fatigue as a causal or contributory factor is largely unknown. Unlike metal fatigue, human fatigue generally leaves no telltale signs, and we can only infer its presence from circumstantial evidence."

Some people, he said, suggest that fatigue causes many of the accidents that have two main features: long periods of inactivity and equipment monitoring, and human error resulting from inattentiveness and poor judgment. But others suggest that there has been an "overeager attribution" of accidents to sleep disorders and fatigue. There is probably some truth in both assertions, Lauber says, and sleep researchers could help accident investigators by developing better methods and theories to determine the role that sleep problems play in causing accidents and by providing realistic, not overblown, assessments of the validity of claims that fatigue, sleepiness or circadian factors have caused accidents or incidents.

Nevertheless, Lauber was able to provide several rather dramatic case studies in which fatigue, sleepiness, irregular work schedules and the monotony of a low-stimulus environment clearly contributed to major accidents in all transportation sectors. Most of these accidents occurred at night, usually in the circadian trough, and in all cases, some combination of long duty hours, irregular work schedules and lack of sleep were at least contributory causes.

## TRAINS

In April 1984, in two separate incidents barely a week apart, four Burlington Northern freight trains were involved in collisions that derailed 12 locomotives and 61 cars, killed seven trainmen and injured four and caused more than $5-million in damage. The first incident, a head-on collision near Wiggins, Colorado, occurred at 3.58 a.m.; the second, a rear-ender near Newcastle, Wyoming, occurred at 4.56 a.m.

In both cases, according to Lauber, crew fatigue and irregular work schedules contributed to the accidents. In fact, the NTSB determined that both accidents were probably caused by the crews' failure to comply with signals because they were asleep. Contributing factors included the use of alcohol and marijuana and fatigue resulting from irregular and unpredictable work schedules and voluntary lack of sleep during off-duty hours. Whether at home or at an away-terminal, the trainmen could not determine when they would next be called to go on duty, Lauber said. Moreover, he added, facilities at the away-terminals for sleep and recreation were inadequate and might be said to encourage drug and alcohol consumption.

Lauber added that the company failed to acknowledge the effects of inadequate rest on performance and crews "were very aware that they would not meet any supervisory personnel at away-terminals and knew they were unlikely to be supervised at night at all."

At least two studies have documented the fact that sleepiness and circadian factors can affect train operations. For example, a Swedish study in which 11 engineers were wired with electrodes to measure brain waves and eye movements found that six of the trainmen dozed while on duty and two slept while the train sailed through a warning signal. And a German study that analyzed more than 2,200 instances in which train engineers failed to respond to warning switches found that the problem occurred most often during the circadian troughs at 3:00 a.m. and 2:00 p.m.

## SHIPS

In February 1985, at 12:20 a.m., a car ferry ran aground on Mona Island, Puerto Rico. The NSTB found that the master failed to monitor the ship's progress or to maintain an adequate lookout and that he assumed watch while fatigued and on medication. Lauber said there was evidence the master suffered from both chronic and acute fatigue; he had not had a single day off in a year, and during the week of the accident, his schedule permitted only 3 hours off each day in addition to 7 to 8 hours allowed for sleep. At the time of the accident, he had gone 42 hours without sleep because of a combination of insomnia and work duties.

More than 200 passengers and crew were evacuated to Mona Island and the $5-million vessel was a write-off.

In April 1988, a Japanese tanker went aground in the Strait of Juan de Fuca off the coast of the state of Washington. According to investigators, the second mate, who was on watch from midnight to 4:00 a.m., fell asleep sometime after 2:15 a.m. and awoke at 3:15 a.m. after the ship had run aground. Lauber quoted a NSTB marine investigator saying that one of his former skippers had had a solution for maintaining alertness on watch: "The watch officer was *never* allowed to sit and seldom was allowed to come inside out of the weather." Lauber noted that while these techniques might prevent people from falling asleep on the job, they are of "dubious value in assuring long-term attention to duty."

The largest oil spill in U.S. history occurred in the early morning hours of March 25, 1989, when the tanker Exxon *Valdez* went aground on a reef off the Alaskan coast and spilled 240,000 barrels of oil in a formerly pristine fjord. The accident occurred shortly after midnight while the ship's third mate was in control of the ship. Several months later, *Time* ran a cover story about the results of its investigation into the accident, in which it suggested that crew fatigue might have been a factor. It said that personnel cutbacks in the merchant marine had led to understaffing of ships and, as a result, 12- to 14-hour workdays had become routine.

## TRUCKS

Driving a truck is tiring business, whether on the open highway or in the city, says Andy Turnbull, editor of *Truck News*, an industry newspaper. "City driving in a big truck is just plain tiring. These trucks can have up to 20 gears. When [a driver] pulls away from a stop sign, he may shift three times before he gets across the street. And the strain of maneuvering a 45-foot trailer around a corner that is built for a 20-foot car is a real problem. On the highway, you have a different type of fatigue: it's just boredom, droning boredom."

Lauber cited several incidents involving trucks that illustrate "some of the more flagrant abuses of physiology and prudence" that have come to the NSTB's attention:

• An intercity bus and a truck collided at 4:15 a.m. on an interstate highway in Arkansas, injuring 28 people. The truck driver had had only 2 hours of sleep in the 21 hours before the accident and there was evidence of alcohol and marijuana use. The NTSB concluded that "the combined effects of fatigue due to sleep deprivation, monotony, and vulnerability to attention lapses at that hour of the day" reduced the driver's vigilance, affected his judgment and contributed to the commission of several errors.

• In North Carolina, a truck collided with two vehicles, one a school bus carrying 27 children. Six were killed, 12 were seriously injured and the rest sustained minor or moderate injuries. Lauber said investigators determined that the truck driver failed to stay to the right of the center line because of inattention owing to a momentary lapse of alertness, falling asleep or an epileptic seizure. The driver had had 1½ hours of sleep in the 36 hours before the accident and had been on duty for 12 hours, 7 of which had been spent driving. Nevertheless, Lauber noted, the driver did not appear to be in violation of U.S. Department of Transportation rules concerning hours of service.

• In Arizona, a truck hit a school bus at 3:15 p.m., killing two children and injuring 26. The NSTB found that the driver was suffering from chronic fatigue owing to sleep loss caused by excessive duty time and a prolonged irregular work schedule. The company's failure to monitor the driver's excessive work hours was cited as contributing to the accident. The driver was found to have kept two sets of conflicting duty logs, one for himself and one for the company. He had slept poorly two nights before the accident, and the night before he'd slept for about 5½ hours (awakening at 3:30 a.m.) on the floor of a motel room shared with other truckers. He'd put in 88½ hours of work during eight consecutive days, in violation of federal rules.

According to David Dinges, the sleep problems associated with trucking in the United States have been exacerbated by a trend toward "just in time" delivery. Because many companies don't want to maintain large inventories in their warehouse, they wait until they're running low and then contract with a trucking company to deliver new inventory from the manufacturer on a guaranteed basis. "They must deliver it by a certain day or they lose their fee," said Dinges. "That's produced tremendous competitiveness and it puts economic incentive directly in conflict with the need to be safe."

The American Insurance Association found that interstate trucking accidents increased by 25 percent between 1983 and 1986, after the industry was deregulated. Driver fatigue was responsible for 40 percent of heavy-truck accidents, according to a study by the American Automobile Association. Trucking is a fiercely competitive industry, and many drivers feel compelled to work long hours to make ends meet. There are regulations governing hours of service, but truckers are known to keep multiple log books — one conforming to legal hours of work and another showing their real hours of work.

"It is chilling to listen to drivers who brag that they keep two or three log books and drive 18 to 20 hours a day," one truck driver commented in *Truck News*. She went on to say that she has often spoken on the CB with drivers whose "voices are thick with sleep, whose thought processes are drastically slowed. I've overheard two drivers where one is begging the other to pull off for sleep and the other, in a sleep-fagged voice, says he can pull for another hour or two."

U.S. regulations require truckers to rest for 8 hours after driving for 10 hours continuously. In 1988, during a debate over proposed federal trucking regulations in Canada, this 10-and-8 rule came under attack by the Canadian trucking industry, which argued that it was inappropriate to Canadian conditions and inherently unsafe because it disrupts circadian rhythms by forcing drivers to follow an irregular (i.e., non-24-hour) sleep/wake pattern.

The 10-and-8 rule does not limit drivers to 10 hours of driving a day; in fact, it allows up to 16 hours of driving in every 24 hours. (Since driving for 10 hours and resting for 8 equals only 18 hours, the driver can squeeze up to 6 more hours of driving into the 24-hour period.) Although the 10-and-8 regulations were introduced for reasons of safety, "in fact they were deadly dangerous," Turnbull says; they literally require drivers who work 16 hours in a 24-hour period to do it in an unsafe way, by forcing them to "sleep irregular hours and in effect, start work 6 hours earlier every day."

As we have seen previously, a daily phase advance of 6 hours in the sleep cycle is very disruptive; in fact, its effect on the circadian system is about equivalent to flying eastbound across the Atlantic every day.* "I'd like to see how well the people who write the rules would do if they had to start work . . . hours earlier every day," one trucker commented in *Truck News*.

"Your sleep pattern is so totally screwed up that when you're supposed to be sleeping, you're not and when you have to drive to make a profit, your body wants to sleep," said Turnbull. "This is, of course, a major safety hazard." He has argued that stringent enforcement of the U.S. regulations actually led to an increase in truck accidents, and "it's probably only a matter of time before the regulations . . . are named as contributing factors in an accident."

He and a number of truckers' groups in Canada advocated regulations that would allow drivers to drive for up to 15 hours in every

---

* Truckers also have to contend with a variant of jet lag on long transcontinental trips accomplished in three to four days. As with jet travel, westbound trips are easiest on the circadian system because they involve a phase delay. On an eastbound trips, truckers are likely to find it hard to sleep well.

24 — which would actually be less than the total number of hours permitted under the 10-and-8 rule — but would allow truckers to maintain a consistent sleep/wake cycle from one day to the next. However, proposed federal regulations call for a 13-and-8 rule and several provinces have already instituted a similar regulation.

Theoretically, a 13-and-8 schedule would still cause a daily slippage in the sleep/wake cycle of about 3 hours, but in practice it would likely permit drivers to maintain a 24-hour schedule, Turnbull says. "After you've fueled your truck and had a couple of meals and coffee breaks, you're up to 24 hours." But he says these regulations are unnecessarily complex and are "presumptuous" in telling truckers how they should sleep. "The regulations force truckers into a sleep pattern that might sound good to the schoolteacher mentality of a civil servant, but which is not necessarily good for everyone," he wrote in an editorial in *Truck News*.

As one driver put it, "I'd sooner sleep when I'm tired. . . . If I drive until I'm tired, then it doesn't matter what time it is. . . . I climb into the bunk and I go to sleep. But if I'm not tired I just can't sleep and if I have to stop driving because the log book says I have to, that doesn't mean I sleep — because if I tried, I'd just get into the bunk and lay there. I might get tired by the time I could start driving again, but I couldn't afford to sleep then and I'd have to drive anyway."

## PLANES

Commercial aviation has a remarkably good safety record, considering the inherent potential for disaster in the fact that thousands of aircraft are in the air all over the world every day. (Airlines, which account for 95 percent of all passenger-miles flown, operate about 9,000 jet aircraft worldwide; the largest can carry up to 450 people each.) But in recent years, several trends have combined to put an unprecedented amount of pressure on commercial aviation and to increase public anxiety about the safety of the airways. These include deregulation, cheap fares, and the resulting boom in air travel; increased economic pressures on airlines to operate at full capacity; intense congestion at major airports and in their control zones; insufficient growth in ground and air traffic control facilities at airports; and the effects of increased security in exacerbating delays and congestion.

Pilots bear the brunt of these pressures. "Every pilot has come under pressure to continue when he felt too tired to go on," says Norman Bindon, president of the Canadian Air Line Pilots Association. Perhaps no other occupation combines so many of the factors that make it difficult to maintain alertness on the job: jet lag, shift work, long work hours and highly irregular schedules, which require people to sleep in different rooms in different environmental conditions nearly every day, at variable times of day and night. They are also required to perform at variable times of day and night, usually with the lives of hundreds of people in their hands.

Airline schedules are designed primarily with economics and passenger preferences in mind; rarely are the circadian rhythms of pilots a consideration. For example, the tendency of airlines to schedule eastbound transatlantic flights at night for economic reasons means that most landings occur in the middle of the pilots' biological circadian trough, a period during which studies have shown that more fatigue-related errors are likely to occur. German researchers Karl Klein and Hans Wegman note that pilots' night-duty hours should be shorter than day-duty hours because they are more stressful, and they say it would be wise to avoid the coincidence of the end of a long duty period with the nocturnal trough. At a time when their circadian system is at its lowest ebb, people should not be required to perform tasks requiring maximum efficiency, such as landing a plane.

Unfortunately, that is precisely what is regularly demanded of many pilots. A 747 captain wrote in the aerospace journal *Aviation Week and Space Technology* that he regularly works 12 to 15 hours at a stretch and that it's not uncommon for his crew to have been awake for more than 24 hours when it makes the final landing of their duty period. He described a trip around the world in eight days in which he crossed every time zone and worked for up to 14 hours at a time; he had fewer than 24 hours off before being assigned to a six-day trip to South America. Describing these working conditions as "disgraceful," he said they will inevitably result in accidents and the loss of lives.

In recent years, two major technological factors have contributed to the problem of maintaining alertness in the cockpit: newer aircraft can fly for up to 16 or 18 hours at a time without stopping, and sophisticated new cockpit computers have transformed the inherent nature of the pilot's job. Cockpit automation is, of course, intended to make flying safer, but its effect on pilot performance and alertness is mixed. On the one hand, machines are usually more precise and better at doing routine tasks than humans are; however, they lack the ability to respond creatively to unexpected problems and they can fail. (They are, after all, manufactured and programmed by human beings; human error once removed can be just as deadly.) This is where the pilot is expected to excel; ingenuity is supposed to be the bailiwick of the human mind.

But pilots can become bored and drowsy during automated flight; instead of actually flying the plane, most commercial pilots of large passenger aircraft now spend long periods doing little more than monitoring the autopilot in a dimly lit and (usually) low-stimulus environment. They may be lulled into a state of "automation complacency" by overreliance on the autopilot. In one survey of 200 commercial airline pilots, nearly half expressed concern about losing their flying skills with too much automation and about nine out of 10 said they manually fly at least some part of each trip just to maintain their proficiency. The U.S. Federal Aviation Administration has embarked on a study of the effects of automation on pilot performance that will include an examination of pilot complacency, boredom and lack of vigilance.

If these conditions are exacerbated by sleepiness caused by sleep deprivation and circadian desynchronization — a common hazard, given their erratic schedules — you have the prescription for potential disaster. Finding creative solutions to unanticipated in-flight problems is what humans do best — and it's something pilots have managed to do many times* — but, as we saw in Chapter 6, there's evidence that creative thinking may be affected by even a single night of lost sleep, and it doesn't take long for reaction time, psychomotor skills and vigilance to be affected as well. The amazing thing is not that accidents happen, but that they don't happen more often.

One of the reasons for this is that pilots undergo intense training in simulators that can safely and realistically (*too* realistically, some

---

* One interesting case occurred on a flight out of Los Angeles when the aircraft lost pitch control — that is, the ability to point the nose up or down. The pilots were able to maintain control of the aircraft and bring it around for a safe emergency landing by carefully manipulating the thrust from a tail-mounted engine (which was above the plane's center of gravity and tended to pitch the plane down) and the thrust from wing-mounted engines (which were below the plane's centre of gravity and tended to pitch the plane up). This technique was not "approved procedure" documented in a manual or practiced in a simulator; it was instead an ingenious spur-of-the-moment solution to a potentially disastrous problem.

say) recreate almost any imaginable disaster. This allows them to experience even rare and unusual events and to practice responding to them until it becomes almost second nature. Commercial aircraft also have at least two and often three or more pilots on board to provide a backup capability. In one case where a pilot actually fell asleep while in the process of landing — the plane was just 200 feet off the ground — the co-pilot wakened the pilot in time and the plane was landed safely.

Bindon says that "incidents of actually falling asleep are rare, but having difficulty in staying awake is very real. It's like driving down the road slapping your face. You don't have the option of pulling over and parking while you have your nap — but you do have another operator."

Unfortunately, having two and even three pilots on board isn't necessarily proof against the vagaries of human physiology: in one rather dramatic case, a Boeing 707 that was supposed to land at Los Angeles continued out over the Pacific for 160 kilometers (100 miles) on autopilot because all three pilots were asleep. Air traffic controllers were finally able to rouse the crew by triggering cockpit alarms, and luckily the plane had enough fuel to get back to Los Angeles. This is not a unique case; a 1987 survey of 800 British pilots, conducted by researchers at the Royal Air Force Institute of Aviation Medicine, disclosed several instances where everyone on the flight deck fell asleep during long-haul flights. One pilot who responded to the survey estimated that the entire crew was asleep for about 20 minutes, but "fortunately" they were between the checkpoints at which they were required to contact air traffic controllers. Another pilot reported waking up after about half an hour asleep and finding that he was the only one awake — "a sobering thought."

Although there have been dramatic cases in which pilot fatigue has clearly contributed to an aviation incident or accident, in many cases it's very difficult to assess the extent to which sleepiness and circadian desynchronization are to blame. Accidents usually involve a complex combination of factors, including technical malfunctions and weather, and are often the result of an unusual confluence of these factors. Sorting out their relative contribution is a major challenge for investigators. Technology, in the form of radar and flight-data recorders, can often provide them with data on weather conditions, technical problems and the actual performance of the crew, but information about the crew's state of fatigue is typically more anecdotal, and even when it's available, investigators often find it hard to determine precisely what role sleepiness played in causing the accident. It's usually much easier to tell *what* went wrong than *why* it went wrong.

An illustrative example is the case of China Airlines Flight 006. On February 19, 1985, this aircraft, a Boeing 747 out of Taiwan, was approaching Los Angeles when it experienced an in-flight upset that resulted in uncontrollable dive from an altitude of 41,000 feet to 9,500 feet. The captain got the plane under control and landed safely at San Francisco. Amazingly, although the plane suffered severe damage during the dive (which created gravity forces five times normal), only two of the 274 people on board were seriously injured.

Lauber noted that the NSTB determined the probable cause of the accident to be the captain's preoccupation with an engine malfunction (one engine had lost power during the flight) and his failure to monitor the flight instruments. As a result, the plane rolled and went into a nosedive. The pilot's overreliance on the autopilot while attending to the engine problem was cited as a contributing factor.

The accident occurred at 3:22 a.m. Taiwan time — a time when the captain would have been experiencing a biological trough and would normally have been asleep for several hours. (During the six days prior to the flight, he'd been going to bed between 9:00 and 10:00 p.m. Taiwan time.) Lauber suggests there is a "high probability" the captain was affected by circadian desynchronization.

Because the flight was so long (11 hours) the crew was "augmented" — i.e., it included a second captain and flight engineer, in addition to the three primary crew members. These three took rest breaks during the flight and were replaced in the cockpit by the extra crew members. During his break, the captain got about 2 hours of sleep in a bunk at the back of the cockpit. He'd been back on duty for about 2 hours when the accident occurred.

Because the flight was long and conducted mostly on autopilot, it would be conducive to fatigue, boredom and probably also a decrease in vigilance, according to Lauber. He also suggested that the quality of sleep obtained in the cockpit bunk could not be as good as that obtained at home or even in a hotel room. However, the NSTB did not list fatigue or boredom as a cause of the accident. Lauber noted that although he could not help feeling that fatigue, sleepiness and circadian desynchronization played major roles, it is "difficult to amass enough evidence to hold that these were causal. We could only infer the causes of the crew's degraded performance."

A similar situation involved a flight out of San Francisco that crashed in Bali in 1974, killing 107 people. The crew's schedule was very disruptive to circadian rhythms. Based on San Francisco time, it went this way: depart San Francisco 7:44 p.m., arrive Honolulu, 1:32 a.m.; next day, depart Honolulu at 3:39 a.m., arrive Sydney, Australia, 2:35 p.m.; next day, depart Sydney 6:21 p.m., arrive Jakarta, Indonesia, 1:30 a.m., depart Jakarta at 2:18 a.m., arrive Hong Kong 6:40 a.m.; next day, depart Hong Kong at 4:00 a.m. The crash at Bali occurred 4½ hours later at 8:30 a.m. (S.F. time). The combination of both night and day flying and crossing 12 time zones may have contributed to the accident, according to Martin Moore-Ede, Frank Sulzman and Charles Fuller in their book *The Clocks That Time Us*. They emphasize the need to allow for circadian factors, and not just total duty time, in designing pilots' work/rest schedules. Regulations that involve only total duty time are based on the assumption that the "human body is a machine running at a constant level through night and day." But we know from studies of the circadian system that such reasoning is wrong — often tragically so.

These scientists note that flight crews are subjected to extremely irregular work/sleep schedules and they live in a world in which external time is "rapidly and randomly shifted on a day-to-day basis" compared with their internal clocks. Meals are also irregular, but they may vary in a pattern different from the work schedule, and this too affects circadian rhythms. Further disruption occurs when shifting back and forth between work and home schedules; this is particularly true for senior pilots, who have a tendency to pick the most disruptive routes — those involving long duty days and overseas flying — because they offer better pay and more favorable time-off provisions. "More senior pilots are more likely to be be flying through time zones because overseas flights pay more than domestic flights," says Bindon. "They also bid for longer flights to get more consecutive days off." Flights involving long duty days and overseas flying also mean that these pilots are more likely to be flying at night. And yet, older pilots are likely to be less adaptable to these disruptive work/rest routines than younger pilots.

No matter how much of a "Right Stuff" mentality pilots may have, they are still subject to the same physiological laws as the rest of us.

While it's true that pilots undergo an intense selection process that weeds out most people who are particularly susceptible to medical problems, this doesn't mean that the ones who do make it onto the flight deck of a commercial airliner have any special immunity to the problems caused by sleep loss and circadian factors. Indeed, studies have shown that aircrews report a high incidence of the same kinds of sleep disturbances and gastrointestinal upsets that afflict other shift workers and transmeridian travelers. Ninety-three percent of 12,000 pilots surveyed by the U.S. Airline Pilots Association reported that fatigue was a problem in their work. Similarly, the survey of British pilots revealed complaints about extreme sleepiness on long-distance night flights, "unavoidably soporific" chores in automated cockpits, long delays in crowded airports and difficulty in sleeping in noisy hotel rooms. The study suggested that aircraft should be equipped with an alerting device that would remain inactive as long as there were voices in the cockpit or controls were being operated; if more than 2 minutes went by without either occurring, then a warning light would come on, and if it were not canceled, an alarm would be sounded in the cockpit.

Between 1984 and 1986, sleep researchers from four countries — the United States, Japan, West Germany and Great Britain — conducted a study of sleep quality among pilots, particularly during layovers away from home base. Participants in the study included several airlines, pilots' associations and government organizations concerned with aviation safety. The project was directed by researchers at the U.S. National Aeronautics and Space Administration's Ames Research Center in California.

Eastbound and westbound flights between San Francisco and Tokyo, Frankfurt and London were studied; they involved time zone changes of between 7 and 9 hours. More than 50 pilots between the ages of 31 and 61 from the four countries volunteered to have their sleep monitored in sleep labs at their home base and during layovers in the other cities. They also kept sleep log books. Subjective and objective (MSLT) measures of sleepiness were also done, and in some cases, measurements were made of body temperature, urine, respiration, heart rate, leg movements. They were allowed to sleep whenever they wanted and as long as they wanted to and to employ whatever techniques they normally used for coping with sleeping during layovers.

The goals of the study were to examine changes in sleep patterns associated with flying across multiple time zones; to compare differences in the quality of sleep at home and during layovers; to determine how these differences were reflected in increased sleepiness during awake periods and whether the pilots could accurately assess their levels of sleepiness; and to identify the most successful sleep strategies to cope with transmeridian flying. This project was unique; although previous research had been done on the effects of jet lag, most of the subjects in those studies were tourist volunteers who did not fly across time zones as regularly as pilots do and, of course, had no flight duties.

The results were consistent among all the pilots, despite differences in culture, age and the ways in which their different airlines operated. Not surprisingly, the pilots experienced fewer sleep problems during layovers after westbound flights than after eastbound flights, when their sleep was more variable and fragmented. In both cases, the crews went to sleep as soon after arrival as they could and usually fell asleep faster than they did during off-duty time at home. However, after eastbound flights, the sleep period was shorter than normal because the subjects tended to wake up spontaneously at what would be late morning at their home base. There was a great deal of individual variation when they started the next sleep period; some delayed it until a time that coincided with their home-base sleep period (i.e., they were deliberately maintaining their biological clocks on home-base time). Subjectively the pilots reported their sleep was worse than at home. After westbound flights, they slept about the same amount of time as they did at home and some reported better quality sleep.

One of the most important findings was that the crews experienced increased daytime sleepiness (as measured by the MSLT) in the new time zone; in fact, there was a steady increase in sleepiness throughout the day during their awake time on the layovers, rather than the usual circadian upswing in alertness that might be expected in the early evening. This was attributed to the fact that their circadian rhythms persisted on home-base time and had not adjusted to local time. In the case of pilots who had flown eastward, sleep fragmentation also contributed to decreased alertness while awake.

The persistence of circadian rhythms on home-base time could be used to predict when it would be easier for crews to fall asleep during layovers "and therefore develop better strategies for sleeping or napping while away from home," the scientists said. However, it appears that pilots might have difficulty doing this without the aid of objective measures; the study found that their subjective ratings of sleep quality and daytime sleepiness on layovers were not always consistent with the objective measures, which suggests they were not very good at predicting their own daytime sleepiness patterns.

The researchers found that age was an important factor; older pilots experienced more sleep difficulties than younger pilots. And the Japanese study suggested that larks (morning types) experienced somewhat more daytime sleepiness than owls (evening types).

After westbound trips, most pilots took a nap on the second day of layover just before going on duty late that afternoon for the return flight. This was considered to be a good strategy because it was likely to reduce drowsiness on the subsequent night flight. The researchers said that pilots could improve their sleep quality after eastbound flights, especially just before the return flight, by adopting a more structured sleep schedule. On the first day of the layover, they should limit their sleep immediately after arrival and prolong the wakeful period until the normal *local* time for sleep. This would increase the likelihood that they will be able to stay asleep longer just before their next duty period.

"It appears that proper sleep scheduling during the first 24 hours is most critical, and crew members should develop the discipline to terminate sleep even though they could sleep longer," the researchers say. "Unless layover sleep is arranged in a satisfactory manner by an appropriate sleep/wake strategy, increased drowsiness is likely to occur during the subsequent long-haul flight." They also suggested that short naps can be helpful in promoting alertness and that "flight deck napping could be an important strategy."

They concluded by noting that this study involved only the first layover of an outbound trip and this is not representative of most long-haul flights, which typically involve multiple flight segments and several layovers in different time zones before returning to home base. A subsequent study by the Japanese researchers found that in pilots doing multiple transmeridian flights, sleep disturbances due to circadian desynchronization continue to occur through the second night of recovery sleep after returning to home base. They concluded that after such flights crews should sleep for at least three nights in their home time zone before flying again.

The U.S. researchers, headed by Curtis Graeber of NASA Ames

Research Center, did another study of sleep patterns among pilots flying short-haul flights in the high-density airspace of the eastern United States. These pilots crossed no more than one time zone. They found that pilots took longer to get to sleep and woke up earlier during trips than during off-duty times at home and their sleep was not only shorter in length, but poorer in quality. More than 90 percent of the subjects reported nighttime awakenings, mostly during and after trips. Posttrip sleep was significantly longer than trip sleep and the pilots fell asleep faster than they did before or during the trip. They also took more naps after the trip than before or during them. These findings suggest that the pilots were trying to recuperate from an accumulated sleep debt.

The poor quality of sleep during the trip was reflected in a significant increase in subjective fatigue and a decrease in positive mood. The length of the trip (three versus four days) did not affect fatigue and mood, but time of day did; early on-duty times and the number of flight segments flown each day also had an effect.

## STRATEGIES TO REDUCE FLIGHT-CREW FATIGUE

Pilots' organizations and sleep researchers are often critical of government regulations and the airline industry for not paying enough attention to the problem of pilot fatigue and to the sleep difficulties caused by jet lag. A 1986 survey by the International Civil Aviation Organization (ICAO) suggests that their concerns may be warranted. Of 70 governments or organizations that responded to an ICAO questionnaire, only 17 (24 percent) said they'd conducted studies on the medical aspects of flight-crew fatigue and only 13 (19 percent) said that regulations covering pilot duty times and rest periods were different for transmeridian flights than for north/south flights. Of the 17 that had conducted studies, only five said that their studies of flight-crew fatigue had affected flight-duty times covered by national regulations. (These five constituted a mere seven percent of all the respondents.) Asked if they'd be willing to participate in an ICAO seminar on medical aspects of flight-crew fatigue, 26 (37 percent) of the respondents said no.

Nevertheless, a variety of strategies have been tried to reduce crew fatigue. At one time, airlines often posted flight crews to different cities around the world for extended periods of time, which made sense from a circadian point of view because it allowed long-term adaptation to different time zones. However, this was expensive and many airlines have discontinued it. Klein and Wegman described this practice as "an elegant solution" for the problems caused by trans-meridian flying and said that abolishing it was "medically unwise." However, some European airlines that fly transatlantic routes allow adaptation to North American time zones and schedule pilots to fly north-south routes (say between the United States and South America) for several weeks before having them fly back across the Atlantic.

Alternatively, some airlines try to return air crews to home base as quickly as possible, before their biological clocks start to reset to different time zones. If this is not possible, they provide sleeping accommodations that are shielded from the distractions of local time, thus helping pilots to remain on home-base time. Another strategy is to rate various routes according to the amount of sleep disruption they are likely to cause (taking into account the direction of travel, the number of time zones crossed and whether the flight takes place at night or during the day) and using these ratings to calculate how much rest pilots need after each flight. The ratings can also be used for equitable distribution of the most disruptive flights among pilots. (It would be wise to assign the most disruptive routes to younger pilots, who are more capable of adjusting to circadian desynchronization than older pilots.)

In recent years, the introduction of new aircraft with flight ranges of up to 16 hours has created new issues and approaches to crew scheduling. Pilots' organizations have lobbied for flight-time limita-tions that take into account not only the length of flights but factors such as the proportion of night flying, the effects of changes in time zones and climate in disrupting the sleep/wake cycle; the availability of adequate sleeping accommodations during layovers and during flight. In a submission to the Canadian government, the Canadian Airline Pilots Association noted that rest accommodations at layover stops should be dark, temperature controlled and quiet. The last may be the most difficult to ensure when crews must sleep during the local day and it should be given a high priority in choosing crew accommo-dations, so attention should be paid to both the location of the hotel and the selection of rooms within the hotel.

As for rest facilities on board the aircraft, a seat at the back of the flight deck is not considered adequate; what's needed is a bunk, separated from the flight deck and the passenger cabin, that permits horizontal sleeping. A number of long-range aircraft are now equipped with these bunks and crews that fly them usually consist of one or two extra pilots (an "augmented" crew) so that everyone can have time off to sleep during the flight.

DC10 Captain Martin Vanstone, a representative of the Canadian Airline Pilots Association and the International Federation of Airline Pilots Associations, flies 14-hour flights between Vancouver and Hong Kong with an augmented crew (an additional first officer), which allows each crew member to have about a quarter of the flight — 2½ to 3 hours — off duty. The plane is equipped with a bunk located above the ceiling in the cabin, extending from the galley into the center portion of the overhead racks.*

"From the outside you wouldn't notice it, thinking it was just an overhead rack, except it doesn't have any doors on it," said Vanstone. "It's entered through a bit of a ladder at one end and you just crawl up into it." The bunk is about three feet wide and eight feet long with about 2½ feet of headroom. "You can't quite sit up in there, but it's enough to get your shoes off. It's a little awkward to get into, but once you're in there there's adequate space and you can have quite a good rest." He describes himself as "an easy napper. I can usually fall asleep fairly easily."

While crew members can spend their break as they choose, "most will spend it sleeping in the bunk," he said. "Cabin noise is not a problem. The only difficulty is that the entrance is near the galley and sometimes if the flight attendants are not thoughtful enough, they might be noisy. But in most cases, the people operating these trips have been on it long enough to be aware of the problem and keep the noise down."

The napping schedule differs slightly on the outbound and return trips. On the Vancouver-to-Hong Kong trip, which leaves at about midday (Vancouver time), each crew member is first given a 1-hour break and then they rotate again through a 2-hour break. "If we just gave everyone 3 hours right off the bat, the guy who got the first break is not going to be able to sleep, because it's the middle of the afternoon, his time, and he's then going to have to spend the next 10 hours on duty, so we break it up," Vanstone said. Coming back the trip is

---

\* Bindon notes that various arrangements have been suggested for these sleep areas, including the use of below-decks modular containers. "It starts to get ridiculous — like 'when needed, break glass.' "

shorter and it leaves Hong Kong at midnight (Vancouver time). "Since we only have a short layover, our bodies are still on Vancouver time basically, and because Vancouver time is coming up to midnight or one o'clock in the morning, we take just a single break each. Everyone will get 2½ hours in rotation."

The rotation starts after the plane has reached cruising altitude. Vanstone takes third place in the rotation, which allows him to be on the flight deck during the early part of the trip and for about 2½ hours before they begin the descent into Hong Kong. As captain, he has his choice of rest periods. "There's no democracy on the flight deck. I determined that to use my abilities the best, that's the period of rest I would like to have."

He has only been awakened from his nap once to deal with a problem — a decision whether to divert to Tokyo because of poor weather in Hong Kong and other alternate airports. "There's enough of an abnormality attached to something like that you become alert fairly quickly. By the time I got onto the flight deck, I was fully awake and fully alert." He felt the same would be true in an emergency situation. "There'd be enough adrenaline to get you right up, I'm sure."

Many pilots, however, feel uneasy about the trend toward in-flight sleeping. "I always felt that it wasn't a good characteristic for a pilot to be able to sleep on an aircraft," says Bindon. "I think he should be awake. I would find it difficult." Similarly, Vanstone says that, as "an old-fashioned thinker," he finds the idea of napping on board the aircraft "a little abhorrent" — but he also acknowledged that he finds naps refreshing (although he said some pilots do complain of feeling worse than they did before going to sleep — probably the result of sleep inertia). He added that sleeping in the bunk reduces but does not eliminate napping in the cockpit, which does occur from time to time. But napping in a chair on the flight deck while the plane in on autopilot can improve alertness a great deal, Vanstone said. A pilot sitting in his seat fighting drowsiness is mentally "quite spooled down, not particularly alert, even though he may be fully awake, because it's such a struggle. It doesn't take very much in the way of a nap to bring you right back up. It's incredible how just a 10-minute period of tilting the seat back and closing your eyes will refresh you practically right back to normal." If a first officer asks to be allowed to do this, "my answer is always, by all means, because if he can be up and refreshed in 10 minutes, then if I happen to doze off accidentally, at least he's there. But if I make him struggle, and maybe I'll be struggling in half an hour from now, that's when there's more probability that both of us are going to doze off together."

Scheduled napping is not yet widespread in commercial aviation and it causes some concern: pilots worry about chain-of-command issues, and sleep researchers raise questions about the potential negative effects of sleep inertia. But a strategy involving augmented crews and scheduled napping seems much preferable to what often happens now — pilots falling asleep in a random and unplanned way on the flight deck while on duty.

Stampi believes that napping by pilots can be a good idea, but "a lot depends on individual characteristics and also on the duration of the nap. We should find a perfect duration for each pilot that is quite restorative but is not too long to produce a high or a long sleep inertia."

On-board sleeping was also used in what was perhaps the most dramatic recent example of long-distance air operations — the British campaign against Argentina in the Falklands War in 1982. The Royal Air Force was required to provide around-the-clock support to British troops over distances of some 13,000 kilometres (8,250 miles) and across five time zones. The Falklands Islands are located off the southeast tip of Argentina, and the RAF's nearest staging base was on Ascension Island, in the mid-Atlantic off the coast of Africa, about 6,400 kilometres (4,000 miles) away — an 18-hour round trip. It was anticipated that missions lasting up to 30 hours at a time, occurring frequently over a period of several weeks, would be required, and that crews would have to sleep on board the aircraft; obviously, fatigue and sleep disturbances were going to be a matter of major concern.

In addition to carrying augmented crews and utilizing on-board sleeping, the RAF also made strategic use of a short-acting hypnotic, temazepam, which was given to off-duty pilots to help them sleep at scheduled times. In the end, the flight crews were able to carry out as many as half a dozen 28-hour missions over a two- to three-week period with no fatalities and the loss of only three aircraft.

The use by pilots of hypnotics and stimulants to regulate sleep (or other drugs that affect alertness) is understandably controversial. The pilots of commercial passenger jets are not allowed to use such drugs in flight or immediately prior to it, although use during off-duty hours is not entirely prohibited. Hypnotics may be used on the ground to promote sleep, provided that the duration of off-duty time is sufficient to permit the drugs to clear the system before the pilot goes on duty again. However, William Hark, a doctor with the U.S. Federal Aviation Administration, said that while occasional off-duty use of the drugs is acceptable, if a pilot were using hypnotics regularly, "we'd have a problem with that."

Some U.S. military pilots are allowed to take stimulants while flying, and this touched off a controversy in West Germany in September 1988, where there was growing concern over the safety of low-level training flights by U.S. Air Force pilots. West German television quoted an unnamed Air Force spokesman as saying that pilots use the stimulant so they can fly "when they haven't gotten enough sleep or don't feel fit enough." The report added that the pilots later take a sedative to counteract the stimulant.

In response, the U.S. Air Force issued a press release indicating that pilots do not take the drugs for normal, day-to-day flying. News reports quoted that statement as saying that "the use of stimulant and sedative medications is limited by regulation to flights in which the length or precise schedule of the mission presents a significant risk of flight safety due to fatigue. [Drug] use almost exclusively involves solo flights to or from the United States and overseas bases." An Air Force spokesman was quoted as saying that the sedative is only used on the ground, to get the pilot's "body clock back in order" and that the stimulants are not recommended for routine use; they are used only if the pilot feels enough fatigue to jeopardize flight safety.

Later, the Pentagon issued a statement defending the use of the drugs, which had been going on for as long as 30 years. It said that dispensing of the medication is "rigidly controlled" and it is used "almost exclusively for transoceanic solo missions in single-seat air-craft. No crashes anywhere have been related to drug use." The Navy medical command issued a statement at about the same time saying that its pilots were not allowed to use such drugs.

## AIR TRAFFIC CONTROLLERS

In late 1988 and early 1989, a series of close encounters occurred between aircraft operating in the busy control zone of Toronto's Pearson International Airport. Several of these near-collisions were attributed in part to overwork and fatigue on the part of air traffic controllers. In one incident, according to the Canadian Aviation

Safety Board, a controller was working his seventh day in a row and his 14th in the previous 16; in another, the controller had been working for four days in a row and 12 out of 13. A supervisor was unavailable to monitor potentially hazardous convergences because understaffing had forced him to relieve other controllers. These incidents were "indicative of a fundamental safety deficiency in arrival procedures" at the airport, the CASB said. "If uncorrected, [these procedures] could lead to more serious occurrences . . . possibly with more serious consequences."

The situation at Pearson International Airport, one of the 20 busiest airports in the world, is by no means unique; Jack Butt, former president of the Canadian Air Traffic Controllers Association (CATCA) warned that similar problems can be expected at other Canadian airports. In 1987, the U.S. Federal Aviation Administration estimated that near-collisions between commercial aircraft in U.S. air space exceeded 400 incidents a year.

During the 1980s, deregulation resulted in an explosive growth in air traffic, particularly in North America and Europe. At the same time, both Canada and the United States have experienced serious shortages of air traffic controllers, especially after the 1981 firing of 11,500 striking controllers by the U.S. government and the 1985 freeze on hiring and training controllers imposed by the Canadian government. Between 1983 and 1989, the traffic volume at Canadian airports almost doubled, while the number of controllers dropped by more than 350, CATCA stated. Canada needs about 400 more controllers and it will take a decade to correct the situation, says CATCA president Carl Fisher. As a result, controllers are locked into a phase-advance shift rotation because switching to a clockwise rotation would cause serious scheduling problems, particularly with overtime. "There's not enough people available to do that. It really restricts overtime." The controllers' union has called for a public inquiry into Canada's air traffic control system.*

All over North America, controllers at major airports are increasingly hard-pressed to handle the increased workload and both gov-

---

* Ground support personnel, including airport firefighters, have similar complaints about overwork. The Union of Canadian Transport Employees says that in some cases workloads have more than tripled in the past decade. "Safety is being compromised because our members are fatigued and are forced to hurry their work," said union spokesman Duncan MacLeod.

ernments are now scrambling to catch up. In 1987, the U.S. Federal Aviation Administration ordered that 950 new controllers be hired and trained. In late 1988, Transport Canada ordered a 70-flights-per-hour restriction at Pearson Airport and said that it would take steps to alleviate the shortage of controllers; these measures include a longer-term recruiting and training program for new controllers, but over the short term, other measures were being taken, including hiring former U.S. controllers, moving controllers from other airports, re-hiring retired controllers and asking them to work overtime.

In fact, overtime and long working hours are already common at busy airports; at Pearson, for example, 135 controllers were doing the work intended for a crew of 194 — including 22 tower controllers doing the work of 36. Roger Burgess-Webb, a spokesman for the Canadian Air Line Pilots Association said that these incidents indicate that controllers are overworked. "It's common sense that fatigue, working such long hours, would adversely affect performance."

Shift schedules can also affect job performance, particularly if they contribute to sleep deprivation. Simon Folkard and Ruth Condon of the University of Sussex analyzed anonymous reports from 435 air traffic controllers from 17 countries* and found that a form of sleep paralysis was far more likely to occur on the night shift. Of the 75 incidents reported (by 26 individuals), fully three-quarters — 56 in number — occurred during the night shift. In contrast, only 12 incidents occurred during the evening shift and seven during the day shift. The number of incidents peaked about 5:00 a.m., in the middle of the circadian trough. Eighteen of the 26 who reported experiencing night-shift paralysis said it had happened only once or twice, but the others reported at least five incidents. Eighty percent of the incidents were reported to have lasted for less than two minutes, but nearly 11 percent (a total of eight incidents) were said to have lasted for five minutes or more. In more than two-thirds of the incidents, the controllers said they felt they were awake at the time (although they felt sleepier than normal), that their vision was not affected, that they remained aware of their surroundings and did not have strange mental reactions such as hallucinations. But some reported that their limbs "felt heavy," and nearly half said they experienced peculiar physical

---

* It is notable that virtually all the shift schedules reported by the controllers involved a phase-advance rotation — evenings to mornings to nights. As we have seen, it's harder for the human circadian system to adapt to a phase advance than to a phase delay.

sensations such as cold or numbness. In 86 percent of the incidents, the controllers said they were sitting down at the time; however, only a few of the controllers reported falling over or slumping forward, and half said they were able to speak or make small finger movements.

Perhaps most worrying was the fact that most of the controllers reported being unaware of their inability to move until they tried to make large movements, usually in response to an external event. Folkard and Condon reported that more than half of the controllers said the paralysis prevented them from responding to a work-related event, and in more than half of those cases, "it was judged that the inability to respond could have resulted in an accident or near-accident." However, they emphasized that this phenomenon is rare and estimated that the potential for an accident to happen as a result of the paralysis occurs only about 0.5 times over an individual controller's entire career.

Folkard and Condon examined a variety of factors to determine which appeared to contribute to incidents of night-shift paralysis. There were no significant differences among countries, nor did the type of facility (e.g., tower, area control, approach control, etc.) make any difference. Perhaps surprisingly, the researchers also found that neither the length of shifts nor the provision of rest breaks within the shift period had a significant effect.

However, working consecutive night shifts did have a major impact: the incidence nearly tripled from 5.5 percent among controllers working only single, isolated night shifts to 15.6 percent among those who worked two or more night shifts in a row. Folkard and Condon note that there's good evidence that people sleep considerably less during the day between two night shifts than they do during normal night sleep periods; thus, sleep deprivation will accumulate over several night shifts and this could account for the higher incidence of night-shift paralysis. Fortunately, most controllers — nearly 88 percent — said their schedules involved only single night shifts and about nine percent said they work two nights in a row, leaving only about three percent who reported schedules involving more than two successive night shifts.

Many of the controllers said their schedules required them to work a night shift on the same day as a morning shift, sometimes with as little as five hours off in between. Folkard and Condon found that this type of schedule — what they refer to as a "single-day M/N shift" — had a "marked effect" on the incidence of night-shift paralysis; it was reported by less than three percent of controllers who did not work such shifts, by more than five percent of those who worked on an irregular schedule that permitted such shifts and by nearly 12 percent of those who worked a regular schedule in which such shifts were enforced. They note that night sleeps before a morning shift tend to be shorter than normal, which again contributes to sleep deprivation.

The researchers found some correlation between night-shift paralysis and individual variations in the flexibility of sleep patterns. Controllers who said they followed a "rigid" sleep schedule reported the highest incidence of paralysis, particularly if they were also evening types. Those who said they were "flexible" sleepers reported a lower incidence. It is notable that flexible morning types had an especially low incidence of less than one percent, about one-tenth of that experienced by rigid evening types, who had the highest incidence at 9.35 percent.

The researchers were somewhat surprised by the high incidence among evening types, because other research has indicated that such people adapt to night work more readily than morning types. However, they noted that the majority of paralysis incidents occurred when these controllers worked a single-day M/N shift and suggested that evening types might have more problems with this type of shift. For one thing, evening types would be more likely to go to bed later than morning types the night before a morning shift, but they would have to get up just as early in the morning. Moreover, evening types would find it more difficult to nap between the morning and night shift because their circadian cycle would be at its peak during this period. Thus, the researchers suggested, schedules involving single-day M/N shifts are likely to cause more sleep deprivation in evening types than in morning types, and their findings back up this hypothesis.

Folkard and Condon did not find any correlation of night-shift paralysis with age and there were too few women controllers in the sample to assess the influence of gender. However, when they compared the results of this study with the one they did on nurses (a mostly female sample) and made adjustments for the much higher rate of consecutive night shifts among nurses, they found the incidence of night-shift paralysis to be three times higher among the men and concluded that night-working males are far more prone to this problem than night-working women. This supports the view that night-shift paralysis is a form of sleep paralysis, which appears to be more common in men than in women.

The researchers conclude that the incidence of night-shift paralysis is dependent on four factors that affect an individual's degree of sleepiness or sleep deprivation: the time of night, the number of successive night shifts, working morning and night shifts on the same day and flexibility in sleep habits. They said that the incidence of night-shift paralysis can be used as an indicator of the amount of sleep deprivation associated with a particular shift schedule or individual controllers. Finally, they said that this "potentially dangerous sleep deprivation" could be reduced by permitting controllers to work only single night shifts and by eliminating single-day morning/night shifts. They also suggest that sleep deprivation caused by night work might be reduced if workers are screened on the basis of sleep flexibility.

· · · · · · ·

In his speech to the Association of Professional Sleep Societies, John Lauber urged sleep researchers to intensify efforts to find counter-measures for fatigue on the job. Since shift work, 24-hour transportation operations and transmeridian flights are inescapable facts of modern life, techniques are urgently needed to help people cope with the "unique biological and psychological demands of such operations," he said. Moreover, public education is essential to counteract the myths and misperceptions contained in statements like, "A few beers and I sleep like a baby . . . " or "I know my limits; I know when it's time to pull over and sleep . . . " Lauber described these as "widely held beliefs which many people use to make practical decisions about their own coping strategies. Strategy founded on ignorance all too often ends in tragedy."

### III. Sports

For a world-class athlete, years of training, a lifetime of effort — everything — may depend on a few minutes of dazzling speed or stunning artistry on the ice, the racetrack, the ski slope, the diving tower or the balance beam. "What it come down to is getting it all perfect for 4½ minutes on that one evening," says world champion figure skater Kurt Browning, who electrified the skating world in

1988 by landing the first quadruple jump in competition. When records are set and medals won or lost in hundredths of a second or tenths of a point, athletes must be at their physiological peak to have any hope of winning — and yet they are routinely required to perform after crossing many time zones and at virtually any hour of the day or night. In 1987, for example, the men's final free-skating competition of the U.S. national figure skating championships wrapped up after 1:00 a.m. and one TV commentator suggested that this was why the competitors were not at their peak. "You can't do it this late."

(Sleep loss and circadian factors might well have an even worse effect on doing school figures, in which skaters are judged on their ability to trace precise lines in the ice with their blades. This requires just as much concentration as a free-skating program, but it is far more tedious and lacks the creative and emotional stimulation of free skating. It is now being phased out of international competitions.)

Richard Coleman, who did a survey of 90 U.S. Olympic athletes before the 1984 Games, found that most of the time, these athletes were pretty good sleepers. They averaged nearly 8 hours of sleep a night and also napped about half an hour each day. Only three percent reported significant insomnia and about 10 percent experienced occasional sleep problems. But on the night before competition, it was a different story: more than half reported having sleep problems. In many cases, they phase-advanced their sleep period to adjust to events scheduled early the next day and, as a result, lost an average of 1 to 3 hours of sleep. Athletes reported that these sleep difficulties affected their performance — they cited symptoms such as anxiety, low energy levels and lack of concentration — but they also said that the stiffer the competition, the better they were able to overcome their fatigue.

Coleman also found that 60 percent of the athletes reported that jet lag and the scheduling of events affected their performance significantly. In recent years, a growing awareness of the deleterious effects of jet lag and sleep loss has prompted coaches and coaching associations to offer athletes more guidance on how to combat the problem. Some of the advice is the same as that given to any transmeridian traveler, but some is more specific to the athlete's needs. For example, a paper distributed by the Coaching Association of Canada says that athletes should schedule their arrival time at their destination during evening hours and then have a light practice to enhance sleep; however, athletes should not practice difficult routines or those requiring high skill levels immediately after arriving at their destination, because their performance is likely to be poorer than usual and this could damage their confidence so badly that they might not recover it for the competition.

Another paper, by physiologist Charles Winget of the NASA/Ames Research Center, gives athletes detailed information about the circadian system and the fact that different circadian rhythms will "reset" at different rates. He focuses on physiological parameters that affect athletic performance — e.g., heart rate, neuromuscular function, oxygen uptake, hormone secretions, carbohydrate storage in the liver, body temperature, even bowel movements (which can take up to a week to resynchronize to the new time zone).

Body temperature and heart rate are two important rhythms for the athlete. Winget notes that an athlete's peak performance on tasks involving muscle coordination will occur at the time of highest body temperature (late afternoon or early evening) and the worst time will coincide with the circadian low in temperature. The heart-rate rhythm adapts to the new time zone more quickly than body temperature. Winget notes that circadian variation in the circulatory system is important because it influences the delivery of oxygen, glucose and hormones to body organs; this is particularly critical for optimal brain functioning. Circadian variations in the neuromuscular system can also affect things like grip strength, reaction time and elbow flexion strength.

Circadian rhythms can cause variability in performance of between 10 and 30 percent over the day, and the amount of this variability increases with increasing complexity of tasks, Winget notes. He lists a number of functions important to athletic performance that exhibit circadian variation — e.g., reaction time, eye-hand coordination, visual acuity and perception. One study found circadian rhythms in the speed of muscular movement and subsequent output of power from muscles and another found that the circadian timing of blood flow to muscles can significantly affect short-duration physical power required for events like weight lifting and gymnastics.

Sleep loss caused by travel, jet lag and disrupted schedules also takes its toll on athletes. Whether the effects are pronounced or subtle, they can affect a gymnast's psychomotor control or cost a runner a few precious seconds, Winget says. Other potentially damaging effects include lack of concentration, lethargy, distractibility, reduced alertness and motivation and loss of coordination. He warns athletes that their bodies will require several days at least to adapt to the new time zone before it will be back in condition to deliver a peak performance.

These days, athletes and their coaches are much more aware of the need to give their bodies time to adapt to new time zones, either before or after the trip. "If we go to Europe, we're talking about 5, 6 hours — what we try to do is reorganize their schedule here, get them on a different schedule that would line up with their competing schedule in Europe," says Ron Ludington, director of the ice skating science development center at the University of Delaware, who has coached 36 U.S. national skating champions. This usually takes place over several weeks and means that skaters often end up training at night. Ludington says they adapt readily enough before competition, but "when they come back, they're usually fatigued and they've got to readapt again to a regular day schedule, so they feel it for a few days. They have a real letdown and we just let them have it."

Competitions in Japan are another matter: "That requires us going earlier, so we get more acclimated. About an hour a day is the best you can do in acclimation. We try to go six days, seven days, before they compete; that's about the best we can do because of the financial problems."

Ludington said that skaters, like other athletes, are subject to the demands of television and this means that many of them compete at night. "We know the events that are held at night in most cases, so we just adapt to it. We usually know far enough in advance. I think the main thing is just getting used to it." He added that, for years, he taught skating all night, but when he recently took his job at the university, "I had to change my schedule, so I just changed it." Whether athletes are morning people or night people, they have little control over the times they have to compete, so they too must learn to adjust. "They have no choice in most cases, but I find these kids are so motivated at this level that they adapt because they want it so badly."

The situation is not much different for professional athletes, except, of course, for the added enticement of very large financial rewards. They also experience problems with sleep loss and circadian desynchronization caused by jet lag and irregular schedules, particularly because they compete all over the world for months on end with

little respite. In November 1988, so many of the top-seeded international tennis players in a major U.S. tournament were suffering from
injuries and jet lag that the competition was described by one journalist as the "survival of the least fit." Several players urged that
changes be made in the $36.5-million professional tour schedule to
allow for a two-month break at the end of the year. At a press
conference, Ivan Lendl blamed the spate of injuries on the fact that
professional tennis has no off-season. "You can't play 12 months a
year for 10 years as I've done and not get hurt."

In June 1987, hockey superstar Wayne Gretzky caused a sensation
when he said he was too tired to play in the postseason Canada Cup
tournament after leading the Edmonton Oilers to their third Stanley
Cup victory in four years — and, not incidentally, winning the National Hockey League's most valuable player award for the eighth
consecutive year. (Since Edmonton is located in the northwestern
reaches of the continent, the Oilers rack up a lot of cross-country
distance during the playing season; in 1989, they logged more than
80,000 kilometers — nearly 50,000 miles — traveling to 23 cities.)
"I'm more mentally and physically tired than I've ever been," Gretzky
told the press. "You show up tired and down and they say, 'We don't
care.' They just want you to perform. That's all they're concerned
about." When it was suggested that his hesitation had more to do with
contract negotiations than with fatigue, the usually even-tempered
Gretzky testily denied the charge and pointed out, not for the first
time, that he was not a machine.

Athletes tend not to comment publicly about being tired — in part,
no doubt, because such complaints are typically greeted with a lack
of sympathy directly proportional to the size of their paychecks.
There's a certain irony in this: in so many ways, athletes are pampered
and catered to and yet one of the most basic requirements for good
performance — quality sleep — is usually all but ignored when travel
schedules and competition times are set up. And the physiological
demands on athletes may be even greater than ever because of the
growing tendency to schedule events and competitions with prime-
time television in mind. Since TV networks pay huge sums for
broadcasting rights, they naturally have a powerful influence on the
timing of sports events.

Hockey and baseball are two games that are played most frequently
at night. In fact, more baseball games are now played under the lights

than during the day — a reversal of the situation that existed prior to the era of TV megabucks. Evening games typically start about 7:00 or 7:30 p.m. and rarely last less than 3 hours; extra-inning games can go on for 4 or 5 hours and can end well past midnight. Baseball teams play nearly every day for six to seven months, and during road trips, they move to a new city every three or four days, usually leaving after a night game. Consequently, players spend a good portion of their time between April and October shuttling back and forth across the North American continent in the middle of the night and rarely getting to bed before 2:00 or 3:00 a.m.* "If you don't like the night work, you get a bank job," said Mike Mitchell, former travel manager of the Toronto Blue Jays.

About the only concession the official schedule makes to this tiring routine is to mandate a day off after a team has traveled from west to east. However, teams will often send the pitcher scheduled to start the first game in the next city on ahead so he can get some rest.

Players generally prefer to travel immediately after a game, rather than wait until morning. They want to be on their way, Mitchell said; their attitude is that "we're done with that city. It's psychologically important to put the series behind you." Still mentally psyched up from the game and full of rich food from lavish postgame meals, they usually aren't very sleepy anyway. Some players may sleep while traveling but most don't, Mitchell said. Some — usually veterans who've learned to pace themselves — will take a nap in the afternoon before the game. "It's a long year," he said.

Doing intense physical exercise at night may also affect an athlete's ability to sleep. While performance tends to peak in the early evening, between about 7:00 and 9:00 p.m., many games run much later. Broughton said this might be an even worse problem for athletes in sports involving heavier exercise than baseball, such as hockey, football or soccer. "Exercise late at night might cause them to have poor quality sleep."

A perfect example of what this kind of schedule entails occurred with the Blue Jays in May 1987, when they returned to Toronto from a western trip. They stopped in Winnipeg on their day off to play an exhibition game and then a delay in their charter flight meant they

---

* The legendary Babe Ruth was a nightowl who didn't like going to bed at night, but he always made it to the ballpark and during his 15-year tenure with the New York Yankees, the team won the World Series four times.

got into Toronto after 4:00 a.m. Moreover, they'd spent 21 of the preceding 23 days on the road. "Not exactly a prescription for a successful homecoming," one sports writer noted. They lost their next game, but in true right-stuff fashion, refused to attribute it to fatigue. "We just didn't score runs," said one player, as though that fact had no conceivable relationship to fatigue. Their manager at the time, Jimy Williams, described in news reports as tired looking, added, "We got into Minneapolis at four in the morning and won; we got into Anaheim at 4:00 a.m. and won. I don't want to use excuses."

Players aren't the only ones who suffer from fatigue because of this schedule. Harvey Moldofsky tells the story of one man who was referred to his sleep clinic complaining of daytime sleepiness. Since the man drove a van for a living, the problem was potentially serious. Tests for apnea, narcolepsy and other sleep disorders proved negative, so Moldofsky took a closer look at the man's daily routine and found the cause of his sleepiness: he was an avid Blue Jays fan who invariably stayed up nights to watch baseball games — including ones broadcast during western road trips, which start about 10:00 p.m. and end between about 1:00 and 2:00 a.m. Toronto time.

## IV. The Space Program

There are times when the exploration of space places extraordinary demands on workers, both on the ground and in orbit. Here, we will examine two situations that provide the most graphic examples of the ways in which sleep problems affect our migration into space: first, the events leading up to the January 1986 explosion of the space shuttle *Challenger* and, second, the sleep problems associated with long-duration space missions.

### THE *CHALLENGER* ACCIDENT

The report of the presidential commission that investigated the *Challenger* explosion contained an appendix entitled "Human Factors Analysis," which examined the excessive amount of overtime among workers and managers at the Kennedy Space Center in the months and days leading up to the flight. Although it drew no conclusions about the effects of these work schedules in causing the accident, it is clear that the entire KSC team, including key decision-makers, were in a state of extreme fatigue by the time the ill-fated shuttle lifted off the launch pad.

Preparing a shuttle for launching "imposes an around-the-clock work requirement on several large groups of workers, including launch-control-center personnel," the report noted. "While shift work is common in many industrial settings, few can equal a shuttle launch's potential for inducing pressure to work beyond reasonable overtime limits." The pressure increases tremendously when the rate of launching increases or when unexpected delays occur, particularly within a few days of liftoff.

The three months leading up to the ill-fated *Challenger* launch on January 28 provided some particularly apropos examples. In its effort to establish the shuttle as a reliable workhorse, NASA had been pushing hard to increase the frequency of shuttle flights and had planned a schedule for 1986 involving an average of more than one launch a month, a rate never before (or since) achieved. But, the flight before *Challenger* was postponed a record seven times before it finally got off the ground in mid-January, and the *Challenger* flight was delayed five times. These events created an exceptional amount of pressure on the more than 5,000 ground workers at the Kennedy Space Center, including senior launch control officials.

During November, December and January, an usually high amount of overtime was required, with some workers putting in seven to nine consecutive 60-hour work weeks. There were about 150 cases where the work week exceeded 80 hours and instances in which two men each worked 96 hours in one week. One of these, a mechanical technician team leader, worked 60, 96½, 94 and 81 hours a week during January.

The commission said that three independent factors contributed to excessive overtime: consecutive days worked, long hours on any given day and multiple shift changes. It found that during a six-week period in November and December, many workers worked two weeks or longer without a day off and one worker put in 50 days straight without time off. In many of these cases, the workday ranged from 10 to 12 hours; in fact, a number of workers put in 12-hour days for periods ranging from 10 to 18 days in a row, some of them more than once during the study period.

Although attempts were made to balance overtime among the workers, some individuals with critically needed skills bore the brunt of the overwork. For example, the mechanical team leader mentioned above worked for 26 consecutive days, only two of which were 8 hours long; 16 were 12-hour days and the remainder were 13 to 16 hours long. In the case of the man who worked 50 days in a row, all his shifts were night shifts, which normally lasted from midnight to 8:00 a.m., although on 38 of the days, he actually worked until about noon.

The commission described these examples as "extreme but by no means isolated. They illustrate a frequent pattern of combining weeks of consecutive workdays with multiple strings of 11- or 12-hour days. Research has shown that either of these factors alone produces worker fatigue, but that together they represent a potential threat to safety and worker effectiveness."

In some cases, shift schedules exacerbated the problems of fatigue and sleep loss experienced by workers putting in long hours, the commission said. Some workers worked 12-hour shifts from 3:00 p.m. to 3:00 a.m. or vice versa, sometimes up to seven days in a row, which caused substantial sleep loss. In the cases cited above, extended workdays of 12 to 16 hours also disrupted sleep by interrupting the workers' adjustment to the current shift schedule.

The commission noted that jet lag was an added factor for workers sent overseas just before a scheduled launch to provide support in case the shuttle had to make an emergency landing. Typically, this travel involved crossing at least five time zones. Many of these workers put in overtime shifts just before traveling. In one case, a man who had worked for 10 consecutive days, seven of which exceeded 11½ hours, went on duty the first day he arrived in Spain. "While the likelihood of a contingency landing may be remote, the performance requirements of the ground crew at the alternate site will be critical if the [shuttle] experiences the type of emergency that dictates such landings," the report noted.

The commission concluded that overtime among KSC workers was not being adequately monitored from the perspective of safety and suggested that an audit system and greater overtime restrictions "might contribute significantly to reducing the potential safety risks associated with shift work, especially that engendered by un-anticipated launch postponements." However, it did conclude that these activities, including assembly and preparation of the shuttle for launching, were "not a factor in the *Challenger* accident."

The commission commented briefly on the teleconference held on the evening of January 27 to decide whether *Challenger* should be launched the next morning in the unusually cold weather that had descended on the Kennedy Space Center. The participants included 13 key managers located at the Kennedy Space Center, the Marshall Space Flight Center and at Morton Thiokol Inc. in Utah, which manufactures the shuttle's solid rocket booster. (It was the failure of a seal on one of these boosters that caused the *Challenger* explosion.) There had already been one launch abort on the morning of January 27. By the time the 3-hour teleconference started at 7:00 p.m., these managers had been awake and on duty for periods ranging from 12 to 19 hours. The two who had been awake the longest (19 and 18½ hours respectively) had slept for only about 2 to 3 hours each the night before. (The others had slept between 5 and 8 hours.)

The commission report suggests that irregular work hours and insufficient sleep may have contributed significantly to a lack of effective communication and exchange of information during the teleconference. (In fact, there was a heated debate about the advisability of launching the shuttle.) It noted that "time pressure, particularly that caused by launch scrubs and rapid turnarounds, increases the potential for sleep loss and judgment errors. This could be minimized by preventing launch support personnel, particularly managers, from combining launch support duty with office work on the same day. The willingness of NASA employees . . . to work excessive hours, while admirable, raises serious questions when it jeopardizes job performance, particularly when critical management decisions are at stake."

The commission did not venture an opinion as to whether the flawed decision to launch *Challenger* was caused by fatigue (and, in fact, *The New York Times* later reported that "Commission staff members said privately that they did not believe that was the case"). Nor did the commission draw any conclusions about the effects of work schedules on performance or management judgment; however, it did suggest that NASA should evaluate the consequences of work schedules in its effort to reform its launch and operational procedures.

A year later, NASA announced that it had set in place a system to reduce overtime among KSC workers and established a special "scrub team" of managers to take over when a launch is postponed and attempted again within 24 hours. According to one KSC official, the team's responsibility would be to "handle the scrub turnaround tasks so we can get a lot of management out and get them rested before they have to come back in on that 24-hour turnaround."

## SLEEPING IN SPACE

Before human beings ever flew in space, doctors wondered whether the most basic physiological functions would be possible in zero gravity. Would astronauts be able to swallow? Urinate? Sleep? It was quickly determined that the simple answer to all these questions was yes. But in the case of sleep, the simple answer is not the full answer. After nearly 30 years of manned space flight, we know that although it's certainly possible for people to sleep normally in space, the demands of running a complex mission in a unique, hazardous and isolated environment often make it very difficult to do so, and this in turn affects the ability of astronauts and cosmonauts to perform their duties.

Sleeping accommodations in space are not luxurious by Earth standards. In the early days (i.e., the 1960s), astronauts and cosmonauts slept in their seats — often poorly. Zero gravity can be a nuisance, as Soviet cosmonaut Gherman Titov discovered during his 17-orbit mission in 1961; he reported that his arms would float up as soon as he fell asleep and his muscles relaxed. After this happened a couple of times, he strapped his arms down with a belt and was fast asleep in seconds. (Titov, the first human to sleep in space, also has the distinction of being the first to oversleep; he woke up 30 minutes late.) Mercury astronaut Gordon Cooper, the first American to sleep in space, was so concerned about monitoring his spacecraft systems that he kept waking up throughout the night and got only about 4½ hours of sleep.

In the 1970s, with the advent of the first rudimentary space stations (the Soviet Salyut station and the U.S. Skylab), there was room enough for sleeping bags attached to the walls of the spacecraft. The same is true for the U.S. space shuttle, although some astronauts prefer to sleep in their seats, while others just float with a leg or arm tethered and still others have no trouble sleeping while floating freely throughout the cabin. (While these astronauts often bump against something, it's usually too light to wake them up. However, waking up nose-to-nose with another crew member is a distinct possibility.) Astronauts who are troubled by motion sickness in zero gravity — a common affliction — will often anchor their heads to the sleeping bag with a strap to prevent them from moving around.

On the space station Freedom, which will be built by the United States, Europe, Japan and Canada and is scheduled to fly in the 1990s, astronauts will have private soundproofed compartments to hang their sleeping bags. It is likely that shift work will be the rule on board the station and the private rooms will make it easier for off-duty crew members to sleep while others are working.

In the future, it's possible that astronauts may try out a new kind of space bed — one that rotates in order to create a gravity load on their feet equivalent to Earth's 1-G. Designing and testing this bed on earth was the thesis project of Peter Diamandis, a graduate student at the Massachusetts Institute of Technology, who was exploring the possibility that rotating astronauts while they sleep, and thus exposing their bodies to gravity loads, might help overcome some of the physiological problems caused by zero gravity, notably muscle wasting and loss of calcium from the bones. The bed rotates at 23 RPM; when it first starts to move, you can feel yourself being pushed toward the foot of the bed, but in a matter of seconds, all sensation of rotation disappears and the bed becomes a surprisingly comfortable place to sleep. "You notice the process of getting there, but once you're there, it doesn't feel that unusual. You don't feel as if you're standing up or anything like that," said Diamandis, who has run overnight sleep tests in his lab with subjects whom he dubs "gyronauts."

· · · · · · ·

Sleep problems are not uncommon on space flights, despite the high motivation and superb physiological condition of crew members; the environment is unusual, the conditions usually cramped and often uncomfortable and the performance demands high. Unforeseen problems are an almost daily occurrence — they frequently disrupt sleep schedules — and life-threatening emergencies are always a possibility. One of the most unusual difficulties stems from the fact that a spacecraft orbits the Earth approximately every 90 to 120 minutes, depending on its altitude, and thus experiences a rapidly alternating light/dark cycle as it repeatedly moves out of the sun into the Earth's shadow. Astronauts usually deal with this problem by pulling down window shades or wearing a mask.

Curtis Graeber of NASA/Ames Research Center notes that the quality of sleep obtained by astronaut crews will always affect performance and safety on space missions; in some extreme cases, astronauts have had to carry on working despite experiencing excessive fatigue caused by sleep loss.

The first EEG sleep measurements were taken on the Gemini VII mission in 1965. Inadequate sleep was common during the nine Gemini missions carried out in 1965 and 1966, according to Graeber. The two-man spacecraft was cramped and the astronauts slept in their seats; excitement and anxiety, noise, staggered sleep periods, intentionally altered day/night cycles and uncomfortable and unfamiliar sleep accommodations all contrived to make sleep difficult. Similarly, crews on the three-man Apollo missions experienced difficulties. Graeber reports that the crew on the first flight, Apollo 7, did not adjust to large shifts in their sleep/wake cycles and mission requirements prevented all three crew members from sleeping at the same time. During the first three days, they reported sleeping poorly and subsequently the quality of their sleep was mixed. Similarly on Apollo 8, the first mission to orbit the moon, the lack of simultaneous sleep and circadian desynchronization caused so much fatigue, particularly just before the crew was scheduled to leave lunar orbit for the return to Earth, that the flight plan had to be changed. On subsequent missions, sleep quality improved because crew members were all allowed to sleep at the same time.

On Apollo 11, the first lunar landing mission, the crew slept well on their trip to the moon, but neither Neil Armstrong nor Edwin Aldrin slept well on the moon's surface because of the cramped, noisy quarters and cold space suits. On subsequent landing missions, high-quality sleep continued to elude crews; when technical problems occurred that required changes in the sleep schedule, the astronauts were forced to rely on their "physiological reserves" until they could get some sleep on the way back to Earth, Graeber said.

More extensive sleep studies were carried out on the three Skylab missions in the mid-1970s. There were three missions, lasting 28, 59 and 84 days. Although the sleep of the crews was, overall, normal and adequate, there were considerable individual variations in sleep latencies and in total sleep time. (In one case, an astronaut's total sleep time averaged less than 6 hours, compared with 7½ hours on earth and sleep researchers suggested this reduction in total sleep time may have had an effect on his performance.)

The Skylab astronauts attributed occasional sleeplessness to noise, poor lightproofing and long work days that did not permit a sufficient amount of time for winding down before bedtime. They reported feeling more affected the next day by a poor night's sleep in space than they were by losing the same amount of sleep on earth. However, none of the sleep changes observed were considered serious enough to jeopardize mission performance.

Graeber reported an interesting incident that occurred on the first flight of the space shuttle. In the week before the mission, the two-man crew phase-advanced their sleep period by an hour a day so they would be adapted to a 2:00 a.m. wake-up on launch day. Once in orbit, they slept in their seats so they'd be within reach of the controls in case of an emergency. On the second night, Mission Control set off an alarm to test their reaction and one of the astronauts flipped the wrong switch. Nothing untoward happened as a result, but the crew member barely remembered the incident later. This situation had all the earmarks of sleep inertia on awakening from deep sleep. Graeber suggested that the depth of sleep experienced by the astronaut on the second night might have been affected by the fact that poor sleep was obtained on the first night because of low temperatures in the space-craft.

## THE SOVIET MANNED-SPACE PROGRAM

Individually and collectively, Soviet cosmonauts have logged more time in space than anyone else. Aboard their Salyut and Mir space stations, they have conducted missions lasting from six months to more than a year and, by mid-1989, they had accumulated about 3½ times more person-hours in space than U.S. astronauts.

Managers of the Soviet space program have paid a great deal of attention to sleep/wake/work schedules and their effect on the phys-iological and psychological well-being of cosmonauts, particularly on long-duration missions.* (Much of this effort reflects their interest not

---

* A comprehensive summary of Soviet documents concerning long-duration missions is contained in a NASA report called *Soviet Space Stations as Analogs*, by B. J. Bluth, a systems engineer in NASA's space station program, and Martha Helppie, a research associate. This report provides the source for much of the following information about sleep/wake and work schedules in the Soviet space program.

only in permanent human habitation of low Earth orbit, but their intention to send manned missions to Mars after the turn of the century.)

Like U.S. shuttle astronauts, Soviet cosmonauts have sleeping bags aboard the Mir station. They wear fur boots in bed to compensate for poor circulation in zero gravity, which can affect their sleep; some have also reported a feeling of suffocation because of the slow air movement in the spacecraft. Cosmonauts generally sleep at least 7 to 8 hours a day and sometimes longer if they need it. Toward the end of a 211-day mission aboard the Salyut space station, crew members were allowed to sleep for 12 hours a day. Cosmonauts rarely need an alarm clock to wake up; one, who had been waking up at 7:00 a.m. all his life, found that "my biological clock works in space too."

The scheduling of sleep and work is carefully controlled on long-duration missions. On some early flights, cosmonauts followed a migrating schedule that involved a daily phase advance or delay of about 30 minutes in their sleep/wake cycle. This caused circadian desynchronization and serious problems with sleep loss and fatigue; consequently, crews on the Mir station now maintain a 24-hour schedule synchronized to Moscow time and a five-day work week with two days off.

In their crew selection process, Soviet space officials try to match cosmonauts with similar biological rhythms, believing that this improves their ability to coordinate spacecraft activities and to operate with maximum efficiency. It also permits them to rest properly during prescribed rest periods.

Not surprisingly, however, fatigue increases as the mission goes on. Around the end of the third month in space, monotony and isolation start to seriously affect cosmonaut crews, and it becomes a challenge for Mission Control to keep them active and motivated. Several cosmonauts have commented that a diversified and interesting work program is essential for a stable working environment. One commented that work provides the best antidote to depression and anxiety.

However, rest breaks are also important, particularly for maintaining vigilance when operating automated equipment. One Soviet report detailed the lapses in attention that can occur: "With prolonged work at a control panel, attention is turned off for a small fraction of a second at first. . . . There are temporary blackouts. . . . Signals are not reaching the operator's consciousness. . . . The percentage of omitted signals increases, despite the growing stimulation of the operator and his willful effort. That is why taking a rest break is important."

These breaks, which often involve physical exercise, reading or listening to music, are taken as soon as signs of fatigue are evident, but they're short so as not to take the cosmonaut's attention away from his or her work for long; it is felt that long breaks would reduce performance. (It does not appear that cosmonauts employ ultrashort napping.) Soviet researchers note, however, that by the end of a long mission, feelings of tiredness do not disappear even after a night's sleep.

Toward the end of a 326-day mission in late 1987, cosmonauts Yuri Romanenko and Alexander Alexandrov were reported to be highly fatigued and they were put on a 4½-hour workday for several weeks before their return to earth. Noting that even two days of rest could no longer restore the cosmonauts, Soviet officials commented that "the crew is not concealing that they feel the monotony of the flight." Mission control was instructed not to press them to work overtime and work that could interrupt a sleep period was halted. In an unusual move, a "safety pilot" was sent up to the space station to escort the fatigued crew when it was time for them to come back to Earth.

Cosmonauts can take sleeping pills, but in at least one case, this appears to have caused a serious problem when one crew member experienced an abrupt personality change; he became irritable and fractious and began complaining about the work schedule and living conditions. His behavior was attributed to taking excessive doses of sleeping pills because he'd been unable to rest.

Managers of the Soviet space program are particularly concerned about the emotional and psychological fallout of fatigue, excessive work, isolation and monotony. Unlike the U.S. program, the Soviet program employs a psychological support group that participates in the selection of crews and provides day-to-day monitoring of crews on long-duration missions. Crew members themselves are also very conscious of the problems that fatigue can cause. In his diary, Cosmonaut Lebedev wrote that the most difficult challenge was "keeping calm in dealing with [Mission Control] and with other crew members because pent-up fatigue could generate serious friction." He admits frankly to a feeling of apprehension as to whether he will be able to live and work with his partner for a long period of time, "whether I will always be able to keep my composure and self-control. With growing fatigue, there is a danger of serious lapses." But tensions "cannot be allowed to explode," he comments. "A crack, once it appears, can widen."

Graeber says that experience to date indicates that the problems associated with sleep loss in space appear to be manageable; however, some individuals appear to have sleep difficulties for long periods of time. Developing selection criteria to minimize this problem "may be warranted," but at the same time, this might result in the loss of valuable talent, so developing ways to help astronauts sleep well on extended missions in space might be useful. He notes that Soviet researchers have already done experiments with sailors in which sleep has been electrically induced.

Looking to the future of permanent human habitation of space, Graeber notes that the threats posed by the harsh environment will not disappear, nor will operational problems. And as we build bigger and more expensive space structures and send more people into space, the potential losses from human error will greatly increase. As on earth, there will be space-based industries requiring 24-hour vigilance. "Consequently, there will always be a need for altered sleep/wake cycles." And if humans venture to other planets, the trip will be made in constant sunlight, in which case "it is arguable that the earth's 24-hour cycle may not be the most advantageous for crews."

He concludes that while sleep problems won't prevent humans from achieving new goals in space, there's no question that they have and will continue to jeopardize efficiency and safety, and better ways must be found to prevent this from happening in the future.

# Conclusion

We expect our sleep/wake system to carry us through virtually any kind of work schedule, anywhere, anytime, regardless of the limitations imposed by physiology. This is often described as treating the human body like a machine, but actually, the opposite is closer to the truth. As Martin Moore-Ede points out, we don't expect machines to function indefinitely if we push them beyond the operating limits for which they were designed. In fact, he argues that in a sense it's a mistake *not* to view the human body as a piece of "highly sophisticated machinery" — one that should be properly maintained and not operated outside its "design specs."

"If you assume people are adaptable and they'll manage somehow," he says, "then you end up asking people to do things which are really — even given unlimited willpower — still beyond their capabilities."

The technologies that so influence the daily conduct of our lives do not alleviate the need for human vigilance and alertness. In fact, despite the level of automation they permit, they have, paradoxically, increased that need — as they have increased the consequences when human vigilance and alertness fail. As long as the symbiotic relationship between humans and machines endures, the stakes will remain high.

"Population surveys and epidemiological studies have clarified the enormous prevalence of sleep problems . . . throughout the world," commented a task force of U.S. sleep experts. "The pervasive role of sleep and wakefulness schedules in modern industrialized society has created a series of public-policy issues related to the well-being and performance of millions of shift workers and others in critical and strategic enterprises."

They said that understanding sleep and its disorders is critical to fully understand human health and disease. The sleep/wake system, they concluded, is equal in importance to the circulatory, digestive and reproductive systems.

If the medical community has been slow to come to grips with sleep's central role in our lives — and its ability to disrupt the conduct of our lives — the public and our political and economic systems have been slower still. Sleep has been viewed as being a bit like the weather — something that everyone talks about but no one does anything about.

Recent advances in sleep research indicate that this need no longer be true.

# REFERENCES AND BIBLIOGRAPHY

In addition to personal interviews with many of the researchers mentioned in this book, source material included numerous books, scientific papers and magazine and newspaper articles. Following is a bibliography for those who may be interested in further reading.

## Scientific papers and books:

Angus, R. G., R. J. Heslegrave, R. A. Pigeau, and D. W. Jamieson. *Psychological Performance During Sleep Loss and Continuous Mental Work: The Effects of Interjected Naps.* Toronto: Defence and Civil Institute of Environmental Medicine, 1987.

Bluth, B. J., and M. Helppie. "Soviet Space Stations as Analogs." Unpublished grant report NAGW-659. National Aeronautics and Space Administration, 1986, 1987.

Broughton, R., et al. "Life Effects of Narcolepsy in 180 Patients from North America, Asia and Europe Compared to Matched Controls." *The Canadian Journal of Neurological Sciences.* November 1981.

Broughton, R. "Performance and Evoked Potential Measures of Various States of Daytime Sleepiness." *Sleep*, Vol. 5. (Suppl. 2), 1982.

Broughton, R., and M. Mamelak. "Effects of Nocturnal Gamma-Hydroxybutyrate on Sleep/Waking Patterns in Narcolepsy-Cataplexy." *The Canadian Journal of Neurological Sciences.* February 1980.

Coleman, R. *Wide Awake at 3 a.m.* New York: W. H. Freeman and Co., 1986.

Czeisler, C. H., et al. "Bright Light Resets the Human Circadian Pacemaker Independent of the Timing of the Sleep-Wake Cycle." *Science*, Vol. 233, August 8, 1986.

Czeisler, C. H., et al. "Human Sleep: Its Duration and Organization Depend on Its Circadian Phase." *Science*, Vol. 210, December 12, 1980.

——. "Entrainment of Human Circadian Rhythms by Light-Dark Cycles: A Reassessment." *Photochemistry and Photobiology*, Vol 34, 1981.

Czeisler, C. H., M. C. Moore-Ede, and R. C. Coleman. "Rotating Shift Work Schedules That Disrupt Sleep Are Improved by Applying Circadian Principles." *Science*, Vol. 217, July 30, 1982.

Dement, W. *Some Must Watch While Some Must Sleep.* New York: W. W. Norton & Co., 1978.

Dinges, D. F. "The Nature of Sleepiness: Causes, Contexts and Consequences," pgs 147-179 in *Perspectives in Behavioral Medicine: Eating, Sleeping and Sex.* Edited by Albert J. Stunkhard and Andrew Baum. Hillsdale, N. J.: Lawrence Erlbaum Associates, 1989.

Dinges, D. F., M. T. Orne, W. G. Whitehouse, and E. C. Orne. "Temporal Placement of a Nap for Alertness: Contributions of Circadian Phase and Prior Wakefulness." *Sleep*, Vol. 10(4), 1987.

Dinges, D. F., W. G. Whitehouse, E. C. Orne, and M. T. Orne. "The benefits of a nap during prolonged work and wakefulness." *Work and Stress*, Vol. 2, No. 2, 139-153, 1988.

Folkard, S. and R. Condon. "Night Shift Paralysis in Air Traffic Control Officers." *Ergonomics*, Vol. 30, 1987.

Graeber, C. "Sleep in Space." *Sleep and Its Military Applications*. Edited by M. Jouvet. NATO DRG Proceedings, 1987.

Hauri, Peter. "The Sleep Disorders." *Current Concepts*. Kalamazoo: The Upjohn Company, 1982.

Herscovitch, J., and R. Broughton. "Performance Deficits Following Short-Term Partial Sleep Deprivation and Subsequent Recovery Oversleeping." *Canadian Journal of Psychology*, 35(4), 1981.

——— . "Sensitivity of the Stanford Sleepiness Scale to the Effects of Cumulative Partial Sleep Deprivation and Recovery Oversleeping." *Sleep*, Vol. 4(1), 1981.

Heslegrave, R. J., and R. G. Angus. "The effects of task duration and work-session location on performance degradation induced by sleep loss and sustained cognitive work." *Behavior Research Methods, Instruments & Computers*. 17(6), 1985.

Horne, J. A. "Sleep Loss and 'Divergent' Thinking Ability." *Sleep*, Vol. 11(6), 1988.

——— . *Why We Sleep*. Oxford: Oxford University Press, 1988.

Horne, J. A., and O. Ostberg. "A Self-Assessment Questionnaire to Determine Morningness-Eveningness in Human Circadian Rhythms." *International Journal of Chronobiology*, Vol 4, 1976.

Ishihara, K. et al. "Differences in Sleep-Wake Habits and EEG Sleep Variables between Active Morning and Evening Subjects." *Sleep*, Vol. 10(4), 1987.

Lauber, J. K., and P. J. Kayten. *Sleepiness, Circadian Dysrhythmia and Fatigue in Transportation System Accidents*. Keynote address, 2nd Annual Meeting of the Association of Professional Sleep Societies, San Diego, 1988.

Lumley, M. et al. "Ethanol and Caffeine Effects on Daytime Sleepiness/Alertness." *Sleep*, Vol. 10(4), 1987.

Magee, Jon, John Harsh, and Pietro Badia. "Effects of Experimentally-Induced Sleep Fragmentation on Sleep and Sleepiness." *Psychophysiology*, Vol. 25, No. 9, 1987.

Mamelek, Mortimer. *Insomnia*. Kalamazoo: The Upjohn Company, 1987.

McCall, T. "The Impact of Long Working Hours on Resident Physicians;" Levinsky, N. G. "Compounding the Error;" Glickman, R. "House-Staff Training — The Need for Careful Reform." *The New England Journal of Medicine*, March 24, 1988.

Moldofsky, H. "Sleep and Fibrositis Syndrome." *Rheumatic Disease*, Vol. 15. No. 1, February 1989.

Moldofsky, H. et al. "Effects of sleep deprivation on human immune functions." *The FASEB Journal*, June, 1989.

Moore-Ede, M. *Shiftwork and Your Health*. Circadian Technologies Inc., 1986.

Moore-Ede, M., F. Sulzman, and C. Fuller. *The Clocks That Time Us*. Cambridge: Harvard University Press, 1982.

Naitoh, P. *Napping and Human Performance During Irregular or Prolonged Work*. NHRC Report. San Diego: Naval Health Research Center, 1988.

Naitoh, P., and R. G. Angus. *Napping and Human Functioning During Prolonged Work*. NHRC Report No. 87-21, Naval Health Research Center, San Diego, 1987.

Reschtschaffen, A. et al. *Sleep* 12(1), 1989 (entire issue).

Roth, B., M. Billiard, R. Broughton, S. Nevsimalova, and A. Vein. *Idiopathic Hypersomnia*. Fourth European Congress on Sleep Research, 1978.

Spielman, A. J., P. Saskin, and M. J. Thorny. "Treatment of Chronic Insomnia by Restriction of Time in Bed." *Sleep*, Vol 10., No 1, 1987.

Stampi, Claudio. "Ultrashort Sleep/Wake Patterns and Sustained Performance." *Sleep and Alertness: Chronobiological, Behavioral and Medical Aspects of Napping*. Edited by D. F. Dinges, and R. J. Broughton. New York: Raven Press, 1988.

Stuss, D., and R. Broughton. "Extreme Short Sleep: Personality Profiles and a Case Study of Sleep Requirement." *Waking and Sleeping* (2), 1978.

Valley, V., and R. Broughton. "Daytime Performance Deficits and Physiological Vigilance in Untreated Patients with Narcolepsy-Cataplexy Compared to Controls." Rev. E.E.G. *Neurophysiology*, 11, 1981.

Webb, W. "The Proximal Effects of Two and Four Hour Naps Within Extended Performance without Sleep." *Psychophysiological Research*, Vol. 24, No. 4, 1987.

Winget, Charles M. "Timing Travel and Athletic Performance." *Sports: Science Periodical on Research and Technology in Sport*. The Coaching Association of Canada, 1984.

———. *Report of the New York State Ad Hoc Advisory Committee on Emergency Services*. New York, October, 1987.

———. *Sleep, Wakefulness and Circadian Rhythm*. AGARD Lecture Series No. 105, Advisory Group for Aerospace.

———. *Sleep and Alertness: Chronobiological, Behavioral and Medical Aspects of Napping*. Edited by: F. Dinges and Roger J. Broughton. New York: Raven Press, 1988.

## Magazine and newspaper articles:

Blakeslee, Sandra. "Sleepers Who Are Prone to Violence Benefit from New Clinics and Drugs." *The New York Times*. July 7, 1988.

Brim, Gilbert. "Losing and Winning." *Psychology Today*, September 1988.

Coleman, R. "Shiftwork Scheduling for the 1990s." *Personnel Magazine*, January 1989.

Gibb-Clark, Margot. "Duties Conflict for Single Fathers." *The Globe and Mail*. January 7, 1989.

Gibbs, Nancy. "The Rat Race: How America Is Running Itself Ragged." *Time*, April 24, 1989.

Goleman, Daniel. "Hitting Bottom When You Hit the Top." *New York Times* Service, reprinted in *The Globe and Mail*, September 2, 1986.

Harris, G. T., and R. J. Trotter. "Work Smarter, Not Harder." *Psychology Today*, March 1989.

Hoffman, Ellen. "Have Office, Will Travel." *Psychology Today*, September 1988.

Horne, J. A. "Why Do We Need to Sleep?" *New Scientist*, November 12, 1981.

Kiechel, W. "The Workaholic Generation." *Fortune*, April 10, 1989.

Landi, Ann. "When Having Everything Isn't Enough." *Psychology Today*, April 1989.

Long, Michael E. "What Is This Thing Called Sleep?" *National Geographic*, December 1987.

Maynard, Rona. "The New Executive Father." *Report on Business Magazine*. March 1989.

Schwartz, Felice N. "Management Women and the New Facts of Life." *Harvard Business Review*, January-February 1989.

Wurtman, R. J. and J. J. Wurtman. "Carbohydrates and Depression." *Scientific American*, January, 1989.

——— . "Are Women Fed Up?" *Time*, October 12, 1987.

——— . "The Mommy Track," *Business Week*, March 20, 1989.

——— . "The Portable Executive," *Business Week*, October 10, 1988.

# INDEX

accidents, 17-18, 51, 83-84, 107-08, 116, 130, 137, 150, 194, 209, 210, 214, 215-16, 220-21, 225, 232, 234-35, 237, 241, 243, 246, 278, 285-91, n293, 293-96, 305-06, 308, 316-20, 326
  and circadian rhythms, 52-53
  and sleepiness, 73, 107-08, 109, 111. *See also* narcolepsy, sleep apnea
actors, 68
advanced sleep phase syndrome, 72-73, 80, 81-82, 255
age, 34-35, 38-39, n46, 46, n49, 50, 86, 88, 92, 100, 104, 108, 110, 131, 174, 180
  and circadian rhythms, 74, 77
  and shift work, 237, 238, 252, 306
  and sleep disorders, 69, n106, 117, 119
  and sleepiness, 135
  and sleep/wake patterns, 74
Agnew, H. W., 129
air traffic controllers. *See* transportation personnel
Åkerstedt, Torbjörn, 235
alcohol, 51, 87, 91, 98, 101, 102-103, 107, 109, 114, 115, 230, 256, 274, 272, 278, 288
  and sleepiness, 135-37
Aldrich, Michael, 220-21
Aldrin, Edwin, 322
Alexandrov, Alexander, 325
Allen, William, 269
American Narcolepsy Association, 110, n112
Angus, Bob, 7, 12, 13, 151-52, 156, 164, 166, 187, 188, 191, 196, 204-05, 206
animals, 26, 27, 28, 29, 30, n32, 32, n39, 43
  diurnal, 43
  nocturnal, 43
  and sleep deprivation, 125-27
  and sleep disorders, 113
  and sleep/wake patterns, 176

apnea. *See* sleep apnea
Armstrong, Neil, 322
artists, 68
Aschoff, Jurgen, 45, 76
Aserinsky, Eugene, 32-33
Association of Professional Sleep Societies, 84, 85, 234, 285
Association of Sleep Disorders Centers, 85
astronauts. *See* space program personnel
athletes, 60-63, n93, 123-24, 168, 169, 183-88, 189, 225, 257, 260, 264, 278, 310-16
automation, 17, 142, 202, 207, 208, 209-10, 214, 215, 223-24, 233-34, 235, 241, 246, 259, 292-93, 295, 297, 303, 324, 327

bed-wetting, 34, 39, 116, 117
Beggs, James, 259
behavior modification, 85, 94, 95-96
Berger, Ralph, 27, 138
Biddle, Jeff, 255, 261, 270
Bindon, Norman, 292, 294, 296, n302, 303
biochemicals, 28-29, 31, 32, 42, 47, 100, 251. *See also* specific types
  and circadian rhythms, 77
  and sleepiness, 134
biofeedback, 86, 94
biological clocks, 16, 40, 41-48, 49, 57, 69, n70, 70, 71, 75, 76-77, 79, 86, 168, 226, 230, 239, 242, 249, 251, 254, 255, 256, 296, 298, 324
  and age, 48
  and disease, 48
  in plants, 41, 42, n43, 43-44
biological rhythms, 20, 41-42, 324. *See also* circadian rhythms
biomagnetism, 205-06
biorhythms, n42
biphasic sleep, 50, 176-77
births, and circadian rhythms, n53
blind people, and circadian rhythms, 76-77

blood pressure, 34, 35
Bluth, B. J., n323
body movements, 34, 107
Bohle, Philip, 165
Bonnet, Michael, 67, 181-82, 183
Bootzin, R. R., 95
breathing patterns, 32, 34, 35, 42, 174,
  217-18, 297. *See also* sleep apnea
bright-light therapy, 74, 76-82, n240,
  239-41, 246-47, 255-57, n256
Brim, Gilbert, 265
Broughton, Roger, 16, 30, 40, 49-50,
  52, 112, 128, 129-30, 132, 138-39,
  170, 172-73, 176, 177, 178, 179,
  188, 201, 210, 218, 219, 221, 315
Burbank, Max, 205
Burell, Gunilla, 275
Butt, Jack, 306

caffeine, 50, 51, 89, 96, 101-02, 113,
  135-36, 229, 239, 255
Canadian Narcolepsy Association,
  n112
Carskadon, Mary, 40, 50-51, 129, 140,
  141-42, 154, 164, 176, 181, 268
Cartwright, Rosalind, 222
cataplexy, 110-13, 218, 219, 220. *See
  also* narcolepsy; sleep attacks
chefs, 143-45
Christensen, Kathleen, 26
chronic fatigue syndrome, 30
chronobiology, 42, 201, 237, 247
chronotherapy, 71, 72-73, 81, 86, 252
chronotype tests, 66-67, 189, 237-38.
  *See also* owls; larks
Churchill, Winston, 177
circadian disorders, 87
circadian rhythms, 20, 30, 42, 44,
  46-47, 48-52, 53-59, 60-61, 65, 68,
  69-70, 72, 74, 76-79, 80, 81-82, 91,
  115, 138-39, 141, 142, 152, 153,
  154, 165, 173, 175, 176, 189,
  190-91, 194, 200, 216, 225-26, 228,
  231, 232, 233, 239, 240, 241, 243,
  245, 247, 248, 249-57, 286, 290,
  293, 294, 295, 296-97, 298, 299,
  300, 301, n307, 307, 311, 312-13,

322, 324. *See also* biological clocks;
  biological rhythms; jet lag; larks;
  owls; shift work; sleep disorders;
  sleep/wake patterns; temperature
  and accidents, 53, 150
  and age, 56, 86, 92
  and body temperature, 55-59, 66, 67
  and death, 53-55
  and jet lag, 249-257. 292, 293,
    295-301, 311-14
  and narcolepsy, 111, 219
  and performance, 52-53, 68, 69,
    141-42, 152, 156, 165, 192, 195,
    322-33, 234-235, 249, 250-51, 252,
    257, 286, 290, 293-96, 307-08,
    311-13, 315, 322
  and shift work, 225-232, 233-235,
    240, 241-44, 245, 247, 307-10,
  and sleepiness, 48-52, 55-56, 57-58,
    66-67, 72-73, 74-76, 81, 105, 119,
    136-37, 138-39, 149, 153-54, 191,
    227, 231-33, 293, 298-300, 303-04,
Coleman, Richard, 37, 50, 65-66, 91,
  n93, n98, 100, 105, 132, 225, 230,
  231, 234, 236, 239, 241-42, 244,
  245, 246-47, 311
Colligan, Michael, 245-46
Collyer, Geoff, 69
Colonerus, Edourd, 143-45
computer operators, 68, 69, 232-33,
  239
Condon, Ruth, 233, 307-10
Conn, Robert, 140-41, 155, 280, 281,
  282-84
continuous positive airway pressure,
  109
Cooper, Gordon, 320
core sleep (anchor sleep), 163, 164,
  174, 189
CPAP. *See* continuous positive airway
  pressure
Crick, Francis, 37-38
Curtis, Carole, 271-72
Czeisler, Charles, 57, 70, 71, 76,
  77-79, 80, 225, 234, n240, 240-41,
  242-43, 256

Dali, Salvador, 180
Dartmouth-Hitchcock Sleep
    Disorders Center, 28, 69, 89
da Vinci, Leonardo, 177, 178
deaths, and circadian rhythms, 53-54
de Candolle, Augustin, 43
delayed sleep phase syndrome, 72-74,
    76, 80, 81, 175, 216, 228, 252, 255
de Mairan, Jean Jacques d'Ortous,
    41, 42, 44
Dement, William, 33, 50, 91, 113, 131,
    140, 155-56, 165, 181, 231
depression, 10, 34, 37, 79, 80, 91,
    98-100, 102, 107, 109, 128-29, 147,
    156, 222, 275, 279, 324
desynchronization, 56-57, 115, 226,
    229, 247, 247, 252, 255, 293, 294,
    295, 299, 301, 313, 322, 324
Diamandis, Peter, 321
DIMS. *See* disorders of initiating or
    maintaining sleep
Dinges, David, 15, 16, 25, 26, 27, 31,
    51, 128, 129, 134, 136, 134, 137,
    141, 142, 147, 148-49, 152-53, 154,
    169, 170-71, 174-75, 177, 191,
    192-93, 194, 196, 200-01, 203,
    207-08, 209, 210, 211, 215-16, 224,
    230, 241, 247, 275, 289
diseases, 87, 100-01, 104, 114
    and circadian rhythms, 53-54
disorders of initiating or maintaining
    sleep, 90, 104
doctors. *See* health care personnel
DOES. *See* sleepiness, excessive
Donohoe, Frank, 162
Downey, Ralph, 181-82, 183
dreams, 36, 37, 87, 99, 101, 118-19,
    124. *See also* REM sleep
drugs, 84, 87, 91, 101, 100, 101, 106,
    108, 109, 110, 114, 115, 118, 227,
    243, 254, 274, 287, 304-05. *See also*
    alcohol; caffeine
    amphetamines, 101
    antianxiety, 100
    antidepressants, 38, 99, 100, 115
    antihistamines, 101
    and circadian rhythms, 55, 75

cocaine, 101
contraceptives, 115
hypnotics, 93, 94, 115, 254, 255,
    304-05
marijuana, 101, 286
and narcolepsy, 112-13, 221
relaxants, 115
and REM sleep, 112, n127,
sedatives, 230, 305
and sleep disorders, 83
and sleepiness, 135
sleeping pills, 83, 85, 93, 227, 243,
    325
stimulants, 112, 115, 154, 305-06
temazepam, 304
tranquilizers, 101, 115
Duhamel, Henri-Louis, 42
dyssomnias, 89

Edison, Thomas, 15, 132, 177
EDS. *See* sleepiness, excessive
electric light, 15, 16, 70, 129, 223,
    240-41 *See also* bright light therapy
endocrine system, 31, 47, 77
entrainment, 46, 48, 56, n70, 70, 71,
    72, 76, 78, 86, n98, 251, 253. *See
    also* desynchronization; bright-light
    therapy; time cues
epilepsy, 117, 118, 289
E-types. *See* owls
evening types. *See* owls
Everson, Carol, 126
evolution, 16, 25, 26, 27, 100, 176-77
executives, 19, 169, 214-15, 224, 257,
    259-76, 278
exercise, 88, 89, 98, 104, 165-66, 237,
    315, 325
eye movements, 32-33. *See also* rapid
    eye movements

firefighters, 169, 194, 214, 224, 235,
    236
Fisher, Carl, 306
Folkard, Simon, 233, 307-10
food, 50-51, 148, 229, 237, 239, 250,
    255, 297, 315
    and sleep disorders, 80

free-running, 43, 45-46, 50, 56-57, 58, 70, 72, 76, 88, 176, 252. See *also* time cues; desynchronization
Friedmann, J. F., 172
Fuller, Charles, 54, 296

gamma-hydroxybutyrate, 112-13
Gardner, Randy, 124, 125, 155-56
gastrointestinal system, 47
gender
    and sleep disorders, 86, 106, 114, 115-16, 119
    and sleep paralysis, 303
    and work, 262, 263, 268, 269-74
Geringas, Eric, 69
Glickman, Robert, 282
Globus, G., 138
Godbout, Roger, n130
Gold, Sylvia, 271
Graeber, Curtis, 299, 322-23, 326
Greenwood Callens, Paula, 231
Gretzky, Wayne, 314

Hamermesh, Daniel, 261, 270
Hark, William, 306
Haslam, Diana, 174
Hauri, Peter, 28-29, 69, 74, 75, 89, 91, 92, 94-95, 98, 100, 101-02, 106, 117, 128, 134
health care personnel, 17, 169, 175, 214, 224, 225, 229, 230-31, 233, 235, 240, 241, 244, 247, 248-49, 260, 278-285, 309
heart attacks, 35, 53, 133, 230, 278
heart disease, 107, 217, 243, 275
heart rate, 34, 35, 42, 204, 207, 235, 251, 297, 312
Helppie, Martha, n323
Hensby, Sharon, 162
Henschel, Arne, 71
Herscovitch, Joel, 172-73
Heslegrave, Ron, 7, 151-52
hibernation, 27, 42
high blood pressure, 108
Hirshkowitz, Max, 108
Hochschild, Arlie, 274
Horne, James, 26, 29-30, 51, 66,

n,129, n139, 157-59, 163-64, 172
hypersomnia, 104-05, 115
    idiopathic, 113-14, 221
hypnotoxins, 28, 134

illness, 87, 100-01, 106
    and circadian rhythms, 53-55
immune system, 31, 47, 54
impotence, n35, 108
industrial personnel, 15, 19, 20, 215, 222-225, 226-27, 231-32, 233-34, 237, 239, 240, 241-44, 275
infradian rhythms, 42
insomnia, 18, 29, 38-39, 56, 69, 71, 75, 86, 88, 89-104, 105, 110, 113, 114, 116, 128, 132, 175, 216, 217, 221, 226, 249, 253, 261, 275, 287, 311
    child-onset, 91
    conditioned, 94-95
    psychophysiological, 92-93
    rebound, 94
    treatment, 91-92, 94-98
International Labor Organization, 238
Ishihara, Kaneyoshi, 67

jet lag, 15, 18, 40, 58, 70, 80, 143, 215, 216, 219, 226, 249-57, 278, n290, 292, 298, 300-01, 311-13, 318. See *also* circadian rhythms; travel
judges. See legal professionals

Keith, Vicki, 60-63, 123-24, 125
Klein, Karl, 250-52, 253, 254, 292, 301
Kleine-Levin syndrome, 115
Kleitman, Nathaniel, 32-33, 36, 45, 153-54
Knight, Sara, 222
Kripke, Daniel, 82
Kronauer, Richard, 256

Lack, Leon, 71
lack of sleep. See sleep deprivation
larks, 56, 65-69, 74, 189, 207, 237, 252, 268, 299, 309, 313
Latham, Robert, 267
Lauber, John, 260, 285-89, 295-96, 310

Lavie, Peretz, 49, 51, 115-16
lawyers. *See* legal professionals
Lebedev (cosmonaut), 325
legal professionals, 260, 271, 276-78
leg movements, 103-104, 180, 297. *See
    also* restless legs
Lendl, Ivan, 314
Lerman, Juan-Carlos, n70
Levinsky, Norman, 282
Lewy, Alfred, 79, 81, 240, 255-56
lifestyle, 16, 19-20, 68-69, 70-71, 86,
    87, 129-30, 236-37, 244-45, 259-60,
    264-65, 268, 269-75, 285
light, and circadian rhythms, 76-82 *See
    also* bright light therapy; time cues
limb movement, 32, 35-36, 103-04,
    118, 297
Linnaeus, C., n43
Long, Michael, 256
long sleepers, 90, 101, 115-16, 132,
    133-34, 162, 163, 172, 207. *See also*
    sleep requirements
Lubin, A., 165
Ludington, Ron, 313

McCall, Timothy, 281, 283-84
McDonald, "Ramblin' Rob", n124, 124
MacLeod, Duncan, n306
Mamelak, Mortimer, 16, 39, 56, 69,
    73, 86, 90-91, 92, 98, 101, 107, 109,
    112-13, 180, 219, 238, 260, 278
mania, 98, 99
marathons, 60-63, 123-25, 128, 129,
    155-56, 165
melatonin, 79, 80-81
Melbin, Murray, 19
Mellor, Earl, 223
menstrual cycle, 42, 114
metabolism, 42, 47
microsleeps, 114, 128-29, 134, 152-53,
    154, 232
military personnel, 7, 169, 174, 194,
    205, 209-10, 223, 228, 233, 304-05
Minard, A., 172
Minnesota Regional Sleep Disorder
    Center, 117
Mitchell, Mike, 315

Mitchison, Graeme, 38
Mitler, Merrill, 118
Moldofsky, Harvey, 15-16, 28, 29,
    30-31, 47-48, 55, 73, 84, 93, 103-04,
    130, 147, 162, 201-02, 238, 255, 316
Monk, Timothy, 58-59
Montplaisir, Jacques, n130
monophasic sleep, 50, 175, 177, 178,
    210
mood, 9, 10, 13, 28, 37, 45, 48, 61-62,
    71, 80, 115, 128-29, 139, 148, 166,
    169, 171, 173, 179, 191, 195, 203,
    207, 219, 237, 250, 275, 279, 282,
    300, 324
Moore-Ede, Martin, 44, n53, 54, 57,
    177, 213, 223-24, 225, 228, 229-30,
    234, 238, 239, 242, 296, 327
Moraes, Mark, 68
morning larks. *See* larks
morning types. *See* larks
motivation, 5, 6, 52-53, 62, 133, 141,
    147, 150, 155, 157, 169, 187, 201,
    260, 313, 321, 324
MSLT. *See* Multiple Sleep Latency
    Test
M-types. *See* larks
Mullaney, Daniel J., 151-52, 171
Multiple Sleep Latency Test, 50, 58,
    105-06, 111, 130, 134, 136, 139,
    140, 149, 152, 227, 297-98. *See also*
    sleep latency
musicians, 68

Naitoh, Paul, 156, 170, 194, 197, 202,
    203, 207, 211, 261
napping, 8, 10-12, 21, 37, 49, 50,
    51-52, 56, 67, 73, 87, 92, 95, 96, 98,
    99, 107, 112, n130, 132, 138, 153,
    162, 168, 169-70, 173, 174-75, 177,
    178, 179-197, 199-211, 219, 226,
    227, 239, 246, 247-49, 268, 280,
    285, 299, 302-03, 309, 311, 315,
    325. *See also* polyphasic sleep;
    sleep/wake patterns, ultrashort
    and circadian timing, 190-91, 195,
    200
    and performance, 11-12, 21, 153,

168, 169, 173, 174, 178, 179-80,
  183-187, 188-90, 191, 192-93,
  195-196, 199-200, 201-202, 203,
  207, 209
  and shift work, 210, 219, 226-227,
  239, 246, 247-249
  and sleep inertia, 191, 193-94, 195,
  200
narcolepsy, 34, 104, 109-14, 116, 180,
  216, 218-216
  treatment, 112-13, 221
Nicholson, Anthony, 249-50
night flying, 117
night owls. *See* owls
night-shift paralysis, 233-34, 307-10.
  *See also* sleep paralysis
night sweats, 107
night terrors, 35, 39, 89, 116, 117, 118
noise, 88, 91, 175, 227, 239, 253, 302,
  322, 323
non-24-hour sleep/wake syndrome,
  75-76
non-rapid-eye-movement sleep. *See*
  NREM sleep
non-REM sleep. *See* NREM sleep
NREM sleep, 31, n32, 32-36, 42, 55,
  99, 101, 111, 114, 118, 138, 139,
  180. *See also* slow wave sleep
nuclear plant personnel, 17-18, 206,
  209-10, 214, 215, 224, 234-35, 241,
  247
nurses. *See* health care personnel

on-call sleeping, 235-236, 279, 280
Ondine's curse. *See* sleep apnea, central
optional sleep, 163, 164,172
Orne, Martin, 194
Orr, William, 105
Östberg, O., 66
oversleeping, 15, 62-63, 74, 84, 114,
  130, 133, 138-40, 170, 173, 196-97,
  320. *See also* recovery sleep
owls, 56, 65-69, 72, 74, 189, 207, 237,
  252, 268, 299, 309, 313

parasomnia, 89, 116-19
performance, 52, n130, 130, 132-33,

134, 139, 141, 143-44, 150-160,
  163, 168-170, 179-80, 181-82, 183,
  184-88, 189-90, 191-97, 199-211,
  215, 232, 246, 247, 249, 250-51,
  294, 307-308, 310-13, 322, 323. *See
  also* accidents
  and circadian rhythms, 52-53,
  190-91, 232-33, 315
  and jet lag, 249, 250-252, 292, 293,
  296, 304, 311, 312
  monitoring, 21-22, 204-11,
  and napping, 11-12, 21, 153, 168,
  169, 173, 174, 178, 179-80,
  183-187, 188-90, 191, 192-93,
  195-196, 199-200, 201-202, 203,
  207, 209
  and shift work, 224-25, 232, 319-20
  and sleep deprivation, 17-18, 20-22,
  40, 150-160, 163, 169-74, 179-80,
  181-82, 183, 191-94, 224-25, 292,
  293, 294, 295-96,
  and sleep inertia, 137, 152, 169-70,
  184, 187, 189, 193-94, 200, 203, 323
  and sleepiness, 141-142, 143-44,
  150-160, 169, 172, 173,
Pham, Pierre, 82
Pigeau, Ross, 7, 8, 9, 10, 11, 12
pilots. *See* transportation personnel
Pirolli, Ann, 159, 160
police officers, 169, 214, 224, 230, 233,
  236-37, 240, 241, 243, 247
politicians, 17, 249, 253, 276-77, n276
polyphasic sleep, 176-78, 188. *See also*
  napping
Post, Wiley, 250
pregnancy, 104, 131
prophylactic napping, 194-197
pseudoinsomnia, 92
psychiatric problems, 85, 87, 91, 98,
  100, 104, 114, 117, 118, 155, 217
psychotherapy, 85, 100, 102

Quick, James, 269

rapid-eye-movement sleep. *See* REM
  sleep
Rechtschaffen, Allan, 25-26, 29, 125,
  n127, 127

recovery sleep, 13, 57-58, 62-63, 124-25, 126, 133, 138-40, 160-64, 170, 172-73, 179, 191-92, 229
relaxation techniques, 86, 94, 104
REM behavior disorder, n36, 119
REM rebound, 37, 163
REM sleep, 31, n32, 32-33, 35-38, 39, 40, 42, 48, 55, 89, 99-100, 101, 106, 110, 111-12, 114, 118-19, 125, 126, 127, 138, n139, 139, 155, 161, 163, 235, 242
and learning, 37-38, 159-60
Renner, M., 43
Reppert, Steven, 79
reproductive system, 47
restless legs, 103-104, 180
Richardson, B.H., 45
Richey, Preston, 242
Roehrs, Timothy, 130, 135, 137
Romanenko, Yuri, 325
Rosa, Roger, 161, 245-46
Roskies, Ethel, 263
Roth, Bedrich, 114
Rylands, Julia, 7-8, 10-11, 12-13

SAD. *See* seasonal affective disorder
safety. *See* accidents
sailors. *See* athletes; military personnel; transportation personnel
Sallot, Jeff, 270
Schenck, Carlos, 117, 119
schizophrenia, 34, 98, 147, 155
and sleep/wake patterns, 76
Schneider-Helmert, Dietrich, 216, 221-22
Schwartz, Felice, 272, 273-74
seasonal affective disorder, 79-81
Sekiya, Tooru, 261
self-employed people, 68, 74, 260, 264, n272
serotonin, 102
Sewitch, Deborah, 56, 89
sexual activity, 87, 270. *See also* impotence
Shearer, Jon, 225, 227, 229, 233, 236, 237-38, 240, 243-44
shift work, 15, 16, 17, 19, 20, 22, 40,

53, 58, 68, 70, 80, 90, 135, 137, 169, 170, 175, 211, 214, 215, 216, 219, 222-235, 236-49, 275, 278, 280, 292, 306, n307, 307-310, 317-20, 327. *See also* sleep/work patterns; specific careers
costs, 224-25
and health, 229-30, 241, 242
on-call, 235-236, 279, 280
recommendations, 239
short sleepers, 90, 100-01, 132-34, 162, 163, 172, 207. *See also* sleep requirements
Siffre, M., 45
sleep, function of, 25-31, 36-38, 40, 126, 133-34, 157, 162, 169
sleep apnea, 102, n106, 106-09, 110, 113, 116, 180, 181, 217, 220, 222
central, 108
mixed, 108
obstructive. *See* sleep apnea, upper airway
treatment, 109
upper airway, 108
sleep attacks, 110, 111-12, 113, 218. *See also* cataplexy; narcolepsy
sleep continuity, 181-182, 188
sleep debt, n139, 194, 195-96, 197. *See also* napping; sleep deprivation
sleep deprivation, 12, 15, 16-18, 20, 21, 37, 53, 60, 62, 104, 119, 123-45, 148, 149, 150-160, 159, 175, 178, 188, 190, 191-92, 195, 196, 201, 206, 207, 208, 215, 216, 217, 219, 224, 230, 246, 248, 249, 263, 255, 276-77, 279-80, 286-87, 288, 293, 297, 307, 309, 311, 312, 313, 318, 322, 324, 326. *See also* specific careers
in animals, 125-26
costs, 18, 20, 21-22, 285, 287. *See also* accidents
effects, 3-6, 9-10, 12-13, 16-18, 20-22, 28, 29-30, 31, 40, 48, 51, 52, 54, 55, 60-61, 62-63, 99, 102, 123-24, 129, 133-34, 139, 151-52, 153-60, 169-70, 174, 179, 181-82,

190-194, 203, 224-25, 260. *See also* performance; sleep deprivation; sleepiness

sleep disorders, 21, 32, 33, 39, 40, 48, 52, 53, 56, 69, 80, 83-119, 134, 135, 136, 149, 163, 175, 176, 183, 200, 201-02, 216, 228, 286, 327. *See also* sleep problems; specific types
   and lifestyle, 221-22
   and performance, 216-19, 220-221
   therapies, 72-75, 80-82, 85-86
   and work, 216-19

Sleep Disorders Center, California, 118

Sleep Disorders Center, Oklahoma City, 105

Sleep Disorders Centre, Sunnybrook Medical Centre, 16, 69, 86

sleep disorders clinics, 69, 75, 83-84, 87-88, 93, 104, 107, 130, 222, 316

sleep efficiency, 38, 201. *See also* sleep-restriction therapy.

sleep environment, 88-89, 239

sleep flexibility, 67, 68, 170, 237-28, 309, 310. *See also* shift work.

sleep fragmentation, 168, 180-183, 187, 217, 236, 298. *See also* sleep apnea

sleep inertia (sleep drunkenness), 34, 114, 137-38, 152, 169-170, 184, 187, 189, 190,191, 193-95, 200, 203, 304, 323

sleepiness, 4, 9, 10-11, 20, 21, 28, 30, 48-49, 50-52, 58-59, 60, 61, 69, 71, 72, 73, 80, 81, 83, 84, 89, 90, 101, 104, 119, 129, 130, 132, 134-42, 147-66, 163, 169, 172, 173, 184, 194, 195, 200-01, 202-204, 220, 226, 227, 231-32, 233, 234, 235-36, 246-47, 284, 285, 286-87, 292-93, 294-96, 297, 298, 307, 310
   environmental factors, 140-42
   excessive, 104-06, 107, 110-11, 113, 114-16, 116-17, 133, 149, 175, 180, 181, 182, 217, 218-19, 222, 247, 249, 316
   measurements, 9, 148, 202-207

sleeping beauty syndrome, 115-16

sleeping pills. *See* drugs, sleeping pills

sleep latency, 33, 48-49, 50-51, 67, 75, 89-90, 96, 105-06, 111, 130, 134, 136-37, 149-50, 227

sleep loss. *See* sleep deprivation

sleep paralysis, 35-36, 110, 111, 112, 233-34, 307-10.

sleep phase disorders, 81. *See also* advanced sleep phase syndrome; delayed sleep phase syndrome

sleep problems, 19, 20-21, 33, 71, 200, 215, 226, 237, 250, 275, 278, 300, 311, 317. *See also* sleep disorders
   costs, 249, 275-78
   environmental factors, 140-42, 227, 321, 322-23

sleep requirements, 129-34, 270

sleep research, 7-13, 21, 22, 25-31, 40, 44-45, 50-51, 55-56, 57, 66-67, 72, 76-77, 77, 79, 81, 85, 86, 90, 91, 96, 105-06, 118-19, 125-26, 127, 128-29, 133-34, 136-37, 139-40, 141, 148, 149-50, 153-54, 155, 156-61, 162, 165-66, 168-70, 171-74, 178, 180, 181-83, 184-87, 191-92, 194-96, 199, 200, 201, 204, 205-06, 207, 209-10, 217-18, 218-21, 222, 226-28, 230, 231-32, 233, 237-38, 240, 241-42, 245-46, 246-47, 241-42, 247-49, 251-52, 259, 261, 276, 297-300, 307-310, 322-23, 328
   equipment, 4, 8, 10, 31-32, 33, 78, 87-88, 204-07

sleep restriction therapy, 96-98

sleep stages, 30, 33-38, 39, 88, 99, 101, 161-62, 181, 189, 220, 248. *See also* NREM sleep; REM sleep; slow wave sleep

sleep/wake patterns (sleep/wake cycle), 12, 16, 18, 20-22, 26, 30, 31, 38-39, 40, 42, 45-46, 47, 48-49, 55-56, 58-59, 62, 63, 69-70, 70-73, 74-76, 78, 79-80, 81-82, 86, 87, 88, 91, 94, n98, 115, 119, n129, 153, 168, 169, 173, 174, 175-79, 184-90,

201, 209, 219, 225-26, 227-28,
228-29, 232, 237, 247, 254, 285,
290, 293, 301, 309, 322, 324, 326,
327. *See also* circadian rhythms
disorders, 69, 74-76, 79-80, 86, 89,
216. *See also* advanced sleep phase
syndrome; delayed sleep phase
syndrome
Type O resetting, 76-79
ultrashort, 153, 169-70, 174, 178,
187, 199, 210, 285, 325. *See also*
napping
sleepwalking, 35, 39, 87, 89, 116,
117-18
aggressive, 116, 118
sleep/work patterns, 16, 18-22, 68-69,
71-72, 74, 87, 170, 179, 210-11,
241-44, 296, 323-24. *See also* shift
work
slow wave sleep (deep sleep), 34-35,
39, 48, 88, 89, 99, 117, 137-39,
n139, 160, 161-63, 181, 182, 189,
193, 195, 235, 248, 250. *See also*
NREM sleep; sleep inertia
Smiley, Alison, 210, 225, 229, 233, 238
Smith, Carlyle, 159, 160
smoking, 102
snoring, 32, 83, 86, 87, 88-89, 106,
107, 222. *See also* sleep apnea
Southmayd, S.E., 128
space, sleeping in, 213, 320-326
space program personnel, 17, n93,
169, 193, 213, 214, 246, 259, 260,
267, 278, 316-26
Speilman, Arthur J., 96
sports. *See* athletes
Stampi, Claudio, 168-69, 178, 179,
183-90, 196-97, 204, 208-09,
210-11, 285, 304
Stanford University Sleep Disorders
Clinic and Research Center, 33, 87,
91
storing sleep, 196-97, 200. *See also*
napping; sleep debt
stress, 87, 91, 92-95, 96, 115, 116, 117,
137, 206, 221-22, 230-31, 236-37,
238-39, 265-66, 269-70, 271,

274-275, 278, 317
Stretch, Bob, 7
Stuss, Donald, 132
sudden infant death syndrome, n106
Sulzman, Frank, 54, 296
SWS. *See* slow wave sleep

Taub, John, 138
teachers, 278
technological advances, 15-16, 19,
176, 204-208, 214-15, 223, 233-34,
262, 266-69, n266, 292-93
temperature
ambient, 35, 42-43, 88, 89, 322, 323
body, 29, 35, 42, 45, 47, 55-59, 59,
66, 67, 76, 77, 78-79, 126, 176, 189,
251, 252, 297, 312
brain, 34, 35
Terman, Michael, 240
Tilley, Andrew, 162, 165
time cues, 43, 44-45, n45, 46, 57, 60,
70, 72, 74, 76, 88, 101, 239, 253,
254, 300-301
Titov, Gherman, 320
Torsvall, Lars, 235
train crew. *See* transportation
personnel
transportation personnel, 17, 53, 169,
175, 194, 205-06, 209-10, 214, 215,
224, 233, 240, 241, 253, 257, 260,
278, 285-310
travel, 12, 19, 69, 80, 87, 95, 168, 249,
250-57, 267, 296-97, 300-01,
311-14, 315-16, 318. *See also* jet lag;
transportation personnel
Tripp, Peter, 124-25
truck drivers. *See* transportation
personnel
tryptophan, 102
Turnbull, Andy, 288, 290-91

ultradian rhythms, 42, 48, 52
ultrashort sleep. *See* sleep/wake
patterns, ultrashort
unemployed people, 74

Valley, Victoria, 218-19

Vanstone, Martin, 302-04
violent sleepers. *See* sleepwalking,
   aggressive

Watson, Robert, 217
Webb, Wilse, 67, 129, 173-74
Wegman, Hans, 250-52, 253, 254, 292,
   301
weight, 100-01, 106, 107, 109, 115,
   126, 229
Weinberg, Hal, 205-206
Weitzman, Elliot, 57, 72
Wever, Rutger, 45, 76

Whittaker, Megan, 159
Wilkinson, Robert, 151, 161, 171
Williams, Jimy, 316
Winget, Charles, 312-13
Wolfson, Amy, n46
workaholism, 20, 210, 260-65, n274,
   274-75
writers, 8, 68, 75-76, 256, 272
Wurtman, Judith, 81
Wurtman, Richard, 81

zeitgebers. *See* time cues